PROGRAMMER'S
GUIDE TO FORTRAN

A Second Course

Michael H. Pressman

Long Island University
C.W. Post Campus

wcb
Wm. C. Brown Publishers
Dubuque, Iowa

To my daughter Laurie, who is such an important part of my life.

Cover design by McCullough Graphics

Library of Congress Catalog Card Number: 87–71182

ISBN 0–697–07835–3

Printed in the United States of America by Wm. C. Brown Publishers
2460 Kerper Boulevard, Dubuque, IA 52001

10 9 8 7 6 5 4 3 2 1

Contents

3 Storage of Numeric Data and Real Numbers 66

Preface

Purpose

The concept of this textbook has been on my mind for many years. As a teacher of computer languages for over twenty years (and as a professional programming consultant in industry), FORTRAN is my "mother tongue." My affection for it stems not only from my long-term relationship to it, but also from its marvelous flexibility. In the early days of programming, with no other language available (other than assembly language), we programmers were engaged in all aspects of writing scientific and commercial programs in FORTRAN. In our academic program, FORTRAN was a required language for our engineering students, and when our computer science program began a few years later, FORTRAN was the major language. In both our undergraduate program and our graduate program in management engineering, our students took elementary and advanced FORTRAN.

The orientation of our department is to train students for industry, and thus we took a very practical approach to our teaching, emphasizing the systems analysis and application aspects of the subject. (Almost all of our teachers have some industrial experience that they bring into the classroom.) However, there were no good books available to cover the many concepts of advanced FORTRAN; the students had to depend on the class notes and expertise of the instructors.

In the last few years, the organization of computer language teaching has changed significantly due to the influence of the Association for Computing Machinery (ACM) and the Princeton Educational Testing Service. Pascal now seems to be the anchor of most computer science curricula, and the more practical languages, like FORTRAN, BASIC, and COBOL, have been shoved aside. Nonetheless, despite the prediction of its demise many years ago, FORTRAN is still alive and kicking and is still the major language in at least the scientific and engineering portions of industrial applications. We do not argue with the idea that students with a good background in one or two computer languages can pick up another language on their own, but they cannot learn of the problems, pitfalls, and advantages of the language without some strong guidance and experience. Industry today is suffering from poorly trained programmers, poorly trained not in theory but in the application of what they have learned.

Audience

This text is designed to satisfy the requirements of a new marketplace. Since most technically oriented students will receive early training in Pascal and probably BASIC and assembly language as part of their undergraduate studies (if not in high school), a student who needs to learn FORTRAN comes to the study of this "ancient" language with many of the necessary tools of logic and structure. This text is aimed at the engineering and science students, as well as the students of finance and statistics, who have a previous programming background and want a sophisticated approach to a computer language.

Generally, this kind of student is able to handle, and usually wants, an approach that does not insult his or her intelligence, but instead is detailed and precise and not afraid to get into the quagmire that exists in the real world. Although no high-level mathematics is required, we do not hesitate to use trigonometry, simple probability, and numerical methods. At the same time, we will demonstrate many of the commercially oriented applications, keeping in mind that the practical aspects of science and engineering include monetary considerations.

No other books on the market take this approach. Most others may attempt to satisfy the market by trying to be all things to all readers; however, the space spent on concepts that the reader has absorbed from other courses takes away from that devoted to the professional aspects of programming. Part of the aim of this text is also to train the professional programmer who is faced with learning a new language without the help of the classroom experience; thus it is intended that the text be a learning manual, not just a classroom aid. One could view this text as an advanced text in the language since so much emphasis is given to the details of implementation and application.

The text is designed to fit into a Computer Science, Science, or Engineering curriculum in which the student has had Pascal and possibly BASIC and/or assembly language. It can also be used as a self-teaching manual for a course in programming languages in which the student must develop familiarity with languages not formally studied.

Organization

This text assumes a degree of sophistication on the part of the student and avoids spending time and space on hardware and logic covered in an introductory text. On the contrary, after a short introduction into the mechanics of running a program, the text leaps right into writing programs; although they are short and of limited value, these early programs get the reader onto the computer as soon as possible. In this way, the reader comes face to face with the fun and frustration of programming. The text emphasizes the necessity for the programmer to experiment with his or her implementation of the language in order to develop a sense of independence, rather than depending on a text that cannot possibly cover the myriad of dialects in the real world.

We begin with the rudiments of FORTRAN, and by the end of chapter 2 the reader is capable of writing some rather useful applications. Next we hop into subprograms in order to begin the development of a structural approach, as well as to allow the student to begin assembling a subprogram library. The next subject treated is one-dimensional arrays, so that by the end of chapter 5 the reader has learned about 85% of the language.

At that point we step back for a chapter and talk of the noncoding aspects of programming in order to give the reader an overall picture of where programming fits into the whole picture of data processing and why our approach must be oriented toward the user. The goal of chapter 6 is to develop a perspective at a time when the reader has enough knowledge to appreciate it but before we get into the real meat of applying what we have learned and will learn.

A second aspect of the organization of this text might be somewhat controversial: we take the approach that FORTRAN 66 is still in existence (certainly it is in industry) and that some readers may have only that version available. Thus we start with this earlier version of the language, making a slow transition to FORTRAN 77; by chapter 7 the reader is conversant in both versions, using the older version through chapter 5, but, where possible, using the higher version from there on. It is our belief that a student trained in a language should be familiar with existing earlier versions, just as the student of English should be able to understand Chaucer and Shakespeare.

Chapter 7 begins our more formalized approach, in contrast to the relaxed approach of the earlier chapters, which involved more spoon-feeding and avoided some complications momentarily. The ensuing chapters are heavy with applications and projects that should meet the needs of the most demanding instructors.

Content

This text covers all of the commands of FORTRAN 77, even those for which the author has found little application (but he's still learning). A survey of the major FORTRAN books in the field will find that many topics of FORTRAN are barely mentioned, if not completely ignored. In addition, the text covers symbolic debuggers, a most useful tool in the real world, as well as a number of debugging techniques used by professionals. Symbolic debuggers are almost never mentioned in most texts, yet most professionals would not be without one.

Approach

The overall theme of this text is that the computer is a tool whose usefulness depends on how carefully the programs are fashioned to the needs of the user. A program is a means of communicating information from the user, through the tool, and back to the user; the program (and the computer) serve as the medium through which the information passes and is manipulated. The program is not created and does not exist for itself, but only to serve the user.

Now this is not to deny that programming can be a creative and satisfying activity; it certainly is. After over twenty years, the author still loves this kind of work. But the ultimate satisfaction should be looked for not in the sophistication of the code but in the ease with which the program can be used.

Thus we look at programming not as a machine-oriented function, but as one deeply involved with human communication. Our first priority is people, not machines. Although the term *user-friendly* has been overused and abused, it describes what we are striving for. Our activities are guided by human psychology and perception.

But we are also concerned with the reader's psychology. This text is a guide, not a map. The reader must look around and learn for him- or herself, which is usually the best way to learn. Our aim is to point the reader in the right direction, not lead him or her by the nose. Most knowledge depends on ''E and E,'' experience and experimentation.

Pedagogy

At the beginning of many of the chapters is a little section entitled ''What the reader needs to know for this chapter''; it indicates some of the prerequisite material that must be known as well as some of the system-dependent information that the reader must find out for him- or herself. Each chapter begins with an introduction that describes how the chapter fits in the overall concept and ends with a summary that reviews what the chapter has done.

Within the chapters are many sample programs; often the same program is enhanced a number of times as new features of FORTRAN are covered. The sample programs are explained in depth so that the reader is not left with any insecurities about the intention and implementation of the code.

Occasionally anecdotal material is included that pertains to the material being covered. The intention is not only to keep a light approach, but to show the reader that the real world also has its foibles.

How to Learn FORTRAN: The Author's Responsibility

Learning requires a contract between teacher and student in order to optimize the process and instruct the student as to what must be done to absorb the information. Unfortunately, there is no way that the student can digest this book and thus learn all that can be learned about FORTRAN; this is partly because the author does not intend to spend the rest of his life writing everything that can be taught about FORTRAN! Thus an agreement of responsibility (a contract) is in order.

The author agrees to present the tools needed to write simple FORTRAN application programs; these will be presented in an orderly fashion and in such a way that the reader is not swamped with details. However, the details will be presented following a thorough discussion of the basic concept (including examples), thus providing the reader with a deeper knowledge. The author will suggest a number of exercises that the reader is urged to try; these exercises will involve both review questions and programs to be written by the reader.

The author agrees to lead the reader through the maze of possible applications by beginning simply and building up the complexity of the programs both discussed and assigned. The author will try to present the material on a slightly more sophisticated level than is possible with a beginning programmer, but has no intention of skipping over necessary explanations. The author would rather insult the reader's intelligence with obvious explanation than leave him or her to search out answers to critical points.

However, the author demands that the reader cover the presentation in order and thoroughly, since it would be wasteful to be repetitive except where absolutely necessary. Furthermore, the author will require the reader to search out the information that pertains to his or her computer with regard to both the implementation of FORTRAN and its relationship to the operating system; at the beginning of each chapter the author will present a list of what the reader must find out in order to fully answer the exercises and write the programs.

There was a time when the number of available computers was small and authors wrote language texts for particular machines. That time is gone, and it is now most important that the FORTRAN programmer be aware of the large number of FORTRAN implementations (dialects) rather than be trained for only one brand of computer. Thus the author agrees to discuss the question of dialects as it applies to different instructions, but he cannot discuss all of the possible implementations.

The author also agrees to build each topic by first discussing the early versions of FORTRAN (1966) and then building up to the newer versions (1977). In this way it is hoped that the reader will first understand the conceptual properties of the instruction and will look upon the new FORTRAN as a timesaver, but not as the only method. Fortunately, the specifications of FORTRAN were written such that earlier versions became subsets of newer versions and thus old FORTRAN programs would run almost without change under new compilers.

The author acknowledges that apparent contradictions may appear in the text for pedagogical reasons. Occasionally a concept is developed more effectively by simplifying it and ignoring the details. Once the concept is understood, the details and exceptions can be described. The author requests that the reader have a bit of faith in those cases where concepts are developed over a span of many pages or even chapters.

How to Learn FORTRAN: The Reader's Responsibility

If the reader wishes to get as much out of this text as possible, there are certain responsibilities that he or she must assume.

First of all, it is expected that the reader has already had a previous course in programming using any language, although BASIC, Pascal, PL/1, or C (especially the latter) is preferred. An assembly language exposure would also be very useful. No time will be spent on logical representations such as flowcharts or pseudocode; it is expected that the reader can set up the necessary logic; we are only concerned with expressing that logic in FORTRAN.

It is also expected that the reader has a rudimentary background in the decimal, binary, octal, and hexadecimal number systems. Although all of our FORTRAN applications will be written using decimal, there are concepts best explained in other systems.

It is expected that the reader will have access to the FORTRAN manual for the computer he or she is using, so that information pertaining specifically to that system may be obtained readily. The reader will also need access to any required operating system instructions necessary for compiling, linking, and running FORTRAN programs. It is expected that the reader will actually write and execute programs on the system. Facility in a language cannot be gained without practice in writing it and the frustration of debugging it.

It is expected that the reader will have patience and realize that all mistakes are of his or her own making. It serves no purpose to complain about features missing in one language that may be present in others; all languages have their advantages and disadvantages—there is no perfect language. One of the nicest features of working with computers is realizing that everything has a rational reason and that all that has to be done is to find that reason. There are no mysteries. The search for an answer requires humility and perseverance, usually in that order.

Finally, it is expected that the reader will read thoroughly, do all of the exercises diligently, write all of the programs completely, and communicate to the author any errors discovered.

A Note to the Instructor

The instructor using this text should feel free to take whatever liberties are necessary to present this material in a fashion of his or her own liking. The order of the presentation and some of the assumptions made by the author certainly are subject to question. A perfect text is somewhat like a perfect program; when no one any longer finds fault with it, it means that no one is using it!

For example, the treatment of alphameric data in chapter 10 can be moved forward once one-dimensional arrays (chapter 5) is completed. The chapter on subprograms (chapter 4) can be moved backward, although this will complicate some of the teaching and exercises. For the instructor who prefers list-directed I/O, the FORMAT statement treatments can also be delayed.

However, it is most important that the instructor be familiar with the operating system and utilities on the computer being used by the student. It will be the instructor's responsibility to aid the student in entering, compiling, and linking programs. If the system has a symbolic debugger, the instructor may find this an excellent topic to add to the syllabus and use as a supplement to this text.

Furthermore, the instructor should hesitate to allow any of the nonstandard language features that may be available in the students' implementation of FORTRAN. The instructor owes it to the students to instill only good programming habits.

Acknowledgements

I would like to thank the various reviewers of this text who pointed out the errors of my ways; in most cases I listened, but in some cases I preferred to remain in error. They were: Dr. Henry Todd, Brigham Young University; Professor Barry Russell, Alvin Community College; Professor Alexander Stoffel, Mayville State College; Professor K. M. Weiss, Jr., Baldwin-Wallace College; Professor Donald Henderson, Mankato State University; Professor Manfred Ruess, Norwalk State Technical College; Professor Stacey Edgar, SUNY at Genesco; Professor Andrea Martin, Louisiana State University; and Professor Richard Rink, Eastern Kentucky University.

Most of all, I wish to thank the employees of Wm. C. Brown who sweated through the production of this text with me, Renee Menne, Jean Starr, Earl McPeek, and especially, Nova Maack.

PROGRAMMER'S
GUIDE TO FORTRAN

1

Introduction to FORTRAN

1.1 Historical background

FORTRAN was developed in the mid-1950s as an experiment to determine whether programming code could be written in an algebraically oriented fashion and translated by computer to efficient machine language. In the days of slow computers, the cost-effectiveness of automatic translation of a high-level language versus handwritten machine or assembly language had yet to be proven. The project went so well that FORTRAN (derived from FORmula TRANslation) became an instant success. By the early 1960s it had become the de facto standard for scientific and engineering work.

Part of FORTRAN's success was due to its ability to be implemented on computers with memories as small as 8 kilobytes. At a time when memory costs were extremely high, a memory of 128 kilobytes was considered a giant and 32 kilobytes was normal. Thus FORTRAN could be implemented on almost all of the computers being mass-produced at that time.

The design of FORTRAN was based on two requirements. First, the language syntax should be easily translated (*compiled*) into machine code, and second, the language should be 'programmer friendly.' Programmers of the day wrote in assembly language, which afforded almost complete programming freedom. FORTRAN, to be useful, had to allow programmers to write code quickly and with a minimum of restrictions. Since the language was intended to be production oriented and used by experienced professionals, there was little thought to what has become today's watchword: *structure*. (On the contrary, good assembly language programmers are used to providing their own structure and do not need language constraints to force good style.)

FORTRAN was first released by IBM, and other manufacturers soon followed by copying the syntax of the uncopyrighted language. One of the advantages of this high-level language was that once compilers were written to translate the FORTRAN into the computer's own machine code, FORTRAN programs written for one computer would be portable and could be moved to another computer. During the early generations of computers, when the life span of a piece of hardware was from two to four years, the cost of reprogramming in machine or assembly language was the major factor slowing down the advance of computer technology. Thus, the concept of a portable program was extremely attractive to industry.

However, the concept of portability almost died a quick death as the various versions of FORTRAN started to diverge. Even within IBM, different versions appeared on different computers. Furthermore, computer manufacturers competed with each other by offering enhanced versions with no standardization of the new features. Additionally, one of the faults in the language was that a different input/output (I/O) command was used for each I/O device, so diverting identical output from a typewriter to a card punch required a program revision.

1.2 Standardization

By the early 1960s, FORTRAN had become a plethora of dialects. Although conversion from one dialect to another was not difficult, it was annoying enough that the promise of FORTRAN becoming the first truly portable language was in danger of being broken. At that time the American Standards Association (ASA) was involved in standardizing many areas of data processing, and it accepted the responsibility for drafting standards for three of the then-used languages, FORTRAN, COBOL, and ALGOL.

X3.9–1966 was the ASA specification for FORTRAN IV, a version that required a medium- to large-size computer to implement. X3.10–1966 was the specification for a subset called Basic FORTRAN IV, which was to be implemented on small computers. FORTRAN IV and its subset were sparse and efficient. All I/O was reduced to two major commands, one for input, the other for output, with the I/O device specifiable as a variable; thus a change in I/O unit required the change of only one value, either in the program or in the data. There was one assignment statement, two conditional branches, one unconditional branch, and one looping command, plus a halt command. The assignment command allowed the use of any valid algebraic expression and could also access functions. The language provided the programmer with a small number of flexible commands, and all program logic was written using these commands.

Due to the sales competition in those days, the FORTRAN compiler was usually supplied without charge by the manufacturer as an inducement to purchase the hardware. As the first high-level language available and the only one that could be implemented on the more reasonably priced small computers, FORTRAN was used in all kinds of applications, commercial as well as technical. Its inherent precision problem when dealing with money (or any real number) was overcome by clever programming techniques. To this day some payroll, accounts payable and receivable, job costing, and estimating programs are still being written in FORTRAN.

Standardization, however, did not solve all of the problems. Because of hardware or cost constraints, some manufacturers did not fulfill all of the ASA requirements for the language. At the same time, some supplied additional features that were nonstandard, often leading to programming practices that destroyed the portability of the program. But more important, the specifications of the ASA (26 pages plus appendices—longer than anything it had previously written) were unclear in many respects and did not specify what should occur if a FORTRAN program did not conform to the standard.

One of the aims of the writers of the FORTRAN standards was to be permissive, i.e., to let the rules specify only the minimum requirements of the language. Experimental extensions were not only permitted but encouraged. All versions of the compilers must treat standard programs similarly but may treat nonconforming code and extensions as they see fit. The only major rule that was sacred was that the full FORTRAN IV must not exclude any of the features included in the Basic FORTRAN IV. Therefore, programs written in the subset would always run under either type of compiler.

Thus, there were many proposed improvements to the language. As the language spread into the academic area, many schools provided their students with versions of FORTRAN that assisted in error detection and debugging. Among the more interesting names were MAD (Michigan Algorithmic Decoder), WATFOR and WATFIV (University of Waterloo FORTRAN and its successor), IITRAN (Institute of Illinois FORTRAN), and NDFOR (Notre Dame FORTRAN). Industry needed to have the language work with some of the newer I/O devices, including graphics hardware. Some of the features of the other production languages (BASIC and COBOL) were also desired.

In time, it became easier to draft a new set of specifications instead of attempting to elaborate on the old. Although this task began in 1970, it was not until 1977 that the new specifications were announced. By then the ASA had become the ANSI (American National Standards Institute), and ANSI X39–1978 covered both the full implementation of the language, which has come to be called FORTRAN 77, and its subset.

By the 1970s, manufacturers had learned that there was more profit in 'unbundling,' i.e., selling their hardware and software separately. Thus it is very unlikely that FORTRAN 77 will ever be given away. Since the cost of a new compiler may run into a few thousand dollars for a mini-, super-mini- or mainframe computer, industry may not consider the movement to the newer version of FORTRAN cost-effective. In the microcomputer field, where a FORTRAN compiler may cost as little as $100, the existing versions of FORTRAN vary all the way from the old Basic FORTRAN IV to a full FORTRAN 77.

Thus it is necessary for the FORTRAN programmer not only to be familiar with the newer and more streamlined features of FORTRAN 77, but also to be able to work with the less elaborate FORTRAN 66. In the real world, there are still millions of old FORTRAN programs that must be maintained.

It is expected that a new set of FORTRAN specifications will be forthcoming very shortly. Already called FORTRAN 8x (the x represents the year of adoption), it will be an enhanced version of the language with new facilities that will permit it to remain competitive with the newer languages being used in production environments.

Whatever the version of FORTRAN, it is imperative that the programmer read the manufacturer's manual very carefully, especially searching out the ANSI specifications that are unsupported on the computer and avoiding the nonstandard features that are so tempting to use but destroy the portability of the program.

1.3 Compilers

A compiler is a program that translates the programming language into machine code so that it can be executed on the computer. Whereas an Assembler substitutes the machine language equivalent of the assembly language statements, which have a one-to-one relationship with the machine code, a compiler must deal with far more complex instructions, usually requiring a number of machine language instructions for each high-level instruction. The portability of a language requires that there be different compilers for each machine language so that the same high-level program produces identical results on each computer.

Like the Assembler, the compiler must assign storage locations and tie all variable and constant references to them. It must also set up the required loops, rework the decisions into the form acceptable by the machine's instruction set, and, most difficult, arrange the formulae into the order that the machine can handle. It must be able to set up subprogram calls for complex processes that the hardware cannot handle simply, such as I/O, or for which no hardware instructions exist, such as mathematical functions and possibly floating-point arithmetic. The compiler should also provide warnings to the programmer about questionable constructions.

Unfortunately, FORTRAN, as the first of the popular compiler languages, was also the training ground for the specification writers and compiler designers. The ASA 1966 standard was rather permissive. It permitted extensions to the language without limit, so that even where it expressly prohibited a feature, that feature could still be included. Furthermore, the specifications did not specify what treatment should be given to statements and logic that did not obey the rules. Thus a nonstandard construction might compile differently under the action of different compilers. It was and still is the responsibility of the programmer to avoid nonstandard code. (The author cannot overemphasize this point, having spent many years debugging programs that ran beautifully on one computer but bombed on others!)

However, this discussion should not detract from the ease of using FORTRAN. Over the years FORTRAN compilers have become more sophisticated and reliable. The warnings given herein are only to suggest that it is impossible to specify a computer language perfectly.

The FORTRAN compiler has a number of roles to play. First of all, it checks syntax. Such errors as unbalanced parentheses, missing commas, invalid characters, and some misspellings are flagged and listed. Branches are checked to ensure that the object of the branch both exists and is unique. Loops are verified to ensure that their range is properly entered and does not conflict with any other loop.

Unfortunately, the compiler is not always able to spot all of the possible errors. No calculations or I/O are performed during the compilation phase; thus, errors that might be caused by invalid data or improper calculations will never be caught in the compilation stage. Nor can the compiler check to see that the logic will treat all of the conditions that might possibly arise. Furthermore, many of the statements involved with I/O are not fully defined at compilation time, and errors may not show up until the execution of the program. Also, the compiler cannot tell whether an external procedure is available; this is determined in the linking phase described in section 1.6.

Ideally, the compiler will at least give a warning about an undefined variable that is used in the program. Usually this error is caused by a misspelling when entering the program. Some compilers consider an undefined variable a "destructive" error and prevent completion of the compilation process, but others ignore it, and when the program executes, the accessed value will be "garbage," i.e., whatever value was left in that assigned location by a previous program. Furthermore, some operating systems clear the memory with zeros prior to executing a program, making an undefined location even harder to spot. Thus the author insists that it is the programmer's responsibility to initialize all variables used. The programmer should always review the list of variables produced by the compilation listing, looking for misspellings; some compilers can provide a cross-reference table, which is extremely valuable for finding unused variables and branches.

Most compilers translate the FORTRAN into assembly language, which the Assembler then converts into machine code. In those cases, the programmer can usually request a listing of the assembly language code as well as the FORTRAN code. This listing is very useful for studying the way in which the compilation is done and whether the code is optimized. Some other systems convert directly to machine code; although this method may speed up the compilation, it requires a more complex compiler.

The necessary operating system commands required to run the compiler are usually found in the manual(s) accompanying the FORTRAN language specifications supplied by the software publisher. Since there are so many different operating systems, it must be the responsibility of the reader to learn about the one used on his or her system.

1.4 Optimization

One of the challenges facing the designers of the first FORTRAN compiler was to optimize the code within practical limits. As an example of optimized code, examine the following expression:

$$\frac{A + B}{C + D}$$

As we will see it written in FORTRAN a little later on, it appears exactly the way it does in algebra:

$$(A + B)/(C + D)$$

Assuming the FORTRAN compiler is programmed to work from left to right on processes of equal priority, the pseudocode might be:

1. Add A and B.
2. Store in T1 (T1 is temporary location 1).
3. Add C and D.
4. Store in T2 (T2 is temporary location 2).
5. Load T1.
6. Divide by T2.

The optimized code for this expression, as it would be written by an experienced programmer, would be:

1. Add C and D.
2. Store in T1.
3. Add A and B.
4. Divide by T1.

The optimized code is one third shorter, thus occupying less space in memory and taking significantly less time to execute. However, the compilation time is significantly extended when the optimization procedure is left to the computer. Even though large memories are now available and computer speeds are quite swift, it still behooves the programmer to utilize memory and computer time efficiently, especially when working on a multiprogramming computer where the resources are shared. At the same time, utilizing the additional compilation time while still in the program development and debugging stages is also wasteful. Many medium-size and large-size systems provide the programmer with a choice of optimizing the code or not. The usual procedure is to use nonoptimized code until the program is ready for use as a production program and then optimize it.

However, as good as optimizers are, the human being is still capable of producing more efficient code (although the programmer may not be too anxious to do it). Thus good assembly code will always be more efficient than even optimized compiled code. In our treatment of programming style, we will emphasize how the programmer can optimize his or her own code, thereby utilizing less memory and time.

1.5 Subprograms

One of the most useful features of FORTRAN is that it is able to access external subprograms, i.e., previously written code that can be easily combined with newer code. Although it is possible for a FORTRAN compiler to directly substitute assembly language instructions for most of the arithmetic formulae and the control statements, the I/O commands require very large sections of code, as do the floating-point computations on those computers that do not have floating-point hardware (hardware that works with real numbers directly). The only feasible way to provide such code was to incorporate it in external subprograms that could be linked with the main program.

A prime advantage of a subprogram is that although it may be accessed a number of times by different sections of the program, the subprogram code resides in memory only once. The compiler generates instructions to branch to the subprogram and to return to the statement following the branch after the subprogram is executed. Although the linking instructions increase execution time slightly, the saving in compiler time and required memory is far more important. The more times the subprogram is used, the more efficient the code becomes.

All computer languages have a subprogram facility; in some other languages they are called *procedures*. There are two types of subprograms: the function, which is primarily used to return a single computed value, and the subroutine, which is used for all other processes. However, every version of FORTRAN can use external subprograms written by the user, that is, subprograms written, compiled, and stored in machine code at some earlier stage in program development. It is not necessary to include the source code of the subprogram with the main program. Therefore, programming time is reduced, and the compilation of the subprogram occurs once, not each time that the main program is recompiled.

The programmer may also set up a program library in which commonly used subprograms are stored. The code for the subprograms needed for a particular application is searched for somewhat automatically, simplifying the programmer's manual effort. The program library can also be accessed by other users of the same disk, making a library of subprograms available to an entire installation.

Since subprograms may also call other subprograms, most programs become a main program with a number of levels of subprograms. This arrangement is usually referred to as a *programming system*. In this way even the longest program can be reduced to a system of small modules.

1.6 Linkers

The process whereby the subprograms are linked to the main program and to each other is called *linking*, and it is performed by a piece of software called a *linker*. The linker also connects the main program, usually called the *mainline*, to the operating system (OS).

The linkage from the operating system to the mainline consists of transferring control to the first executable instruction of the program and, upon the completion of the program, returning to the proper location in the OS to prompt or wait for the next command. As we will see, the last logical instruction in a FORTRAN program is the STOP instruction. In the early days when FORTRAN ran on a card-based computer without an operating system resident in memory, it was necessary for the system to come to a halt, since the manual push of a button was required to define and begin a new process. Later on, when memories were large enough to house an operating system (or at least the shell of one), new processes could be triggered by control cards that were read in prior to the program to be compiled or executed; these cards contained what was called the *Job Control Language* (JCL) and allowed for the continuous running of one process after another without manual intervention, a procedure called *batch processing*. In some cases the instruction STOP was replaced with something else; in all cases, the concept of STOP merely meant a return to the operating system.

The linker, after connecting the operating system with the mainline, goes on to scan that mainline for any calls to external subprograms. These subprograms may be those called intrinsically by the FORTRAN language to implement the more complex procedures, such as I/O, and supply the common functions, called library functions, which are supplied as part of the language, and/or they may be the user-written subprograms previously stored by the programmer or by others at the programmer's installation. The linkage to each of these subprograms is set up by the linker. The linker then goes on to the next level of subprograms, where it repeats the process for those programs. This process continues until all subprograms have been linked.

If a linkage is not possible, e.g., if there is a call to a subprogram that does not exist, the linker will provide a message about this undefined reference. It becomes the programmer's responsibility to either define the missing routine or correct the calling statement to that routine. If the programmer desires it, many linkers will also provide a map, i.e., the name of each routine used and where it is located in memory at execution time; this map can be very useful during the debugging stage of program development.

1.7 Statement syntax and style

FORTRAN was developed during the period of punch card operations, and thus it utilizes an 80-column record. The column ranges are rigidly defined, but within those ranges there is a degree of freedom. The sections of the FORTRAN instruction will be described briefly here, without going into the details that will be presented in a later section.

The character C in column 1 indicates that the rest of the record, columns 2–80, is a comment and is not to be treated as a FORTRAN instruction. The purpose of the comment is documentation, a very important part of program writing. Some implementations will accept a completely blank line as a comment, and others will accept an asterisk (*) in column 1 in place of the C.

Columns 1–5 are used for statement numbers, better called statement labels. These integer values are used to provide connections between related statements in the program. Not all statements need be labeled; only those accessed by other statements must be. Each label must be unique, i.e., no two statements may have the same label. The labels themselves appear as numbers in the range 1 to 99999. They may be placed anywhere in the field (right-justified, left-justified, centered, or however the programmer desires). Blanks and leading zeros have no effect; thus 00213 is treated the same as 213.

Column 6 is used to indicate that a given record is a continuation of the previous record. Although the first record of an instruction must never contain any entry in column 6, all continuation records must. In old compilers, the character in column 6 can be any nonzero digit; in newer versions, any nonblank character or nonzero digit may be used. A continuation record is treated as though column 7 of that record follows right after column 72 of the previous record. Although there are distinct limits on the number of continuation records that can be used, almost all compilers allow at least five continuation records.

Columns 7–72 contain the FORTRAN instructions in what is called free format. There are no rules as to what columns to use, and since blanks are completely ignored, the programmer has complete freedom to develop a style of instruction layout that he or she finds satisfying. Because blanks are ignored, instructions can be indented and spacing within the instruction can be arbitrary. However, some implementations have restrictions on the case of the letters used and will not accept lowercase letters; to play it safe, it is best for programmers to always use uppercase letters for FORTRAN instructions.

Columns 73–80 are comment columns and may contain any information the programmer wishes to place there. When FORTRAN was a card-based language, it was the usual procedure to identify (number) the cards in those columns just in case a card got misplaced or the deck of cards was dropped. In disk-based systems, the columns are not used as often, but one suggestion is to place the date of a modification in those columns on the statement modified; this is a very useful documentation technique. The FORTRAN 77 specifications ignore these columns, but most implementations will use them as previously defined.

The actual layout of the FORTRAN instructions is a matter of style, and like most things that are a matter of style, there is no right or wrong. Throughout this text, the author will present and discuss his style and the rationalization for it. However, it must be said in all honesty that the author's style continues to change (and to improve, he hopes) even after over 20 years of FORTRAN programming. The intent of developing a style is of no concern to the FORTRAN compiler; the style's purpose, like the purpose of any documentation, is to make it easier for a human being to read the program. Thus the author's rationalization of his style is that it serves as additional documentation for the reader of the program, whether that reader is the author himself, another programmer, or a student who strives to understand the logic of the program.

As far as statement labels (numbers) are concerned, the author always right-justifies them so that they are easier to scan when looking for a given value. For the same reason, he tries to keep the numbers in numerical order, where possible. To help preserve that order, the author initially numbers the necessary statements in steps of 20 (20, 40, 60, etc.), thus leaving numbers available for any necessary insertions required if the program needs modification. An exception is made in the case of Format statements, which are given numbers 1000 higher than the preceding statement number.

When using continuation indicators in column 6, the author uses the digits 1–9 consecutively as needed and continues with the alphabet, should that be necessary in FORTRANs that accept more than nine continuation lines.

Since it is always safest to use uppercase letters for FORTRAN instructions, the author uses lowercase letters for comments so that they stand out a little better. Furthermore, after the C in column 1, the rest of the comment is placed after column 20 for the same reason. Blank lines (with a C in column 1) are also used quite often for better readability and to separate different modules of a program.

1.8 Summary

Because the reader already has a programming background, we will move right into the language without the usual explanation of what computers are or how important they are. We will also skip the usual treatment of logic and algorithms, since the reader is familiar with those concepts.

However, we emphasize that the reader should be familiar with the process of program preparation, which will probably require a text editor, compilers, and linkers. The history we have covered is not critical to the study of the language, but it does explain why some of the structures are the way they are. The concept of optimization should be familiar to any user of a calculator or even a slide rule. The reader should now review subprogram (or procedure) structure in any previously studied language(s).

The only new information at this time is the layout of the FORTRAN instruction. The simplicity of the layout should allow the reader to become familiar with it easily. Although we do not indicate column 6 in our program listings, we cannot overemphasize its importance in providing the only rigidity in our statement syntax: **statement numbers to the left, statements themselves to the right.** The only time an entry appears in column 6 is if it is a continued statement or as part of a comment.

2

Rudimentary FORTRAN programming

2.1 Introduction

The intent of this chapter is to get the reader into FORTRAN programming in the fastest possible way. The essence is simplicity—we will not begin with gory details or problems of dialect or implementation beyond what is absolutely necessary. Instead, we will start out using the lowest practical version of FORTRAN. However, as the chapter develops, we will move toward more detailed explanation, a forecast of the rest of this text.

We assume this lowest version to be the full FORTRAN IV as described in the 1966 specifications. Although there are still plenty of programs written in the subset, Basic FORTRAN IV, it is very unlikely that any computers still require that reduced version. If so, the reader will find only some minor problems; in the beginning this text will work mostly within the subset, and exceptions will be noted.

By the end of the first few sections of the chapter, the reader will be asked to write simple programs. Of course, these programs will be of limited value in the real world, but pedagogically they will force the reader to go through the exercise of entering, compiling, linking, and executing a FORTRAN program and thereby learning how FORTRAN interfaces with the operating system on his or her computer. Once the mechanics of compiling and linking are learned, there will be no need to refer back to these mechanics until such time as additional techniques are required.

Likewise, the critical topics of structure and style will be somewhat ignored at this time. Structure is necessary in complex programs, but not in the simple programs that we will present at this point in our study. The point here is to get into writing programs quickly, developing a familiarity with the essentials of the language and becoming comfortable with it. The importance of actually writing the programs and running them cannot be overemphasized. As any programmer knows, the feeling of satisfaction from seeing a program execute correctly is the best reinforcement to both the learning process and the ego.

2.1.1 What the reader needs to know for this chapter

1. How to use a text editor or keypunch to prepare the source program.

2. If a program name is required in the program and, if so, the syntax.

3. The control records or commands necessary to compile, link, and run a FORTRAN program.

4. On a disk system, the required file names or partial names, if any.

5. How a compiled listing of a program is obtained.

6. If the compiler error messages are fully explained on the listing or if a listing of error messages is necessary (and where the list can be found).

7. The logical unit numbers (device numbers) for the primary input and output devices that the reader will use (where there is a choice, use terminal input and output).

8. The key used for end-of-record in a terminal system. Usual ones are ENTER, NEW LINE, CR (Carriage Return), or some down/left arrow symbol.

9. If list-directed (format free) I/O is available.

10. How a programmer accesses simple input and output disk files.

11. If a random number generator is available and how it is used (optional).

2.2 The structure of a FORTRAN program

The whole problem, according to some critics, is that FORTRAN has no structure! That's somewhat true, but it is also what gives the language its flexibility and efficiency.

However, there are some rules about the order of certain types of FORTRAN instructions. First of all, a FORTRAN program must end with an END statement so that the compiler realizes that it has reached the physical end of the list of instructions. As we will see, it is possible to batch a series of FORTRAN programs one after another, either in a punch card deck or on a disk file, and it is important that the computer be able to separate one program from another; the END statement does just that.

Another required statement—the STOP command—involves the logical end of a program, that is the end of a logical path when no more statements are to be executed. Normally the logical end will be just before the physical end of a program, but it need not be. On some systems, CALL EXIT is used instead of STOP. Basically, STOP and END are the only required statements in a FORTRAN program. Thus, the shortest possible program is:

```
6
 STOP
 END
```

As we described in section 1.7, the FORTRAN command is placed in columns 7–72 in free format.

The program above consists of only one instruction, STOP; when executed, this instruction causes the computer to cease execution of the FORTRAN program and return to the operating system. The END statement does not cause anything to be executed; it just serves as information to the compiler. The END statement is often called a pseudoinstruction because it looks like a FORTRAN statement but serves other purposes.

This program is rather useless; however, it does serve as a starting point for our first exercise. (In all exercises, it is the reader's responsibility to determine which processes are system dependent.)

2.2.1 Exercises

Exercise 2-1

Enter the above program on your computer through whatever editor is available. Find out what control records are needed for your compiler. In some cases, the program must be stored in a disk file with a certain file name or file name suffix. In other cases, a control record may have to precede the program to tell the operating system that a FORTRAN program is coming and that the FORTRAN compiler is needed; this method is usually required in card-based systems. The system may also require a program name within the program.

Next, find out what commands must be given to the operating system to compile the program and supply you with a listing of the compiled programs (not just a listing of the source program that you entered into the editor, but the listing produced by the compiler, which includes your source program, any error messages the compiler finds, as well as other information produced by the compiler about program storage). Compile the program and print out the compiler listing.

If there are errors (and don't be too discouraged if there are—even STOP can be spelled wrong!), correct the errors in the editor and recompile the program. Continue this process until all errors are removed. At this point, the disk should also contain an *object* (sometimes called a *binary*) or machine language version of your program. Examine the listing file and see if any of the compilation information has any meaning to you.

Next, determine the operating system command necessary to link your program and do so. It is unlikely that you will get any linking errors for so simple a program, but then, nothing is impossible! Upon a successful link, another disk file is produced—an executable version of your program, linked with the operating system.

Now execute (or run) the program. If you are not on a terminal, you may see nothing happen. If you are on a terminal, you will probably see some kind of message that the program has executed a STOP; however, some systems will just supply the operating system prompt.

Find out how a file directory is obtained and enter the appropriate commands. Look for the various versions of the program in your directory; there should be a source file, an object or binary file, and an executable or run file.

You should now start a system logbook, documenting how the FORTRAN language is implemented on your system. First, save a record of any additions that must be made to your source program file before the FORTRAN compiler will accept it. Then record the operating instructions that you used to compile, link, and run. Finally, make an entry about what happens when a STOP is executed. Is there a message? What can someone else running your program expect to happen?

Actually, this exercise may prove to be the most frustrating one in this book. You are responsible for learning much on your own that the text cannot teach, and the chances for error are manifold. However, once the process of compiling and linking is learned, it can be used almost without modification throughout the text.

Exercise 2–2

Revise your program from exercise 2–1 and put in some errors, such as misspellings, or remove one of the statements. Recompile the program and examine the error messages produced. Find out how to look up error messages if your compiler simply indicates an error number.

2.3 Output of literal data

Input and output (I/O) is usually the hardest part of any language, and thus this text will develop the topic very slowly and carefully. Literal data refers to a character string that is to be output as is, that is, literally, and is the easiest I/O concept to teach in most languages.

FORTRAN I/O consists of pairs of instructions, the I/O statement and the FORMAT specification. Among other things, the I/O statement specifies:

1. The I/O mode, input or output, as implemented by READ or WRITE.
2. The logical unit number (LUN) or device number of the I/O device to which the I/O applies.
3. The statement number of the associated FORMAT specification.
4. The list of variables, if any, being I/Oed.

Thus the I/O statement tells how and what is to be I/Oed.

It will be necessary for the reader to learn what logical unit or device numbers are used on his or her system. As we will see later, a variable may be used to make portability easier. At this point we need to know the device numbers for the principal input and output devices to be used. On a terminal system, we are interested in the numbers for the screen (output) and the keyboard (input); the same number, or even a symbol such as an asterisk (*), may be used for both. On a card-based system, we would need to know the numbers for the card reader and the printer or typewriter. For the purposes of this text, we will assume that the principal output device number is 1 and the principal input device number is 2.

The statement to output literal data might have the form:

```
WRITE (1,1000)
```

The number 1000 is an arbitrarily chosen FORMAT reference number. The parentheses and comma are required, but the spacing in columns 7–72 is arbitrary.

The FORMAT specification describes what the I/O record looks like or where the information is to be found or placed. Literal data to be output must be described just the way it is to be seen.

2.3.1 Hollerith descriptor and carriage control

FORTRAN uses a literal format descriptor (also referred to as a format specification) called H or Hollerith (for Herman Hollerith, the man who thought of storing census data on punch cards and invented early versions of punch card equipment back in the 1890s), in which the programmer must indicate the number of characters to be output, the character H, and then the character string. Thus the FORMAT to print out the word FORTRAN would appear as:

```
1000 FORMAT (1H , 7HFORTRAN)
```

The 1H followed by a blank at the beginning of the format specifications causes a blank to be placed in the first output column; with printer output, this first column occurs *before* print position 1 and is not actually printed. As we will describe in great detail in section 2.14, any output that eventually goes to a printer that has such features as new page commands, skipped lines, and so forth, requires that a symbol be used to control that vertical movement. A blank means move to next line before printing; the 1H blank places that blank in the first column of output, which is used by the printer for *carriage control*. If your principal output device is a printer, all output formats must have this carriage control in them.

(Some implementations strive for compatibility of all output devices, and even though carriage control has no meaning to a display screen or typewriter, it must be included in all output formats for any device on those systems. It will be necessary for the reader to determine how his or her system reacts. An easy test is presented in exercise 2–6.)

The seven characters following the second H are to be output literally. The parentheses are required; the comma and the space following the 1H blank are not required but are used for greater readability. Of course, the H format specification is very prone to error. First of all, the programmer must be able to count the desired number of characters; if 6 is entered instead of 7, the FORTRAN compiler would accept only FORTRA and would produce an error message, not knowing what the extra N is for; if the number 8 is used instead of 7, the compiler would look at the string as FORTRAN) and the error message would indicate a missing closing parenthesis.

An alternative method combines the first blank with the rest of the literal string:

```
1000 FORMAT (8H FORTRAN)
```

but this is considered poor style, because the programmer may lose count of the actual number of characters being output and the columns in which they are being placed. The author has always made it a matter of consistency to keep the 1H blank separate from any other output descriptions to avoid some very interesting errors (which will be described later).

2.3.2 Literal specification

Because of the problems with character counting, a second version of the literal specification was introduced as an extension to FORTRAN 66. This version allows the programmer to insert the string between apostrophes so that the FORMAT statement would have the form:

```
1000 FORMAT (1H, 'FORTRAN')
```

The blank after the comma is optional and was inserted to improve readability. Furthermore, the blank specified by the Hollerith can also be specified with the literal:

```
1000 FORMAT (' ', 'FORTRAN') or (' FORTRAN')
```

As a matter of style, the author uses Hollerith to define the first blank and literal for the rest of the literal information, as in the next example.

However, literal specification also has its problems. How does one represent an apostrophe as a valid character in the string? This problem was solved by assuming that two adjacent apostrophes represent a single apostrophe in the string. Thus the FORMAT specification

```
1000 FORMAT (1H , 'FORTRAN''S GOT PROBLEMS!')
```

will output

```
FORTRAN'S GOT PROBLEMS
```

2.3.3 Skip specification

Another available literal specification is used to skip columns, i.e., to leave undefined columns blank. It has the form wX, where w is the number of columns
to be skipped. The FORMAT:

```
1000 FORMAT (1X, 'FORTRAN''S', 10X, 'GOT', 10X, 'PROBLEMS')
```

will output

```
FORTRAN'S          GOT          PROBLEMS
```

The 10X specifications cause 10 blank spaces to be left between each of the three
words, resulting in a total of 40 output columns being used. Note that the 1X at
the beginning of the FORMAT leaves a blank in the carriage control column;
thus, we now have three ways of putting a blank there.

2.3.4 FORMAT statement (nonexecutable)

The FORMAT statement is a specification statement; it is never executed but
only accessed by an I/O statement. Thus, a single FORMAT may be accessed
by multiple I/O statements. Furthermore, the physical location of a FORMAT
in the program is of no significance; it may be placed anywhere prior to the END.
This author's style is to place the FORMAT immediately after the first I/O
statement that accesses it. In the early versions of FORTRAN, FORMATs had
to be positioned before the first executable statement and thus were placed in the
beginning of a program. Other programmers like to place their FORMATs at
the end. There's no accounting for style!

In this text, the 1H blank or its equivalent will always be included so that
the same FORMAT can be used to write to either a printer or the screen, thus
saving the programmer a certain amount of effort when sending identical output
to both.

(The FORTRAN 77 specifications do not include Hollerith as part of their
regular specs, but for the sake of compatibility with earlier versions of
FORTRAN, they are included in the appendix. It is possible, although very unlikely, that some version of FORTRAN 77 will not permit the use of Hollerith.)

2.3.5 Exercises

Exercise 2-3

Write a complete FORTRAN program that outputs your full name in capital
letters on the principal output device; don't forget the STOP and END statements. Use Hollerith specification; however, if your compiler also accepts literal
specification, enter a second set of I/O commands to perform the same task, thus

printing out your name twice. Compile, link, and run the program, checking the output to make sure that your name was spelled correctly.

Exercise 2–4

Revise the above program using lowercase letters in the literal string. Recompile, link, and run to see if your output device handles lowercase characters.

Exercise 2–5

If exercise 2–4 was successful, revise your FORTRAN instructions to use lowercase letters. Recompile, link, and run to see how your system handles lowercase instructions. It's possible they will not compile, and even if the program does compile, it might not execute. (On a Prime, the error shows up during execution of the output due to the lowercase h in the 1h .)

Exercise 2–6

Revise the program from exercise 2–5, leaving out the 1H blank in the FORMAT and rerun. If your system requires carriage control for your principal output device, the first character of the string will be missing. If the first character is still there, you may leave out the 1H blank permanently when writing to that device in the future.

Exercise 2–7

Revise exercise 2–3 so that it has a single FORMAT statement accessed by three WRITE statements. Put the FORMAT anyplace before the END and run the program. You should get the same output line three times.

2.4 Integer constants and variables

In FORTRAN, as in most other computer languages, information is expressed in different modes. Of the two primary numeric modes, integer and real, we are interested only in integer mode at this time. Integer information is limited to whole numbers within a certain restricted range. Integer mode has particular applications not only as data but as part of the language itself. For example, the logical unit number used for I/O devices must be integer. The FORMAT statement number is also an integer, as are other statement numbers.

Integer and real information are stored differently (as will be discussed in the next chapter) and used differently; it is critical that the FORTRAN programmer be constantly aware of the difference. Integer constants are always written *without* a decimal point. Although the range of integers is restricted, for our present purposes we can say that as long as integers are within the range of −32,000 to +32,000, all will be well.

In FORTRAN, variables or symbolic names (more properly called symbolic locations, that is, memory addresses that the programmer accesses using convenient symbols) are selected by the user, although FORTRAN has some defaults that come into effect if the user makes no previous specification of mode. FORTRAN (and BASIC) differ from the "structured" languages (Pascal, COBOL, and so forth) in that variable names may be used as needed without prior mode specification. Thus, the first appearance of a FORTRAN variable in a program may be at that point where it is first needed. (This feature is highly criticized by purists who, somewhat rightfully, believe that all variables should be mode-defined or at least stated at the beginning of a program.)

A variable name begins with a letter and can be followed by up to 5 additional alphameric (alphabetic or numeric) characters. Although "standard" FORTRAN has a limit of 6 characters, some older subsets have a lower limit and some advanced versions allow up to 32 characters. The programmer can usually be safe with a limit of 6. Of course, the choice of the name is completely at the user's discretion, but it should be an acronym, mnemonic, abbreviation, or other self-documenting letter-number combination. As we will discuss in a later section on documentation, it is good practice to define each variable name publicly; nonetheless, the choice of descriptive names is an additional documentation aid.

The programmer can declare the mode of any variable name or range of names. If the programmer does not do so, the FORTRAN language provides a default, which states that any variable name starting with a letter in the range I–N (note: *IN*teger), that is, I, J, K, L, M, or N, stores integer mode information; all other starting letters default to real mode. Although the default method can lead to some unusual names, many programmers use this default mode as a self-documenting scheme in which the program reader need only look at the variable name to determine its mode, rather than searching through the mode specifiers at the beginning of the program to find out what mode the programmer is using for that variable.

The assignment of an integer value to a integer variable is done with a very simple assignment statement, such as:

```
     ISCRN = 1
     WRITE  (ISCRN,1000)
1000 FORMAT  (1H ,'USING A VARIABLE LOGICAL UNIT NUMBER')
```

This example illustrates a technique used by many programmers to allow easy portability to a computer system that uses a different set of logical unit numbers for its I/O devices. The only required change would be in the assignment statement—there would be no need to modify the many WRITE statements that normally exist in a program. The variable name ISCRN is an abbreviation for SCREEN that obeys the six-character restriction; it is an integer because it begins with one of the integer characters, in this case an I.

2.5 Simple loops (the DO statement)

Every computer language has a construct for looping; unfortunately, each language uses its own terminology. The FORTRAN construct is called the DO loop, the word DO derived from the abbreviation for "ditto" ("do"). Although the DO loop has many powers and is somewhat flexible, we will restrict ourselves for the present to the simplest of cases, a loop from 1 to some higher limit with an increment or step of 1.

The syntax of the DO statement is as follows:

DO *nn   i = m1, m2, m3*

where:

nn is the number of the statement at the end of the loop

i is an integer variable (called the index or counter)

m1 is the initial value of *i*

m2 is the final value of *i*

m3 is the increment or step.

m1, m2, and *m3* may be integer constants or variables.

m2 must be greater than or equal to *m1*.

If *m3* is not specified, it is assumed to be 1.

All statements after the DO and up to and including the statement labeled *nn* will be executed.

The program below, which prints out the same message a number of times, illustrates how a DO loop operates.

```
     DO 20 L = 1,10
  20 WRITE (1,1020)
1020 FORMAT  (1H ,'LET''S WRITE IT AGAIN, SAM!')
```

In the program, we did not specify a value for *m3,* so the computer assumes it to be 1. However, if we wanted to play it safe, we could have written it as:

```
DO 20 L = 1,10,1
```

As we might expect, the message is written ten times on succeeding lines.

There are a number of features of the operation and use of DO loops that we are not prepared to describe until we cover a number of other FORTRAN commands. These features will be discussed in sections 2.12 and 2.13.

2.6 Integer output

The output of integer values is the simplest of output routines. Integer values are automatically output right-justified in the specified field (range of columns) with leading blanks. For example, the number -14 in a specified field of six columns

consists of three blanks, the minus sign, the 1, and the 4. Positive values are never preceded by a + sign. If the specified field is too small for the value, the results are system dependent, but most compilers will flood the entire field with asterisks. Thus the value −12345 in a field of four will yield ****.

To output an integer value requires two additions to our WRITE/FORMAT pair: the variable name in the WRITE statement and an integer field specification in the FORMAT statement. All integer field specifications, regardless of the variable name used, are in the form In, where n is the number of columns of output set aside for the value.

In the sample program below, the DO loop index or counter is used as the output variable.

```
      DO 20  L = 1,10
  20 WRITE  (1,1020) L
1020 FORMAT (1H ,'COUNT =', I3)
```

In each of the ten lines of output, the string COUNT = will be in columns 1 through 7 and the value of L, ranging from 1 to 10, will be right-justified in columns 8 through 10. The field of I3 was chosen so that there would be a blank between the equal sign and the value of 10 in the last line. The output would look like:

```
COUNT =    1
COUNT =    2
COUNT =    3
COUNT =    4
COUNT =    5
COUNT =    6
COUNT =    7
COUNT =    8
COUNT =    9
COUNT =   10
```

Alternative FORMATs would be:

```
1020 FORMAT (1H ,'COUNT = ', I2) or
             (1H ,'COUNT =', 1X, I2)
```

However, most programmers would choose the first version of the FORMAT for two reasons: (1) the instruction is one character shorter, so the typing is slightly less work, and (2) more importantly, the field of three columns is big enough to output values up to 999 without overflowing.

Also note the commas that separate the FORMAT specification fields. Although in one case the comma is not necessary, it does provide readability, as does the arbitrary blank the author generally places after the comma.

2.7 Simple integer input

The rules of integer input are fairly simple, but some implementations break those rules, resulting in some degree of machine dependency. The rules will be described below, and it will be the reader's responsibility to determine how closely these rules are followed on his or her computer.

In FORTRAN the statement used for input is called a READ statement; it follows the same syntax and rules as the WRITE statement, except that the list of variables is almost always used. The logical unit number is also machine dependent; we will assume here that the main system input device, whether it is a keyboard or a card reader, is a 2. Thus the FORTRAN statements to read in an integer value might look something like this:

```
     READ (2,1000) N
1000 FORMAT (I4)
```

Note that input FORMATs do *not* have a 1H blank as the first specification.

The I/O commands above will look for a value in the first four columns of the input record and store it in the variable N. In FORTRAN, any blank column is considered to contain a zero. Thus an entry of (blank) one (blank) four should produce a value of 0104 or 104 according to the rules of FORTRAN. An entry of eight followed by three blanks should produce 8000. An all-blank entry field will produce a 0 in any implementation. Thus it is considered necessary to enter integer input right-justified in the field, with no embedded blanks; the value 14 should be entered as (blank) (blank) one four.

However, we have couched our explanation very carefully because of the variety of machine-dependent implementations. In order to make integer data entry easier at a terminal keyboard, manufacturers have taken exceptions to the FORTRAN rules and made a number of nonstandard "enhancements" that confuse the issue. For example, on a Prime computer, all blanks are ignored; on a VAX, leading and trailing blanks are ignored but embedded blanks are treated as zeros; on most computers, trailing blanks after the last value in the input record are ignored. And the rules may be different when reading from a disk file! (Card systems do not have this problem, since all records are 80 columns and cannot be shorter.) Our general rule, which we will emphasize throughout this text, is to follow the specifications of standard FORTRAN (right-justification) and take no machine-dependent shortcuts unless absolutely necessary. In fact, some data entry people always use leading zeros to ensure right-justification.

The sample program below was written for a terminal; it prompts for the input of two integer values, shows the size of the fields, inputs the values, and displays them. On a card system, the same program can be run without the prompts. This program is useful for testing the implementation of integer input on your machine.

```
C                 display prompt
      WRITE  (1,1000)
 1000 FORMAT  (1H ,'ENTER TWO INTEGERS IN 2I4 FORMAT')
      WRITE  (1,1002)
 1002 FORMAT  (1H ,'--->--->')
C                 input data
      READ   (2,1004) M, N
 1004 FORMAT  (I4, I4)
C                 output data
      WRITE  (1,1006) M, N
 1006 FORMAT  (1H , I4, I4)
C                 termination
      STOP
      END
```

In this program, two lines of prompts are displayed first, then the computer halts until the user enters the data on the keyboard and presses the end-of-record key (ENTER or NEW LINE or CARRIAGE RETURN or CR, etc.). The characters entered are then examined and formatted as specified by the FORMAT statement, which, in this case, will first look at the characters in columns 1–4 and get a value to be placed in the variable location M; then it will look in columns 5–8 to get a value for N. The information is then output in columns 1–4 and 5–8, respectively.

A sample screen will look like:

```
ENTER TWO INTEGERS IN 2I4 FORMAT
--->--->
  12 -18
  12 -18
```

Note the use of comment statements to describe the program.

2.7.1 Repetition factor

In a FORMAT statement, the use of two or more adjacent, similar fields (such as I4, I4) can be simplified by using a repetition factor in the form mIn. In the last example, we might have used the FORMATs:

```
1004 FORMAT (2I4)
```

and

```
1006 FORMAT (1H , 2I4)
```

In fact, the prompt FORMAT has two identical literal fields, and it could have been written as:

```
1002 FORMAT (1H , 2('--->'))
```

where the parentheses surrounding the literal field are required.

Another application of integer input would allow us to input the upper limit of the DO loop example shown in the previous section:

```
C                 prompt and input for limit of loop
      WRITE  (1,1000)
 1000 FORMAT  (1H ,'ENTER TWO-DIGIT LIMIT')
      READ  (2,1002) LIMIT
 1002 FORMAT  (I2)
C                 loop
      DO 20  L = 1,LIMIT
   20 WRITE  (1,1020) L
 1020 FORMAT  (1H ,'COUNT =', I3)
C                 termination
      STOP
      END
```

The choice of the variable name LIMIT is completely arbitrary—it could just as easily be NUM.

A sample screen would look like:

```
ENTER TWO-DIGIT LIMIT
03
COUNT = 1
COUNT = 2
COUNT = 3
```

2.7.2 List-directed (free-format) input

In addition to the FORMATted READ, many FORTRANs have a list-directed or format-free input that simplifies the entering of data, especially in some of the small test programs that we will be suggesting. The usual form, with some system-dependent variations, is:

```
READ (2,*) IN1, IN2, IN3
```

where the asterisk (*) indicates that the data is to be entered without a format. The data itself must consist of a series of values separated by blanks and/or commas. Thus the person entering the data could enter

```
-12, 18 24
```

for the three expected values.

However, the free-format READ does have a few disadvantages. First, there must be as many values entered as the input list specifies; otherwise, the system will just sit and wait until the missing data is entered. Second, blanks do not substitute for zeros—zeros must be entered explicitly. Nonetheless, this feature of the language is undoubtedly a major convenience, and the reader may substitute this version of the READ where desired in future exercises.

2.7.3 Exercise

Exercise 2–8
Enter the first full program in this section on your computer and run it with appropriate test data to see how your FORTRAN implements the blank = zero rule of the FORTRAN specifications. Below are some suggested test data, although you should add any data you think of to cover any other conditions.

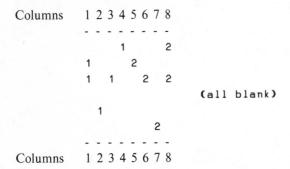

```
Columns   1 2 3 4 5 6 7 8
          - - - - - - - -
                1       2
          1         2
          1   1     2   2
                        (all blank)
             1
                      2
          - - - - - - - -
Columns   1 2 3 4 5 6 7 8
```

2.8 Assignment and integer arithmetic

Earlier in the chapter we assigned a value to ISCRN with the statement

```
ISCRN = 1
```

Now we will move ahead to assign values that are stored in variables or computed from a combination of constants and variables. However, the reader should understand very clearly just how the assignment statement works. The statement

```
I = I + 1
```

does not mean that the equation is to be solved for a value of I. Obviously there is no solution (other than possibly infinity). The equal sign was a poor choice of symbols, but it was the only logical symbol available on the old keypunch keyboards. (Other languages have tried to eliminate the confusion by slightly changing the structure of the statement. BASIC allows and sometimes requires the programmer to precede the assignment statement with LET; Pascal, C and Modula-2 use :=, and APL uses a reverse arrow.)

The author thinks of the assignment statement as an "equation of storage." Keeping in mind that variable names are merely symbols for memory locations, the symbol on the left of the equal sign represents the location where the computed value will be stored; the symbols on the right are the memory locations from which values will be taken. Thus the above assignment statement tells the computer to take the value in I, add 1 to it, and put the new value into I. It is important for the programmer to keep in mind just how "stupid" (maybe "simple" is a better word) the computer is, for it can never look too far ahead. In the case of an assignment statement, the operations on the right side of the equal sign are performed first; once the new value is determined, that value is placed into the storage location on the left. The computer is not confused by looking at the entire statement at once.

Another critical point is that the only memory location affected by an assignment is the one on the left. Memory locations from which values are read are unchanged.

2.8.1 Algebraic expressions and evaluation

On the right side of the assignment statement we find the most powerful part of FORTRAN, the ability to write any algebraic expression in a form not too different from what we use in arithmetic. There are five processes available in FORTRAN:

process	symbol	priority
addition	+	3
subtraction	−	3
multiplication	*	2
division	/	2
exponentiation	**	1

The priorities, just as in arithmetic, indicate the order of evaluation of the expression if no other guidelines are given. Thus

```
I = 6 + 3 * 2 ** 4
```

will be evaluated by first exponentiating 2, then multiplying by 3, and then adding 6 for a value of 54. Where priorities are equal, the order of evaluation is from left to right.

However, the order of evaluation can be controlled by the programmer by using sets of parentheses; as in algebra, anything within a set of parentheses will be evaluated first. Sets of parentheses may be embedded within one another; evaluation starts with the innermost set and continues outward. Thus

```
I = (6 + 3) * 2 ** 4      will yield 144
I = 6 + (3 * 2) ** 4      will yield 1302
I = ((6 + 3) * 2) ** 4    will yield 104,976
```

One of the basic suggestions given to programmers is that if there is any doubt, use parentheses. The FORTRAN compiler is very understanding and will compensate for human insecurity. Furthermore, the parentheses may make the statement easier to read, thus serving as documentation.

2.8.2 Integer arithmetic

With the exception of division, all the arithmetic is standard. Division, on the other hand, depends on the mode of the variables and constants used. At this point we are considering only integer values, so the quotient obtained will always be truncated. For example, 8/3 is 2. And, of course, anything divided by zero will yield a wrong answer; this situation will be discussed in more detail in the next chapter.

There is one other symbol that must be discussed more fully. Placing a minus sign in front of a variable or constant in a situation where subtraction is obviously not intended indicates multiplication by -1. For example,

```
I = -K + 4
```

is shorter but the same as

```
I = -1 * K + 4
```

Another FORTRAN rule is that two symbols cannot be next to each other, but they can be separated by parentheses. Thus exponentiating to a negative power has to be written as

```
I = K ** (-M)
```

Integer division with its truncating feature may seem like a rather useless procedure, but when applied to whole numbers only, it can lead to some very efficient code, for example:

```
C                 The Change Maker
C
C         input:   a value from 0 to 99 cents
C         output:  the number of quarters, dimes, nickels,
C                         and pennies.
C
```

```
C                     input amount of change
      WRITE   (1,1000)
 1000 FORMAT  (1H ,'ENTER AMOUNT OF CHANGE IN I2 FORMAT')
      READ    (2,1002) ICHNGE
 1002 FORMAT  (I2)
C                     calculate change
      NQRTR = ICHNGE / 25
      LEFT  = ICHNGE  -  25 * NQRTR
      NDIME = LEFT / 10
      LEFT  = LEFT  -  10 * NDIME
      NICKL = LEFT / 5
      NPENS = LEFT  -  5 * NICKL
C                     output
      WRITE   (1,1004)
 1004 FORMAT  (1H ,'CHANGE: QUARTERS   DIMES  NICKELS  PENNIES')
      WRITE   (1,1006) ICHNGE, NQRTR, NDIME, NICKL, NPENS
 1006 FORMAT  (1H ,I4, ' = ', 4I9)
C                     termination
      STOP
      END
```

First, notice that the mode of all of the variables and constants is integer; the variables all start with a letter in the range I–N, and the constants do not have decimal points. Thus all the division truncates. The value of the input variable, ICHNGE, is not changed so that it can be output with its original value at the end of the program; this is considered good programming practice. A single temporary variable, LEFT, was used to hold intermediate calculations. Finally, the FORMATs for the output were purposely chosen so that the results, with the exception of the original amount, are printed out right-justified under the headings. The headings were set up in fields of 9 so that we could use an I9 specification with a repetition factor of 4. Sample output for this example would look like:

```
CHANGE: QUARTERS   DIMES  NICKELS  PENNIES
   68 =         2       1        1        3
```

Of course, this is not a perfect program (few are). Input of a value greater than 99 cents will yield a correct answer so long as paper money is not considered. Even 0 will yield a correct answer. But a negative input, rather impossible in this practical example, will not yield correct answers (GIGO, "garbage in, garbage out"). A good program screens or edits the input data to ensure that it is in the right range and provides an error message instead of incorrect answers. Later on, we will be very involved with the quality of data.

2.8.3 Exercises

Exercise 2-9

Write a self-generating program (no input) that outputs a table of squares and cubes for the numbers from 1 to 25. Provide headings for the three columns of output. Use a DO loop rather than constructing your own loops.

Exercise 2-10

Write a program to accept two positive numbers, divide the first into the second and produce a *rounded* quotient, for example, $7/3 = 2$, but $8/3 = 3$. When your program is completed, revise it to handle both positive and negative divisors and dividends. (This can be very easily done in integer arithmetic, once an algorithm is found, and there are many possible algorithms, some more elegant than others.)

Exercise 2-11

Write a program to accept a value from 1 to 7 and compute the factorial of that number. For example, 4! (4 factorial) $= 4 * 3 * 2 * 1 = 24$. Use a DO loop, initializing the product to 1 so that the multiplication will work.

Exercise 2-12

Write a program to accept a whole dollar amount and break it down to $1000, $500, $100, $50, $20, $10, $5, and $1 bills. Allow for five-digit input and devise test data from $1 to $30,000.

2.9 Simple decisions (the IF statement)

Thus far all of our programs have been linear, that is, each statement is executed in order from the first to the STOP, the last logical statement. If we want to edit the input data, we must be able to branch to alternative logics and execute some statements and not others depending on the conditions. We can do this using a conditional branch statement called the IF statement. First we will look at the oldest version of the IF, which appeared in the initial FORTRANs. It was the only version available then; now, there are better ones, which we will cover subsequently.

The syntax of the IF statement is:

```
IF (expression) n1, n2, n3
```

The *expression* can be any valid FORTRAN expression, as simple as a single variable or as complicated as FORTRAN allows. That expression is evaluated and the result compared to zero. The program then proceeds according to the following rules:

If the result is less than zero (negative), the program branches to the statement numbered *n1*.

If the result is zero, the program branches to the statement numbered *n2*.

If the result is greater than zero (positive), the statement branches to the statement numbered *n3*.

This IF statement has become known as the arithmetic IF because the expression can only be arithmetic in nature. It is also known as the three-branched IF. If our logic requires it, the branches need not be unique, that is, two branches can have the same number, as we will show below. (All three branches could be to the same statement, but that wouldn't make any sense!)

Since the arithmetic IF can only compare the expression to zero, it may seem difficult, for example, to compare two variables. But this is not difficult, as any assembly language programmer knows; it is merely a matter of subtracting one variable from the other. For example, to compare ICHNGE to 99, we would code:

```
IF (ICHNGE - 99) n1, n2, n3
```

If ICHNGE is less than 99, the subtraction will yield a negative result, branching to *n1;* if ICHNGE is equal to 99, the result will be zero, exercising the second branch, *n2;* and if ICHNGE is greater than 99, the result will be positive, and the third branch will be taken.

Let's now apply this new statement to our change program:

```
C                 The Change Maker, with Editing
C
C            input:   a value from 0 to 99 cents
C            output:  the number of quarters, dimes, nickels and
C                           pennies.
C
C                 input amount of change
      WRITE   (1,1000)
 1000 FORMAT  (1H ,'ENTER AMOUNT OF CHANGE IN I2 FORMAT')
      READ    (2,1002)  ICHNGE
 1002 FORMAT  (I2)
C                 edit input
      IF  (ICHNGE)  20, 40, 40
   20     WRITE   (1,1020)
 1020     FORMAT  (1H ,'ERROR IN INPUT')
          STOP
```

```
C                     calculate change
   40 NQRTR = ICHNGE / 25
      LEFT  = ICHNGE  -  25 * NQRTR
      NDIME = LEFT / 10
      LEFT  = LEFT  -  10 * NDIME
      NICKL = LEFT / 5
      NPENS = LEFT  -  5 * NICKL
C                     output
      WRITE   (1,1040)
 1040 FORMAT  (1H ,'CHANGE: QUARTERS   DIMES  NICKELS  PENNIES')
      WRITE   (1,1042)  ICHNGE, NQRTR, NDIME, NICKL, NPENS
 1042 FORMAT  (1H ,I4, ' = ', 4I9)
C                     termination
      STOP
      END
```

This program branches into two logical paths, an error message if the input is negative, or the calculation if the input is zero or positive. If we wanted to restrict the input to numbers less than 100, the program could be modified as follows:

```
   IF (ICHNGE) 20, 40, 10
10 IF (ICHNGE - 99) 40, 40, 20
```

Notice that there are two STOPs in this program. This is perfectly logical, but some programmers may question the style. There are two logical paths and two logical endings—very logical! The error routine was indented to emphasize that it is a separate logical path.

2.9.1 Review question

2–1. For values of $I = 5$, $J = -5$, $K = 7$, $L = 2$ and $M = -2$, determine the number of the statement to which the program will branch as a result of the following IF statements:

    a. IF (J) 10, 20, 30
    b. IF (I - J) 10, 20, 30
    c. IF (2 * I - M * J) 10, 20, 30
    d. IF (L / K) 10, 20, 30
    e. IF (M / L + J / I) 10, 20, 30
    f. IF (7) 10, 20, 30

2.10 Unconditional branching (the GO TO statement)

We now come to the most abused statement in programming, the four letters that strike fear into the minds of many purists, the instruction that gives

FORTRAN its bad name: the GO TO. The problem with this unconditional branch is that it allows the programmer to write code in which loops may overlap, branches may conflict, and logic can go both upward to preceding statements and downward to later statements. The often-heard term *spaghetti code* has nothing to do with pasta or Italy—it refers to the look of the convoluted code produced by some novice programmers or programmers with no concept of structure.

However, the GO TO allows a degree of flexibility not found in the "structured" languages. If the GO TO is used properly, the code produced is as fine as that produced by Pascal, Modula-2, or any other restrictive language. Throughout this text the GO TO will be used with discretion and under restrictions placed on it not by the language but by a programmer guided by a structured mind.

The GO TO allows the programmer to build unrestricted loops; with the DO statement, the loop must have an upper value. The specification of that upper value may require a very restrictive program in which the user must supply information about the number of times the loop is to be executed; sometimes the user doesn't know how much data is coming in or doesn't want to restrict the amount of data. Our aim is to write "user-friendly" software that makes the running of the program as simple as possible, even if the programmer must do a lot of work to satisfy that aim. Now let's show how the GO TO allows us to modify our change program to provide an input loop.

```
C                   The Change Maker, with Editing and Multiple Input
C
C              input:      a value from 1 to 99 cents
C                          0 to terminate
C              output:     the number of quarters, dimes, nickels and
C                                      pennies.
C
C                    input amount of change
   20 WRITE    (1,1020)
 1020 FORMAT   (1H ,'ENTER AMOUNT OF CHANGE IN I2 FORMAT')
      WRITE    (1,1022)
 1022 FORMAT   (1H ,'  0 TO TERMINATE')
      READ     (2,1024) ICHNGE
 1024 FORMAT   (I2)
C                    check for end-of-data and edit input
      IF  (ICHNGE)  40, 90, 60
   40     WRITE    (1,1040)
 1040     FORMAT (1H ,'ERROR IN INPUT')
          GO TO 80
```

```
C                       calculate change
   60 NQRTR = ICHNGE / 25
      LEFT  = ICHNGE  -   25 * NQRTR
      NDIME = LEFT / 10
      LEFT  = LEFT   -   10 * NDIME
      NICKL = LEFT / 5
      NPENS = LEFT   -    5 * NICKL
C                       output
      WRITE   (1,1060)
 1060 FORMAT  (1H ,'CHANGE: QUARTERS    DIMES   NICKELS   PENNIES')
      WRITE   (1,1062) ICHNGE, NQRTR, NDIME, NICKL, NPENS
 1062 FORMAT  (1H ,I4, ' = ', 4I9)
   80      GO TO 20
C
C                       termination
   90 STOP
      END
```

There some programmers who believe that having one GO TO branch to another GO TO is redundant. But a program is easier to follow if only one backward branch exists for any single destination statement. The error routine and the GO TO 20 are indented to produce more readable code.

One new technique has been introduced in this program. It is easy enough to build a multiple input loop into a program like this one, but a way to get out of the loop is also needed. In due time we will describe some very fine end-of-data techniques, but in our attempt to keep everything on a very rudimentary level, we have used the concept of a *sentinel* value, that is, a data value that indicates to our program that the end of data has been reached, i.e., the previous value was the last valid piece of data. Now, of course, any value could be picked, but we want a value that would not be likely to occur as input. In this case, zero is a good choice; we would not expect anyone to use it as data since the answer for that input is so obvious. Another reason for using zero is that a null entry, a blank, or on some terminals just hitting the end-of-record key (ENTER or RETURN) will yield the value of 0.

Here we have used the GO TO for two purposes: (1) to rejoin our logical paths at a common point (statement number 80) and (2) to loop back for more input. Actually, the arithmetic IF produces three GO TOs, and that is one reason why it also has a bad reputation. In a FORTRAN program, statement numbers (except those on FORMAT statements) are needed only to serve as the destination of some kind of GO TO, whether explicitly stated or hidden within another instruction.

We will not duck the issue—GO TOs can lead to problems! But languages without a GO TO must often use rather convoluted logic to solve certain problems. Straightforward, direct logic, even if GO TOs are used, is still preferable to stilted code.

2.11 Alternate conditional branching

The arithmetic IF statement can be a difficult statement to appreciate because it is almost always necessary to do a calculation to make the comparison with zero. However, later versions of FORTRAN improved greatly on the statement and eased not only the programmer's work but the program reader's effort. The full FORTRAN IV set included a statement called the logical (or the two-branched) IF based on the truth or falsity of an expression. With the logical IF, the power of the expression was also expanded by adding relational operators:

symbol	relational operation
.LT.	less than
.LE.	less than or equal to
.EQ.	equal to
.NE.	not equal to
.GT.	greater than
.GE.	greater than or equal to

These symbols allow the programmer to make comparisons relationally rather than arithmetically.

In addition, the logical IF allows the programmer to combine arithmetic or relational operations with logical operators. The three operators available in all versions of FORTRAN IV and higher are:

symbol	logical operation	priority
.NOT.	negation	highest
.AND.	conjunction	
.OR.	inclusive disjunction	lowest

The rules followed by the operations are the same as those taught in any language or philosophy course, namely, an .AND. relation is true only when both assumptions are true, an .OR. relation is true when either or both assumptions are true, and the .NOT. operator is used to reverse true and false.

2.11.1 Logical IF

The logical IF statement has the general form

```
IF (condition) statement
```

While the arithmetic IF permits only branching, the logical IF permits any FORTRAN statement (other than a DO or another IF) to be executed if the tested condition is true. The logical IF branches to its auxiliary statement if the tested condition is true and to the next sequential statement if the tested condition is false. Thus the logical IF allows the programmer to execute a single statement with relative ease.

Before we demonstrate our change-making program again, let us mention two rules: (1) within an expression, arithmetic operations take precedence over relational ones and relational ones take precedence over logical ones; however, the use of parentheses gives the programmer control over those priorities; (2) there is no restriction on the number of combinations that can be used.

```
C                       The Change Maker, with Editing and Multiple Input
C
C               input:    a value from 1 to 99 cents
C                         0 to terminate
C               output:   the number of quarters, dimes, nickels and
C                         pennies.
C
C                  input amount of change
   20 WRITE    (1,1020)
 1020 FORMAT   (1H ,'ENTER AMOUNT OF CHANGE IN I2 FORMAT')
      WRITE    (1,1022)
 1022 FORMAT   (1H ,' 0 TO TERMINATE')
      READ     (2,1024) ICHNGE
 1024 FORMAT   (I2)
C                  edit input
      IF (ICHNGE .EQ. 0) STOP
      IF (ICHNGE .GT. 0 .AND. ICHNGE .LE. 99) GO TO 60
C                  error routine
      WRITE    (1,1040)
 1040    FORMAT  (1H ,'ERROR IN INPUT')
      GO TO 80
C                  calculate change
   60 NQRTR = ICHNGE / 25
      LEFT  = ICHNGE  -  25 * NQRTR
      NDIME = LEFT / 10
      LEFT  = LEFT  -  10 * NDIME
      NICKL = LEFT / 5
      NPENS = LEFT  -  5 * NICKL
C                  output
      WRITE    (1,1060)
 1060 FORMAT   (1H ,'CHANGE: QUARTERS   DIMES  NICKELS PENNIES')
      WRITE    (1,1062) ICHNGE, NQRTR, NDIME, NICKL, NPENS
 1062 FORMAT   (1H ,I4, ' = ', 4I9)
   80    GO TO 20
C
C
      END
```

The first logical IF, when true, terminates the program by executing the STOP. Seeing the last logical statement of a program in any physical location other than prior to the END may perturb some programmers, and even the author is not happy with it, but it must be recognized that the STOP need not be near the end. The alternative is to place it prior to the END with a label, say 90, and have the true result of the IF yield a GO TO 90.

The second logical IF edits the input value and permits only those that are greater than 0 *and* less than or equal to 99 to be processed; any value less than 0 *or* greater than 99 will "fall through" to the next sequential statement and enter the error routine. The program demonstrates two applications of the logical IF; one causes the execution of a single command (STOP), and the other causes the execution of a series of commands. If execution of the single statement does not cause a branch or a STOP, processing continues with the next sequential command.

Since most FORTRANs now implement the logical IF, we will continue to use it throughout the text; for those few implementations that still do not have it, the substitute construction requires one or more arithmetic IFs and a few more statement numbers.

However, the logical IF presents a serious structural problem: if we wish to execute a body of instructions when the expression is true, we actually must test for the opposite conditions and skip around the desired series of steps. In the program above, we test for valid data and skip around the routine for invalid data. Thus the programmer must primarily test for a false condition. Although there are ways the programmer can do this fairly logically by wrapping the true conditions in a .NOT., this solution becomes a "kludge." A better solution exists in FORTRAN 77 and is so excellent a solution that the author not only presents it at this point but recommends its use whenever writing in the higher level of FORTRAN. The construction is called the block IF.

2.11.2 Block IF

There are two general forms that can be used for the block IF.

```
IF   (condition) THEN
          statements executed if condition is true
                        :
     ELSE
          statements executed if condition is false
                        :

ENDIF
```

or

```
IF   (condition) THEN
            statements executed if condition is true
                        :
ENDIF
```

The IF..THEN..ELSE..ENDIF structure allows the programmer to encapsulate a series of statements to be executed when the condition is true and to place these statements immediately after the IF; it also allows the same structure to treat the false condition, although the ELSE block is optional. Let us again use the change-making program to illustrate:

```
C                      The Change Maker, with Editing and Multiple Input
C
C              input:    a value from 1 to 99 cents
C                        0 to terminate
C              output:   the number of quarters, dimes, nickels, and
C                              pennies.
C
C                      input amount of change
   20 WRITE    (1,1020)
 1020 FORMAT   (1H ,'ENTER AMOUNT OF CHANGE IN I2 FORMAT')
      WRITE    (1,1022)
 1022 FORMAT   (1H ,'  0 TO TERMINATE')
      READ     (2,1024)  ICHNGE
 1024 FORMAT   (I2)
C                      edit input
      IF  (ICHNGE .EQ. 0)  STOP
      IF  (ICHNGE .GT. 0  .AND.  ICHNGE .LE. 99)  THEN
C                      calculate change
         NQRTR = ICHNGE / 25
         LEFT  = ICHNGE  -  25 * NQRTR
         NDIME = LEFT / 10
         LEFT  = LEFT  -  10 * NDIME
         NICKL = LEFT / 5
         NPENS = LEFT  -  5 * NICKL
C                      output
         WRITE    (1,1060)
 1060    FORMAT   (1H ,'CHANGE: QUARTERS    DIMES  NICKELS  PENNIES')
         WRITE    (1,1062)  ICHNGE, NQRTR, NDIME, NICKL, NPENS
 1062    FORMAT   (1H ,I4, ' = ', 4I9)
      ELSE
```

```
C                      error routine
          WRITE   (1,1064)
  1060    FORMAT  (1H ,'ERROR IN INPUT')
      ENDIF
C
      GO TO 20
C
C
      END
```

Note the reduction in statement numbers and the superior structure provided by this implementation—a significant improvement!

The FORTRAN syntax for the block IF statement considers the THEN part of the command to be in the same instruction as the IF part. If the programmer prefers to place the THEN on a separate line, a continuation indicator is required. Furthermore, some programmers prefer the construction END IF to ENDIF; this is purely a matter of taste.

2.11.3 Exercises

Exercise 2–13

Write a program to accept multiple input, terminating on zero and editing out any negative values, to find all of the factors of the input value. Keep the input value within the range 1 to 32000.

Exercise 2–14

Write a program that accepts multiple input until a sentinel value of -9999 is read, counts the number of input values while it adds them up, and then generates a truncated average before terminating. Don't forget to initialize both the counter and the sum to zero; otherwise, the program may not produce correct results. Output the counter and the input value during the input routine so that the values are verified.

Exercise 2–15

Write a program for multiple input that accepts a year as input and prints one of the following messages: NOT A LEAP YEAR or LEAP YEAR. Remember, leap years are those years evenly divisible by 4, *except* those that are evenly divisible by 100, which are not leap years, *except* those evenly divisible by 400, which are leap years! For example, 1900 was not a leap year; neither will 2100, 2200, or 2300 be leap years, but 2000 and 2400 will be.

2.12 DO loop implementation

Although this chapter serves as an introduction to FORTRAN, some time must be spent on the details of DO loops because of their universal importance in so many programming applications. The simple applications shown in previous sections only scratch the surface of the many ways in which this iterative command is used.

The DO structure itself may be simulated by the use of IFs and GO TOs. For example, the loop:

```
DO mm i = m1, m2, m3
      work of the loop
mm last work statement
```

can be replaced by:

```
i = m1
mm work of the loop
      i = i + m3
  IF  (i .LE. m2)  GO TO mm
```

In many implementations of early versions of FORTRAN, this was the machine code developed. However, what if the values set up for $m1$ and $m2$ are such that $m1 > m2$? If the logic of the loop is followed, it can be seen that the work of the loop is performed once, for $i = m1$.

In other implementations, the logic was as follows:

```
i = m1
mm IF  (i .GT. m2)  GO TO nn
      work of the loop
      i = i + m3
  GO TO mm
nn      etc.
```

With this logic, the work of the loop is not executed at all if $m1$ is greater than $m2$.

(As a personal note, when the author was writing his first professional FORTRAN programs, most information about the language came from the manufacturer's manual. The FORTRAN implemented by the Control Data Corporation (CDC) used the latter method of implementing DO loops, and the author would set the value of $m2$ to zero if he didn't want the loop executed. Some years later, the program was to be translated to an IBM computer by the author and a colleague. The colleague, schooled on IBM manuals, claimed that this "gimmick" would not work. The argument became one of "Yes, it will," "No, it won't," until both of us reached for our manuals, mine, the gospel according to CDC, his, the gospel according to IBM. Lo and behold, the manuals differed! This experience was the author's first taste of the different dialects of the FORTRAN language.)

One of the faults of the specifications of 1966 was that they detailed what should happen only if the DO instruction was used according to the rules, that is, if *m1* was less than or equal to *m2*. But the specifications did not tell what would happen if the rules were not followed. As we will see, there are a number of instructions that became machine dependent when improperly used. The DO loop was one of them.

Fortunately, the 1977 specifications were far more precise about how the loop should work. In fact, the loop can perform many more functions under this revision. However, within the definition of the 1966 loop (that is, an increasing index), the implementation used in FORTRAN 77 is the second one, where the work of the loop is not done when the initial value exceeds the final value. The code generated is something like this:

```
      i = m1
      n = maximum ((m2 - m1 + m3)/m3, 0)
mm IF  (n .EQ. 0) GO TO nn
         work of the loop
         i = i + m3
         n = n - 1
   IF  (n .GT. 0)  GO TO mm
nn       and so forth
```

However, we want to avoid problems with conflicting dialects and thus must insist that the programmer control the execution of the loop by the appropriate logic so that the program is universally accepted in all versions of FORTRAN. Thus we will always make sure that *m2* is equal to or greater than *m1*.

2.12.1 DO loop exhaustion

Another interesting situation reflects the FORTRAN language developers' attitude that if the loop is exhausted, that is, all values of the index have been executed, then the value of the index is no longer needed. The logic illustrated in all the DO loop cases presented above implies that at the end of the execution of

```
      DO 100 I = 1,10
              :
100 end of loop
```

the value of the index I would be 11. However, in many of the early computers, the index of the loop was put into a high-speed register to speed up processing of the program, and since the specifications allowed the destruction of the index for exhausted loops, many of the implementations, notably IBM, never transferred the value from the high-speed register to the variable location, stating that the index is "indeterminate." Thus many of the older programs were forced to restate the index value if it was needed for any later calculation.

For example, let's look at a program that reads in up to 30 values and averages them. Input is terminated by a value of -9999 or by reading 30 values, whichever comes first.

```
C                      Read up to 30 values and average
C
C               initialize sum
      ISUM = 0
C               input loop
      DO 20  I = 1,30
           READ  (2,1000)  NUMBER
 1000     FORMAT  (I5)
           IF  (NUMBER .EQ. -9999)  GO TO 40
   20 ISUM = ISUM + NUMBER
C               reset index
      I = 31
   40 NUMVAL = I - 1
      IAVERG = ISUM / NUMVAL
C               output
      WRITE  (1,1040)  NUMVAL, IAVERG
 1040 FORMAT  (1H ,'With', I3,' values, the average is', I5)
      STOP
      END
```

In this program, the amount of input is controlled by the DO loop parameters, but the loop can be branched out of if the data ends before 30 values have been read. In all FORTRANs, when a branch is made out of a loop *before* exhaustion, the value of the index is available and can be used to calculate the amount of input.

Using the index to determine the number of data items requires a decrementation of its value (NUMVAL = I − 1) because the end-of-data value is also read. Consider the sample data below:

I	value read
1	82
2	98
3	79
4	85
5	−9999

On the fifth read, the end-of-data value is input and the loop is terminated by the IF statement; the value of I is one greater than the number of pieces of valid data read and must be decremented to obtain the correct number of pieces of valid data.

However, if the programmer cannot count on the system to place the appropriate value back into I when the loop is exhausted, programming to set the correct value is required. For example, the statement

```
I = 31
```

before statement 40 sets the value of I if the loop is exhausted.

2.12.2 Testing DO loop implementation

The program below is useful for determining the method of implementation used for the DO loop in any particular machine. Another alternative is to compile the program and list it in assembly language so that it can be studied.

```
C               Test of DO Loop Implementation
C
   20 WRITE  (1,1020)
 1020 FORMAT (1H ,'Enter lower and upper DO loop parameters (2I3)')
      READ  (2,1022)  M1, M2
 1022 FORMAT (2I3)
      IF  (M1 .EQ. 0  .AND.  M2 .EQ. 0)  STOP
C               execute loop
      DO 100  I = M1, M2
  100 WRITE  (1,1100)  I
 1100 FORMAT (1H ,'Index =', I4)
C               exhaustion
      WRITE  (1,1102)  I
 1102 FORMAT (1H ,'Exhaustion value of index =', I4)
          GO TO 20
C
      END
```

Entering values of 3 and 2 for M1 and M2, respectively, will test the implementation to see if the work of the loop is executed once or not at all when the initial parameter is greater than the final parameter. This program also displays the exhaustion value.

2.13 More on DO loops

And there is still more to talk about with DO loops!

In the previous section, we saw that it is permissible to branch out of the range of a DO loop at any time; that branch can be a GO TO or a STOP. However, it is *not* permissible to branch into the range of a DO loop from outside its range; all entrances to a DO loop *must* be made at the DO statement. If a DO

loop is entered in the middle of its range, the index and loop control are not set
up, and indeterminate results and sometimes an infinite loop can result.

```
                        . . . .  GO TO ii          valid
                        . . . .  GO TO jj          invalid
          ii      DO mm i = m1, m2, m3
                              :
          jj                  :
range of                . . . .  GO TO nn          valid
the loop                . . . .  GO TO jj          valid
                        . . . .  GO TO ii          infinite loop
                              :
          mm      last statement in range of loop
                              :
                        . . . .  GO TO jj          invalid
                        . . . .  GO TO ii          valid
      nn                      :
```

The only valid branch to statement *jj* is from within the range of the loop itself;
the other branches to *jj* come from outside the range and are invalid.

Of course, if the programmer attempts to branch into the loop from outside
the loop, some compilers will issue a warning message. (There are some circumstances where branching into the range of the loop after having branched out of
it is legal and logical.) Some systems will abort the execution of the program
when the improper branch occurs, and some will just let the error go undetected
and leave the program to do its thing, which can't possibly yield correct answers!

Keep in mind that DO loops are used so often that some systems try to optimize their execution by using special high-speed registers for the index. Thus
if a programmer tries to set the value of the index outside the range of the loop
before branching into the middle of its range, that value may not go into the
appropriate register; that is why this type of branch is not permitted.

There are some other rules that relate to the index and the controlling parameters. Although these parameters can be accessed, that is, output or used in
calculations, their values must *never* be reset inside the loop. To do so would be
to attempt to take control of the loop from the already set up logic, and this can
only lead to disaster. If the index has been put into a high-speed register, it cannot
be reset by an assignment statement. In FORTRAN 77, the number of iterations
(repeats) are calculated at the beginning of the loop, and modifying the index
later will have no effect on how many times the loop will execute.

The rules are straightforward: always enter a DO loop at the DO statement
and let the DO loop logic control the loop operation!

Another restriction of the DO loop structure is that the last statement in the
loop, the one on which the final statement number is placed, cannot be a transfer,
branch, or nonexecutable statement such as IF, GO TO, STOP, or FORMAT;
nor can it be another DO statement. If one of those forbidden statements should
logically be at the end of the loop, another statement with the final statement
number is added to the loop.

2.13.1 CONTINUE statement

The CONTINUE statement is a do-nothing command (similar to the NOP in assembly language) that in no way affects the logic of the program but on which a statement number can be hung. Many programmers use it for documentation by placing it at the end of every DO loop, whether needed or not. Many also use it to indicate the rejoining of logical paths. Its use when not necessary is strictly discretionary.

A DO loop with a CONTINUE statement has the following form:

```
      DO mm i = m1, m2, m3
              :
              :
         IF (expression) GO TO nn
mm CONTINUE
```

2.13.2 Nested DO loops

FORTRAN allows DO loops to be nested within other DO loops provided their ranges do not conflict.

Example of nonconflicting ranges

```
         DO   mm   i = m1, m2, m3
                     :
            DO   nn   j = n1, n2, n3
                        :
                        :
   nn last statement of nn loop
                     :
   mm last statement of mm loop
```

Example of conflicting ranges

```
         DO   mm   i = m1, m2, m3
                     :
            DO   nn   j = n1, n2, n3
                        :
                        :
   mm last statement of mm loop
                     :
   nn last statement of nn loop
```

A large number of nested loops is permitted, usually 50 or more, depending on the compiler. Seldom do programmers find the necessity for more than 5 nested loops.

The branching rules discussed earlier apply to nested loops as well. Because an inner loop is completely within an outer one, branching from the inner loop to anyplace in the range of the outer loop is permitted; but entrance to the inner loop from the outer can only be made through the inner loop's DO statement.

As an example of nested loops, here is a program that a consultant uses to figure his weekly earnings for various fees and hours worked:

```
C                    Consulting Fee Table
C
      DO 100  IRATE = 36, 44, 2
          WRITE  (1,1000)  IRATE
 1000     FORMAT  (1H ,'Rate = $', I3, 4X, 'Hours      Fee')
          DO 80  IHOURS = 20, 40, 5
              IFEE = IRATE * IHOURS
   80     WRITE  (1,1080)  IHOURS, IFEE
 1080     FORMAT  (1H ,15X, I5, 3X,'$',I4)
  100 CONTINUE
      STOP
      END
```

The output would be:

```
Rate = $ 36      Hours      Fee
                    20   $  720
                    25   $  900
                    30   $1080
                    35   $1260
                    40   $1440
Rate = $ 38      Hours      Fee
                    20   $  760
                    25   $  950
                    30   $1140
                    35   $1330
                    40   $1520
Rate = $ 40      Hours      Fee
                    20   $  800
                     :
                     :
Rate = $ 44      Hours      Fee
                    20   $  880
                    25   $1100
                    30   $1320
                    35   $1540
                    40   $1760
```

We can make a variation in this program to utilize a feature of the compiler. When the outer of two nested DO loops ends with a CONTINUE statement immediately after the last statement of the inner loop, the CONTINUE statement can be eliminated and the two loops can share the terminating statement of the inner loop without any conflict. In this case, the shared terminating state-

ment "belongs" to the inner loop and the compiler generates a terminating CON-
TINUE for the outer loop. Thus the above program can be modified to:

```
C                 Consulting Fee Table
C
      DO 80  IRATE = 36, 44, 2
           WRITE  (1,1000)  IRATE
 1000      FORMAT  (1H ,'Rate = $', I3, 4X, 'Hours      Fee')
           DO 80  IHOURS = 20, 40, 5
               IFEE = IRATE * IHOURS
   80 WRITE  (1,1080)  IHOURS, IFEE
 1080 FORMAT  (1H ,15X, I5, 3X,'$',I4)
      STOP
      END
```

We will see this technique used later on for multiply nested loops all sharing the
same terminating statement.

2.13.3 Review question

2–2. For each of the following DO loop setups, determine the final value of
N:

a.
```
      N = 1
      DO 20 I = 1,15,7
   20 N = N * I
```

b.
```
      N = 1
      DO 20 I = 1,20,7
   20 N = N * I
```

c.
```
      N = 0
      DO 40   I = 2,5
         DO 20   J = I,7,2
             IF  (J .EQ. 3) GO TO 20
             N = N + J
   20    CONTINUE
   40 N = N / 2
```

d.
```
      N = 5
      DO 40 I = 10, 12
         DO 20   J = 1, 5, 2
             IF  (I .EQ. 11 .AND. J .EQ. 3) GO TO 40
   20    N = N + I / J
   40 N = N + 1
```

2.13.4 Exercises

Exercise 2–16

Using a doubly nested set of DO loops, output a multiplication table. The outer loop should run from 2 to 12 and the inner loop from the value of the outer loop to 12 so that there is no repetition in the table. The output will run from 2 x 2 to 2 x 12, then 3 x 3 to 3 x 12, and so forth, up to 11 x 11, 11 x 12, and 12 x 12. No IF statements should be necessary.

Exercise 2–17

Using a doubly nested set of DO loops, output an integer division table. The outer loop should control the numerator and run from 1 to 10, and the inner loop should control the denominator; the table should be limited to nonzero answers. Again, no IFs are necessary.

Exercise 2–18

Modify the multiplication table in exercise 2–16 to output only answers greater than or equal to 20. IFs will be necessary here.

2.14 Carriage control and additional formatting

Earlier in this chapter (section 2.3), we introduced the concept of carriage control and the use of the 1H blank (or the literal blank or the 1X) at the beginning of the output format. The printers used on today's computers can be given various instructions for vertical movement of the paper before any printing operation. The first character sent to the printer controls that movement and is thus responsible for *carriage control,* that is, control of the carriage that holds the printer paper.

 Most printers have the capacity to handle at least 132 print columns, and some are able to handle 144 columns. The WRITE and FORMAT statements first place the information to be printed into a *printer buffer,* then the information is transmitted to the printer for the physical printing. The buffer has one more column than there are print positions in order to accommodate the carriage control character. Since this carriage control is specified first but is not actually printed, we will call the carriage control column column 0 so as not to confuse it with the 132 or 144 valid print positions. For example, the statements:

```
      N = -12
      M = 8
      WRITE  (1,1000) N, M
1000 FORMAT  (1H ,2I4)
```

first blank out the buffer and then set up the following:

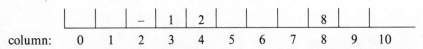

The blank in column 0 causes the printer to move to the next line prior to printing the contents of the rest of the buffer.

There are four specified carriage control characters in both the 1966 and the 1977 specifications; some manufacturers have additional nonstandard controls:

character	vertical movement before printing	method
blank	One line	(1H , or (' ', or (1X,
0	Two lines (skips a line)	(1H0, or ('0',
1	Top-of-form (new page)	(1H1, or ('1',
+	No advance (print on same line)	(1H+, or ('+',

The 1X alternative for 1H blank skips over the already blanked-out column 0.

For example, if FORMAT 1000 in the above example had started with (1H0, the buffer would have held:

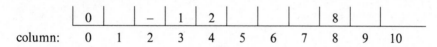

and a line would have been skipped before printing. If the last printed line was line 10, this output would have been on line 12.

The statements

```
      WRITE    (5,1000)
1000 FORMAT    (1H1, 'NEW PAGE AND TITLE')
```

put the heading NEW PAGE AND TITLE on a new page, and

```
      WRITE    (5,1000)
1000 FORMAT    (1H0,'SECRET')
      WRITE    (5,1002)
1002 FORMAT    (1H+, 'XXXXXX')
```

overprints XXXXXX on top of SECRET.

The carriage control character can also be entered as literal output with the apostrophes or even combined with other literal output:

```
1000 FORMAT ('1NEW PAGE AND TITLE')
```

However, the author does not recommend this method, as it often leads to miscounted characters or, worse yet, forgotten character control. Look, for example, at what might happen if carriage control were combined with a numeric field:

```
      DO 20    I = N1, N2
  20 WRITE    (5,1020)  I
1020 FORMAT    (I4)
```

In this case (an actual case taken from the author's long history of stupid bugs), the values of N1 and N2 were expected to be less than 1000 and it was expected that each of the numbers would occupy print positions 1, 2, and 3 and column 0 would have the leading blank that is automatically inserted with integer output. However, the actual value of N2 was over 999 and the following output occurred:

```
                    :
                    :
                    995
                    996
                    997
                    998
                    999

new page            000

new page            001

new page            002
                    :
                    :
```

The remarks the author made at the time are unprintable! From that time on, however, it has always been his style to use the Hollerith specification at the beginning of every output format.

Although carriage control has no meaning to screen or typewriter output, some manufacturers maintain consistency for all output hardware by expecting the carriage control character. On the screen, the carriage control characters 0 and blank act as they would on a printer; the + wipes out the previous line as it overwrites a new line; the 1 may cause a skip of either 6 or 12 lines, depending on the system.

2.14.1 End of I/O record

The final parenthesis at the end of the Format statement indicates the end of the I/O record. When there are more format field specifications than variables in the I/O list, the rest of the format is ignored. Should there be a longer list of variables than available format field specifications, control goes to the next I/O line and to the specifications following the opening parenthesis. If there is more than one set of parentheses, control returns to the rightmost opening parenthesis and includes any repetition factor before that opening parenthesis. For example:

```
    READ (4,1000) I, J, K
1000 FORMAT (2I5)
```

will read:

record	columns 1–5	columns 6–10
1	I	J
2	K	

Another means of indicating end of I/O record is the slash (/) in the Format statement. In output formats, there must be a new carriage control character immediately following the slash, since each I/O record is still independent. For example, the statements

```
      I = 10
      J = 20
      K = 30
      WRITE (1,1000) I, J, K
1000 FORMAT (1H1,'NEW PAGE'//1H0,'HEADINGS'/(1H ,2I5))
```

will yield the following output:

page	line	
1	1	NEW PAGE
1	2	
1	3	
1	4	HEADINGS
1	5	10 20
1	6	30

The 1H1 causes a jump to line 1 of a new page. The first slash indicates the end of line 1, and the second slash indicates the end of line two. There are no specifications between the two slashes. Since the printer buffer is first blanked out before any characters are placed in it, the absence of specifications places a blank in column 0, causing the printer to move to the next line, line 2. (The general rule is that n consecutive slashes will cause $n-1$ skipped lines if the slashes are not at the end of the FORMAT. At the end of the FORMAT, the closing parenthesis also serves as an end of I/O line so that n consecutive slashes with the parenthesis will cause n skipped lines.) The 1H0 causes line 3 to be skipped, so the next output is on line 4. The next slash marks the end of line 4, and the ensuing 1H blank causes a movement to line 5. The closing parenthesis indicate the end of line 5. When the FORMAT is exhausted and there is still more to be output, control returns to the rightmost opening parenthesis, and the 1H blank causes movement to line 6, where the last variable is output.

Changing the FORMAT slightly to leave out the internal set of parentheses

```
1000 FORMAT (1H1,'NEW PAGE'//1H0,'HEADINGS'/1H ,2I5)
```

would result in the following output:

page	line	
1	1	NEW PAGE
1	2	
1	3	
1	4	HEADINGS
1	5	10 20
2	1	NEW PAGE
2	2	
2	3	
2	4	HEADINGS
2	5	30

since format control would go all the way back to the 1H1.

Skipping lines after printing can be forced by placing slashes before the closing parenthesis, one for each line to be skipped. Thus

```
FORMAT (1H0,'HEADINGS'///)
```

will cause three blank lines to be placed after HEADINGS is printed.

(One quick note: in some versions of FORTRAN 66, in particular IBM and Prime, a consecutive slash and closing parenthesis was considered a single end of I/O line, so that only two blank lines would be placed after the literal. One solution is to place a 1H blank or 1X between the last slash and the closing parenthesis to force the third blank line.)

2.14.2 List-directed output

On some systems there is also a list-directed (format-free) output, which is very handy for test programs. The spacing of the output is system dependent and not under the control of the programmer. The general form is:

```
WRITE (1,*) I, J, K
```

2.14.3 Review question

2–3. For the following program, write out the output, indicating pages, lines, and columns.

```
      I = 12
      J = 24
      K = 36
      WRITE  (5,1000) I, J, K
1000 FORMAT  (1H1,'SAMPLE OUTPUT'////1H ,3X,'I', 3X,'J'//
     1                (1H+,2I4//))
```

2.15 Simple data files

As we proceed to more extensive programs, using only a terminal for data input and output becomes more unworkable. The reader using a card-based system can place test data on cards, and the reader who has direct access to a printer can get a hardcopy (printout) of the computer run. But on most minicomputers and on mainframes there is neither card input nor direct access to the printer, and we must now consider elementary methods that the reader can use to set up permanent input files and printable output files. This section is not meant to be a definitive explanation of files and file structure (chapter 7 will do that), but it should provide as much guidance as necessary to enable the reader to set up the minimum files needed to run and test programs efficiently.

The input and output files we need are defined as sequential, formatted, character files; in these files information is stored just as it is entered or as it would be printed. The records in the file are of variable length, containing just as much information as required followed by an end-of-line (EOL) character, an internal code invisible to the user. Thus, even if we are using a 132-character printer, an output line of 70 characters requires only a 72-character record (the additional characters are for carriage control and end-of-line). Using a fixed-length record is permissible but wasteful of disk space.

Input files may be generated by using a text editor or as the output file of a program written to generate the data. In a classroom situation, the instructor often sets up an input file to be used by the students. Output files are generated by the program and may be designed for either screen or printer output or both.

The process of accessing a disk file involves three steps:

1. Opening the file for either reading or writing.
2. Accessing the file with READ or WRITE.
3. Closing the file before termination of the program.

2.15.1 OPEN and CLOSE

On some systems, any file used must be specifically opened and closed. FORTRAN 77 specifies an OPEN instruction; other FORTRANs will have some other method for performing the same functions. The purpose of the OPEN statement is to provide the name of the file (according to the file naming provisions of the particular system), assign it a logical unit number to be used in the FORTRAN I/O commands, and specify whether it is an input or output file; the OPEN statement has the subcommand STATUS=, which is to be followed by either OLD for input or NEW for output. (There is one problem with using NEW—the file must not already exist; depending on the system, it may be necessary to either delete the output file or change the status to OLD before running the test program the second time.)

The general form of the OPEN statement is:

```
OPEN (n, FILE='aaaaaaa', STATUS='bbb', FORM='FORMATTED')
```

where n is the desired logical unit number to be used by the READ or WRITE commands, '*aaaaaaa*' is the file name and '*bbb*' is either 'OLD' or 'NEW'.

On the IBM PC and compatibles, the printer can be accessed directly with the statement:

```
OPEN (n, FILE='PRN')
```

where the desired logical unit number is substituted for n.

Prior to the termination of the program, any files used must be closed. In FORTRAN 77, the command is:

```
CLOSE (n)
```

where n is the logical unit number of the file. In non-77 FORTRANs there will be some other mechanism for closing the file. Some FORTRANs will automatically close all open files upon termination of the program (STOP), but some will not. Thus the user must find out the operating system command for closing files accidentally left open by programs that bomb out prematurely or files not closed by the program.

Some systems provide a default series of numbers that automatically open and close files used during the running of a FORTRAN program. For example, on the VAX super-mini, any unspecified logical unit number except 5 or 6 automatically accesses a file of the name FOR*nnn*.DAT, where *nnn* is the unspecified number; the numbers 5 and 6 are excluded since they are used to address the screen and keyboard of the user terminal on that system. Some other systems do similar things, making the programming effort much simpler, since the user no longer must be concerned with the specific opening and closing of files but need only use the READ and WRITE commands.

The reader will need to determine the procedure required for these two files on his or her computer. The reader will also have to find out how disk files are printed; in some cases, those developed by FORTRAN programs must have an additional option stated so that the carriage control character is properly handled.

Oftentimes, especially during the program development cycle when much testing is done, it is expedient to have simultaneous output to both screen and printer/disk so that the programmer can see the results immediately and possibly save the printing of erroneous results. This is one situation where it is advantageous to have consistent carriage control for all output devices, because the programmer can have simultaneous output with two WRITE statements but only one FORMAT. On the other hand, since the screen is usually only 80 characters wide, it might still be necessary to have two sets of WRITEs and FORMATs.

There are some screens available that will operate in 132-character format, eliminating the inconsistency.

2.15.2 Echo check and END= clause

Providing an *echo check* of input data is another useful technique. An output file should communicate the complete data to the user; the user should not have to examine the input file to see what the input data was. The echo check outputs the input data into the output file and thus provides a complete picture of the computation in one place. As an example of this procedure, we will repeat a program from section 2.12, reading the input data from a file numbered 6 and writing the output data to a file numbered 7.

When data is written to a file, an end-of-file (EOF) mark is placed at the end of that file (it is invisible to the user). This mark is readable by FORTRAN and enables us to end our input routines without requiring the artificial sentinel value. Our input statement now becomes:

```
READ (n,numf, END=ns) I/O list
```

where *n* is the logical unit number, *numf* the FORMAT statement number and *ns* the number of the statement to be branched to when the end-of-file is detected. The EOF is contained in a separate record, so the number of valid data records is still one less than the number of records read. The program below also illustrates the use of the end-of-file mark.

```
C                 Read up to 30 values and average
C
C                 open files  (if necessary)
      OPEN  (6, FILE='DATAIN', STATUS='OLD', FORM='FORMATTED')
      OPEN  (7, FILE='OUTFILE', STATUS='NEW', FORM='FORMATTED')
C                 initialize sum
      ISUM = 0
      WRITE  (7,1002)
      WRITE  (1,1002)
 1002 FORMAT  (1H1,'Input Values')
C                 input loop
      DO 20  I = 1,30
          READ  (6,1000, END=40)  NUMBER
 1000     FORMAT  (I5)
C           echo check
          WRITE  (7,1004)  NUMBER
          WRITE  (1,1004)  NUMBER
 1004     FORMAT  (1H ,I6)
```

```
C               add to sum
   20 ISUM = ISUM + NUMBER
C               reset index
      I = 31
   40 NUMVAL = I - 1
      IAVERG = ISUM / NUMVAL
C               output
      WRITE  (7,1040)  NUMVAL, IAVERG
      WRITE  (1,1040)  NUMVAL, IAVERG
 1040 FORMAT  (1H0,'With', I3,' values, the average is', I5)
C               close files  (if necessary)
      CLOSE  (6)
      CLOSE  (7)
      STOP
      END
```

2.15.3 Journal or log files

The are some alternative ways of producing hard copies of computer runs. Some computers provide for a journal or log file that, when opened, keeps a record of everything that is displayed on the screen. The file can later be closed and printed (or displayed) when desired. Some of the microcomputers allow the I/O devices to be linked. For example, by linking the screen and the printer, everything that is programmed to appear on the screen also goes to the printer. This is useful for obtaining an immediate printout of the computer run when debugging.

2.16 Generation of random test data

The generation of test data can be a very boring task, especially when a large amount of it is needed. In addition, there is always the psychological problem— when a programmer selects data to test a program, he or she picks data similar to the data the program is expected to work with. In professional environments, the designer of test data is usually someone other than the programmer in order to try to get a true test.

One way of getting somewhat unbiased test data is to use a random number generator. Although it is true that it is impossible to generate real randomness on a computer, the pseudorandom numbers that we get are often sufficient for our purposes.

FORTRAN 77 and its predecessors do not specify a random number generator as part of FORTRAN, but almost all manufacturers supply one. Thus there is no consistency between the various generators available. However, almost all of them require a seed or beginning value; the series of "random" numbers obtained from a given seed is always constant, so it is necessary to vary the seed if you need different values each time. Some programmers access certain system functions like the clock, for example, and use the seconds for the seed.

This method provides a certain degree of randomness and 60 different series of values.

The random number generator supplies a real number between 0.0 and 1.0, and the programmer must multiply by the appropriate constant and perhaps add a constant to get the desired range. The illustrative program below generates 80 integer values from 50 to 100 and stores them in file 8. The function used requires a negative value as the seed and a positive number to continue the sequence.

```
C                     Generate 80 Random Values for Test Data
C
C               open file
      OPEN  (8, FILE='TESTDATA', STATUS='NEW', FORM='FORMATTED')
C               generate first value
      NUMBER = RAN(-1.0)*51.0 + 50.0
      WRITE  (8,1000)  NUMBER
 1000 FORMAT  (I3)
C               generate balance of numbers
      DO 20  I = 2,80
         NUMBER = RAN(1.0)*51.0 + 50.0
      WRITE  (8,1000)  NUMBER
C               close file and terminate
      CLOSE (8)
      STOP
      END
```

2.17 Summary and additional exercises

This chapter should provide enough basic FORTRAN for the reader to begin programming with very little concern about the level of implementation on his or her computer. However, as the chapter developed, the more detailed explanations gave a foretaste of the rest of the text. The review questions and exercises below will give the reader a chance to test his or her knowledge of the material and to write some useful programs, developing some useful techniques while testing the FORTRAN compiler being used. In all cases, the only arithmetic used is in integer mode. The programmer should strive for a clearly designed program (including comments for documentation) and a fully annotated output where all values are identified.

In summary, we have touched upon the following FORTRAN topics, commands, and subcommands:

topic	section
Assignment	2.8
CLOSE	2.15
CONTINUE	2.13
DO	2.5
ELSE	2.11
END	2.2
END = (in READ statement)	2.15
FORMAT	2.3
GO TO	2.10
IF, arithmetic	2.9
IF, logical	2.11
IF..THEN..ELSE..ENDIF	2.11
Integer arithmetic	2.8
OPEN	2.15
READ	2.7
STOP	2.2
WRITE	2.3

2.17.1 Review questions

2–4. What are the errors in the following Format statements?

```
a. 1000  FORMAT (1H ,14HERROR MESSAGE)
b. 1000  FORMAT (1H ,'IT'S A GREAT DAY!')
c. 1000  FORMAT (1H ,17HNOW WHAT'S WRONG?)
```

2–5. Which of the following variable names are valid for integer mode?

a. NOW   f. IF
b. IS   g. IN2
c. THE   h. L
d. TIME   i. NTGER
e. 2GO   j. HELPME

2–6. For what values of the index I will the DO loop be executed?

```
a. DO 20 I = 3, 20, 3
b. DO 20 I = 1, 1
c. DO 20 I = 40, 50, 5
```

2–7. For the following nested loops, what values of N will be displayed?

```
      N = 0
      DO 10  I = 1, 5
         DO 10  J = 2, 6, 2
            N = N + 1
   10 WRITE  (1,1010) N
 1010 FORMAT  (1H ,I6)
```

2–8. Evaluate the following expressions according to the rules of FORTRAN:

   a. 3 + 4 * 5
   b. 3 / 4 + 5
   c. (3 + 4) * (5 + 6)
   d. (3 + 4) * 5 + 6
   e. 3 + 4 * 5 + 6
   f. 3 / 4 + 5 / 6
   g. 68 / 3 / 6

2–9. For L = 8 and M = 9, determine if the following expressions are true or false:

   a. IF (L / 2 * 2 .EQ. L)
   b. IF (M / 2 * 2 .EQ. M)

   What is this type of instruction useful for?

2–10. Determine if the following expressions are true or false:

   a. IF (5 .GT. 0 .AND. 5 .LE. 10)
   b. IF (5 .GT. 20 .OR. 5 .LT. 10)

2–11. Give the algebraic equivalent of each of the following FORTRAN expressions:

   a. I / J + K
   b. I + J * K / M * N
   c. I + J / (K + L)
   d. (I + J) / (K + L)
   e. N * (N − 1) / 2
   f. J ** 3 − 4 * M * N
   g. I / K ** M
   h. I * K ** (−M)

2.17.2 Exercises

Exercise 2–19

Write a program to input an integer number (positive or negative) and, using only integer arithmetic, determine if it is a multiple of 5. The output should consist of the number itself and the message 'MULTIPLE OF 5' or 'NOT A MULTIPLE OF 5'.

Exercise 2–20

Write a program to input two integer numbers and determine if the numbers are of like or unlike sign. Assume that 0 is positive. The output should consist of the two numbers and the message 'LIKE' or 'UNLIKE'.

Exercise 2–21

Write a program to input two integers (positive or negative) and determine if they are of like or unlike parity. Two even numbers or two odd numbers are of like parity, one even number and one odd number are of unlike parity.

Exercise 2–22

Write a program to input a non-negative integer number and determine, only by using integer arithmetic, whether this number is a perfect square or not.

Exercise 2–23

Write a program to read in integer numbers (positive and negative), preferably from a randomly generated data file, and count the number of positives, negatives, and zeros. Calculate the total count, that is, the sum of the number of positive numbers, negative numbers, and zeros, and see if it agrees with the total number of pieces of data read.

Exercise 2–24

Write a program to read in positive integers and determine whether they are prime numbers. Display the number and the appropriate message.

3

Storage of numeric data and real numbers

3.1 Introduction

In this chapter we begin our detailed look at the FORTRAN language and how it is commonly implemented on a variety of computers. We take the approach that a good programmer can write good application code with but a smattering of knowledge of the language but always desires the full understanding that thorough study yields. It is the author's contention that a professional programmer is interested in not only how but why; the more knowledge, the better the programmer.

This chapter illustrates how knowledge of numeric storage in a digital computer enables the programmer to understand problems that arise, to get around "impossible" situations, and to use FORTRAN in applications that might be out of the question otherwise. Although FORTRAN was not designed for commercial applications, it was the only high-level language available for a number of years, so it was used by many programmers who used their knowledge of the language to develop techniques that expanded the usefulness of FORTRAN beyond the dreams of its creators. Its inherent imprecision was conquered, and to this day there are still environments where FORTRAN handles all of the commercial applications, including payroll, cost accounting, and financial reports, without losing a penny!

This chapter includes rather detailed descriptions of how numeric information is stored in the computer, whether in memory, on disk, or on tape. Usually some of this detail is covered in a course in assembly language or machine architecture; we are including it here not only for those readers who need the background but also because of its influence on FORTRAN programming.

While debugging, it is often critical to view the actual storage of data in memory (regular or peripheral) to determine whether the data or the program code is causing the problem. Some FORTRANs have facilities for binary-oriented (octal or hexadecimal) output format specifications as a further aid to the programmer, and most operating systems have a dump facility that displays or prints the binary representation of the data. The material in this chapter will enable the reader to interpret this information.

3.1.1 What the reader needs to know for this chapter

1. How to convert integers from the decimal number system to binary and back.

2. The maximum storage size for integer numbers on the computer in use, in terms of either bits (16 or 32) or bytes (2 or 4).

3. The number of bits or bytes used for both single precision and double precision reals and how they are allocated.

4. The availability of Byte mode (optional).

5. The availability of Logical mode (optional).

3.2 The binary number system

Even though the programmer working in a high-level language such as FORTRAN is primarily interested in decimal-based numbers, it is critical that he or she be aware of the exact method of storage of numeric data in order to understand the restrictions of range and the problems of precision. The binary number system is used because digital computers can store information most accurately in a *bipolar state,* that is, a state based on two mutually exclusive conditions. The binary number system is a base 2 system in which there are only two binary digits (*bits*), 0 and 1.

Within a computer, all arithmetic is based on the binary number system. The addition and multiplication tables are quite simple, and as a result, the electronics necessary to perform the arithmetic is both inexpensive and extremely fast.

addition				*multiplication*		
+	0	1		×	0	1
0	0	1		0	0	0
1	1	0 + carry		1	0	1

$$1 + 1 + 1 = 1 + \text{carry}$$

It has become common nowadays to base hardware and software design (the "architecture" of the computer) on a multiple of 8 bits. This 8-bit module is called a *byte.* Thus we hear of 8-bit computers, 16-bit computers, 32-bit computers, 64-bit computers, and even higher. At first we will work with 8-bit numbers in order to keep our explanations and examples simple.

The numbers that can be expressed in 8 bits range from 00000000 to 11111111 or, in decimal, from 0 to 255. However, this leaves no room for negative numbers. There are some unusual implementations of FORTRAN that use *unsigned* numbers, but *signed* numbers are far more important in general calculations.

3.3 Complementary arithmetic

Complementary arithmetic is a method in which negative numbers are stored in such a way that addition can be performed on any two numbers by the same process regardless of sign. If you were to perform the addition of +23 and −58, the normal procedure requires a number of decisions (which absolute value is higher? what sign should the answer have?). The theory and development of complementary arithmetic is usually covered in a course in computer mathematics, Boolean algebra, or computer architecture, so it will not be presented here. Suffice it to say that positive numbers are represented with the first bit of the grouping equal to zero, so that the range becomes 00000000 to 01111111 or 0 to 127 in decimal, effectively half of the unsigned range.

The method described here is called *two's complement*. A negative number is stored in *complementary* form, which in binary means that the bits are reversed (zeros become ones, ones become zeros) then one is added. Thus, -18 is derived by first determining the binary equivalent of $+18$ and then complementing the number.

$$
\begin{array}{rl}
+18 = & 00010010 \\
\text{reversing:} & 11101101 \\
\text{adding 1:} & +\ \underline{00000001} \\
-18 = & 11101110
\end{array}
$$

A negative number will always have the first bit "on" or equal to one. This is the way that -18 will be stored in a computer (or a calculator), although it will be displayed in its more usual representation as a decimal number when we users see it. Because the first bit indicates whether a number is positive or negative, it is called the *sign bit*.

Demonstrating the application of complementary arithmetic, we will add $+25$ to -18:

$$
\begin{array}{rl}
+25 = & 00011001 \\
-18 = & \underline{11101110} \\
& 00000111 = +7
\end{array}
$$

We very casually ignored the fact that there was a bit left over when the leftmost addition was done. This bit is called the *carry bit*, and it has no effect on the validity of our answer.

Now what would happen if we had added -18 and $+7$?

$$
\begin{array}{rl}
-18 = & 11101110 \\
+7 = & \underline{00000111} \\
& 11110101 = ?
\end{array}
$$

Our answer is a negative number (the sign bit is on) stored in complementary form. Thus we must "uncomplement" the number; this process happens to be identical to complementing it, that is, we reverse the bits and add one:

$$
\begin{array}{rl}
\text{reversing:} & 00001010 \\
\text{adding 1:} & \underline{00000001} \\
& 00001011 = +11
\end{array}
$$

Thus, 11110101 represents -11.

Notice how simple the arithmetic is! There is no need to concern ourselves with the signs of the numbers involved in the addition, as we must with the normal manual method. The required hardware is very simple, consisting of a complementer to reverse the bits of a number and an adder to add them, with a mechanism for the carry from one bit position to another. A computer doesn't even have hardware to subtract; the subtrahend is complemented and added to the minuend. Thus, $9 - 5$ is treated as $9 + (-5)$.

At this point we must redefine the allowable range of numbers storable in 8 bits. The smallest number (or the largest negative number) is 10000000, which becomes -128 when uncomplemented. Adding one continuously increases the number until 11111111 is reached, which is the two's complement for -1. Continuing to add one brings us through zero and into the positive numbers until we reach 01111111 or $+127$. So the possible range of signed numbers storable in 8 bits is -128 to $+127$. Another way of expressing the range is:

-2^7 to $+2^7-1$
$-(2$ to the 7th power$)$ to $+(2$ to the 7th power$)-1$

(Another method of treating negative numbers uses *one's complement,* in which the bits are reversed, but one is not added. In this system there are two representations of zero, $+0 = 0000\ 0000$, $-0 = 1111\ 1111$; $-1 = 1111\ 1110$, $-2 = 1111\ 1101$, and so forth. Obviously, the hardware needed to do the arithmetic is slightly different. This method is not used as frequently as it once was.)

3.3.1 Review questions

3–1. Convert the following decimal integers to 8-bit binary, representing the negative numbers in two's complement.

    a. 100   b. -2 c. 64   d. -64 e. 80   f. -128

3–2. Convert the following binary numbers to decimal. Two's complement is used to store the negative values.

    a. 1111 0110   b. 1001 1100   c. 0001 0111   d. 0111 1000

3–3. Determine the range of a 16-bit signed number. Express that range in both integers and powers of 2.

3.4 Overflow and division by zero

We now must examine one of the major problems that occurs in the use of computers—exceeding the allowable range storable in the defined bit pattern. (We will continue to work with 8-bit numbers for the sake of simplicity.) What happens if we ask the computer to perform the addition of 125 and 5? We would expect to get 130, but we do not—instead we get −126. What seems like nonsense very quickly makes sense if we examine the addition process:

$$
\begin{array}{r}
125 = 01111101 \\
+\ \ 5 = \underline{00000101} \\
10000010
\end{array}
$$

This answer is a negative number stored in two's complement; when converted to decimal, it turns out to be −126.

This invalid result occurs when we overflow the allowable number of bits that the storage location can hold. It occurs in all mechanical calculation devices, whether a computer or an abacus. The problem is that sometimes we get no warning that such an overflow has taken place! The computer does "know" that the overflow exists. (If the computer is aware of the overflow, why do some systems not warn the programmer?) There is a fairly simple rule that states that if a carry takes place into, but not out of the leftmost bit, an overflow has taken place; also, if no carry takes place into the leftmost bit, but one does take place out of it, an overflow has occurred. In our example above, a carry takes place into the leftmost bit position but not out of it; thus, there is an overflow. Try adding −126 and −3 and you will see a carry out of the leftmost bit, but not into it; the overflow there results in the answer +127.

There is a geometrical analogy that also illustrates this concept. If one were to consider the number line not as a ray extending from negative to positive infinity but rather as a loop in which −128 is one higher than +127 with addition moving clockwise and subtraction counterclockwise, all of the "overflow" calculations work. For example, moving clockwise five numbers past +125 will bring us to −126; then moving counterclockwise three numbers brings us back to +127.

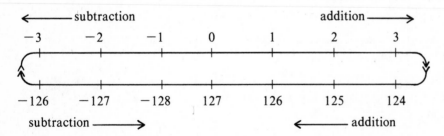

Notice (and you should go through the process just to convince yourself that we're on the level) that a double overflow actually can yield a correct result! (This will not always happen; it depends on the nature of the calculation.) Thus programmers who allow this kind of error to happen on systems that permit it may have a very difficult time tracking it down. Overflow also occurs during multiplication if an attempt is made to generate a product (either positive or negative) outside the range of allowable storage.

Obviously, the programmer must prevent overflow when writing code. That is why it is so important to understand the available range of integer constants and variables. All versions of FORTRAN have a 16-bit integer (usually called INTEGER*2 to indicate the 2-byte size) that provides a range of -32768 to $+32767$. This rather restrictive range is sufficient for most applications, but there are times when the programmer will need more. Many systems also provide a 32-bit integer (called INTEGER*4), providing a range of $-2,147,483,648$ to $+2,147,483,647$, which solves most of the programmer's problems but again not all.

Although it may be of little consolation to the programmer debugging a program that is producing "mysterious" results, all of the invalid sums and products caused by overflows can be predicted and computed manually if one is familiar with the way the arithmetic is done within the hardware.

3.4.1 System error handling

We now get into the never-never land of how FORTRAN should treat executable errors. Executable errors cannot be found during compilation, since the compiler cannot predict what values are to be input and computed. For example, the compiler cannot know that the expression $I + J$ will yield an overflow if I and J are to be read in during execution of the program. Nor are there any standards as to how execution errors are to be handled, so each implementation of FORTRAN may have entirely different error-handling techniques.

What are the choices? (1) The computer can spot the overflow and abort the execution with an error message to that effect. (2) The computer can set an indicator on but continue with the execution using the invalid result calculated. (3) The computer can ignore the error, continuing to use the invalid result. (4) The computer can allow the programmer to set up an overflow error branch and control the logic (as COBOL allows) in case of an overflow.

At this point it is up to the programmer to find out how the implementation he or she is working with handles such an error. It is most unlikely that the fourth method is used, unless the version of FORTRAN is a very advanced one. It is somewhat unlikely that the first method is used, since the computer can still calculate a value, albeit an invalid one. Methods (2) and (3) are most commonly used. Method (2), however, requires a subprogram that the programmer can access to determine if the overflow has occurred.

Method (2) generally uses a one-bit location in the computer called the *overflow indicator*. If it is on ($= 1$), it indicates that an overflow has occurred, and of course, it is left off ($= 0$) if the calculated result is within range and correct. A subroutine or function may be supplied by the manufacturer to access this indicator from FORTRAN. (It is always possible to access it from assembly language, which means that the hardware is there to do it; in a pinch, a FORTRAN programmer can write his or her own assembly language subprogram callable from FORTRAN.) Different hardware designs treat the overflow indicator differently. In some architectures, the overflow indicator, once on, stays on until it is reset by programming, usually by accessing it; in these systems the programmer must initialize it to 0 at the beginning of execution to ensure that it is off. In such implementations, it is possible to write a program that accesses the indicator at the end of execution; if it is on, it means that an overflow has taken place somewhere during execution. In other implementations the indicator is set off just prior to any type of calculation that might turn it on (such as addition, subtraction, and multiplication); in this situation the overflow indicator must be checked after any addition, subtraction, or multiplication.

The test program given below was run on a VAX computer to illustrate method (1) described above; a copy of a test run follows. The IMPLICIT INTEGER*2 (I–N) statement forces all variables starting with letters in the range I through N to be 16-bit integers; the VAX default of 32-bit integers would necessitate using very large numbers for test data. On the VAX, 5 and 6 are the LUNs for the screen and keyboard; end-of-data is triggered on the keyboard with control-Z.

```
C                       TESTADD:  tests overflow during addition
C
      IMPLICIT INTEGER*2  (I-N)
C
C
   20 WRITE  (5,1020)
 1020 FORMAT  (1H0,'Enter two integers in free format')
         READ  (6,*, END=900)  I1, I2
         N = I1 + I2
         WRITE  (5,1022)  N
 1022    FORMAT  (1H ,I7)
      GO TO 20
C
  900 STOP
      END
```

Test run

```
Enter two integers in free format
12, -18
      6

Enter two integers in free format
32767, 2
%SYSTEM-F-INTOVF, arithmetic trap, integer overflow
```

This procedure is known as an *arithmetic trap*; the error is displayed and the program is aborted. Although the VAX aborts the program immediately, other systems may not. For example, the same program run on the Prime yielded a result of -32767, and the program continued to run.

Under any circumstances, it should be obvious that the FORTRAN programmer (and programmers in most of the high-level languages) must exercise extreme care when dealing with integer numbers to ensure that they do not extend beyond their range. We can only advise that the programmer learn the method of handling overflow errors on his or her system and utilize whatever assistance that computer gives. It is always advisable for the programmer to run some test programs that force overflow and watch what happens!

3.4.2 Division by zero

Another concern of the FORTRAN programmer is what happens when division by zero is attempted. Although we all know that division by zero is not defined in our number system, there are times when imperfect logic will ask the computer to compute it. Again we are faced with a system dependent situation. On earlier IBM systems, division by zero was ignored; that is, 8/0 yielded 8. On a Prime, a positive number divided by zero yields 0, a negative one yields -1. On VAX, the program bombs with a "arithmetic trap, integer divide by zero" error message; the same thing happens on Radio Shack and many other machines.

Thus it is obvious that the programmer must check the value of the divisor prior to a division to ensure that division by zero is *not* attempted.

3.4.3 Exercise

Exercise 3–1

Write a program TESTDIV, similar in structure to TESTADD, to see how your system responds to division by zero; run it on your system with appropriate test data.

3.5 Hexadecimal notation

In the above examples, we have restricted ourselves to 8-bit bytes, which are easy to view in binary form. However, as we move to 16-, 32-, and 64-bit patterns, such a long string of bits is difficult for the human mind to analyze. It has become common to group the bits into groups of 4 bits (half a byte, sometimes called a "nibble"), with each group represented by a character from the base 16 number system, which is called *hexadecimal* or *hex* (for those on familiar terms with it). In this way a byte reduces to two characters and a 32-bit real, which we will be looking at shortly, to 8 hex characters, certainly a lot easier to communicate.

The hexadecimal number system contains the counting numbers from 0 to 15 and now uses the letters A, B, C, D, E, and F to provide single character representations of the numbers from 10 to 15, respectively. Although the high-level programmer is primarily concerned with decimal numbers, there are several different situations in which the knowledge of bit patterns and their representation is useful. Sometimes it is necessary to look at the actual method in which the computer has stored information. If the system allows for a dump of information stored either in memory or in a disk file, it will not display it in binary but will use a more condensed notation like hex. In addition, some systems allow the user to patch files by modifying existing information with revised data; the patch is made in hex, and the user must know the applicable hex pattern or code. Furthermore, there are times when the programmer uses bit patterns to store other kinds of information; it is much easier for the programmer to specify those patterns directly in hex than to compute the decimal equivalents.

There are still some systems (CDC, PDP, Prime, and so forth) that use octal (base 8) notation. In this notation the group size is three, and because three is not a factor of the normal configurations of 8, 16, and 32, octal representations is not as neat. Normally the grouping is started from the right end of the bit pattern, and whatever is leftover on the left is placed into its own octal character.

Conversion table

Binary	Hexadecimal	Octal	Binary	Hexadecimal	Octal
0 = 0000	0	0	8 = 1000	8	10
1 = 0001	1	1	9 = 1001	9	11
2 = 0010	2	2	10 = 1010	A	12
3 = 0011	3	3	11 = 1011	B	13
4 = 0100	4	4	12 = 1100	C	14
5 = 0101	5	5	13 = 1101	D	15
6 = 0110	6	6	14 = 1110	E	16
7 = 0111	7	7	15 = 1111	F	17

For example, -125 in decimal is 1000 0011 in binary (because of hex conversion, most programmers write a binary number in groups of four bits), 83 in hex, and 203 in octal. A negative number, which has its first bit on ($= 1$), will have as its first hex character a value of 8 or above. In octal, there is no easy rule, since the value of the first character depends on the number of bits being represented.

Many programmers familiar with hex use it in place of binary whenever possible. For example, converting the 16-bit number 0111 1001 1100 0110 to decimal is a nuisance, but by converting it to hex (79C6) and knowing the appropriate powers of 16 for each of the positions (4096, 256, 16, and 1), the conversion becomes:

$$
\begin{array}{rrcr}
   & 7 \times 4096 &=& 28672 \\
 + & 9 \times \quad 256 &=& 2304 \\
 + & 12 \times \quad 16 &=& 192 \\
 + & 6 \times \qquad 1 &=& \underline{\quad 6} \\
   & & & 31174
\end{array}
$$

Complementing in hex is also not difficult. Merely subtract the number from FFFF and add 1. For example, -31174 is:

$$
\begin{array}{r}
 \text{FFFF} \\
 -\underline{79\text{C}6} \\
 8639 \\
 +\underline{\quad 1} \\
 863\text{A}
\end{array}
$$

The sign of a hex number can be determined very easily by looking at the first character. If it is 7 or less, the first (sign) bit is zero and the number is positive; if it is 8 or above, the first bit is one and the number is negative.

3.5.1 Review questions

3–4. Convert the 8-bit values from in review question 1, section 3.3, to 2-character hex.

3–5. Convert the following 16-bit numbers expressed in 4-character hex to decimal, remembering to complement the negatives:

    a. FEED   b. 7FFF   c. ABED   d. 1234   e. 8000

3.6 Integer storage

Both the 1966 and the 1977 specifications of FORTRAN duck the issue of precise definition of storage. In the earlier days of computers, the basic word size came in many variations, including 8, 12, 16, 24, 36, 48, 60, and 64 bits. Thus any attempt to standardize would have caused preferential treatment to a particular manufacturer. The only rule specified was that once a manufacturer defined a standard numeric storage unit, all numeric storage was to be based on that unit. According to the specifications, the number of bits allocated for the storage of real numbers must be equal to that for integer numbers.

For the large computers that used word lengths of 32 bits or more, these specifications caused no real problem, since this is the minimum bit configuration addressable. But as the smaller machines (minicomputers) came into the picture, most had a word size of 16 bits, which, as we will see, is too small to store real numbers. Yet, because of the minicomputer architecture, supporting an integer larger than 16 bits would have been expensive for a computer designed to be more economical in memory use and cost than its big brothers. Thus the minicomputer manufacturers took immediate exception to the equal-size specification and stuck with a "half-size" integer of 16 bits with its restrictive range. (In an attempt to satisfy the specifications and still use their computers efficiently, the IBM 1130 and 1800, unless the user specified the operating system to use "one word integers," used 32 bits of storage for each integer, but only 16 bits were accessible by FORTRAN.)

In all fairness, it must be remembered that FORTRAN was invented to be a scientifically oriented language emphasizing computations involving real numbers. The language inventors did not realize that FORTRAN would be used in a wide range of applications in which the 16-bit integer would pose a severe restriction.

Today, having moved toward a byte (8-bit) definition of storage size, we talk of a short integer (INTEGER*2) of 2 bytes or 16 bits and a long or double integer (INTEGER*4) of 4 bytes or 32 bits. (The ANSI specifications do not refer to these two classes of integers, but in order to maintain compatibility with earlier systems, most manufacturers include this distinction.) However, those FORTRANs that have both modes available are not consistent in their default mode. On the Prime, for example, the default is INTEGER*2 and the programmer must specify those integer variables that are to be in long form; on the Digital Equipment Corporation VAX series, the default is INTEGER*4 and the user must specify those variables that are to be treated as short. (To emphasize the inconsistency, in VAX BASIC the default is short, but in VAX Pascal there is no short.)

Under any circumstances, integer numbers are stored in pure binary, using complementary form for negative numbers. The number of bits allocated for their storage is machine and compiler dependent. All FORTRAN implementations have a 16-bit integer, with a range from $-32,768$ to $+32,767$. Where the larger integer is available, the programmer may choose the method of storage desired for each variable and should do so in such a way that memory and disk storage are optimized.

Although some programmers have become lazy due to the availability of very high speed computers with large memories, it is still wise to optimize programs so that they use as little of the computer's resources as possible. This is extremely important in multiprogramming environments where inefficient programs can cause a severe degradation in operations. It is the responsibility of the programmer to strike a good balance between ease of coding and operating efficiency. A program that runs inefficiently once a month is not as serious a problem as one that must run twice a day.

Thus a good programmer will choose to store integer values in 16-bit or short integers when assured that the values will not approach the 32,767 limit. However, if there is any danger of overflow, it is then best to play it safe with the longer integer. The shorter integer not only uses less storage space but also calculates significantly faster. Furthermore, on some systems long integers are not fully implemented and cannot be used as arguments to some supplied library functions.

On some implementations, there is even a shorter method of integer storage using 8-bit bytes called BYTE or INTEGER*1. With this method the range is from −128 to +127.

In FORTRAN 77 and some extended versions of FORTRAN 66 there is also a mode of storage called LOGICAL, in which the values stored are either true or false. Only a single bit is really necessary to store either true or false, but since the architecture of computers makes it difficult to access individual bits of a grouping, an entire group of bits is used to store a representation of this bipolar state. Although the programmer may never need to worry about it, the representations vary from system to system. Some use 0 for false, 1 for true; others use 0 for false, −1 for true; and yet some others use 0 for true, nonzero for false. Still others may only utilize one bit of the grouping and treat, for example, any even number as false (last bit is 0) and any odd number as true (last bit is 1). Under any circumstances, the use of logical storage does not save space, but it is useful to simplify coding, as we will see later on.

Table of integer storage

Type	Bits used	Range	Comments
LOGICAL	1	0 to 1	limited availability
BYTE	8	−128 to 127	limited availability
INTEGER*2	16	−32768 to 32767	universal
INTEGER*4	32	−2, 147,483,648 to 2,147,483,647	usually available

Note: This table refers to those architectures based on 8-, 16-, or 32-bit word sizes. Other architectures (12-, 24-, 36-, 48- or 64-bit words) will have different ranges.

3.7 Real numbers

Real numbers can contain a decimal point. Although real numbers may be integer valued, they appear to be virtually unlimited in range and need not be whole numbers. However, deriving a method that allows for the storage of extremely small and extremely large numbers without using excessive memory requires an approach quite different from that used with integer numbers.

Real numbers are stored in normalized, exponential form, that is, a given number is not stored as we normally see a decimal number; instead it is stored with the decimal point shifted to the left of the first significant digit (normalized) and multiplied by the appropriate power of 10 (exponential) to maintain its value. For example:

$$3.14159265 = 0.314159265 \times 10^1$$
$$5280. = 0.5280 \times 10^4$$
$$-0.00254 = -0.254 \times 10^{-2}$$

Of course, if we are dealing with a number like the first one above, an approximation of pi using nine significant digits, we must realize that a nonterminating transcendental number would use an infinite number of digits; for practical reasons, we must set a limit and accept a certain lack of precision. Integer-valued reals, if within the allowable range, are a notable exception to this rule; they are stored precisely; also stored precisely are those decimals that are expressible as combinations of the powers of $1/2$ (such as 0.25, 0.1875, and so forth).

Since the computer uses the binary number system, we are faced with the additional complication that the decimal portion of most noninteger valued reals is not precisely convertible to binary. Although 0.25 in decimal is exactly equal to 0.01 in binary, conversion of 0.40, for example, yields a nonterminating binary number, 0.011001100110. . . .

Just as with integer numbers, FORTRAN sets up a limited number of bits to contain a real number. A real number is stored as two integer numbers, the normalized digits (including the sign) and the power of the base. Thus pi would be storable as 314159265 and 1, if it were stored in decimal. The first number is called the mantissa or significand; the second, the characteristic or exponent. The real number is first converted to binary, then it is normalized and stored as two binary integer numbers. In determining storage capacity, a certain number of bits are used for the characteristic and the rest for the mantissa.

In general, the storage form for a real number is $0.nnnnnnnn \times 2^m$, where the n's are either zeros or ones and m is the power of two that maintains the value. In most implementations, 8 bits are used to store the characteristic, and the range of numbers that can be stored is:

$$2^{-128} \text{ to } 2^{127} = 10^{-38.5} \text{ to } 10^{38.2}$$

Where 32 bits are used as the standard precision real, 24 bits are left for the mantissa, of which one is used for the sign. Thus with 23 bits left, only six significant decimal digits can be stored precisely. Fortunately, most implementations of FORTRAN have a double precision real that is stored in 64 bits. With $64 - 8 - 1 = 55$ bits, precision can be raised to about 16 significant digits.

As a rough guide to the number of significant decimal digits, the number of bits available for the mantissa, exclusive of the sign bit, can be divided by 3.3219; the antilog, base 10, of the result yields an approximation to the largest value that can be stored precisely. For example, with a 23-bit mantissa, $23/3.3219 = 6.9237485$ significant digits or, taking the antilog, 8,389,739 (the actual value is 8,388,607; our approximation is in error by less than 0.014%). Thus any integer valued real larger than 8,388,607 cannot be stored precisely.

However, the method of storing reals differs from implementation to implementation. Some computer manufacturers will allocate their bits differently, getting a greater characteristic at the expense of a less precise mantissa. Others will "steal" a bit by using the fact that the first bit in the mantissa is always 1 (since the binary point has been normalized to its left), thus grabbing a little additional precision in the mantissa at a sacrifice of execution speed.

3.7.1 Two methods of storing reals

Let us examine two methods commonly used for the storage of real numbers. In both, the decimal real is first converted to binary, truncating after the bit limit is reached. Then the binary number is converted to normalized binary form. Finally, the characteristic is *biased,* that is, a constant is added to it so that it always has a positive value; this simplifies the calculation algorithms used by the computer. Assuming an 8-bit characteristic with a normal range of -128 to $+127$, biasing adds 128 to the characteristic. Thus, a characteristic of -128 stores as 0, 0 stores as 128, and 127 stores as 255; the characteristic becomes an unsigned integer value ranging from 0 to 255. It is easier to add the 128 in decimal if the characteristic is negative or in binary or hex if the characteristic is non-negative. Biasing by $+128$ is quite easy in binary or hexadecimal; it is done by adding either 1000 0000 (binary) or 80 (hexadecimal) to the unbiased characteristic; thus, in binary one only needs to reverse the first bit.

We will start with the 'nonprecise' version of pi:

$$3.14 = 11.0010\ 0011\ 1101\ 0111\ 0000\ 10 \qquad \text{(truncating after 24 bits)}$$
$$= 0.1100\ 1000\ 1111\ 0101\ 1100\ 0010 * 2^2 \qquad \text{(2 = 0000 0010)}$$
$$= \text{1000 0010 biased}$$

The final bit pattern will consist of a sign bit, in this case 0 for positive, 23 bits of mantissa and 8 bits of characteristic.

The first method of storage we will look at is one favored by IBM, in which the characteristic is stored first, followed by the sign combined with the first 23 bits of the mantissa, with negative numbers stored in two's complement:

$$3.14 = 1000\ 0010\ 0110\ 0100\ 0111\ 1010\ 1110\ 0001 = 8264\ 7AE1$$

Had the number been -3.14, the last 24 bits would have been complemented (reverse the bits and add 1).

$$-3.14 = 1000\ 0010\ 1001\ 1011\ 1000\ 0101\ 0001\ 1111 = 829B\ 851F$$

On the Prime, the sign and mantissa are stored in the first 24 bits, the characteristic in the last 8.

The second method of storage, favored by the Digital Equipment Corporation (DEC) on their 16- and 32-bit computers, stores the mantissa in sign magnitude form, in which the value is always absolute and the sign bit contains the only information related to sign. Furthermore, since the binary number is normalized such that the binary point is always to the left of the first significant bit and that bit is always 1, there is no need to store that bit—it is treated as an implied 1 bit. Thus one additional bit position is freed for the low order end of the number; the 24th bit is used and the first bit, always a 1, is not stored. This is an attempt to provide just a bit more precision to the storable real, increasing the number of significant digits from 6.924 to 7.225 and allowing the manufacturer to claim a full 7 significant decimal digits.

Of course, if the first bit is implied and not stored, the mantissa generated for a power of 2 is always all zeros, leaving no method for the representation of that most important constant, zero. The method used by DEC is to store zero as:

$$0.5 * 2^{-128}$$

or all zeros, including the characteristic. When the hexadecimal string 0000 0000 is encountered, it is treated as zero, not as the extremely small number that the bit pattern really represents.

There is a further adjustment, far more annoying, made in this method of storage. The order of storage is sign bit + characteristic + mantissa; when the number is converted to hexadecimal, the characteristic becomes difficult to isolate since it is distributed over three hex characters. In this method of storage, we get:

$3.14 = 0100\ 0001\ 0100\ 1000\ 1111\ 0101\ 1100\ 0010 = 4148\ F5C2$
$-3.14 = 1100\ 0001\ 0100\ 1000\ 1111\ 0101\ 1100\ 0010 = C148\ F5C2$

Shown below are a few additional examples. Method 1 refers to two's complement, method 2 to the sign-magnitude method with implied first bit.

$27.375 = 1\ 1011.0110\ 0000\ 0000\ 0000\ 000$
$\qquad\quad = 0.1101\ 1011\ 0000\ 0000\ 0000\ 0000 * 2^5 \qquad (5 = 0000\ 0101)$
$\qquad\qquad\qquad\qquad\qquad\qquad\qquad\qquad\qquad\qquad = 1000\ 0101\ biased$

method 1: $1000\ 0101\ 0110\ 1101\ 1000\ 0000\ 0000\ 0000 = 856D\ 8000$
method 2: $0100\ 0010\ 1101\ 1011\ 0000\ 0000\ 0000\ 0000 = 42DB\ 0000$
-27.375
method 1: $1000\ 0101\ 1001\ 0010\ 1000\ 0000\ 0000\ 0000 = 8592\ 8000$
method 2: $1100\ 0010\ 1101\ 1011\ 0000\ 0000\ 0000\ 0000 = C2DB\ 0000$
$0.00254 = 0.0000\ 0000\ 1010\ 0110\ 0111\ 0110\ 0010\ 0000$
$\qquad\qquad = 0.1010\ 0110\ 0111\ 0110\ 0010\ 0000 * 2^{-8}$
$\qquad\qquad\qquad\qquad\qquad\qquad\qquad -8 + 128 = 120 = 0111\ 1000$

method 1: $0111\ 1000\ 0101\ 0011\ 0011\ 1011\ 0001\ 0000 = 7853\ 3B10$
method 2: $0011\ 1100\ 0010\ 0110\ 0111\ 0110\ 0010\ 0000 = 3C26\ 7620$
-0.00254
method 1: $0111\ 1000\ 1010\ 1100\ 1100\ 0100\ 1111\ 0000 = 78AC\ C4F0$
method 2: $1011\ 1100\ 0010\ 0110\ 0111\ 0110\ 0010\ 0000 = BC26\ 7620$

There is one final complication, as we mentioned with integer values, in that the order in which the bytes are displayed when output or dumped may not be exactly the same order as shown above. For example, on the DEC VAX, the first two bytes appear after the last two; this display was rearranged to maintain a compatibility with one of their previous computer series, the 16-bit PDP 11s. Other manufacturers may similarly move the bits around for some good reason, although we are not always privy to that reason.

The reverse procedure, converting from the storage method to decimal, requires that the steps be reversed and, if using method 2, the implied bit be placed back into the number. In the example below, the bits making up the characteristic have been underlined to make it more illustrative.

Method 1

7EA0 0000 = <u>0111 1110</u> 1010 0000 0000 0000 0000 0000
       0111 1110 = 126

unbiasing   126 $-$ 128 = -2
        1010 0000 0000 0000 0000 0000

complementing -0.1100 0000 0000 0000 0000 000 $* 2^{-2}$
       -0.0011 0000 0000 0000 0000 0000
       $-0.$ 3   0 (hex)
       -0.1875 (decimal)

Method 2

4149 OFCF =   <u>0100 0001 0</u>100 1001 0000 1111 1100 1111
      1000 0010

unbiasing   0000 0010 = 2
   = $+$ 0.1100 1001 0000 1111 1100 1111 $* 2^2$
   = $+$ 11.0010 0100 0011 1111 0011 1100
       3. 2 4 3 F 3   C (hex)
       3.14158987 (decimal)

It is therefore critical that the FORTRAN programmer consult the specifications given by the manufacturer of the software in order to determine exactly what ranges (in terms of significant digits and power of ten) are supported on a particular computer. For general purposes, we will assume the following ranges, which is a safe rule on the majority of computers:

	number of bits	significant digits	exponent range
standard precision real:	32	6	-38 to $+38$
double precision real:	64	16	-38 to $+36$

Some manufacturers may distribute the bits of double precision reals to attain a larger exponent at the expense of some significant digits in the mantissa; this information is usually found in their manuals.

3.7.2 Review questions

3–6. For each of the four reals below, convert to both storage methods shown in the preceding section:

   a. −2.0   b. 38.015625   c. −287.046875   d. 123.4

3–7. For each of the four reals shown as stored in the two methods discussed, find their values in decimal. The answers should be identical for each pair (use this fact to check your answers).

method 1	*method 2*
a. 8040 0000	0000 4000
b. 8160 0000	0000 40C0
c. 8191 0000	0000 C0DE
d. 889B E000	4000 C448

3.8 I/O of real numbers

To output real numbers, the programmer must specify not only the number of digits to be output but also the location of the decimal point. The general form of the decimal Format field specification is F$w.d$, where w is the total number of columns allocated for output (field width) and d is the number of columns to be to the right of the decimal point. In a simple case:

```
      A = -12.347
      WRITE   (1,1000) A
1000 FORMAT   (1H ,F8.2)
      STOP
      END
```

will output −12.35 right-justified in columns 1 through 8 (columns 1 and 2 will be blank for this value).

The F format specification comes from the term floating-point, an earlier term used to describe real numbers. The decimal point could be located anywhere within the number; thus, it "floated." Calculators that allow the user to insert a decimal point anywhere are described as floating-point calculators. Integer numbers were called fixed-point numbers because the decimal point, if there was one in an integer number, would always be fixed at the end of the value.

Note that the number in the example above has been rounded; this is required by the 1977 specifications, but not by earlier versions. Thus some implementations rounded, as above, while others truncated (they would output

−12.34). It would be wise for the user to try the above program to ascertain whether his or her implementation rounds or truncates. The internal value of the number remains unchanged; only its appearance in the output differs.

Note also that only as many decimal places as requested are displayed; it is not considered a field overflow if additional decimal places exist. However, if the number had been −12345.347, the integer portion of the number would overflow the number of columns available to it and the field overflow output (usually the field is filled with asterisks) would result.

Positive numbers are output without a plus sign; thus, the value 12345.347 would fit the F8.2 field. Numbers less than 1.0 are usually output with the zero before the decimal point. Specified fields that show no decimal places (such as F8.0) will print out the integer portion (usually rounded) and a decimal point. There is a general rule that takes account of the fact that the decimal point, at least one digit before it, and the minus sign (when needed) will always appear; the rule states that the field width (w) should always be greater than or equal to three more than the requested number of decimal places (d). Rule: $w \geq d+3$.

3.8.1 Exponential specification

There is also an exponential form for real I/O; it is usually reserved for very large or very small numbers. The specification has the form E$w.d$, where again w is the field width and d the number of decimal places. The general form of the output is $s0.nnnnnEsmm,$ where the s's are signs (the first of the mantissa, the second of the characteristic), 0 is the zero that most implementations place just before the decimal point, the n's are the significant or decimal digits (d) requested, and mm is a two-digit power of 10. This form is identical to the normalized, exponential form discussed earlier in the chapter. In most implementations, blanks are used in place of the plus signs. Thus:

−12.3856	with an E10.3 appears as	−0.124E 02	in columns 1–10
0.0002	with an E10.3 appears as	0.200E-03	" " "
0.0002	with an E10.0 appears as	0.E-03	" " "

Note the round-off in the first number and the zero padding to generate the requested three significant digits in the second.

There will always be some output, regardless of the size of the number, when E format is used (in the second case, F8.2 would have yielded 0.00). Thus, most programmers, when dealing with problems whose answers may be of unknown size, first use exponential format and later switch, if possible, to the more readable decimal format. Since there will always be a four-character exponent, a decimal point, a leading zero (usually), and a possible minus sign, the general rule becomes: $w \geq d+7$.

3.8.2 Input

Input provides a great deal of flexibility. As in integer input, blanks are treated as zeros and thus a blank record will be read as a zero or zeros. With F or E field specifications, either a decimal or an exponential number may be entered as data and the program will interpret the number according to the way it was entered. However, some systems require that an exponential number be right-justified in the input field, since blank columns to the right of the characteristic become zeros and may cause the attempted generation of an exponent out of the range allowed (usually -38 to $+38$), thus producing an error, since the number of digits allowed for the exponent is usually two.

The definition of the number of decimal places in input F$w.d$ specification provides a default in case the data does not already contain a decimal point. The programmer is always free to override the default by entering the decimal point anyplace in the field. Thus in a field of F5.2, entering 12345 would store 123.450 (assuming six significant digits) in memory; entering 12.34 would store 12.3400; entering 1. would store 1.0000. Thus the data enterer need not worry about right-justification and should be encouraged to enter real data with a decimal point.

The D$w.d$ specification is specifically designed for double precision I/O, but it provides nothing different from E format and is usually considered synonymous. However, when entering data that is intended to be stored to the full capacity of double precision, some systems require that either D specification be used or the value be entered in E format using D instead of E, such as 3.14159265D+00. The same rule applies to constants within the program; otherwise the system will truncate the value to the six or seven significant digits storable in standard precision before it transfers it into the double precision location. For example, the assignment of X $=$ 3.14259265, where X is defined as a double precision variable, may first define the constant, by default, as single precision (approximately 3.14159) and then, when converting to double precision, merely add the necessary number of zeros to pad to the number of bits used by the system for double precision (approximately 3.1415900000000).

Exponential input has a large degree of freedom, as shown by the examples below. An exponential number can be entered with the decimal point anyplace in the field. Furthermore, leading zeros may be left out, as may leading plus signs before both the mantissa and the exponent. Even the E may be left out if a sign is there.

The main system-dependent dialectical differences usually occur during keyboard input of real numbers without a decimal point. Here again, many manufacturers, in an attempt to be user-friendly, shift the input value to the right if a full field of columns is not entered before the end-of-record. Thus an entry of 12 followed by a carriage return in a field of F8.2 may yield 0.12 or it may yield 120000.00. Again, the user must run a number of tests in order to see how his or her implementation of FORTRAN works and must be prepared to alter operational instructions if the program is moved to another system.

Examples of real output

```
      WRITE (1,1000)
1000 FORMAT (1H ,aw.d)
```

<u>internal value</u>   <u>specification</u>   <u>output by column</u>

```
                                                  11111111112
                                        12345678901234567890
-10.25                      F10.4          -10.2500
                            E20.10         -0.1025000000E 02
132767.55                   F10.4       **********
                            E10.4        0.1328E 06
-132767.55                  E10.4       **********
                            E20.10         -0.1327675500E 06
0.00254                     F10.3           0.003
                            E12.4        0.2540E-02
```

Examples of real input

```
      READ   (2,1000)
1000 FORMAT   (F12.2) or (E12.2) or (D12.2)
```

```
              111
123456789012     internal value

1                1000000000.00
1.               1.000000
      1.         1.000000
                 0.000000
         3E2     0.03E+2 = 0.300000E+01
         3+2     0.03E+2 = 0.300000E+01
          3-2    0.03E-2 = 0.300000E-03
         3.E2    3.00E+2 = 0.300000E+03
-3.E-2          -3.00E-02 = -0.300000E-03[1]
```

---

1. This entry could lead to overflow if the system treats trailing blanks as zeros (-3.E-2000000), since only a 2-digit exponent is permissible.

3.8.3 Review questions

3–8. For the value of -12345.678, show the output resulting from the following FORMATs:

1	2	3	4	5	6	7	8	9	10	11	12

a. FORMAT (1H ,F10.2)

b. FORMAT (1H ,E10.2)

c. FORMAT (1H ,E12.4)

d. FORMAT (1H ,E12.5)

e. FORMAT (1H ,F8.0)

f. FORMAT (1H ,F12.4)

3–9. For the READ and FORMAT given, determine what will be stored for X for each of the following input records:

```
        READ   (2,1000) X
1000 FORMAT   (F12.2)

                  111
        123456789012
```

a. 123.45
b. 12345
c.   12345
d.   12345E-2
e.   1.2345E+2

3.9 Intrinsic functions

A collection of functional relationships, much like the function buttons on a calculator, is built into FORTRAN. These subprograms are considered part of the language and require no special linking into a program; in some references they are called *library functions* because they are members of the library of FORTRAN subprograms that make the language work. Although there are different extensions to the library depending on the implementation, there is a basic group of routines built into all versions of the language.

The intrinsic functions' names are reserved words in the sense that any attempt to use them as regular variable names may cause problems and thus should be avoided. Otherwise they are formed under the same rules as variable names, with the first letter of the name dictating the mode (real or integer) of the returned value.

A function can be used in the expression portion of an assignment statement; the function name is followed, in parentheses, by the list of arguments sent to the function. The answer, that is, the result calculated by the function, is returned to a memory location addressed by the function name. The number, mode, and order of the arguments is rigidly fixed, and any modification will cause serious errors either in the running of the program or in the answer returned. Furthermore, there are limitations on the values sent to many of the functions, and it is the responsibility of the programmer to make sure that the values sent are within the proper range. As mentioned previously, error handling is very system-dependent, and whereas an attempt to take the square root of a negative number, for example, will cause a program to bomb on one system, another system will continue, using some erroneous result (such as the square root of its absolute value or maybe even zero).

The majority of the intrinsic functions are used for computational purposes and thus are real-number oriented. This group consists of:

ABS	absolute value
SQRT	square root (limited to non-negative numbers)
EXP	exponential, raising of e to a power
ALOG	natural logarithm (limited to positive numbers); base 10 logarithm = ALOG * 0.4342945
SIN	sine of an angle, in radians
COS	cosine of an angle, in radians
ATAN	arctangent
TANH	hyperbolic tangent

In FORTRAN 77, the additional real computational functions supplied include:

TAN	tangent of an angle, in radians
ASIN	arcsine
ACOS	arccosine
SINH	hyperbolic sine
COSH	hyperbolic cosine
ALOG10	base 10 logarithm

Functions may use other functions as arguments and may be as complex as an algebraic expression. It would not be unusual to see, for example,

```
S = SQRT (ABS (Y))
A = ABS (SIN (X) - COS (Y))
```

(In the earliest versions of FORTRAN, the library functions ended with an F; thus, old programs contain functions called SQRTF, ABSF, and so forth, which carry out the same actions as the current functions).

On all systems there are separate functions for standard precision and for double precision. However, their implementation may differ in that some systems may require the programmer to specify a double precision routine by its own name (DABS for ABS, DSQRT for SQRT, and so forth), whereas other systems will access the appropriate routine, where possible, based upon the mode of the arguments. Again, the programmer must determine how double precision routines are implemented on his or her system.

A number of functions also exist for integer values; they include:

IABS   absolute value

MOD   has two arguments; provides the remainder of argument 1 divided by argument 2. For example, MOD (39,5) yields 4.

There is also a function that has both integer and real versions and that might be called "sign transmission"—the sign of the second argument is placed on the absolute value of the first argument:

SIGN (arg1, arg2) and ISIGN (iarg1, iarg2)

There are a number of highly specialized applications of these functions, but the prime usefulness of SIGN is found in those implementations where output is not automatically rounded. In those situations, it is the responsibility of the programmer to apply the rounding factor. For example, in the case of money, which is rounded to two decimal places, it is usual to add 0.005 to positive numbers and −0.005 to negative numbers, a process that would normally require two-branched logic; however, the SIGN function takes care of this automatically with statements such as:

```
ROUND = AMOUNT + SIGN (0.005, AMOUNT)
```

However, even more useful are those functions that allow the user to change the mode of a value within an expression.

FLOAT   converts an integer argument to a real value.

IFIX   converts a real argument to integer, truncating.

The names of the functions derive from the former names of real and integer mode. On most implementations, the alternative for FLOAT is REAL (not in Prime FORTRAN, where it has another use) and the alternative for IFIX is INT.

Every programmer should acquaint himself or herself with the functions available in the FORTRAN being used. Many systems have a rather large collection of very useful additions to those mentioned above, such as finding maximum or minimum values from a list of variables or doing bit shifting or logical bit operations (AND, OR, and so forth). However, where portability of a program is one of the criteria, the use of specialized functions available only in one or two implementations is best avoided.

3.10 Mixed-mode arithmetic

As we saw in the change-making program, integer arithmetic has valuable applications when we deal with practical problems involving whole numbers. Other applications include the conversion from units to gross, dozen, and units; seconds to hours, minutes, and seconds; seconds to degrees, minutes, and seconds, and so forth. Later we will see even more useful applications.

Real numbers, on the other hand, are most useful in mathematical applications where we are not restricted to whole numbers, such as statistical means and standard deviations, scientific measurements, and engineering applications. However, there are times when we will have to combine integer values and reals, and it is important for the programmer to understand exactly how the language works when the modes are not the same.

Mode conversion can always be accomplished with an assignment statement. For example:

```
IDOL = AMOUNT
```

extracts the integer portion of AMOUNT, thus truncating it. An AMOUNT of 12.99 will yield an IDOL of 12. This kind of conversion is useful for breaking numbers into parts. FORTRAN implements this assignment by automatically invoking the intrinsic function IFIX (or INT).

The reverse conversion, integer to real, can also be done with an assignment statement when it is necessary to store a whole number as real. Again, the FORTRAN compiler automatically invokes the appropriate intrinsic function, in this case FLOAT (or REAL).

However, an area of major concern is the *mixed-mode expression,* in which both modes, integer and real, exist in an expression either on the right side of the assignment statement or within a decision statement. For example, in the change-making program, the assignment statement that converts the number of quarters to an amount of money might be written as:

```
AMOUNT = 0.25 * NQRTR
```

In that expression, 0.25 is real, NQRTR is integer.

Today most FORTRAN compilers handle mixed-mode arithmetic according to a very strict rule—each part of an expression is evaluated independently, and whenever a conflict of mode occurs, the integer value is automatically converted to real (using the intrinsic function FLOAT) within the working area of the computer (the stored value is unchanged) and the result of the calculation becomes real. Thus in the above mixed-mode expression, the computer will convert the integer value (NQRTR) to real and then multiply it by the real (0.25). The result of the calculation is then assigned to the location on the left of the equal sign *according to the mode of that assigned variable*. For example, if the storage location had been IAMNT, only the integer portion of the answer would be stored (if NQRTR held the value 15, AMOUNT would become 3.75, but IAMNT would become (integer) 3).

It might be tempting to do the calculation as:

```
AMOUNT = NQRTR / 4
```

which would result in a value of 3.0. (The .0 is not necessary to indicate that the number is real—only the point is needed. The extra zero is added to emphasize the presence of the decimal point and distinguish it from a period or spot on the paper.) When the compiler examines this expression, it sees an integer divided by an integer and thus does the calculation by integer arithmetic, yielding a 3; when assigned to a real value, the 3 becomes 3.0. If the instruction had been written

```
AMOUNT = NQRTR / 4.0
```

the right answer would have been obtained since the expression would have been evaluated as mixed mode. (However, it is a poor programming practice to divide when multiplication is possible, since the latter executes much, much faster.)

Many experienced programmers avoid mixed-mode expressions, since there is always the possibility of having a calculation performed not quite in the way intended. As an example, examine the following assignment statement:

```
I = 8 / 5 + 8.0 / 5
```

Since the divisions have a higher priority than the addition, they will be performed first from left to right. The first division is in integer mode and will yield the result 1; the second division is mixed and will yield the result 1.6. The addition now is mixed mode and yields 2.6. The value stored in I is 2. The obvious answer of 16/5 or 3.2 never appeared. Thus, experienced programmers prefer to control mode conversion themselves and not leave it to the compiler. The programmer-controlled method of converting quarters to money is:

```
AMOUNT = FLOAT (NQRTR) * 0.25
```

There is one exception to the mixed-mode rule: an integer exponent on a real base is *not* considered mixed mode. Thus the statement:

```
A = X ** L
```

is a perfectly valid statement. It is good programming practice to use an integer exponent wherever possible because the computation is far more efficient and precise. With an integer exponent the algorithm uses multiplication, while a real exponent requires the conversion of the base to its logarithm, the multiplication of the base, and then taking the antilog.

(*Hint*: if you have a compiler that can show the compiled assembly language and if you know the assembly language on your machine, it would be very instructive to write some mixed-mode instructions and observe how your computer compiles them.)

3.10.1 Review questions

3–10. Given the following values, I = 5, J = 8, A = 12.5, B = 25.0, calculate the values stored in either N or X:

      a. `N = (I * J) / B`
      b. `X = I + (J / B)`
      c. `X = I / J + J / I`
      d. `N = A / B`

3.11 Problems of precision

As we illustrated in a previous section, the storage of real numbers leads to imprecision in the case of any decimal number that is not constructed of the powers of 1/2. Thus values like 18.50, 18.75, 18.25, 18.125, 18.375, and so forth, are perfectly convertible to pure binary; a value like 18.40 is not and is stored as approximately 18.39997. Furthermore, a variable assigned as 18.40 and another computed as 2.0 * 9.20 may differ by a bit and thus not yield a perfect equality. Thus when the programmer deals with real numbers (not just in FORTRAN, but in all the other languages that store reals in pure binary, such as BASIC, Pascal, PL/1, Modula-2, C, and so forth), special techniques must be employed.

Now just what does this imprecision represent? The error in storing 18.40 is approximately 0.00016%, certainly within the error tolerance of most financial, scientific, and engineering applications. A very safe estimate of error with standard precision FORTRAN is less than 1.0 in the sixth significant digit or $<$ 1.0E-06. With double precision, the error is reduced to $<$ 1.0E-14 on most systems. Thus, in the technical fields, little fault is found with the "imprecision" of FORTRAN.

Nonetheless, any comparison for equality must invoke the concept of tolerance. As any machinist knows, a part of a given size must fall within a certain range or tolerance; imagine what would happen if a 2-inch piston and a 2-inch cylinder were both exactly 2 inches—one would not fit within the other! Therefore a comparison of the equality of two reals should be written as:

```
IF (ABS (AMT1 - AMT2) .LT. 1.0E-02) GO TO {logic for equality}
```

According to this statement, if the difference between AMT1 and AMT2 is less than 0.01, they are to be considered equal.

The important idea here is that when dealing with real numbers, 0.00 is not a point but is a range. When trying to avoid division by zero, it is not only necessary to consider a value of 0.00 but also a value so small that division by it would generate a quotient that overflows the allowable range of real numbers. A properly written check for division by zero would be:

```
IF (ABS (DVSR) .GE. 1.0E-06) QUOT = DVDND / DVSR
```

The concept of a zero range is not so alien to many practical applications in the commercial area. For example, the United States federal income tax form states that if the amount owed is less than $1.00, it may be ignored; likewise, if a refund to the taxpayer is less than $1.00, it will not be made unless specifically requested by the taxpayer. In other words, if the tax indebtedness ranges from −0.99 to +0.99, it can be treated as 0.00:

```
IF (ABS (TAX) .LT. 1.00) TAX = 0.00
```

3.12 Money calculations

When FORTRAN appeared as the first high-level language, it was an immediate success because it reduced programming effort by a factor of at least 5. However, its use in commercial applications was restricted because of the imprecision problem. Nonetheless, the trade-off was in favor of writing in FORTRAN and developing techniques to conquer the problem.

One solution (still used in many instances by both FORTRAN and assembly language programmers) was to work in cents by multiplying the two decimal place money values by 100.0 and adding a very small round-off to correct for the imprecision. Then all further calculations were done in integer, which is significantly faster and had no precision problem. Each multiplication required that the product be divided by 100 to maintain accuracy. It was even possible to write a rounded division routine in which the quotient would be incremented rather than truncated if the remainder was equal to or greater than half the divisor. For output purposes, values were converted to real and divided by 100.

The integer system had distinct limitations. With a FORTRAN that only has the short 16-bit integer available, the highest storable value is $327.67. With a 32-bit integer, the limit is over $21,000,000.00, which was sufficient for many situations but still could produce a problem; keep in mind if that a value produced by multiplication was limited to 1/100th of that amount, it would be a little over $210,000.00. Furthermore, when dealing with tax and interest rates, it was often necessary to work in mils (one tenth of a cent or one thousandth of a dollar), requiring a further reduction of the limit by one tenth. Thus the use of the integer system described above was only partially successful.

Another method was to convert the pure binary into binary coded decimal (BCD), in which each digit of a number was stored as a separate integer (as in the commercial languages COBOL and RPG). For example, the number 12345 is stored as 0001 0010 0011 0100 0101. In this method, special conversion routines had to be called after input and before output, and all calculations had to be done one process at a time (as in RPG or assembly language) using called subprograms. Not only was the programming little more than a lengthy and tedious sequence of CALLs to subprograms, programs were extremely slow in operation.

A third method was to work with integer-valued reals, for which greater precision was possible, at least in addition and subtraction. But problems still crept in with multiplication and division.

3.12.1 Round and strip

However, a more direct solution is available, one in which a calculated value can be reduced to an almost perfectly precise two-decimal-place number. To illustrate the problem and its solution, consider the following example involving the pricing of item in a retail application:

quantity	unit cost	calculated value	rounded	desired output
4	$0.077	$ 0.308	$ 0.313	$ 0.31
7	1.234	8.638	8.643	8.64
1	0.187	0.187	0.192	0.19
8	0.556	4.448	4.453	4.45
total		$13.581	$13.601	$13.59
rounded		13.586		
truncated		13.58	13.60	

As you can see, neither the sum of direct calculation rounded nor the rounded values truncated produces the desired answer of $13.59. What is needed is some way of calculating the desired output as precisely as possible to the nearest penny.

The truncation property of integer assignment comes to our rescue. First we apply the proper round-off, then multiply the value by 100, convert to integer to truncate, and then reconvert to real.

```
AMT = FLOAT (IFIX (100.0 * (AMT + SIGN (0.005,AMT)))) / 100.0
```

Unfortunately, in those FORTRANs that support only the short 16-bit integer or in which there is no version of IFIX that will generate a long 32-bit integer, the largest value that will work without overflow is $327.67; with 32-bit integers, the largest supportable value is $21,474,836.48.

However, the algorithm can be extended to satisfy even larger values:

```
AMT = FLOAT (IFIX (AMT)) + FLOAT (IFIX (100.0 *
1                (AMT - FLOAT (IFIX (AMT)) + SIGN(0.005,AMT)))) / 100.
```

In this algorithm, the dollars and cents are separated, the dollars on the left side of the + sign, and the rounding, multiplying, truncating, and division applied only to the cents; then the dollars and cents are added together to yield the final value to two decimal places. Unfortunately there is still a limitation of $32767.00 in those FORTRANs that support only a 16-bit integer; the limitation on those systems that support a 32-bit integer and have the appropriate versions of IFIX and FLOAT to deal with them is $2,147,483,648.00, which is sufficient for all applications except those dealing with the federal government!

A final method, which has no limitation in any FORTRAN implementation, cannot be reduced to a single statement as we did for the preceding method. Later we will see how these routines may be generalized and stored for easier access using subprograms (chapter 4), and then they will not be as unwieldy to use as they seem now. Thus, this next method would not be used quite as shown here, but bear with it as we develop the algorithm. The technique is similar to measuring a 20-foot room with a 6-foot rule. We subtract from our measurement the whole number of 6-foot intervals until we get a distance of 6 feet or less; that is, we lay our 6-foot rule down three times successively until we are left with a measurement of less than 6 feet, in this case, 2 feet. We take our final fine measurement, let's say 1 foot 11¾ inches and then add it to the three 6-foot measurements (18 feet) to get a total of 19 feet 11¾ inches. The algorithm below assumes a limitation in integer size of 16-bits or 32767.

```
C                 round AMT to exactly two places
    SGN = SIGN (1.00,AMT)
    AMT = ABS (AMT)
    NUM = AMT / 32767.0
    AMT = AMT - FLOAT (NUM) * 32767.0
    AMT = FLOAT (IFIX (AMT)) + FLOAT (IFIX (100.0 *
1                (AMT - FLOAT (IFIX (AMT)) + 0.005))) / 100.0
    AMT = SGN * (AMT + FLOAT (NUM) * 32767.0)
```

The calculation is simplified by working with the positive value of AMT, having saved the sign in the variable SGN; the sign is reapplied at the end of the computation.

To illustrate the logic, assume a value of -910843.576 for AMT

SGN = -1.00
AMT = 910843.576
NUM = 27
AMT = $910843.576 - (27 * 32767) = 26134.576$
AMT = $26134.00 +$
            truncated $(100 * (26134.576 - 26134.00 + 0.005)) / 100$
      = $26134.00 + (58 / 100) = 26134.58$
AMT = $-1.00 * (26134.58 + (27 * 32767)) = -910843.58$

3.12.2 Exercises

Exercise 3–2

Test the above algorithm by writing a program that includes it; provide a multiple input loop (with a means of exiting from the loop with some sentinel value), and output after each statement so that the inner workings of the algorithm may be observed. It would be instructive to use a format like E16.7 to see how closely precision is obtained, but on the last output also display AMT with a decimal format like F10.2 to see what will be printed. Use only single precision reals of up to six significant digits at this time.

Exercise 3–3

Research the reference manuals for your system to see how to convert the above program to use double precision reals. Study carefully the documentation on FLOAT and IFIX (or REAL and INT) with regard to the mode of the arguments to the function and the mode of the answers returned. Your system might even include special functions to simplify this calculation, like the DINT function on the Prime, which converts a double precision real to its integral value, but still as a double precision real. It is also possible, however, that your system cannot do this and will require an entirely different approach.

3.13 Summary and additional exercises

In this chapter, we have delved into the details of numeric storage and its implications for FORTRAN programmers. In addition, we have studied the use of real numbers. The following chapters will build programming techniques based on this material. The intrinsic library functions have been introduced, and they too will be considered part of the tools in our future applications. But most notably, we have begun to look at some of the programming problems that exist in the real world and have begun to give a professional outlook to our study.

In summary, we have touched upon the following FORTRAN topics and commands:

	section
topic	
BYTE	3.6
division by zero	3.4
FLOAT and IFIX (REAL and INT)	3.9
hexadecimal notation	3.5
INTEGER*2, INTEGER*4	3.6
intrinsic functions	3.9
LOGICAL	3.6
overflow	3.4

3.13.1 Exercises

Exercise 3–4

Write a self-generating program (no input) that outputs a table of square roots and cube roots for the numbers from 1 to 50. Use the intrinsic function for square root and avoid any mixed-mode arithmetic by using the appropriate conversion function. Output to four decimal places. The output should be fully described with a title and headings over each of the columns.

Exercise 3–5

Write a program to read in multiple two-value records representing hours worked and hourly rate paid. (If possible, read from a data file.) Compute the salary as hours $\times$ rate for those hours less than or equal to 40, hours $\times$ rate $\times$ 1.5 for those hours greater than 40 and less than 60, and hours $\times$ rate $\times$ 2.0 for those hours greater than 60. Make sure your test data covers all three possibilities. Also compute and output the sum of the hours worked and salaries paid to all employees.

Exercise 3–6

Expand the program in exercise 3–5 to compute withholding taxes on the following basis:

weekly salary	*tax computation*
< $160.00	$0.00
$160.00 to 320.00	5% of salary greater than $160.00
> $320.00	$8.00 + 8% of salary greater than $320.00

Also output total taxes withheld.

Exercise 3–7

Develop a table of compound interest based on the equation

Total Amount $=$ Principal $*$ $(1 + n)$ $**$ number of years

Use a principal of $1000. and embed the equation in a doubly nested DO loop, the outer loop going from 6% to 18% by 2 and the inner loop going from 5 years to 25 years by 5. The output should be completely described by proper annotation and/or headings.

Exercise 3–8

The general equation for a second order curve is:

$$y = a * x ** 2 + b * x + c$$

Write a program that will input values of *a, b,* and *c* and solve for the two values of *x* at *y* $= 0$ as derived from the quadratic formula. Take into account the situation where the discriminant is negative and complex values result. Also treat the case of *a* $= 0$, which reduces the equation to that of a straight line, and the erroneous case of *a* $= 0$ and *b* $= 0$. The output should include an echo check and full description of all answers.

4

Subprograms

4.1 Introduction

When FORTRAN was first implemented, it was compiled into a series of subprogram-accessing statements, except for very basic integer operations. Very few computers had floating-point hardware, so real calculations had to be performed by calling integer subprograms to do them by software means; even today, many computers leave the installation of floating-point hardware as an option to the user. Furthermore, I/O operations are very complex, and the simple READ and WRITE statements that we use in FORTRAN in no way indicate the work that the computer must do; again, extensive subprograms must be called.

Because the designers of the language realized that subprogram access was a very necessary function of FORTRAN, they not only built into it the ability to access subprograms written in the computer's assembly or machine languages, but they also provided the mechanism to link up with subprograms written in FORTRAN. Unlike the subprograms of many other languages (such as BASIC or Pascal), the FORTRAN subprogram is external to the program calling it, that is, the FORTRAN subprogram is an independent piece of code that can be compiled separately and stored in machine language, ready to be linked with the calling program at some later time. Although the designers of FORTRAN may have intended to speed up the compilation of a large programming system by breaking it into smaller modules, they also provided the language with a convenience and facility that is valuable beyond estimation.

In this chapter, not only will we go into the application of subprograms, but we will also examine the details of how subprograms work and how they are linked into the main program. This chapter represents the beginning of *structured* programming—we will now be able to modularize large programs into small, workable, and easily testable code; this modularized code is also easier to document and utilize in many different programming systems.

4.1.1 *What the reader needs to know for this chapter*

1. How to link a mainline with user-written subprograms.

2. Whether his or her implementation can handle subprograms stored in the same source file as the mainline.

3. How to build and access a subprogram library.

4.2 Concept of the subprogram

A subprogram is an independently written piece of code, packaged so that it can be compiled separately and stored apart from the programs that will utilize it. The user need not know anything about the logic of the subprogram, the variables used, or the statement numbers used; all the user must know is the name of the subprogram and the structure of its argument list, that is, the number, order, and mode of the variables used to transmit information back and forth between the calling program and the subprogram.

Placing a piece of code into subprogram form has many advantages. First of all, it allows a large program to be broken into modules, thus aiding in the structuring of the program. Each module can be independently tested without concern for the integration of that module, which can be done at some later time.

Furthermore, the subprogram may be accessed many times within the same programming system, yet its code only occupies memory once. For example, a program may use the square root function (SQRT) many times, but the same code is used over and over; repeated access to the subprogram does not cause the code to be inserted into the program each time the subprogram is accessed. Especially in small computer systems, this space savings is significant.

Once a subprogram is written, it may be accessed by many different programs. Thus a properly generalized subprogram is valuable not only to the writer of the subprogram, but also to the other programmers who have access to it. Most systems provide a means by which subprograms can be stored in a common library easily accessible to all system users.

A final advantage of subprograms is that a subprogram can call another subprogram. Thus we talk of calling and called programs without the need to differentiate between a mainline program and its subprograms. The only limitation is that a circular reference cannot be set up, that is, subprogram A cannot call subprogram B, which calls subprogram A. Similarly, recursion (in which a subprogram calls itself) is allowed only in some very advanced versions of FORTRAN. (Recursion is a favorite topic of many theoretical computer scientists, but a study of the linkage procedures used in most computers will show that recursion uses an exorbitant amount of memory compared to other ways of solving a problem. Only in very few instances is the use of recursion efficient both in memory use and execution time.)

Because this is an advanced programming text, we can take the time and effort to fully explain just how subprogram linkage works. In so doing, the reader will become conscious not only of the effectiveness of subprograms, but also of their pitfalls.

We use the term *programming system* to represent the mainline program plus its called subprograms. Every system must have a mainline, which is the anchor of the system. Subprograms cannot be executed separately; they must be accessed from a mainline. During the linking operation, the machine language versions of the mainline and the called subprograms are tied together, and the subprograms contained in the FORTRAN subprogram library are added automatically, along with the necessary parts of the operating system.

4.2.1 Subprogram linkage

In our study of subprogram linkage, we are interested in three elements:

1. How transfer is made to the subprogram.
2. How information is transmitted back and forth between calling and called programs.
3. How return is made to the proper location in the calling program.

Let us illustrate subprogram linkage with a simple program that calls one of the intrinsic library programs a number of times. The SQRT function requires one real argument; that argument must be a real constant, a real variable, or a real expression. The function returns a real value that can be assigned to either a real or an integer location (truncating for the latter).

```
X = SQRT (C)
N = SQRT (A + B)
Y = SQRT (2.5 * D - E)
Z = X - SQRT (Y - 2.00)
```

In this example, the subprogram SQRT is accessed four times, yet, as we have previously mentioned, the actual code for SQRT resides in memory only once. The linkage mechanism for subprograms requires that there be a way of saving a "return address" so that the logic continues at the appropriate point after the subprogram is executed. Furthermore, each time the subprogram is used, a different value of the argument is transmitted to it; thus, there must be a mechanism that ensures that only the appropriate value is used for the calculation.

And, of course, the beauty of the subprogram linkage is that the mechanisms used by the computer are transparent to the programmer and of no concern, *provided that the code is correctly written*. The details provided here are to show the programmer the internal workings so that if a problem occurs, the programmer has some idea where to look and furthermore will understand the cause of the error.

There is one other concern to the user of the subprogram, and that is how the routine handles an error condition. For example, there is no rational solution to the square root of a negative number. When we write our own routines a little later in this chapter, we will discuss various error handling techniques. But here we are using someone else's routine, and we have no control over it. In most cases the manufacturer will document the range of the argument(s) to the function (in this case, non-negative), but seldom will they describe what happens if that range is abused. On the old IBM 1130, the square root was taken of the argument's absolute value so that the square root of -4 was 2. On other systems, a zero is returned; others display an error message and abort the program. This is, unfortunately, another one of those system dependent situations, and we can give no rule other than to be careful.

4.3 Types of subprograms and argument handling

There are two main types of subprograms:

1. *Functions* are used to return a single value. There are three types of functions. All functions are accessed in the same way; only the physical location of the code is different.

   Intrinsic functions are supplied by the manufacturer and automatically linked into the calling program. They usually are high-speed, very efficient algorithms written in assembly language.

   Arithmetic statement functions consist of a single assignment statement and are placed directly into the calling program.

   Function subprograms are independently compiled code with no restriction in logic except that only one value is to be returned.

2. *Subroutines* are used in all other situations.

   The function must have at least two arguments. One is the returned value, which is stored in a location whose label is the name of the function itself. Thus, if the SQRT function is accessed, the calling program sets aside a location labeled SQRT to store the returned value. The other arguments, numbering one or more (virtually without limit), identify the values sent to the function. These arguments may be constants, variables, or expressions. The function is accessed in an assignment statement and looks just like a function used in algebra. (There are some unusual system-dependent functions that have no arguments.)

   The subroutine transmits all of the information going back and forth in the argument list; the name of the subroutine is only for identification, and thus there is no need for the compiler to set aside a storage location for its name, as is necessary with functions. The number of arguments for a subroutine can be as little as none or as many as desired. Furthermore, the arguments may represent the information going to the subroutine, the variables being modified in the subroutine, or the variables being generated in the subroutine. These arguments may be specified in any order and also may be constants, variables, or expressions for information sent to the subroutine, but only variables for information being modified or generated in the subroutine. The subroutine is accessed by its own statement, a CALL statement.

There are some very critical rules governing the placement of arguments in subprograms. The programmer who writes the subprogram dictates the name of the subprogram and the arguments used (after all, it is his or her subprogram, and if we want to use it we must abide by the programmer's terms). First of all, the number of arguments in the calling and called programs must agree. (There are exceptions to this rule in some advanced implementations where the accessing statement may have fewer arguments and the number of arguments is transmitted to the subprogram, but these cases usually involve intrinsic functions that are written in assembly language.) Secondly, the order of the arguments must agree, that is, the first argument in the calling program must correspond to the first argument in the called program, the second argument in the calling program must agree with the second argument in the called program, and so forth for the rest of the arguments. As we will see, communication between routines is done by the order in the argument list, not by the names of arguments. Thirdly, the mode of the corresponding arguments must agree; if the calling program transmits a real value and the called program treats it as integer, the value worked with will be wrong because of the different methods of storage. (Try, for example, writing a program with the statement:

```
X = SQRT (9)
```

and print the value of X. The SQRT function expects a real value like 9.0, but 9 is an integer value; the returned value will be nowhere near what is expected.)

The mechanism used in FORTRAN for transmitting information to a subprogram consists of transmitting the address of the information, not the value. Then the subprogram uses that address to reach into the memory and get the value. The same rule is used for information to be returned from the subprogram; the address of where to put the result is sent to the subprogram, which uses it to locate the repository of the modified or generated information. For this reason, only a variable should be in the argument list for any argument that is to be modified. If the argument for information sent to a subprogram is an expression, that expression is first evaluated and the result placed in a temporary location; the address of that temporary location is then sent to the subprogram. Thus a mode change is not possible during subroutine linkage, since the only means of communication is an address and there is no way to differentiate the address of an integer from that of a real.

Whenever a variable appears in the argument list, a location is set aside for it in the calling program, but not in the called subprogram; the transmitted address is moved into some location in the subprogram, but it is transparent to the FORTRAN programmer.

4.4 The arithmetic statement function

The arithmetic statement function is a user-written function that consists of a single assignment statement. Despite its limited length, it is a very useful construct in many situations; it also will serve as a very good example of just how a subprogram works.

The required elements of this abbreviated subprogram are:

1. *The name of the function.* Since the name of the function also serves as the storage identification for the value derived, the mode (integer or real) of the function must agree with the mode of the value to be returned. The name of a function follows the same rules as the name of a variable.

2. *The argument list.* The argument list contains the variable names for the information to be sent to the function and with which the function will perform the calculation. However, the arguments listed only serve as temporary identifiers, since different information may be sent to the function each time; thus, they are called *dummy arguments*. As we will see, no storage locations are set aside for them, and they are useful to the programmer only to describe just what the function does. Most implementations require that the dummy arguments be unique from the variables used in the rest of the program. Again, they must reflect the mode of the information being sent.

3. *The work of the function.* This FORTRAN expression describes what the function does. It can contain only the dummy variables specified in the argument list, constants, and intrinsic function names. As might be expected, it must follow all of the rules for FORTRAN expressions.

The arithmetic statement function, like the function in BASIC or the procedure in Pascal, is placed immediately before (exclusive of comments) the first executable statement. A program may contain more than one statement function.

As an example, let us assume that we are writing a program that must calculate the square root of the sum of two squares a number of times and that we have decided to use a statement function to avoid constantly repeating the same type of expression.

```
                    :
C              statement function for square root
C              of the sum of squares
      ROOT (XXX, YYY) = SQRT (XXX * XXX + YYY * YYY)
                    :
```

```
                    :
        HYPOT = ROOT (DX, DY)
                    :
                    :
        SIDE3 = ROOT (X2-X1, Y2-Y1)
                    :
                    :
        DIST = XLNGTH + ROOT (2.86, HEIGHT)
                    :
```

In this program segment, the statement function is specified once but accessed three times, each time with different arguments. XXX and YYY are the dummy arguments in the function itself. To access the function, the accessing statement must specify the name of the function and an argument list corresponding in length, order, and mode to that of the function. The value of the first argument in the accessing statement is represented in the function by the first dummy argument, the second with the second, and so forth with any other arguments. Thus the first time the function in the above program is accessed, the value of DX is "substituted" wherever XXX appears in the function and the value of DY is "substituted" wherever YYY appears. The second time the function is accessed, the dummy arguments are "replaced" by the values of $X2-X1$ and $Y2-Y1$, respectively, and the third time by 2.86 and HEIGHT.

Note how the function's expression can contain an intrinsic function; it can even contain a previously defined arithmetic statement function. The squaring of the arguments was done by multiplication rather than exponentiation because the former is both faster and more accurate.

4.4.1 Details of subprogram linkage

Now it is time to look at the details of what actually occurs within the subprogram linkage. The addresses of the transmitted arguments are sent to the subprogram, and the subprogram accesses the values of the arguments through their addresses. For example, assume that DX is stored in location 182 and DY in location 176. During execution of the program, an address table is set up somewhere in the computer's memory; in this case it consists of 182 and 176 in the order specified by the argument list. The subprogram accesses that table and uses it during execution. Thus the function becomes, on its first access:

1. Multiply the contents of address 182 by the contents of address 182 and store the result in a temporary location, say address 753.

2. Multiply the contents of address 176 by the contents of address 176, leaving the answer in whatever hardware register the computer uses for calculations.

3. Add to that register the contents of address 753 (the temporary location).

4. Store the results in a temporary location, say address 753 again.

5. Access the SQRT function, transmitting address 753.

6. The SQRT function will return its calculated value into whatever location had been assigned to it, say address 1332.

7. Transfer the contents of address 1332 into the location assigned to the arithmetic statement function, say address 1334.

8. Return to the accessing statement and continue its execution. In this case all that is left is to move the value stored in address 1334 into the address set up for HYPOT, say 612.

The contents of the locations used by the function are:

Address:	176	182	612	753	1332	1334	
Label:	DY	DX	HYPOT	temp	SQRT	Root	register
Step 1:	4.5	6.4		40.96			
Step 2:	4.5	6.4		40.96			20.25
Step 3:	4.5	6.4		40.96			61.21
Step 4:	4.5	6.4		61.21			61.21
Step 5:	4.5	6.4		61.21			61.21
Step 6:	4.5	6.4		61.21	7.827		61.21
Step 7:	4.5	6.4		61.21	7.827	7.827	61.21
Step 8:	4.5	6.4	7.827	61.21	7.827	7.827	61.21

Although there may be system-dependent differences, this process is similar during all subprogram accesses. FORTRAN stores constants in such a way that their addresses can be sent to a subprogram in the same way as the address of a variable. From the above description, it is obvious that FORTRAN has no way of controlling or checking programmer errors in number of arguments or modes. If our ROOT function is called with only one argument, the routine will use for the second argument the garbage stored in whatever location the next address in the table points to, an address left there during a pervious use, not placed there by our accessing statements. Furthermore, a difference in the number of arguments may cause a return to a wrong address in the accessing program, since the address computation on many systems depends on the length of the list; the result will often be a mysterious bomb-out with no explanation other than a possible "illegal instruction" or maybe an infinite loop.

On the other hand, the transmission of a value of wrong mode (real for integer or integer for real) will not cause a bomb-out as long as the argument lists are of the same length, but it will generate a wrong answer.

4.4.2 Exercises

Exercise 4–1

Write an arithmetic statement function to calculate a rounded integer quotient; use no real arithmetic. Embed the function in a testing program (often called a *driver*) that will accept multiple sets of data. The testing program should test to ensure that the divisor is nonzero before sending it to the function. The function can first be written for positive values only, but if that should prove too simple, expand it to cover mixed signs.

Exercise 4–2

Write an arithmetic statement function to generate the tangent of an angle as a function of the sine and cosine. There should be a second arithmetic statement function to convert from integer degrees to radians. The driver program should accept the angle in degrees, use the second function to convert it to radians, and then use the first to determine the tangent. Once your program is working, modify it so that the first function accesses the second directly instead of through the driver.

Exercise 4–3

Write a series of arithmetic statement functions to be used to generate the cotangent, the secant, and the cosecant, all as functions of the sine and cosine. Again, a driver program should surround them for testing purposes.

Exercise 4–4

Write two arithmetic statement functions, one to convert an angle in degrees and decimals of a degree to radians (D2R) and the other to convert radians to degrees and decimals of a degree (R2D); pi (3.14159265) radians = 180 degrees. Both functions are to receive a real argument and return a real result. Incorporate both into a driver program for testing.

4.5 The function subprogram

The function subprogram is a true external subprogram that is compiled separately from the calling program. Like the arithmetic statement function, it can return only one value, but it is not limited to only one assignment statement, and it can contain any kind of logic including branching, looping, and I/O. The function subprogram is primarily used for computational purposes, not for I/O, but there is no inherent restriction on such use.

A perfect example of the use of a function subprogram (or simply a *function*) is the routine we described in the previous chapter (section 3.12) to develop a "pure" two-decimal-place number. This is a routine that will be very useful and thus is a perfect candidate for generalization and storage in a library.

Remember that a function subprogram is an independent piece of code; thus, the algorithm must be "packaged." The package consists of:

1. A header identifying the program as a function, specifying its name and its (dummy) argument list.

2. The necessary terminating statements: the last logical statement, RETURN, and the last physical statement END. A subprogram may also have a STOP in it, ending the run of the program, but it must contain at least one RETURN.

```
C        Function RND2:
C        returns a real value trimmed to two decimal places
C
       FUNCTION RND2 (AMT)
C
C               arithmetic statement function to trim cents
       TRIM(Y) = FLOAT (IFIX(Y)) +
      1       FLOAT (IFIX (100. * (Y - FLOAT (IFIX(Y)) +
      2                            0.005))) / 100.
C
C               get sign and make working variable positive
       SGN = SIGN (1.0, AMT)
       AAA = ABS (AMT)
C               divide by 32767 to get number of whole units
       NU = AAA / 32767.0
C               reduce to value less than 32767, then trim
       AAA = AAA - 32767. * FLOAT(NU)
       AAA = TRIM (AAA)
C               add trimmed value to base value and return
       RND2 = SGN * (AAA + FLOAT(NU) * 32767.0)
       RETURN
       END
```

Note that the function subprogram contains an arithmetic statement function that in turn contains two intrinsic functions. The variable SGN was chosen instead of SIGN because the latter is the name of an intrinsic function; the programmer cannot use the names of intrinsic functions as regular variables without interfering with their use as functions.

The function subprogram is accessed in the same way as any function. The calling program may contain statements like:

```
AMT = RND2 (AMT)

TAX = RND2 (0.075 * PRICE)

PRICE = RND2 (RND2 (UNITS * UNITPR) * PROFIT)

TOTAL = PRICE + RND2 (TXRATE * PRICE) + DLIVRY
```

In each of the above statements, the address of the argument, whether it be the address of AMT in the first statement or the temporary address containing the values of the expressions in the others, is transmitted to the subprogram. The contents of that address is accessed from the subprogram and utilized in the calculation.

One of the general rules of designing functions is that the arguments sent to the function are not to be changed. Thus the value transmitted to the function is moved into a working location (AAA) that is local to the subprogram so that the modifications done to it will not affect the value in the accessing program. Of course it is possible to write a function that will modify one of the arguments, since the subprogram has the address of each argument. For example, if the function had the statement:

```
AMT = 2.0 * AMT
```

placed after the AAA assignment statement, not only would the trimmed value be returned to the calling program, but the value of the argument in the calling program would also be doubled! It is considered a bad programming practice to modify the argument in a function, but that does not mean that some programmers don't take shortcuts once in a while. However, we will see in the next section how this practice can have disastrous results!

Another example of a function is presented below; this one has two dummy arguments and accesses the function above:

```
C         Function SALSTX:
C         Applies sales tax to purchases greater than $1.00
C
      FUNCTION  SALSTX (AMT, RATE)
C
      IF  (AMT .LE.  1.00) SALSTX = 0.00
      IF  (AMT .GT.  1.00) SALSTX = RND2 (AMT * RATE)
      RETURN
      END
```

4.5.1 Subprogram storage and libraries

Although some disk-oriented systems allow the programmer to place subprograms in the same source file as the mainline, thus compiling them simultaneously and linking in easily, this is efficient only when the subroutine is useful with just that application. It is a more general practice to store subprograms in their own source files and compile them separately. In that case, however, an additional step is required to link the subprograms with the mainline: it is necessary during the linking operation to specify any user-written, external subprograms, otherwise the linker will be unable to find the routine. (There are some systems that search the entire disk and require no special subprogram references, but they are unusual.)

Another alternative is the use of subprogram libraries. In this method, the machine language version of the subprogram is stored along with other subprograms in a named library. During the linking operation, the name or names of the desired libraries are given and the linker extracts from those libraries just the routines called by the system. Most production shops use this method to simplify the work of the programmers.

4.5.2 Exercises

Exercise 4–5

Enter the routine RND2 into your system and compile it. Then write a driver program for it; a driver program is a mainline program used to test the subprogram. For example, the driver for the RND2 function should allow the tester to enter multiple data until an end-of-data indicator is entered, access the RND2 function, and display both the input value and the returned value each time. The input value should be entered and displayed to more than two decimal places, preferably with both E- and F-formats, so that the actual number representation can be seen as well as what will be output to two decimal places.

If your system has a library facility, load the compiled version of the subprogram into the library, delete the compiled version (not the source files) from your directory, and link it with its driver from the library.

Exercise 4–6

Write a function subprogram (DMS2R) to accept as arguments integer values for degrees and minutes and a real value for seconds and return the angle in radians. Also write a driver to test it.

Exercise 4–7

Write a function subprogram (SALARY) to accept as arguments real values for hours worked and hourly rate paid. Compute the salary as hours × rate for those hours less than or equal to 40, plus hours × rate × 1.5 for those hours greater than 40 and less than 60, plus hours × rate × 2.0 for those hours greater than 60. Also write a driver to test it.

4.6 Subroutines

The subroutine is quite different from the function in a number of ways. First of all, it can return more (or less) than one result. All information going to the subroutine and coming from it is placed in the argument list. The name of the subroutine is for identification only; even though the name must follow the rules of FORTRAN variable names, the mode of the subroutine name has no significance. It is also considered proper for a subroutine to change the value of the arguments if that is the intention of the routine.

Secondly, since the subroutine may return multiple answers, it cannot be placed in an assignment statement as the function can. The subroutine is accessed through the CALL statement, which specifies the subroutine name and the argument list. But as is the case with the function, the arguments in both calling and called programs must agree in number, mode, and order.

In no way are input arguments (values sent to the subroutine) differentiated from output arguments (values returned from the subroutine) or updated arguments (values modified by the subroutine). The order in which they are placed in the argument list by the writer of the subroutine is purely a matter of style (or whim). Thus the caller of the subroutine must clearly understand what each argument stands for and what the subroutine will do with it or to it.

As an example, let us look at a subroutine that receives a unit cost, a number of units, a rate of profit, and a tax rate and returns the price, the tax, and a variable delivery charge (nothing if price is $100.00 or more, 2% of price if price less than $100.00):

```
C                       Subroutine FIGURE:  prices items and computes tax
C
      SUBROUTINE  FIGURE  (UCOST, NUNITS, PRFRAT, TAXRAT, PRICE,
     1                     TAX, DLIVRY)
C
C                Glossary
C                --------
C           UCOST:   unit cost                           input
C           NUNITS:  number of units                     input
C           PRFRAT:  profit rate (in decimal)            input
C           TAXRAT:  tax rate (in decimal)               input
C           PRICE:   price                               output
C           TAX:     computed tax                        output
C           DLIVRY:  delivery charge                     output
C                    if price >= $100.00, delivery free
C                    if price < $100.00, = 2% of price
C
C
      PRICE = RND2 (PRFRAT *  RND2 (UCOST * FLOAT(NUNITS)))
      TAX   = RND2 (TAXRAT * PRICE)
      IF  (PRICE .GE. 100.00)  DLIVRY = 0.00
      IF  (PRICE .LT. 100.00)  DLIVRY = RND2 (0.02 * PRICE)
C
      RETURN
      END
```

Although the same results could have been obtained by three functions, the subroutine is more efficient in this situation. The subroutine is accessed by a statement like

```
CALL FIGURE (UC, NUMBER, 1.25, 0.075, SELLPR, TAX, DCHRGE)
```

Notice how the argument lists agree in number and mode and how the order of the arguments must correspond. Only the input values may be constants or expressions, otherwise the results will be incorrect.

4.6.1 Constant modification

As we mentioned before, the subroutine is very useful if we wish to modify arguments, and we will be doing much of that subsequently. For the moment, let us look at a very simple example in which two values sent to a subroutine are returned with the larger one in the first argument:

```
C       Subroutine GETMAX: places larger of two values first
C
        SUBROUTINE GETMAX (K, M)

        IF  (K .GE. M) RETURN
C               interchange
            ITEMP = K
            K = M
            M = ITEMP
C
        RETURN
        END
```

Notice how the interchange is done! A temporary location is usually required; any other method could destroy one of the values.

Now there is a very dangerous situation that can arise in any subroutine that modifies a value. Let us assume that the above code is accessed as follows:

```
            :
LL = 8
CALL GETMAX (2, LL)
            :
            :
NEW = 2
WRITE (5,1000) NEW
            :
```

Let us assume that LL is stored in location 817 and the constant 2 in location 932. The addresses 932 and 817 are sent to the subroutine GETMAX in that order. In the subroutine, the values in locations 932 and 817 (2 and 8 respectively) are compared by the logical expression IF (K .GE. M) and the resulting value is false; the logic proceeds to the next sequential statement and the interchange takes place. The contents of location 932 are placed in the temporary location (ITEMP), the contents of location 817 are placed in location 932, and the temporary contents then placed into location 817. The two locations 932 and 817 now contain 8 and 2, respectively, as return is made from the subroutine to the calling program. Later on in the calling program, the contents of 932, the location that originally contained the constant 2, is placed into the location labeled NEW; however, location 932 now contains an 8. From now on in the program, whenever the constant 2 is accessed, the value of 8 will replace it! I don't think it is necessary for me to tell how many programmer hours can be spent debugging this kind of situation.

The combined code of the calling program and the subprogram are shown below, along with the contents of the critical locations. The symbol (2) stands for the constant 2 as stored by the compiler. The change in that location caused by the subroutine is the source of the problem.

```
                            location:   932      817
                            label:      (2)      LL
LL = 8                                   2        8
CALL GETMAX (2, LL)

SUBROUTINE GETMAX (K, M)                  K        M      ITEMP
IF (K .GE. M)  RETURN
     ITEMP = K                            2        8        2
     K = M                                8        8        2
     M = ITEMP                            8        2        2
RETURN

                                         (2)       LL      NEW
NEW = 2                                   8         2        8
WRITE  (5,1000)  NEW
```

Some of the more modern languages such as Pascal prevent this situation as part of the language, but this is not done in FORTRAN. However, there are some implementations that do prevent this kind of disaster. On the DEC VAX system, for example, constants are stored in a "no write" program section so that any attempt to modify a location containing a constant yields an "access violation" bomb-out. Other implementations, such as Microsoft's TRS-80 Model 4 compiler, move the constant first into a temporary location and then transmit the address of the temporary location, leaving the original constant still in its memory location. The Prime FORTRAN 66 allows the error to occur. Regardless of the implementation, the programmer must exercise extreme care when transmitting a constant to a subprogram.

The linking of subroutines with the mainline program is done in the same way as with functions, and of course, subroutines can also be stored in libraries.

4.6.2 Exercises

Exercise 4–8

Write an error message subroutine called ERRMSG that displays different error messages based on a single input argument. Use the table below as a starting point for a table of errors and messages, and add to it any messages that you think will be valuable.

input	message
1	value out of range
2	invalid input
3	excess data
4	insufficient data
< 1 or > 4	undefined error

As an added touch, if the input value is negative, skip a line in the output both before and after the message. Thus a 2 will display (or print) the message "invalid input," but a -2 will surround the message with blank lines.

Exercise 4–9

Write a subroutine (R2DMS) that receives an angle in radians and returns the angle in degrees, minutes, and seconds, the first two as integer, the last as real. The driver program should display the reals to at least two decimal places.

Exercise 4–10

Write a subroutine (TIMBRK) that accepts a real value for time in the form HR.MN and returns the hours and minutes as integers.

Exercise 4–11

Write a subroutine (EGGBRK) which accepts an integer number of eggs and returns a breakdown in gross, dozen, and units (1 gross = 144 units, 1 dozen = 12 units).

4.7 Error handling

Certainly one of the most abused phrases in the computer field and yet the one that contains the most truth is GIGO (garbage in, garbage out). Yet the probability of an invalid argument being sent to a subprogram at some time is so high that the writer of a subprogram *must* consider what to do in case an invalid value is sent to his or her subprogram. The alternatives are:

1. Abort the run immediately upon detecting invalid data, with an informing error message.

2. Continue the run after displaying an error message, returning a nonvalid answer.

3. Use an error indicator in the argument list that can be set with one value if all is well or another value indicating the type of error, if any.

4. Return a ridiculous answer that the caller can test.

Each of the above methods has its advocates. Although all professional programmers believe it to be the responsibility of the caller of the subprogram to ensure that only good data is sent, the subprogram must also be written defensively, that is, it must protect itself from bad data and not return an invalid answer that might be construed as a correct one. The programmer, of course, has no control over how the system implements the intrinsic functions, but he or she ought to find out just what happens when an invalid argument is used. Try sending a negative value to the SQRT routine and see what the response is!

The disadvantage of alternative 1 is that it prevents the program from discovering any later errors that might arise. It is very frustrating for the debugging programmer to correct an error in either the program or the data and find that the same error crops up again when rerunning the program. This becomes a waste of both computer and programmer time.

Alternative 2 requires a careful eye on the screen (assuming the screen is used) to ensure that no errors pass by. One variation on this method causes the execution to PAUSE (an instruction we will describe later) and requests a response from the user as to whether to proceed or to abort the program. This tends to keep the user awake and is a very useful procedure in the right circumstances.

Alternative 3 requires an additional argument in the list and is handy when more than one type of error can come in; thus this method provides the most flexibility. The programmer can add an error message routine to his or her system (see exercise 4–8 in the preceding section) and provide very sophisticated error notification, but it will lengthen the program considerably. However, this method places responsibility on the programmer to test the returned indicator; the lazy programmer, too lazy to check the information sent to the subprogram in the first place, may fail to do this. For this reason, alternative 1 has many advocates. Alternative 3 cannot be used with functions (theoretically).

This writer prefers alternative 4 in a professional environment because it keeps code to a minimum and still gives the caller two chances to check the operation, first by checking the data going in and second by checking the answer coming out.

We will illustrate the use of the "ridiculous" result with a function for calculating factorials. (A factorial is the product of the numbers from 1 to an integer input value and is indicated with an exclamation point. Thus 4! = 4 * 3 * 2 * 1 = 24. By definition, 0! = 1, and negative factorials are undefined.) Since factorials get very large very quickly, the result will be computed as an integer-valued real, although the input to the routine must be integer. If the input value is negative, a value of -1.0 will be returned; for a factorial, this is a "ridiculous" number and the caller can test it.

```
C                       Function FACTL:  generates factorials
C
      FUNCTION FACTL (N)
C
```

```
C               if N < 0, return value of -1 indicating invalid input
      IF  (N .LT. 0)  FACTL  =  -1.0
      IF  (N .LT. 0)  RETURN
C               initialize factorial as 1
      FACTL = 1.0
C               return if N less than or equal to 1
      IF  (N .LE. 1)  RETURN
C               loop for N > 1
      DO 20  I = 2,N
   20 FACTL = FACTL * FLOAT (I)
C               return
      RETURN
      END
```

Error handling is one of the most controversial issues in professional programming, and there is no perfect method. The user must use a subprogram (like a car) with care; it is impossible to expect the writer of the subprogram to take care of all eventualities. One can only hope that writing a defensive subprogram and checking data carefully before the subprogram is called will prevent garbage from proliferating.

4.7.1 Exercise

Exercise 4–12

Enter the routine FACTL into your system and compile it. Then write a driver program for it. For example, the driver for the FACTL function should allow the tester to enter multiple integer data until an end-of-data indicator is entered, access the FACTL function, and display both the input value and the returned value each time.

Test data should include numbers less than zero. The output of the returned values should use E-format because the numbers do get very large and will overflow the range of allowable real values somewhere around 33! It would be a good idea to modify the FACTL function so that any attempt to input a value in excess of the maximum value your computer can handle would return a value of 0, another ridiculous value for a factorial.

Another FACTL driver might be written to generate a table of factorials from 1 to this maximum input value. A touch of sophistication would be to use decimal output (F-format) while the factorial is within a reasonable range and exponential output (E-format) for the rest.

If your system has a library facility, load the compiled versions of the subprogram into the library, delete the compiled version (not the source file) from your directory, and link it with its driver from the library.

4.8 Summary and additional exercises

In this chapter we have covered most of the critical features of subprograms. As we develop more of the FORTRAN language, most of the applications discussed will utilize subprograms, since they allow the programmer to develop more efficient, modularized, and structured programming systems. In later chapters we will cover some of the more intricate details of subprogram use and some of the sophisticated subprogram techniques used by programmers, as well as some of the additional features offered by FORTRAN 77.

The exercises below, although rudimentary, give the novice programmer exposure to software that will be useful in future applications. It is critical that the exercises be actually run on any computer being used so that the linking operation can be checked out. Furthermore, if any of these systems has a library mechanism, the reader can get a very valuable experience by trying it out.

In this chapter, we have touched upon the following new FORTRAN commands:

topic	section
CALL	4.3, 4.6
FUNCTION	4.5
RETURN	4.5
SUBROUTINE	4.6

4.8.1 Exercises

Exercise 4–13

Write the programming system necessary for the following application:

A food establishment needs a computerized system that will allow the cashier to input the net amount of a bill (before tax and tip) and the amount the customer is paying in cash; the output should consist of the net amount, the tax, the tip, the total cost, and the change to the customer broken down into $20s, $10s, $5s, $1s, quarters, dimes, nickels, and pennies.

The tax is to be computed with a statement function that uses two arguments, the tax rate and the net amount of the bill. The tax rate should be a variable that is set by an assignment statement. If possible, incorporate the RND2 routine for greater precision.

The tip is to be computed in a function according to the rules below:

If net < $5.00, tipping rate is 25%

If net > $25.00, tipping rate is 15% of the full amount

Otherwise, tipping rate is 18% of the full amount

Again, the RND2 function would allow greater precision.

A subroutine is to be used to break down the change into its components. The input to the subroutine will consist of a real number for change, but it will return integer numbers for the eight categories of change. The output for the change might be placed in this subroutine, and it would be preferable to display only the nonzero categories.

The mainline program can use ERRMSG (exercise 4–8) when checking the validity of the input data, which must be positive. Also, the amount of the bill plus tax and tip must be equal to or less than the amount paid; if not, an error message should be displayed rather than sending negative change into the subroutine.

Exercise 4–14

Write the programming system necessary for an application in which goods are sold in quantities of gross, dozens, and units. The specifications for the mainline program, a subroutine to classify the number of items, and a function to compute a total cost are given below.

The subroutine is computational only and should contain no I/O. Also assume that error checking for negative NITEMS is unnecessary.

SUBROUTINE BASE12 (NITEMS, NGROSS, NDOZEN, NUNITS)

Input:	NITEMS—the number of items to be broken down.
Output:	NGROSS—the number of gross in NITEMS.
	NDOZEN—the number of dozen left after NGROSS is removed from NITEMS.
	NUNITS—the number of items left after both NGROSS and NDOZEN are removed from NITEMS.

For example,

352 items = 2 gross, 5 dozen, 4 units.

The function subprogram is computational only and should contain no I/O. It should also contain *no mixed-mode* arithmetic.

FUNCTION COST (NGROSS, NDOZEN, NUNITS, UCOST)

Input:	NGROSS, NDOZEN, NUNITS as described above.
	UCOST—the cost per individual unit, a real number with two decimal places.

Output: COST—the cost of the input quantities, computed as
               follows:
               each gross at 100 times the unit cost
               each dozen at 10 times the unit cost
               each unit at the unit cost

For example, using the above quantities and a unit cost of 0.08:

$$COST = 100 \times 0.08 \times 2 + 10 \times 0.08 \times 5 + 0.08 \times 4 = \$20.32$$

Mainline (called MAIN1.FOR)

Input: NITEMS, UCOST from the keyboard in free format (if pos-
               sible). The input for above example would be 352,0.08

               The program must be written for an unlimited amount of
               multiple input and should be prompted.

               Error checking should be done for negative input with an ap-
               propriate error routine.

Calculation: Use the above subprograms to compute the cost.

               Include an arithmetic statement function to compute the total
               cost as a percentage of the standard cost as computed by the
               unit price times the number of items. For example, using the
               above values:

$$20.32 \,/\, (0.08 \times 352) \times 100 = 72.16\%$$

Output: NITEMS, NGROSS, NDOZEN, NUNITS, UCOST,
               COST, PERCENTAGE

5

One-dimensional arrays

5.1 The need for additional structures

With what we already know, we could write a program that would input examination scores and determine average, maximum, and minimum scores. Such a program would be considered a very minor programming effort; it could be easily written and would provide a significant analysis of the data with very little code. The program could handle an unlimited amount of data, and furthermore, it could also prepare a distribution of the scores, that is, count the number of scores between 90 and 100, between 80 and 89, between 70 and 79, between 65 and 69, and below 65 and tabulate the frequency.

However, there are many things the program cannot do. What if the passing score was not fixed at 65, but at 15 points below the average grade? Or what if the scores were to be graded on a curve, with the top 10% getting an A, the next 35% a B, the next 35% a C, the next 10% a D, and finally the lowest 10% an F. We will not get involved in the pros and cons of variable grading schemes, since there are almost as many schemes as there are professors to implement them; the important point here is that any variable scheme requires a method in which the data can be reexamined *after* certain parameters such as the average have been determined.

In our examples and exercises thus far, we have used the so-called HIPO (hierarchy: input, processing, output) scheme, in which each data item is input, massaged, and output prior to inputting the next piece of data; the next data value then erases the preceding value. Thus each new piece of data destroys its predecessor. How then can we look at that data again?

Of course, there is one obvious method: rereading the data, either by entering it again manually (a ridiculous method), by refeeding the same cards back into the read hopper, or "rewinding" the disk file (moving the file pointer back to the beginning of the file) and repeating the input code. Now there are some circumstances where the latter option has some merit, but fortunately for the programmer, there is another construct available in FORTRAN that is not only far more sophisticated but is also faster and (more importantly) leads to better code— better because it is structured and easier to write, debug, and understand!

This new construct involves the handling of blocks of data all resident in memory simultaneously, and it opens up new horizons of programming applications. This construct—the array—will be found in almost every programming language, and its importance cannot be overstressed. Thus we will spend considerable time and effort to develop it in all its detail.

5.1.1 Professional approach to programming

With this new construct, we can handle an extremely large amount of data, but input and output from and to the keyboard and terminal are very inefficient. For example, imagine a situation in which we want to analyze temperature data for a year by inputting up to 366 numbers representing the mean temperature for each day. A program that accepts 365 or 366 manually inputted values would probably never run correctly because of the very great chance that at least one entered value would be incorrect, thus negating the whole effort. The usual method is to prepare the data in advance in a disk file (or on punch cards) and write the program to read from the file. Each line or card of data is called a *record*.

Similarly, our results should also be sent to a disk file or a printer so that they may be viewed in some form other than the fleeting image on the screen. This final output should contain not only the answers but also a listing of the input; the user can then see the complete problem, input and output, at once without having to look at two different files. The listing of the input data is called an *echo check*, that is, an echoing of what comes into the machine; not only does it provide the human user with a listing of the input, but it also tells us what values the machine thinks it has, enabling us to correct input errors much more easily. Furthermore, the output should not only be self-contained, but it should also be properly annotated so that the reader is not confused by the myriad of numbers but is made cognizant of what each one represents. The input file, on the other hand, can just be a collection of numbers without annotation, arranged in a convenient format for input.

In this chapter, we will cover the basic methods of block I/O and also look at many variations so that the reader can see the tools available for providing flexible and artistic output. Keep in mind that the purpose of an output report is to convey information; for good communication, the information must be provided in a clear and concise fashion so that there is no confusion on the part of the reader. We mention *artistic* output to emphasize the importance of good form design as an aid in communication. The professional programmer often spends more time on the design of the output than on the calculations; after all, the calculations are a matter of fact, the artwork a matter of taste. Unfortunately, the taste of the programmer and that of the user may often differ, and the former is many times asked to redesign the output form; little does the nonprogrammer realize how much programming effort goes into this.

We will also be concerned with the form or layout of the input. The professional attitude is that the programming effort must be aimed at making the program, a tool for the user, as easy to use as possible. The program is written and debugged during the development cycle and the programmer seldom looks at it again, except possibly to expand it. But the user will be using it day in and day out; for a program (or any tool) to be useful and productive, the user must be kept in mind. Thus the programmer should spend as much time as practical on the program so that it is "user friendly."

(When the author first entered the computer field in 1963, most systems used the typewriter as their principal output device. These typewriters were very slow by today's standards, printing only about 8 to 10 characters/second. Since the computer itself was slow and relatively expensive to run, early output was a collection of numbers without identification, and the user had to refer to a table showing the layout in order to track down what the values meant. As the hardware improved and high-speed printers with 132 columns rather than the 80 typewriter columns became the principal output device, there was a distinct move toward more expressive and annotated output. At that time the author was working for a supervisor who often facetiously said, "I don't care if the numbers are right or wrong, so long as they look good!" Throughout this text, we will be concerned with the presentation of the output, but we also will demand accuracy in the answers.)

As this chapter develops, the reader should notice a trend toward concern for the end product in a production environment. Instead of writing practice programs to build experience or to satisfy an instructor, we will aspire to developing good, professional, programming systems, usable in the real world and at the same time satisfying to their creator.

5.1.2 Structure of this chapter

The new construct that we are about to introduce opens up so many programming applications that this chapter has been divided into two parts. The first part (chapter 5) presents the theory with limited applications; the second part (the appendix to chapter 5) is concerned with applying the theory to some of the myriad of real-life applications.

5.2 Concept of the array

An array is a block (or matrix) of memory locations addressable by a single variable name. To differentiate among the members of the array (the array *elements*), a numeric subscript is used to indicate the location of the element in the array. Just as we might refer to the first house on a block or the first seat in a row, in an array we talk about the first element, the second element, and so forth. An array allows us to store the input "permanently" (that is, as long as the program is running) so that we can have access to it from any place in the program.

Because of this "permanence," we can restructure a program in an entirely different way. Instead of the HIPO approach mentioned above, we can input *all* of the data first, then massage *all* of the data in the next section of the program, and finally output *all* the data and results at one time. Thus the program can have three distinct modules, each separate from the other in terms of branches and loops, but all sharing the data. This segmentation of code lends itself very nicely to a subprogram approach and also results in highly structured code.

There is, however, one problem associated with arrays; the size of the array is bound by the size of the available memory, and thus the amount of data that can be stored may be limited. In these days of large memories, even on the microcomputers, only extremely large data samples will cause a problem. For the moment, we will ignore this limitation, assuming that the kinds of problems we will solve are well within the memory capacities of our systems.

Although we have called the element locator a subscript, the lack of a subscripting mechanism on our keyboards and on most of our printers has caused the inventors of computer languages to adopt another symbol. The earlier languages, such as FORTRAN, COBOL, RPG and BASIC, use parentheses to surround the subscript, which is written on the same line as the array name; some of the later languages, such as Pascal, C, and Modula-2, use the square bracket in the same way. In the pseudocode below, we will use the construct used in FORTRAN, a set of parentheses.

5.2.1 *Program segmentation*

To illustrate the use of an array, we will now develop the pseudocode for a program that inputs examination scores and determines (and outputs) the average score and the highest score. The input module reads in the data until the end-of-data is reached. Of course, another method would be to tell the computer just how much data is coming in so that a controlled loop could be set up; however, that method is considered rather unprofessional, since it requires the user to count the data and then enter that count, creating two chances for human error (after all, if the machine is so smart, it should be able to count the data itself!).

Input module
array is labeled M
number of pieces of data is labeled ND
counter is labeled counter

1. counter = 1

2. read data into M(counter)

3. if end-of-data, go to step 6

4. counter = counter + 1

5.   go to step 2

6. number of pieces of data, ND = counter − 1

Step 5 is indented to provide easier readability. Notice how the number of pieces of data is determined in step 6. It might seem strange to have a counter that is counting ahead and must be decremented to obtain the number of pieces of data, but the human brain works in a very similar way. If we are given a list of numbers, our eyes may scan the numbers very quickly without realizing just how much work our brain does in absorbing the information. Imagine that the numbers are being read from a distance through a telescope and only one number at a time can be viewed; it is not until we try to read the number following the last one that we realize that there are no more values. For example, when viewing a list of four numbers, we do not know until we attempt the fifth read that there are no more numbers. Thus the number of values is one less than the number of attempted reads.

The next process would be to determine the average of the numbers. Since the values are always available, there was no need to keep a running accumulation during the input module; instead, we can keep each process separate and distinct. The pseudocode for the averaging module is:

Determine average

7. sum = 0

8. counter = 1

9. add M(counter) into sum

10.   counter = counter + 1

11.   if counter is less than or equal to ND, go to step 9

12. average = sum / ND

Actually, since there is no branching between this module and the input module above it, we could have begun our numbering again at 1. We would have done this if each of the modules were to be placed in a separate subprogram, but since we have not yet defined the program structure, we will number continuously. Moving on to find the highest score:

Highest score

13. high = M(1)

14. if ND = 1, go to step 19

15. counter = 2

16. if M(counter) > high, then high = M(counter)

17.   counter = counter + 1

18.   if counter is less than or equal to ND, go to step 16

19. continue

Because step 19 was provided just to complete this module, we could actually begin numbering the next module with 19. The output module lists the input and the results.

Output module

19.   counter = 1

20.   output M(counter)

21.   counter = counter + 1

22.   if counter is less than or equal to ND, go to step 20

23.   output average, high

As you will see in a few more pages, the implementation of this program in FORTRAN is disgustingly short and simple!

5.3 Array variables and the DIMENSION statement

Arrays may be used to store any mode of information possible, and array names follow the rules for single variable names. The array variable must be followed by a subscript in parentheses. Since that subscript points to a distinct element in the array, its value can only be integer. The rules of FORTRAN state that the subscript may be:

1. An integer constant

2. An integer variable

3. An integer expression

In the early versions of FORTRAN, including FORTRAN IV, the use of subscript expressions was very limited; subscript expressions could only be of the form:

$$n * I \pm m$$

where I was an integer variable that could be multiplied first by an integer constant (n) and/or have an integer constant (m) added to or subtracted from the product. Typical applications would include such array notation as:

BLOCK (3 * N)   GROUP (N − 1)   LENGTH (2 * N + 5)

A subscript expression such as LENGTH (N * 2 + 5) would be considered invalid since the multiplying constant is not before the variable, even though the evaluation of the expression would give the same result as evaluation of (2 * N + 5).

In some expanded versions of FORTRAN IV and in FORTRAN 77, the subscript expression may be any valid integer expression; some systems even allow real expressions, which will be truncated to integer before being used to locate an array element. Thus, the array syntax IJK $(X * 3.2 - 9.6)$ with X equal to 5.4 would indicate the value stored in array element IJK (7).

For compatibility of implementation, we will use the restricted subscripting of FORTRAN IV. This method may occasionally require an additional statement when a complicated subscript expression is encountered, as in

```
ISUB = X * 3.2 - 9.6
NN   = IJK (ISUB)
```

Note the similarity of IJK (ISUB) in the last instruction to the notation used in accessing a function. From the syntax of the statement, neither the computer nor a human being can determine whether IJK is a function or a subscripted variable. Thus we need another FORTRAN construct to tell the compiler just what IJK represents. Furthermore, for efficient storage, the FORTRAN compiler must know how many elements an array is going to have.

5.3.1 DIMENSION

The DIMENSION statement is a nonexecutable (or specification) statement that declares that:

1. A variable represents an array.
2. The array has a particular number of elements.

The DIMENSION statement appears before any of the executable statements. The statement

```
DIMENSION I(4), J(2), K(3)
```

sets aside four locations for I, two for J, and three for K, a total of nine locations. Furthermore, the syntax I(2), for example, is now understood to be an array element, not a function.

Deciding how big to make the dimension of an array is always a problem. If the exact amount of data is known or limited (for example, the mean temperature for each day of the year has an upper limit of 366 data items), there is no problem. But if we are dealing with a body of data whose size varies from application to application, the programmer must make some estimate of a reasonable size. Although our computers today have fairly large memories, it is still possible to overload them. Thus the programmer's estimate must be a balance of what is truly necessary and reasonable for future expansion against what is not excessive. This programmer has always doubled, where possible, the dimension specified by the program user as the "maximum amount of data that will ever come in"! And many times, over years of use, even that was not sufficient.

Under any circumstances, to prevent the program from yielding erroneous results, the programmer must ensure that arrays do not extend beyond their bounds.

5.4 The mapping function

The computer memory is actually a single one-dimensional array with addresses from 0 to the highest location, which varies according to the amount of available memory. The variable names that we use are temporary symbols that represent a numeric memory address; this is the origin of the term *symbolic location*. During the compilation phase, these symbols disappear from the program as they are replaced by their addresses, and a *symbol table* containing the equivalent address for each symbol is developed. This table can usually be obtained with the program listing and is often useful for locating misspelled variables and unintended modes of storage.

One reason for specifying the size of the array in the DIMENSION statement is to allow the computer to assign contiguous locations to the elements. Thus I(2) is stored next to I(1), I(3) next to I(2), and so forth. Although it might be possible to store arrays dynamically by setting up a location for each element as it is needed, this system would produce a considerably larger symbol table; even worse, it would require allocations to be set up during execution, definitely causing an increase in processing time and possibly causing a memory overflow during execution. Thus the savings in memory by not having to leave room for unused array elements would be countered by the negative aspects of dynamic allocation.

FORTRAN stores array elements contiguously (although some machines store them in reverse order) and is thus able to have a single entry in the symbol table for the array name. As we will see, we need only reference that single name when transmitting an array to a subprogram. The individual elements of the array are accessed by adding a displacement to the location of the first element of the array. For example, I(4) is displaced by three integer allocations from I(1). (The term *integer allocation* is used to precisely define the allocation size since, for example, some computers are byte-addressable and a short integer has an allocation of 2 bytes. Thus I(4) is displaced from I(1) by six bytes. This is all transparent to the programmer, who is only interested in getting FORTRAN to work; for those of us who want to know how it works, the details are important.) Thus the address of the first element of the array is all the computer needs to know in order to access the entire array.

This "mapping" of elements is done by an algorithm called the *mapping function*. For one dimension, it is a very simple matter of subtracting 1 from the subscript to determine the displacement, but for higher-order arrays the procedure is more complex. Understanding the mapping function clarifies how the computer accesses the array elements and also allows the sophisticated programmer to perform a number of handy tricks and develop more flexible subprograms for handling a wide variety of applications. It also trains a programmer to develop his or her own mapping functions for unusually shaped matrices.

Referring to the DIMENSION statement specified in the preceding section

```
DIMENSION I(4), J(2), K(3)
```

and laying out the arrays in forward order, we might expect to see the following memory layout (in bytes):

array element:	I(1)	I(2)	I(3)	I(4)	J(1)	J(2)	K(1)	K(2)	K(3)
memory address:	301	303	305	307	309	311	313	315	317

I(4) is located $2 * (4 - 1) = 6$ byte locations from I(1), which is synonymous with the address of the array. Thus I(4) is located at $301 + 6 =$ byte address 307. The scheme is simple and easy to implement.

However, there are serious problems that occur when programming becomes sloppy. For the same DIMENSION statement, the FORTRAN instruction

```
I(7) = 22
```

should yield a compiler error, since the compiler can compare the dimension of an array with the constant subscript to ensure that the subscript is within the proper limit, just as it can also verify that the subscript is neither negative nor zero. But the compiler cannot check the array bounds if the subscript is a variable or an expression, because the compiler does not do any of the calculations that are done during the execution of the program. Thus the following program code can lead to interesting results:

```
N = 7
I(N) = 22
```

During the execution phase, the mapping function will calculate a displacement of $2 * (7 - 1) = 12$, add it to the base of the array I, and get an address of $301 + 12 = 313$ for the location of I(7). The value of 22 will be placed in that address, and the net result is that the value of K(1) will be modified!

The same kind of erroneous result would occur if N contains the value -2. The mapping function would calculate the displacement as $2 * (-2 - 1) = -6$ bytes and add it to 301 to get address 295, thus modifying some other location in the memory. One can see how disastrous this result might be—it could modify the program instructions or the operating system, which are also sitting in memory.

(One prank often played by some fiendish programmers was to write a program in which the value of N varied from 1 to the size of memory and wipe out the memory.) As with integer numbers, the memory addresses also work in a wraparound fashion, so exceeding the top address by 1 yields an address of 0.

Some advanced versions of FORTRAN 77 have a bounds-checking option that checks a subscript each time it is computed to ensure that it is within the limits specified by the DIMENSION statement, but this option can add a significant amount of code to a program as well as cause a serious degradation of execution speed. Professional programmers often use the option while testing and debugging a new program, but then remove it when the program is put into production.

Obviously, it is the responsibility of the programmer to ensure that the program does not generate out-of-bounds subscripts, and in our examples we will be very careful to do so!

5.4.1 Review questions

5–1. Lay out the memory for the following DIMENSION statement and then indicate what values will be placed in the locations, assuming that the mapping function takes priority and no bounds-checking is in effect. Assume two-byte integers:

```
      DIMENSION I(4), J(2), K(5), L(3)
C
      N = 0
      L(N) = 1
      N = -2
      K(N) = 2
      N = 8
      I(N) = 3
      N = 3
      K(N) = 4
```

5–2. Assuming two-byte integers and four-byte reals, how many bytes of memory must be allocated for each of the arrays in the DIMENSION statement below?

```
DIMENSION I(18), X(22), Y(22), J(7)
```

5.5 Input/output of arrays

There are three basic methods of I/Oing arrays, each of which has its advantages and disadvantages. To illustrate, we will begin with input and assume that we have a file of up to 366 integer mean temperature values. The first method requires that the information be "stacked" one value per record, and we will assume that the value is right-justified in columns 1–3, allowing a range in values from −99 to 999 degrees. However, to give our program flexibility, we could write it so that it would accept an input file with less than 366 values for non-leap years, or a file with only 28–31 values for analysis of a month, or a file with only 7 values for analysis of a week. So our program will accept up to 366 values, but as few as 1 value.

```
C           Analysis of Temperature Data
C           read in up to 366 mean temperatures (integer)
C           compute average, maximum, and minimum
C
      DIMENSION MEANTM(367)
```

The overly dimensioned array (367 elements) allows us to attempt to read a 367th temperature so that we can be assured that the file does not contain too much data.

5.5.1 Method 1: DO loop

```
      DO 20 I = 1,367
  20  READ  (3,1020, END=40) MEANTM(I)
1020  FORMAT  (I3)
         WRITE (1,1022)
1022     FORMAT (1H ,'EXCESSIVE INPUT - ABORT!')
         STOP
  40  NUMTMP = I - 1
```

From here on, we will be using the END= clause of the READ statement, which allows us to terminate input upon reaching the end-of-file; for the reader without that facility, the code will have to be expanded slightly to provide a check for a sentinel value (see section 2.10).

In this method, each trip around the loop causes a new READ operation; each new READ starts at a new record. Thus for 365 days, there are 366 READs issued, the last checking for either the end-of-data or the sentinel value. The output of this data (the echo check) would result in 365 output lines, one piece of data per line. If we wanted to spread out the data, say seven values per line, we would need a fairly complicated code to take care of the last week, which could contain anywhere from one to seven values. Rather than illustrating this unsophisticated code, we will look at method 2, which does a better job.

5.5.2 Method 2: implied DO loop

The implied DO loop looks like a DO statement without the DO and the end-of-loop statement number; it generates the variable list for an I/O command. The variables can be regular or subscripted variables; in the latter case, the DO index can be the same as the subscript. The general syntax is shown below with a WRITE statement, although it is the same for a READ statement. The index and the two or three DO loop parameters (the third is optional, assumed to be 1 if not specified) are enclosed in a set of parentheses:

```
WRITE (. . . .) (list of variables, index = m1, m2, m3)
```

Now we can implement the implied DO loop in our code:

```
      READ   (3,1020, END=40) (MEANTM(I), I=1,367)
1020 FORMAT   (I3)
          WRITE (1,1022)
1022      FORMAT (1H 'EXCESSIVE INPUT - ABORT!')
          STOP
  40 NUMTMP = I - 1
```

The implied DO loop (MEANTM(I), I=1,367) actually is similar to the code:

```
 READ   (3,1020, END=40) MEANTM(1), MEANTM(2), MEANTM(3),
1        MEANTM(4), MEANTM(5), MEANTM(6), ...
:              :
Z        MEANTM(364), MEANTM(365), MEANTM(366), MEANTM(367)
```

With only a single READ statement, the implied DO loop generates a variable list of 366 elements. (This method works only when the END= clause is available; however, it does not work in Microsoft FORTRAN.)

Method 2 works because of a rule that applies to an I/O situation in which there are more elements in the list than specified in the FORMAT statement. In such a situation, reaching the final parenthesis of a FORMAT statement tells the computer that this is the end of the record and to proceed to the next record, starting at the beginning of that record (column 1). Thus, when the instruction to read MEANTM(2) is executed and the only specification in FORMAT 1022 has been used up, the computer assumes that record 1 has been completely read and moves to the next record, record 2, to read MEANTM(2). This process continues until the end-of-file (or 367th record) is reached.

The implied DO loop is even more valuable if we want to output the data in rows and columns instead of in columnar form. Suppose we want to echo check the input in rows of seven, so that each row contains a week's data. We can use the following code:

```
      WRITE   (4,1040)
1040 FORMAT   (1H ,'Listing of Input Data')
      WRITE   (4,1042) (MEANTM(I), I=1,NUMTMP)
1042 FORMAT   (1H , 7I5)
```

With only seven output specifications per line, the computer will output seven values per line until it reaches the last line, which might contain less than seven. (It is perfectly valid for a FORMAT to contain too many specifications; any unnecessary ones are ignored.) Thus 365 days will output 52 lines of seven values and a 53d line with only one value.

5.5.3 Method 3: entire array

The code

```
DIMENSION MEANTM(366)
READ  (3,1020, END=40) MEANTM
```

would be useful only if we had exactly 366 pieces of data. When we state the array name only, the compiler refers to the DIMENSION statement and generates the code for an implied DO loop whose upper limit is the total number of elements in the array. Effectively, we are saving ourselves the effort of coding:

```
READ (3,1020, END=40) (MEANTM(I), I=1,366)
```

This method is useful only when the program is working with full arrays, and thus it is limited to certain applications such as the grading program below.

5.5.4 Multiple-item records

When using multiple-item records, we need to consider a very important point about when the end-of-file is found and what is assumed by FORTRAN for unspecified fields. Let us assume that the input data is filed not as a column of numbers but as rows of seven columns, right-justified in fields of five, for example,

```
78    82    85    75    68    90    86
88    85    72    77    89    90    84
87    79
```

Here we have sixteen values arranged seven per row for two rows, with two values in the last row. If we used the implied DO loop (the most logical approach for this arrangement), our code would be:

```
      READ  (3,1020, END=40) (MEANTM(I), I=1,367)
1020 FORMAT  (7I5)
        WRITE (1,1022)
1022    FORMAT (1H ,'EXCESSIVE INPUT - ABORT!')
        STOP
  40 NUMTMP = I - 1
```

However, NUMTMP would end up with the value 21! Let's look at what happens: FORTRAN reads an entire record, in this case 35 columns, and assumes that any column not containing a character actually contains a zero. Thus it "fills in" columns 11–35 of the last row with blanks that become values of 0. The end-of-file is assumed at the beginning of the next line, and thus 21 values are recorded, the last five of which are zero. Now the programmer could add additional code to "trim" the zeros off the end of the array, but then it would also trim winter (or Celsius) temperatures that actually are zeros.

There is a distinct problem here that requires some techniques beyond our present knowledge, so we will save them for later. A quick and dirty solution is to put a sentinel value after the last valid temperature, some number like 999 or −99, which is well out of the range of standard temperatures; the DIMENSION value would also have to be incremented by 1 to allow for the sentinel value. Then the program could scan for that value and know that it, and any values beyond it, are invalid.

Another point must be brought up here. What would happen if we read in only 365 values but output 366?—what will be output as that last value? The answer will vary from computer to computer, and on some computers, it will vary in each execution. FORTRAN compilers are not supposed to modify any locations other than those specified by the program, so undefined locations will contain "garbage," that is, data left from the previous use of the location. However, there are some computer systems (DEC and Prime, for example) that do zero out all locations as part of the execution phase, regardless of the language being executed. Now RPG and BASIC zero out numeric locations and blank out alphameric ones as part of the compilation of the language, and the programmer can count on these languages to do so. However, programmers in FORTRAN (and COBOL) are responsible for initializing memory locations, even if zeros are placed there. Don't allow a computer that "does something for you" let you become too lazy to write portable and valid code!

Now let's continue with another file structure and see how it can be I/Oed. Suppose we have a file of temperature and humidity, arranged in two columns with the data right-justified in columns 1–5 and 6–10. Again assume that our program is to read up to 366 days. The most efficient code to input and echo check the data is:

```
      DIMENSION MEANTM(367), IHUMID(367)
C                   input from file
      READ  (3,1020, END=40) (MEANTM(I), IHUMID(I), I=1,367)
 1020 FORMAT  (2I5)
          WRITE (1,1022)
 1022     FORMAT (1H ,'EXCESSIVE DATA - ABORT!')
          STOP
   40 NUMTMP = I - 1
```

```
C                        echo check
      WRITE  (4,1040)
 1040 FORMAT  (1H ,'Day     Temperature  Humidity')
      WRITE  (4,1042) (I, MEANTM(I), IHUMID(I), I=1,NUMTMP)
 1042 FORMAT  (1H ,I3, I15, I10)
```

Note carefully the syntax of the implied DO loops. In the READ statement, the order of input is MEANTM(1), IHUMID(1), MEANTM(2), IHUMID(2), MEANTM(3), IHUMID(3), and so forth, alternating the variables. This allows for a very logical input data layout. In the WRITE statement, we use the implied DO loop not only to output the two arrays in an alternating fashion but also to print out the day number (a nonsubscripted variable) corresponding to each record. The output layout is such that the values are right-justified under the headings:

```
Day    Temperature  Humidity
 1              78         80
 2              75         63
 3              82         91
 .               .          .
 .               .          .
 .               .          .
```

Note that the output command

```
WRITE (4,1044) (MEANTM(I), I=1,NUMTMP), (IHUMID(I), I=1,NUMTMP)
```

would output all the values of temperature followed by all the values of humidity; the layout of this output could not be arranged as nicely.

The implied DO loop can also be used with nonsubscripted variables, for example,

```
      WRITE  (1,1050) (I, I=10,100,10)
 1050 FORMAT  (1H ,10I5)
```

This would output the values 10, 20, 30, . . . , 90, 100 right- justified in five-column groups:

```
  10   20   30   40   50   60   70   80   90  100
```

Another shortcut can be used here. When an I/O command runs out of format, end-of-record is transmitted and control returns to the rightmost opening parenthesis in the Format. Thus in the above example, we could have written:

```
      WRITE  (4,1040) (I, MEANTM(I), IHUMID(I), I=1,NUMTMP)
 1040 FORMAT  (1H ,'Day     Temperature  Humidity'/
     1          (1H ,  I3,          I15,        I10))
```

Since the slash (/) also means end-of-record, the literal data would be printed on line 1, the slash would indicate the end of line 1, then the first temperature and humidity record would print with day 1 on line 2. Reaching the end of the FORMAT, which the computer translates as end of line 2, control returns to the rightmost opening parenthesis (the one before the 1H blank) and continues printing the values for day 2 on line 3. This process continues until all the data is output.

5.5.5 Sample program

In the introduction, we described a simple grading program. We will now present one of its many possible forms. In later sections we will expand on part of it as new facilities are introduced. Assume the input file is numbered 3 and the output file 4.

```
C               Grade Analysis & Distribution
C
C      Abstract:  Program inputs up to 60 examination grades.  Grades
C               are edited for proper range (0 to 100).  Average is cal-
C               culated and a grade distribution determined as follows:
C                     90 to 100:  A     IDISTR(1)
C                     80 to 89:   B        :
C                     70 to 79:   C        :
C                     60 to 69:   D        :
C                     < 60:       F     IDISTR(5)
C
      DIMENSION  IGRADE(61), IDISTR(5)
C
C                 initialize distribution counters, error counter and sum
      DO 20  I = 1,5
   20 IDISTR(I) = 0
      NUMERR    = 0
      ISUM      = 0
C                 input module
      READ  (3,1000, END=40)  (IGRADE(I), I=1,61)
 1000 FORMAT  (I3)
         WRITE  (1,1020)
 1020    FORMAT  (1H ,'Excessive input  -  ABORT')
         STOP
   40 NUMREC = I - 1
C                 echo check
      WRITE  (4,1040)  (IGRADE(I), I = 1,NUMREC)
 1040 FORMAT  (1H1,'GRADE DISTRIBUTION'//1H0,'Grades'//(1H ,I3))
```

```
C              edit data for proper range
      DO 60  I = 1,NUMREC
           IF  (IGRADE(I) .GE. 0  .AND.  IGRADE(I) .LE. 100)  GO TO 60
           WRITE  (1,1040)  I, IGRADE(I)
 1040      FORMAT  (1H0,'Record',I3,' has invalid grade of',I4)
           NUMERR = NUMERR + 1
   60 CONTINUE
C              abort if errors
      IF  (NUMERR .EQ. 0)  GO TO 100
           WRITE  (1,1060)  NUMERR
 1060      FORMAT  (1H0,'Program aborted with at least',I2,' errors')
           STOP
C              compute average
  100 DO 120  I = 1,NUMREC
  120 ISUM = ISUM + IGRADE(I)
      AVRG = FLOAT (ISUM) / FLOAT (NUMREC)
C              distribution  (one of many ways)
      DO 160  I = 1,NUMREC
           DO 140  J = 1,4
                IGRBRK = 100 - 10 * J
                IF  (IGRADE(I) .GE. IGRBRK)  GO TO 160
  140      CONTINUE
           J = 5
  160 IDISTR(J) = IDISTR(J) + 1
C              output module
      WRITE  (4,1160)  NUMREC, AVRG, IDISTR
 1160 FORMAT  (1H0,'Average of', I3,' grades =', F5.1/
     1              1H0,'Distribution:  A  B  C  D  F'/
     2              1H ,13X,          5I3)
C              termination
      STOP
      END
```

A sample output would have the form:

```
Average of 52 grades = 82.7

Distribution:  A   B   C   D   F
               8  18  13   9   4
```

Notice how this program is modularized. First the initialization module sets the necessary values to zero; in the next section, this module will be reduced to one statement. The input, echo check, edit, average, distribution, and output modules follow. They are separate modules because each one can be isolated from the others with no branching from one to another; only the data is shared. This program could have been written by a programming team—each member would need to know the names of the variables common to all modules and the range of statement numbers to use and could then write a complete module.

Another interesting point is that once the input and edit modules are complete, the order of the average and distribution modules is not critical; one does not depend on the other. Also note the use of I/O method 3 in the last WRITE statement.

The programmer will generally find the implied loop method the most useful one, although the other two methods have their advantages under certain circumstances.

5.6 The DATA statement

The DATA statement allows the programmer to define initial values for a given location or set of locations; it is useful for speeding up program execution as well as reducing coding effort. The general syntax is:

```
DATA   list of variables/, list of values/, list2/values2/,
       and so forth
```

The DATA statement should be placed after other specification statements (like the DIMENSION statement) and before any executable statements in the program. The variables initialized by the DATA statement may be modified either by input or by assignment at some later time in the program, and although the DATA statement can be used to define constants, the locations defined by the DATA statement should not be thought of as unchangeable.

In the grading program shown in the previous section, the initialization of various locations in the first four executable statements can be replaced by a DATA statement or statements in a variety of ways:

```
DATA   IDISTR/ 0,0,0,0,0/, NUMERR/ 0/, ISUM/ 0/
```

or

```
DATA   IDISTR, NUMERR, ISUM/ 5*0, 0, 0/
```

or

```
DATA   IDISTR, NUMERR, ISUM/ 7*0/
```

Note the use of the repetition factor when the values are all the same, and note that both arrays and single variables may be combined in one DATA statement.

We will illustrate the DATA statement in a vote-tabulating program in the next section of the text. Locations will be set up for the total votes for each candidate; these locations must be initialized to zero since the program will be accumulating totals in them. The program will have a capacity of twelve candidates; it will check for positive values for number of votes and will verify that votes are not reported for more than the actual number of candidates. Should any errors occur, the program will both count and display them, and a final message will warn that the tabulation is invalid. Furthermore, the program will compute the percentage of the total vote for each of the candidates. The DATA statement will be used to initialize the total vote count for each candidate and the number of errors.

```
DIMENSION   NVOTES(12)
DATA        NVOTES/ 12*0/, NERR/ 0/
```

Another way of writing the DATA statement would be

```
DATA        NVOTES, NERR/ 13*0/
```

which uses a single variable list and combines the values into one group. Although this statement may require slightly less coding effort, it is harder to read and thus provides poorer documentation.

Of course, the program would work just as well with the coding:

```
    DO 10 I = 1,12
10  NVOTES(I) = 0
    NERR = 0
```

However, more coding is involved, and execution time is required whenever the program is run. When a DATA statement is used, the compiler places the values in their locations at compilation time. Thus the compilation time may be slightly longer and the machine language code longer, depending upon the size of the DATAed array, but since a production program is usually executed far more times than it is compiled, the saving in execution time becomes more significant, especially when initializing very large arrays.

There are some strict rules regarding DATA statements:

1. The number of variables and the number of values must agree. There is a one-to-one correspondence between the list of variables and the list of values, that is, the first value goes with the first variable, the second value with the second variable, and so forth. The use of an array name in the list of variables implies that the whole array is to be defined. (There are some implementations of FORTRAN that permit fewer values than variables, leaving the remainder of the variable list undefined, but this practice is not in agreement with the FORTRAN standards.)

2. The mode of the variables and values must agree. (The full FORTRAN 77 specifications do allow numeric mixed mode in the DATA statement,

but the advantage of this is not apparent to the author.) The programmer must be careful in differentiating between reals and integers, for example,

```
DATA     NTOTAL/ 0/, TOTAL/ 0./
```

3. A variable must not appear in more than one DATA statement.
4. The full FORTRAN 77 does allow the use of an implied DO list to define partial arrays, for example,

```
DATA     (NVOTES(J), J=4,10)/ 7*0/
```

There are implementations where the programmer might place the DATA statement with the executable statements instead of before them, giving the mistaken impression that the variables listed will be reset. Again, we repeat that the DATA statement acts during the compilation phase and *cannot be used to reset the value of any variables once the program is executing.*

5.6.1 Review questions

5–3. Use a DATA statement to initialize all the arrays in the given DIMENSION statement to zero.

```
DIMENSION  TOTALS(6), ICOUNT(10), SUBTOT(6)
```

5–4. Use a DATA statement to initialize the locations in the array IGRBRK to 90, 80, 70, and 60.

```
DIMENSION  IGRBRK(4)
```

5.7 A one-dimensional example

Proceeding to the voting example described in section 5.6, we will input (LUN = 4) the raw data from a disk file and write output (LUN = 3) to a disk file with some output going to the screen. The file structure is as follows:

Record 1:   Columns   1–2: number of candidates (header record)

Records 2–*n*:   Columns   1–4: precinct number

                 Columns   6–10: number of votes for candidate 1

                 Columns 11–15: number of votes for candidate 2

Columns 16–20: number of votes for candidate 3

.   .   .
.   .
.   .   .

Columns 61–65: number of votes for candidate 12

Input terminates on end-of-file.

We will edit to ensure that each record after the header record (the one with the number of candidates) contains a unique precinct; that is, no precinct is entered more than once.

In this program we will introduce a new feature of the READ statement, the ERR= clause. As some readers may have learned the hard way, an alphabetic character in a numeric field will cause termination of the program with (we hope) some kind of informative error message. The ERR= clause gives the programmer the power to branch to an error routine of his or her own choice when such an error occurs and, if so desired, to return to the program and continue processing. This latter option allows the editing of all of the data, not just up to the first record with an error. In the following program the errors are counted and the final computations and output are suppressed if any of the data is in error.

```
C          Vote Counter
C
C     Abstract:  inputs a file containing votes by precinct, accu-
C                mulates total votes and computes percentages.
C                Determines winner.
C
C     Edits for:  1.  positive values.
C                 2.  duplicate precincts.
C                 3.  excessive candidates.
C                 4.  invalid input character in vote record.
C                     error messages sent to output file.
C
C     Aborts if:  1.  number of candidates not in range 1 to 12
C                 2.  excessive precincts (> 100)
C                 3.  invalid input character in header record.
C                     error message sent to screen.
C
C     Glossary:   IN(12):     temporary input array
C                 NPRCNT(101): precinct numbers
C                 NVOTES(12): vote accumulators by candidate
C                 PRCNT(12):  percentages of total vote
C                 NCAN:       number of candidates
C                 NERR:       error counter
```

```
C                          NPRE:        number of precincts
C                          NTVOTE:      total vote
C
      DIMENSION   IN(12), NPRNCT(101), NVOTES(12), PRCNT(12)
      DATA               NTVOTE/ 0/,  NVOTES/ 12*0/,  NERR/ 0/, I/ 0/
C
C                   open files and input header record
C                   OPEN INPUT  DATA FILE as File 4  (system dependent)
C                   OPEN OUTPUT DATA FILE as File 3  (system dependent)
      READ  (4,1000, ERR=800)  NCAN
 1000 FORMAT  (I2)
      IF  (NCAN .GT. 0 .AND.  NCAN .LE. 12)  GO TO 20
          WRITE  (1,1004)
 1004     FORMAT  (1H ,'INVALID NUMBER OF CANDIDATES  -  ABORT')
          GO TO 900
C                   new page, title and headings
   20 WRITE  (3,1020)  NCAN, (J, J=1,NCAN)
 1020 FORMAT   (1H1,'Vote Tabulation for', I3,' Candidates'/
     1             1H0,'Precinct', I4, 11I6)
C
C                   loop through input records
      DO 200  I = 1,101
          READ  (4,1022, END=220, ERR=180)  NPRCNT(I), IN
 1022     FORMAT  (I4,1X, 12I5)
C                        echo check
          WRITE  (3,1024)  NPRNCT(I), (IN(J), J=1,NCAN)
 1024     FORMAT  (1H ,I4,2X, 12I6)
C                      check for duplicate precinct
          IF  (I .EQ. 1)  GO TO 60
          N = I - 1
          DO 40  J = 1,N
              IF  (NPRCNT(I) .NE. NPRCNT(J))  GO TO 40
                  WRITE  (3,1026)
 1026             FORMAT  (1H ,'DUPLICATE PRECINCT NUMBER')
                  NERR = NERR + 1
                  GO TO 200
   40     CONTINUE
```

```
C                       check for excessive candidates
    60      IF (NCAN .EQ. 12)  GO TO 100
            N = NCAN + 1
            DO 80   J = N,12
                IF  (IN(J) .EQ. 0)  GO TO 80
                    WRITE (3,1060)  IN(J), J
  1060              FORMAT (1H ,I5,' INVALID VOTES FOR CANDIDATE', I3)
                    NERR = NERR + 1
                    GO TO 200
    80      CONTINUE
C                       check for negative votes
   100      DO 120   J = 1,NCAN
                IF  (IN(J) .GE. 0)  GO TO 120
                    WRITE (3,1100) J
  1100              FORMAT (1H ,'NEGATIVE VOTES FOR CANDIDATE', I3)
                    NERR = NERR + 1
                    GO TO 200
   120      CONTINUE
C                        add to counters
            DO 140   J = 1,NCAN
   140      NVOTES(J) = NVOTES(J) + IN(J)
                GO TO 200
C                          input error
   180      WRITE (3,1800)  I
            NERR = NERR + 1
C                          end of loop
   200 CONTINUE
C
C                     excessive records
            WRITE (1,1200)
  1200      FORMAT (1H ,'EXCESSIVE PRECINCTS  -  ABORT')
            GO TO 900
C
C                    check for data errors
   220 IF  (NERR .EQ. 0)  GO TO 240
            WRITE (1,1220)  NERR
            WRITE (3,1220)  NERR
  1220      FORMAT (/1H ,'AT LEAST',I3,' ERRORS:  INVALID TABULATION')
            GO TO 900
```

```
C                      compute percentages and output with totals
   240 DO 260  J = 1,NCAN
   260 NTVOTE = NTVOTE + NVOTES(J)
       DO 280  J = 1,NCAN
   280 PRCNT(J) = FLOAT (NVOTES(J)) / FLOAT (NTVOTE) * 100.0
       WRITE  (3,1280)  (NVOTES(J), J=1,NCAN)
  1280 FORMAT  (1H0,'Totals', 12I6)
       WRITE  (3,1282)  (PRCNT(J), J=1,NCAN)
  1282 FORMAT  (1H0,'%',5X, 12F6.1)
C                      find winner (maximum value routine)
       IWIN = 1
       IF  (NCAN .EQ. 1)  GO TO 320
       DO 300  J = 2,NCAN
           IF  (NVOTES(IWIN) .LT. NVOTES(J))  IWIN = J
   300 CONTINUE
   320 WRITE  (3,1320)  IWIN, NVOTES(IWIN)
  1320 FORMAT  (1H0,'Candidate', I3,' wins with',I6,' votes')
       GO TO 900
C
C                      invalid input character routine
   800 WRITE  (1,1800)  I
  1800 FORMAT  (1H ,'INVALID INPUT CHARACTER IN RECORD', I4)
C
C                      close files and terminate
   900 CONTINUE
C                      CLOSE INPUT DATA FILE  (system dependent)
C                      CLOSE OUTPUT DATA FILE  (system dependent)
       STOP
       END
```

A few explanatory comments on the program are in order. We used the technique discussed in section 5.5 and made the dimension of NPRCNT(101), one larger than the maximum number of records in order to permit a read attempt beyond the expected records. If there are exactly 100 records, the 101st read will cause an EOF (end-of-file) branch to statement 220. If there is a 101st record, or even more, the 101st precinct number will have an array element to go into and thus will not exceed the array bounds and destroy other information; the program will terminate after treating that data with an "excessive input" mes-

Each of the READ statements includes the ERR= clause so that invalid characters in the expected numeric input will be trapped. To provide the user with an indication of which record has the bad data, the main loop counter I is used, thus providing a record number corresponding to the vote records. By initializing the value of I to zero at the beginning of the program (in the DATA statement), the header record giving the number of candidates would be identified as record zero in any error message appearing due to a character error in that record.

The output statement that prints the heading uses the implied DO loop working on a single variable. The input and echo check routine in the main loop use all three of the I/O methods described in the previous section. The READ statement inputs NPRCNT by the DO loop method and IN by the entire array method. The following WRITE statement uses the implied DO loop so that only the valid values are output and not the zeros for the nonexistent candidates.

Error messages indicating the necessity for aborting the run are sent to the screen; messages about invalid data go to the disk (or printer) file. However, the error message indicating the invalidity of the tabulation due to invalid values goes to both the screen and the disk file. In this way, the error is apparent during the run and in the final file. One "bug" in the program is that two types of errors in the same vote record are not noted; the first error found and annotated causes a branch to the end of the loop.

The maximum value routine is a standard one that assumes that the first array element is the maximum value and then checks it against the rest of the array. If by any chance there is only one candidate, the coding is sufficient to take care of that circumstance; otherwise the DO loop that follows would be checking against nonexistent data.

For the following sample data:

```
3
1001    123    417    323
1002     54     45     87
1003     16      8     74
```

the following output is generated:

```
Vote Tabulation for 3 Candidates

Precinct    1      2      3
1001      123    417    323
1002       54     45     87
1003       16      8     74

Totals    193    470    484

%        16.8   41.0   42.2

Candidate  3 wins with    484 votes
```

As is obvious from a study of this example, more coding is required for the editing of the data than is needed for the input, calculation, and output. This is not unusual. In any programming system, it is critical that bad data not be allowed to influence the results, and it is the programmer's responsibility to ensure that bad data does not sneak in.

5.7.1 Exercises

Two programs will be written in the following two exercises; the first will generate the file needed by the second. The second program consists of a series of modules, so it can be built up in a piecemeal manner or shared by a programming team. The modules need not be written in order (the prerequisite module is stated for each).

Exercise 5-1

Write a program to generate a random data file of 20 X, Y, and Z coordinates. These coordinates may be thought of as representing points (measured in feet) on a map. The desired ranges are:

X: 8000.00 to 20000.00

Y: 10000.00 to 20000.00

Z: 50.00 to 250.00

The coordinates should be written to the file with two decimal places and should be formatted in columns 1–10, 11–20, and 21–30, respectively.

    If your FORTRAN does not have a random number generator, the file can be generated using a program written in another language (BASIC or Pascal, for instance). Otherwise, the file must be generated manually.

    Make a printout of the file to be used for checking.

Exercise 5-2

a. For the first module in the program, write an input routine able to read up to 50 coordinates into three one-dimensional arrays (X, Y, and Z) and print out an echo check, complete with headings and title. The output should list the point number (corresponding to the record number in the file) and the X, Y, and Z coordinates to two decimal places. Verify that the echo check agrees with the hardcopy of the file both in values and in number of points. The implied DO loop should be used for both input and echo check.

b. Add a module to the program to compute the mean X, Y, and Z coordinates. Add the results to the output. (Requires module a.)

c. Add a module to calculate the maximum and minimum values for each of the coordinates; add these values to the output. (Requires module a.)

d. Add a module to determine the borders (to the nearest 100 units) of a map containing all the points. Some integer arithmetic will be required. Make sure that the borders completely enclose the points by comparing the border values with the minima and maxima computed in module c. Also determine the midpoint of the map as the mean of the borders. The result should not be *too* far away from the mean coordinates computed in module b. (Requires module c.)

e. Generate a new array of the same length as the coordinate arrays to store an integer quadrant number. Using the mean border computed in module d and moving clockwise, number the upper right quadrant 1, the lower right quadrant 2, the lower left quadrant 3, and the upper left quadrant 4. Each point is to be assigned a quadrant number according to its location, assigning points on the centerlines to the upper and/or right-hand quadrant. For each quadrant output a list of the point numbers in the quadrant and their elevations; verify that your logic worked by checking the quadrant assignments manually. (Requires module d.)

f. Generate two new arrays—one real, one integer—containing four elements each, in which the highest elevation in each quadrant and its corresponding point number are to be stored. Output the results. (Requires module e.)

g. Determine the longest horizontal distance between any two points on the map. Set up the necessary loops so that no distance is calculated more than once. Output the distance. (Requires module a.)

5.8 Equivalence

The EQUIVALENCE statement allows the programmer to

1. Lay out memory in a desired fashion
2. Overlap arrays to save memory
3. Simulate a data structure
4. Have multiple names for the same location

Usually the first property is not of much interest to anyone other than system programmers who might be interfacing with machine or assembly language code. We will therefore not take the time to describe it, although its implementation will become obvious from the forthcoming discussion.

The second property is extremely useful in computers with limited memory in situations where two or more large arrays will not be needed simultaneously. Elements of the two arrays can share the same memory locations, as shown in the following example:

```
DIMENSION I(10), J(8)
EQUIVALENCE (I(1), J(1))
```

The EQUIVALENCE statement makes I(1) and J(1) equivalent, that is, they share the same memory location; then, because of the way arrays are stored in memory, I(2) and J(2) automatically share the same location, as do I(3) and J(3), and so forth, up to I(8) and J(8). Actually, the same layout can be obtained by equivalencing any of the eight elements; it need not be only the first ones. For example,

```
EQUIVALENCE (I(4), J(4))
```

defines the same layout.

The memory layout is as follows:

I(1) I(2) I(3) I(4) I(5) I(6) I(7) I(8) I(9) I(10)
J(1) J(2) J(3) J(4) J(5) J(6) J(7) J(8)

```
|   |   |   |   |   |   |   |   |   |   |
```

Any modification to I(3), for example, also modifies J(3). Thus, the two arrays cannot be accessible simultaneously if they are to contain different information.

The EQUIVALENCE statement need not line up the arrays. They can be offset, if the programmer so desires, and more than two arrays may be equivalenced:

```
DIMENSION I(10), J(8), K(6)
EQUIVALENCE (I(4), J(1)), (I(1), K(2))
```

yields a memory layout of:

I(1) I(2) I(3) I(4) I(5) I(6) I(7) I(8) I(9) I(10)
                  J(1) J(2) J(3) J(4) J(5) J(6) J(7) J(8)
K(1) K(2) K(3) K(4) K(5) K(6)

```
|   |   |   |   |   |   |   |   |   |   |   |   |
```

Any attempt to specify a 'memory warp' by adding an inconsistent equivalence such as (K(5), J(2)) would yield an error message. As a guide, to equivalence N arrays, use N-1 equivalences.

Abilities 3 and 4 are illustrated by the following example. Assume an input record consisting of five integer values:

Elements 1–3: date (month,day,year)

Element   4: low temperature for the day

Element   5: high temperature for the day

A program using this data structure might look like this:

```
                    :
      DIMENSION  INREC(5), IDATE(3)
      EQUIVALENCE  (INREC(1),IDATE(1)), (INREC(4),LOW),
                   (INREC(5),IHIGH)
C
```

```
C                 input record
      READ  (8,1000)  INREC
 1000 FORMAT  (3I2, 2I3)
      MEAN = (LOW + IHIGH) / 2
      WRITE  (1,1002) IDATE, MEAN
 1002 FORMAT  (1H ,'Date: ',I2,'/',I2,'/',I2, 5X,'Mean =',I3)

                           :
```

It is also possible to equivalence two single variables, such as:

```
EQUIVALENCE (IHIGH, IHGH)
```

Such statements used to be very handy when adjusting for spelling errors before the days of disk file editors that could make global changes.

5.8.1 Review question

5–5. A program consists of the following statements:

```
        DIMENSION I(10), J(5)
        EQUIVALENCE (J(1), I(4)), (KK, I(1)), (LL, I(5))
C
        DO 20 N = 1,10
   20 I(N) = N
C
        WRITE (1,1000) J, KK, LL
 1000 FORMAT (1H , 3I5)
C
        STOP
        END
```

Describe fully the storage locations and values printed by the WRITE statement.

5.9 Array access in subprograms

In section 5.7 we presented a rather lengthy sample program illustrating a number of programming techniques. However, the professional programmer would not write the program quite that way. As we will see later, the program could have been broken down into smaller modules than the long DO 200 loop, which included input, echo check, editing, and accumulating; each of these routines will eventually become a separate module once we learn something about multidimensional arrays. Secondly, the routine for maximum value is so standard that most programmers would store the code in a subprogram so that it can be accessed easily and does not have to be written ad nauseam.

The technique of accessing an array in a subprogram may seem to contain a problem in that the array variable must be defined in a DIMENSION statement, yet we do not know the size of the array in the calling program when we write a general purpose subprogram. But with a full understanding of the linkage between the calling and called programs, the programmer will see that there is no problem. As we described in section 4.3, FORTRAN transmits only the address, not the value, of the data being shared. Thus when an array is transmitted to a subprogram, only the address of the array is transmitted, not the myriad of values in the array. The computer then uses the mapping function to access any element in that array.

Since the subprogram needs only the address of a single variable or of an array, no locations are set aside by the subprogram for any of the variables or array elements in the transmission list. Thus the dimension given for a transmitted one-dimensional array is of no significance. (The dimension is significant for multidimensional arrays, as we will see.) Nonetheless, an array must be dimensioned so that the compiler knows it is an array, not a single variable or, when used with a subscript, a function. Although some implementations of FORTRAN allow a variable to be used as the dimension, many professionals use a dimension of 1 as an implied method of documentation indicating that the size of the array comes from the calling program. FORTRAN 77 also allows the use of an asterisk (*) as the dimension of a transmitted array in a subprogram.

Once the issue of the DIMENSION statement in the subprogram is settled, the coding of the subprogram is very similar to that for the mainline except for the "packaging," that is, the header and the RETURN. In addition, the programmer must select a subprogram name that is different from the intrinsic functions supplied with the system. Since our subprogram is going to return only the maximum value in an integer array, it can be implemented as a function. The name MAX is available and describes the function well.

```
C          Function MAX: returns the maximum value
C          in an integer array
C
      FUNCTION  MAX (IRAY, NELEM)
C
C        Glossary:   IRAY: an integer array
C                    NELEM: number of elements in the array
C
C
      DIMENSION IRAY(1)
C
      MAX = IRAY(1)
      IF  (NELEM .EQ. 1)  RETURN
C                    loop through rest of elements
      DO 100 I = 2,NELEM
          IF (MAX .LT. IRAY(I)) MAX = IRAY(I)
  100 CONTINUE
C                         return
      RETURN
      END
```

Of course, this function does not solve the problem in our previous example, where we wanted the location of the maximum value. Not despairing, we will write a function for that purpose:

```
C           Function LMAX: returns
C               the location of the maximum value in
C               an integer array
C
      FUNCTION LMAX   (IRAY, NELEM)
C
C          Glossary:   IRAY:  an integer array
C                      NELEM: number of elements in the array
C
C
      DIMENSION IRAY(1)
C
      LMAX = 1
      IF  (NELEM .EQ. 1) RETURN
C                     loop through rest of elements
      DO 100  I = 2,NELEM
           IF  (IRAY(LMAX) .LT. IRAY(I)) LMAX = I
  100 CONTINUE
C                         return
      RETURN
      END
```

Now, going back to the vote-tabulating program, the five lines ending with statement number 300 can be replaced with:

```
IWIN = LMAX (NVOTES, NCAN)
```

In all honesty, including this maximum value routine as an external function results in longer linking time, less efficient code, and slightly longer execution time. Of course, we are talking about a few more bytes and some microseconds, but where time or memory is critical, calling a subprogram only once is inefficient. However, the programming and debugging time (debugging time because the programmer is incorporating previously tested code) is significantly reduced, and this is usually far more critical.

Most programmers establish a rather comprehensive library of useful functions and subroutines. For example, building on the above routine, one could expect to find MAX, LMAX, MIN, LMIN, RMAX, LRMAX, RMIN, and LRMIN (the latter four are for real arrays).

There are some caveats that must be served up in this topic. First of all, if an array is local to the subprogram, that is, if it is not in the argument list, it must be properly dimensioned for its full value. Secondly, using the DATA statement, for example, to initialize a sum, may cause a problem in a subprogram. Consider the following function, which returns the average of a real array:

```
C          Function AVER:  computes an average of a real array
C
      FUNCTION  AVER  (ARRAY, NELEM)
C
C          Glossary:     ARRAY:  an real array
C                        NELEM:  number of elements in the array
C
C
      DIMENSION  ARRAY(1)
C
      SUM = 0.0
C               loop through values
      DO 40  J = 1,NELEM
   40 SUM = SUM + ARRAY(J)
C               get average and return
      AVER = SUM / FLOAT (NELEM)
      RETURN
      END
```

If SUM had been initialized with a DATA statement and the routine accessed more than once in the same run, the value of SUM at the beginning of the second entry would be whatever it was after the first execution of the routine, that is, SUM would not be reset to zero. The DATA statement is not an executable statement—it is a specification statement that is acted upon by the compiler. Therefore, the value of SUM must be set by assignment.

5.9.1 Exercises

Exercise 5-3

Write real versions of the maximum and minimum functions called RMAX and RMIN and place them, along with the function AVER, into your program library. Revise the program in exercise 5–2 to utilize these routines.

Exercise 5-4

Place the logic used in module g of exercise 5–2 (maximum distance between any two of the points) into function form. Arguments should include the two array names and the number of elements in the arrays. Incorporate the function into the program, ignoring the output of the point number.

Exercise 5-5

Write a subroutine that accepts a real array and number of elements and returns the average, the maximum, and the minimum values.

5.10 Summary and additional exercises

Although this is a rather long chapter, we have not covered everything about arrays. Much more will be covered in the appendix to this chapter and in the chapter on multidimensional arrays; in addition, every chapter beyond this one will use the material covered here. There is still much to learn about arrays.

In this chapter, we have covered the following new FORTRAN commands and programming concepts:

topic	section
DATA	5.6
DIMENSION	5.3
EQUIVALENCE	5.8
ERR =	5.7
HIPO	5.1
implied DO loop	5.5
mapping function	5.4

5.10.1 Exercises

Exercise 5–6

Write a program to do a grade distribution based on the following curve:

Top 10% A

Next 30% B

Next 30% C

Next 20% D

Last 10% F

The program should read a file consisting of two values per record, the student number (a four-digit integer) and the student grade. The output should list each of the grade ranges and the student numbers and grades within that range.

Exercise 5–7

Modify the program in exercise 5–6 to have two curves, the one given above and another for less than 10 students:

Top 20% A

Next 35% B

Next 25% C

Next 20% D

Test by applying to two student files, one with less than 10 students, one with 10 or more.

Exercise 5–8

Write a program that will input two real arrays of the same length and generate a third array of similar length in which each new element is the sum of corresponding elements of the original arrays.

Exercise 5–9

Write a program that will input a real array and a constant from the keyboard and generate a new array of the same length as the first, where each element of the new array is the product of the constant and the corresponding element of the old array.

5A

One-dimensional arrays (appendix)

5A.1 Simple sorting

One of the most frequently used procedures in data processing is the sorting of data so that its access and presentation are more orderly. Sorting is not a complicated process, but it is time-consuming; in fact, it probably consumes more computer time than most other processes combined. Thus the programmer can find volumes written on different sort algorithms, along with the results of many benchmark tests. We will describe three well-known sorting techniques just to acquaint the reader with what is involved; in the chapter on multidimensional arrays, we will present a fairly sophisticated general purpose sort that has weathered the ravages of time.

Data can be sorted in many ways. The data in a telephone book is sorted alphabetically by name, although there are other versions (not necessarily in book form, but in a computer data file) that are sorted by address (for the convenience of telephone salespersons) and by telephone number (for the convenience of the telephone company).

The information in reports is usually presented in some order, with subtotals and totals. An ordered presentation makes it easier for the reader to find information about a specific item. Even scientific data is often sorted to provide information that is not obvious from the raw data.

To illustrate, let us take a raw (unsorted) list of examination grades and sort them in descending order, that is, the highest grade first, then descending to the lowest:

unsorted	*sorted*
82	98
98	85
79	82
85	79

The human eye can sort these few values very easily, almost without thinking. However, to program a sorting process for a computer requires us to develop some general algorithm that will work for all numbers. Probably the most obvious method would be to think in terms of two lists and follow the instructions below:

1. Find the largest value in the first list and transfer it to the first location of the second list.

2. Ignoring that first transferred value, find the largest value of those remaining and transfer that into the second position.

3. Continue the process, ignoring the transferred values, until all values have been transferred.

Let's watch the process and see what happens:

original		pass 1		pass 2		pass 3		pass 4	
82	—	82	98	82	98	—	98	—	98
98	—	—	—	—	85	—	85	—	85
79	—	79	—	79	—	79	82	—	82
85	—	85	—	—	—	—	—	—	79

To implement this sort, we must place some value in the vacated positions so that they will be "ignored" on later passes. One easy method is to place a very small value into the location so that it never competes for the "maximum." When the sort is used for examination grades, -1 would be sufficiently low; however, since we want the sort to be more general purpose, we will use the value -9999.

```
C                       Descending Sort Using Two Arrays
C
      DIMENSION  IOLD(10), JNEW(10)
      DATA       IOLD/ 82, 98, 79, 85, 6*0/,  NELEM/ 4/
C
C                       loop through positions to be filled
      DO 100  I = 1,NELEM
           LMAX = 1
           DO 80  J = 2,NELEM
                IF  (IOLD(J) .GT. IOLD(LMAX))  LMAX = J
   80      CONTINUE
           JNEW(I) = IOLD(LMAX)
  100 IOLD(LMAX) = -9999
C
      WRITE  (1,1100)  (JNEW(I), I=1,NELEM)
 1100 FORMAT  (1H , 10I6)
      STOP
      END
```

Although this sort looks very simple, and it is, it is also very time-consuming. To sort four items, $12 = 4 \times 3$ comparisons are needed. For this sort, the general rule is that $N * (N-1)$ comparisons are required for N items. Furthermore, twice as much memory is required as the size of the array; unless it is necessary to save the original order in memory, a good sorting routine works within the original array, replacing it with a sorted array.

This sort program also illustrates a number of points about the testing of algorithms. The use of DATA statements saves time and effort during testing and assures that the data is the same in all tests; the need for an input routine disappears, and there is no need for input from either the keyboard or a file. The DIMENSION of the array can exceed the amount of data tested by using a variable for the actual amount of data; in this way, the algorithm is ready to go when it is time to package it as a subprogram or place it in a mainline with I/O routines. However, the array must be padded with garbage data (in our case, zeros) in the unused positions, since most compilers expect that the number of elements in the DATA statement agrees with the dimension of the array. A useful alternative for more complete testing is to fill the array with good test data and prompt the tester for the number of elements to be entered from the keyboard during each run. The output format also leaves room for the full 10 values, if they are all used.

5A.1.1 Simple one-array sort

Working within one array requires an interchange of values. Once the maximum value is found on the first pass, it is interchanged with the value occupying the first position; thus at the end of the first pass, the first position has the maximum value in it. On the second pass, the first position is ignored and the second highest value is obtained by comparing the values from the second position on, eventually interchanging the highest value found with the original contents of the second position so that the next highest location becomes filled. The process continues until the next to last position is filled with the second lowest value; the last position automatically has the last value as a result of all of the interchanges. Let's look at the array as it is sorted:

original	pass 1	pass 2	pass 3
82	98	98	98
98	82	85	85
79	79	79	82
85	85	82	79

Now the program:

```
C                    Descending Sort Using One Array
C
      DIMENSION   IARRY(10)
      DATA        IARRY/ 82, 98, 79, 85, 6*0/,  NELEM/ 4/
C
```

```
C                              loop through positions to be filled
      N = NELEM - 1
      DO 100  I = 1,N
          LMAX = I
C                        compare with following positions
          NN   = I + 1
          DO 80  J = NN,NELEM
              IF  (IARRY(J) .GT. IARRY(LMAX))  LMAX = J
          CONTINUE
C                        interchange, if necessary
          IF  (I .EQ. LMAX)  GO TO 100
          ITEMP = IARRY(I)
          IARRY(I) = IARRY(LMAX)
          IARRY(LMAX) = ITEMP
  100 CONTINUE
C
      WRITE  (1,1100)  (IARRY(I), I=1,NELEM)
 1100 FORMAT  (1H ,10I6)
      STOP
      END
```

This sort is far more efficient than our first sort; fewer comparisons are needed since the list becomes reduced in length by one element each time a new pass is started.

Another version of this algorithm is 25% shorter in code, but it requires an interchange each time an element out of order is found. We present it for general interest, only because it is the easiest code for most programmers to remember and duplicate when they need shortness but not efficiency.

```
C                   Sloppy Descending Sort Using One Array
C
      DIMENSION  IARRY(10)
      DATA       IARRY/ 82, 98, 79, 85, 6*0/,  NELEM/ 4/
C
C                        loop through positions to be filled
      N = NELEM - 1
      DO 100  I = 1,N
C                        compare with following positions
          NN   = I + 1
          DO 100  J = NN,NELEM
              IF  (IARRY(I) .GE. IARRY(J))  GO TO 100
```

```
C                       interchange
                ITEMP    = IARRY(I)
                IARRY(I) = IARRY(J)
                IARRY(J) = ITEMP
   100 CONTINUE
C
                etc.
```

5A.1.2 Bubble sort

Another popular and more efficient sort is called the *bubble sort* because the highest values "bubble" up to the top while the lowest values move down to the bottom, position by position, with the intermediate values moving accordingly. The algorithm consists of comparing adjacent locations only, interchanging when necessary; thus on each pass, partial sorting takes place within the whole array, not just at the end points. Using our given values in slightly different order (to make the demonstration more illustrative), let's see what the bubble sort would do:

original	*pass 1*		*pass 2*	
82	82	82	98	98
79	98	98	82	85
98	79	85	85	82
85	85	79	79	79

Two interchanges take place in pass 1, and two more in pass 2. If a pass is run and no interchanges take place, then the sort is finished; the bubble sort can thus terminate before all the apparently necessary passes are made. Furthermore, since the lowest value ends up on the bottom at the end of the first pass, that location need no longer be considered, so the list shortens with each pass.

```
C                 Descending Bubble Sort Using One Array
C
      DIMENSION  IARRY(10)
      DATA       IARRY/ 82, 98, 79, 85, 6*0/,  NELEM/ 4/
C
C                      loop through maximum number of passes
      N = NELEM - 1
      L = NELEM
      DO 100  I = 1,N
          NUMI = 0
```

```
C                     compare adjacent positions
         DO 80   J = 2,L
              IF  (IARRY(J-1) .GE. IARRY(J))   GO TO 80
C                     interchange
              ITEMP      = IARRY(J-1)
              IARRY(J-1) = IARRY(J)
              IARRY(J)   = ITEMP
              NUMI = NUMI + 1
   80      CONTINUE
         IF  (NUMI .EQ. 0)  GO TO 120
  100  L = L - 1
C
  120              etc.
```

5A.1.3 Shell sort

A study of these sorts indicates that the basic concept of interchanging is necessary in all one-array sorts, but as the bubble sort shows, the order of making the comparisons differs. There is yet another simple sort, often called the *Shell sort,* which uses a complicated method of determining the order of the comparisons that even the author would find difficult to describe. Yet this sort is faster than the preceding sorts by a factor of about four. Without further discussion, here is the Shell sort:

```
C                  Descending SHELL Sort Using One Array
C
      DIMENSION   IARRY(10)
      DATA        IARRY/ 82, 98, 79, 85, 6*0/,  NELEM/ 4/
C
C                  select records to be compared
      M = NELEM
   20 M = M / 2
      IF (M .EQ. 0)  GO TO 200
C
   40 K = NELEM - M
      J = 1
C
   60 I = J
C
   80 L = I + M
C                  comparison
      IF (IARRY(I) .GE. IARRY(L))  GO TO 120
```

```
C                     interchange
      ITEMP     = IARRY(I)
      IARRY(I) = IARRY(L)
      IARRY(L) = ITEMP
C                          reset for next comparison
  100 I = I - M
      IF  (I .GE. 1)  GO TO 80
  120 J = J + 1
      IF  (J - K)  60,60,20
C
  200           etc.
```

All of the sorts shown are descending sorts. Any of them can be converted to an ascending sort by changing only part of a statement: in the first two sorts, the .GT. in the comparison becomes .LT., and in the remaining three sorts, the .GE. becomes .LE. In the next section we will present an ascending Shell sort.

5A.2 Sorting techniques

As mentioned in the previous section, sorting is one of the most used procedures in data processing, so it behooves us to spend some time on sorting techniques. It is more efficient to generalize a sort package into subroutine form than to enter the coding each time a sort is desired. Furthermore, this sort package should be as general as possible so that it can be applied to a large number of programs.

In our previous sorts, we were concerned with sorting one array. But in most practical applications, there is usually more than one array to be considered. Take, for example, the telephone book. The one we see is sorted alphabetically by last name, then by first name. Associated with each name is an address and a telephone number. The item the records are sorted on is called the *key;* in the case of the telephone book, the key is the character string of *last name, comma, first name.* While the sort algorithm works on the key, the other two arrays, the address and the phone number, must be carried along so that they maintain their association with the name. Thus, if our sort calls for an interchange of the key, it must also interchange the carry-alongs.

Of course, the telephone book involves alphameric data (alphabetical and numeric mixed), and our study has yet to treat anything but numeric data. (Alphameric data is treated in chapter 10.) But even with numeric data there are complications, namely those of mode. Because integer and real data are not stored the same way, nor are they computed similarly, we must write sorts for integer keys and for real keys. Furthermore, there must be ascending sorts and descending sorts. Thus we have a minimum of four numeric sorts to concern ourselves with: ascending integer key, descending integer key, ascending real key, and descending real key. Fortunately, we can combine the carry-alongs into each sort in such a way that the sort will handle either a real or an integer carry-along, or both, or neither.

Let's review our terminology. The *key* is the array on which the sort is based, that is, the array elements that are compared. The carry-alongs are arrays whose elements correspond to those of the key and must be interchanged when the key is interchanged.

5A.2.1 Ascending integer sort

Now on to our general purpose ascending integer sort using the Shell algorithm. There are provisions for both an integer and a real carry-along. Although this sort is limited to the three arrays mentioned, later in chapter 9 we will expand it to handle multidimensional arrays, giving it the power to sort and carry along far more data.

```
C                     SORTIA:  1-D Ascending integer sort with carry-alongs
C
      SUBROUTINE  SORTIA  (KEY,NREC, ICARY,INDI, RCARY,INDR)
C
      DIMENSION  KEY(1), ICARY(1), RCARY(1)
C
C                         Glossary
C                         --------
C             KEY:      the integer array upon which the sort works
C             NREC:     the number of records in the arrays
C             ICARY:    the integer carry-along array
C             INDI:     the indicator for the integer carry-along
C                         0 = no carry-along, >0 = carry-along
C             RCARY:    the real carry-along array
C             INDR:     the indicator for the real carry-along
C                         0 = no carry-along, >0 = carry-along
C
C
      M = NREC
   20 M = M / 2
      IF  (M .EQ. 0)  RETURN
C
      K = NREC - M
      J = 1
C
   60 I = J
C
   80 L = I + M
C                    comparison
      IF  (KEY(I) .LE. KEY(L))  GO TO 120
```

```
C                        interchange key
         ITEMP   = KEY(I)
         KEY(I) = KEY(L)
         KEY(L) = ITEMP
C                        interchange integer carry-along, if necessary
         IF  (INDI .LE. 0)  GO TO 90
             ITEMP    = ICARY(I)
             ICARY(I) = ICARY(L)
             ICARY(L) = ITEMP
C                        interchange real carry-along, if necessary
   90    IF  (INDR .LE. 0)  GO TO 100
             TEMP     = RCARY(I)
             RCARY(I) = RCARY(L)
             RCARY(L) = TEMP
C                        reset for next comparison
  100 I = I - M
         IF  (I .GE. 1)  GO TO 80
  120 J = J + 1
         IF  (J - K)  60,60,20
C
      END
```

A few comments are definitely in order about this routine! Using a dimension of 1 as we described in section 5.9 is certainly correct. But how do we write the calling statement if there is, for example, no integer carry-along? Remember that the rules of subprogram access require a one-to-one correspondence in the argument lists of both the calling and the called programs. The answer lies in the fact that FORTRAN transmits only an address during a subroutine call; thus the calling argument could be a single unused (or dummy) variable name. Its address will be transmitted to the subprogram as that of an array, but since the indicator (INDI) will be zero, that theoretical array will never be touched. (Maybe we should say that that array will theoretically never be touched, because the programmer could improperly place a positive value in the indicator and cause all kinds of havoc. The subroutine would treat the address of the single variable as the base of an array, and thinking it is writing into the various locations of the array, it will actually be destroying the contents of other variables and arrays. Thus one can easily see that a careless mistake can have serious repercussions that are often difficult to debug.)

Some purists may object to the appearance of the RETURN near the beginning of the code rather than at the end. Of course, they would probably also object to the use of a GO TO to branch to a RETURN at the end. (There is no satisfying some people!) Putting criticism aside, the code works, and that is more important to the professional programmer than petty rules of style. Also, some may object to the arithmetic IF used after statement number 120; if so, it could be replaced by a logical IF and a GO TO.

To convert this sort into a descending one (SORTID), one need only change the comparison IF statement to:

```
IF (KEY(I) .GE. KEY(L)) GO TO 120
```

To convert to real (SORTRA and SORTRD), it is necessary to replace KEY by a real variable such as RKEY, revise all four statements containing KEY to contain RKEY, and change the temporary location used in the key interchange to TEMP.

5A.2.2 Accessing sort

Now on to an application. Suppose we have two arrays, one containing student grades, the other containing student identification numbers; the arrays correspond to each other in that the first grade goes with the first student number, and so forth. We will first sort the arrays using the grades as a key, outputting the grades and the corresponding student number in ascending grade order. We will then resort the arrays using the student number as the key and output in ascending student number.

We will also calculate the mean (average) and the median. The median is the middle grade of a sorted list if there is an odd number of values in the array and the average of the middle two if there is an even number of values. The median represents the number at the halfway point in the grade array such that half the grades are higher and half are lower. The median is often a good indication of the validity of a test since it ignores the effect of extremely low or extremely high grades, which significantly affect the mean. Calculation of the median is very difficult if the array is not sorted, but quite simple if it is.

```
C              SORTML:  to test Subroutine SORTIA
C
      DIMENSION  NUMBER(10), IGRADE(10)
C
      DATA  NUMBER/ 5546, 4859, 1435, 7861, 6*0/
      DATA  IGRADE/  82,   98,   79,   85, 6*0/
      DATA  NELEM/ 4/
C
C              two passes:
C                    1.   sort by grade, find average and median
C                    2.   sort by student number
C              output results of both passes
```

```
C
      DO 100  IPASS = 1,2
           IF  (IPASS .EQ. 1)
     1          CALL SORTIA (IGRADE,NELEM, NUMBER,1, RCARY,0)
           IF  (IPASS .EQ. 2)
     1          CALL SORTIA (NUMBER,NELEM, IGRADE,1, RCARY,0)
           WRITE  (4,1000)
 1000      FORMAT  (1H0,'Student  Grade')
           WRITE  (4,1002)  (NUMBER(I), IGRADE(I), I=1,NELEM)
 1002      FORMAT  (1H , 2I7)
                IF  (IPASS .EQ. 2)  GO TO 100
C                       compute average
           ISUM = 0
           DO 20  I = 1,NELEM
   20      ISUM = ISUM + IGRADE(I)
           AVER = FLOAT(ISUM) / FLOAT(NELEM)
C                       find median
           MIDDLE = NELEM / 2
           IF  (MOD (NELEM,2) .EQ. 0)
     1          MEDIAN = (IGRADE(MIDDLE) + IGRADE(MIDDLE+1)) / 2
           IF  (MOD (NELEM,2) .NE. 0)
     1          MEDIAN = IGRADE(MIDDLE) + 1
  100 CONTINUE
C                 output average and median
      WRITE  (4,1100)  AVER, MEDIAN
 1100 FORMAT  (1H0,'Average =', F6.2, 5X, 'Median =', I3)
C                 termination
      STOP
      END
```

The variable RCARY is a nondimensioned, single variable that serves as a dummy (never to be used) variable; using DUMMY might be more illustrative. Note the use of the MOD function to determine if the number of elements is even or odd. The median determined for an even number of elements is truncated, not rounded.

The output from the above program appears as:

```
Student  Grade
   1435     79
   5546     82
   7861     85
   4859     98
```

```
Student   Grade
   1435     79
   4859     98
   5546     82
   7861     85

Average = 86.00   Median = 83
```

5A.2.3 Exercise

Exercise 5A–1

Write subroutine SORTRA, an ascending sort with a real key in the same form as SORTIA above. Use the random X, Y, Z file generated in exercise 5–1 and produce two listings, one sorted by X coordinate and one by Y coordinate. Each listing should show the X-coordinate, the Y-coordinate, and the point number (corresponding to the record number in the file). Ignore the Z-coordinate.

5A.3 Searching

One reason why sorting is so important is that searching through sorted information for a particular record is much easier than searching through unsorted information. Imagine searching for a name in a telephone book if it were not sorted alphabetically!

Consider an application in which account numbers are stored along with the monetary balances in the accounts. Such an application could occur in a retail operation that keeps track of monies owed by customers or in a bank that wants on-line access at all times to the balances in each account. We will allow for up to 10,000 records. The program will read in the entire file and store the account number and balance in memory. The user will be prompted to enter the account number, and the program will display the balance if the account number is on file and an error message if the account number is not on file. We will assume at first an unsorted file.

```
C               Program to display balance in account
C
      DIMENSION  NMACCT(10001), BALNCE(10001)
C
C                         Glossary
C                         --------
C             NMACCT:   account number
C             BALNCE:   balance in account
C
```

```
C                      input routine
      WRITE  (1,1000)
 1000 FORMAT  (1H0,'Reading in file')
      READ  (4,1002, END=20)  (NMACCT(I), BALNCE(I), I=1,10001)
 1002 FORMAT  (I4, 1X, F10.2)
          WRITE  (1,1004)
 1004     FORMAT  (1H0,'Excessive Input  -  Abort!')
          STOP
   20 NREC = I - 1
C                      prompt for desired account number
  100 WRITE  (1,1100)
 1100 FORMAT  (1H0,'Enter desired account number')
  120 READ  (1,1120, ERR= 800, END=900)  IACCT
 1120 FORMAT  (I4)
C                      search through file
      DO 200  I = 1,NREC
          IF  (IACCT .EQ. NMACCT(I))  GO TO 220
  200 CONTINUE
C                      account not found
      WRITE  (1,1200) IACCT
 1200 FORMAT  (1H ,'Account',I5,' not on file')
      GO TO 100
C                      account found
  220 WRITE  (1,1220)  IACCT, BALNCE(I)
 1220 FORMAT  (1H ,'The balance in account',I5,' is $', F9.2)
      GO TO 100
C
C                      error routine
  800 WRITE  (1,1800)
 1800 FORMAT  (1H ,'INVALID CHARACTER IN INPUT  -  TRY AGAIN')
      GO TO 120
C
C                      termination
  900 STOP
      END
```

We are particularly concerned with the algorithm used for the search. For an unsorted array, we must check every record for an account number not on file. However, if the array is sorted, then the search algorithm could be changed as follows:

```
                   :
                   :
C                              search through file
      DO 200 I = 1,NREC
            IF (IACCT - NMACCT(I)) 210, 220, 200
  200 CONTINUE
C                              account not found
  210 WRITE  (1,1200) IACCT
 1200 FORMAT  (1H ,'Account',I5,' not on file')
                   :
                   :
```

This algorithm basically says that if you are looking for a name in the telephone book starting with L and you have reached the M's, then the name is not there! Thus the search is significantly speeded up for an account number not in the file; on the average, only about half of the records will have to be searched.

There are many ways of setting up a file so that searching through it is more efficient. For example, the file might be indexed like a telephone book or a dictionary, where the range of entries for each page is given at the top of the page. The index would be searched first, then the given page. But this approach involves more programming and is usually used only when a file is so large that it cannot fit into the computer's memory.

5A.3.1 Binary search

The binary search is an extremely fast search method that requires very little coding; it does require, however, that the array be sorted. The basic idea is to look at the middle record and determine on which side of it the desired record must fall, then eliminate the other side. The process continues until the array is reduced to one record; if that record is not the correct one, then the desired record is not in the array. Using this method is like opening the telephone book to the middle page and eliminating half the book immediately based on what is on the middle page. Then the good half is split in the middle, again eliminating half of what is left (one quarter of the book). The process continues until the desired record is found.

Now this method may sound a little like Zeno's paradox, which states that since motion can be constantly broken up into smaller and smaller fractions until there are an infinite number of movements to be made, the movements cannot be made in a finite time. But there is no paradox here because we are dealing with a finite (integer) number of records. However, the algorithm is such that if the record is not in the file, the program could run into an infinite loop unless we program some means of stopping it. Fortunately, we can not only do that, we can compute the maximum number of comparisons needed to search the entire array until it is broken down into that final record. The formula is:

N = natural logarithm (number of records) * 1.4427 + 1

or, in FORTRAN:

```
N = ALOG (FLOAT (NREC)) * 1.4427 + 1.00
```

This formula determines the logarithm, base 2, of the number of records by taking the natural log times 1.4427; then 1 is added to raise to the next integer. A little playing with this formula indicates that only 15 trials are needed to search through a sorted file of 32,766 records!

The binary search is demonstrated in the following program, which reads a file of up to 10,000 numbers sorted in ascending order and searches for a desired value. The file used for this demonstration contains numbers ranging from 0 to 30,000 as generated by a random number function and sorted prior to filing. Following the program is a sample run that tests for the smallest possible value, the largest possible value, and some value in the file.

```
C               Binary Search Demonstration Program
C
      DIMENSION  NUMBER(10001)
C
C                   input from file
      READ  (8,1000, END=20)  (NUMBER(I), I=1,10001)
 1000 FORMAT  (I5)
          WRITE  (1,1002)
 1002     FORMAT  (1H0,'EXCESSIVE DATA  -  ABORT')
          STOP
   20 NNUM = I - 1
C               compute number of required passes
      NPASS = ALOG (FLOAT (NNUM)) * 1.4427  +  1.0
      WRITE  (1,1020)  NNUM, NPASS
 1020 FORMAT  (1H0, I4,' numbers on file requiring',I3,' passes')
C                  enter desired number
   40 WRITE  (1,1040)
 1040 FORMAT  (1H0,'Enter desired number')
      READ  (2,1000, END=990)  NUMDES
C               set up initial limits
      LBOT = 1
      LTOP = NNUM + 1
C               loop through passes
      DO 100  IPASS = 1,NPASS
          MIDDLE = (LBOT + LTOT) / 2
          WRITE  (1,1042)  IPASS, LBOT, LTOP, MIDDLE
 1042     FORMAT  (1H ,'Pass #',I2,'   Limits are',I6,'-',I5,
     1          5X,'Middle subscript =',I6)
          IF  (NUMDES - NUMBER(MIDDLE))  60, 120, 80
```

```
C                number in lower half
   60      LTOP = MIDDLE
           GO TO 100
C                number in upper half
   80      LBOT = MIDDLE
       CONTINUE
C              number not found
       WRITE  (1,1100)  NUMDES
 1100 FORMAT  (1H ,'Desired number',I6,' not on file')
           GO TO 40
C              number found
  120 WRITE   (1,1120)  NUMDES, IPASS
 1120 FORMAT  (1H ,'Desired number',I6,' found in',I3,' passes')
           GO TO 40
C                termination
  990 STOP
       END
```

Sample run


```
5000 numbers on file requiring 13 passes

Enter desired number
2222
Pass # 1      Limits are        1- 5001      Middle subscript =    2501
Pass # 2      Limits are        1- 2501      Middle subscript =    1251
Pass # 3      Limits are        1- 1251      Middle subscript =     626
Pass # 4      Limits are      626- 1251      Middle subscript =     938
Pass # 5      Limits are      626-  938      Middle subscript =     782
Pass # 6      Limits are      626-  782      Middle subscript =     704
Pass # 7      Limits are      626-  704      Middle subscript =     665
Pass # 8      Limits are      626-  665      Middle subscript =     645
Pass # 9      Limits are      645-  665      Middle subscript =     655
Pass #10      Limits are      655-  665      Middle subscript =     660
Pass #11      Limits are      660-  665      Middle subscript =     662
Pass #12      Limits are      662-  665      Middle subscript =     663
Desired number  2222 found in 12 passes

Enter desired number
0
Pass # 1      Limits are        1- 5001      Middle subscript =    2501
Pass # 2      Limits are        1- 2501      Middle subscript =    1251
Pass # 3      Limits are        1- 1251      Middle subscript =     626
Pass # 4      Limits are        1-  626      Middle subscript =     313
Pass # 5      Limits are        1-  313      Middle subscript =     157
Pass # 6      Limits are        1-  157      Middle subscript =      79
Pass # 7      Limits are        1-   79      Middle subscript =      40
Pass # 8      Limits are        1-   40      Middle subscript =      20
Pass # 9      Limits are        1-   20      Middle subscript =      10
```

```
Pass #10      Limits are            1-   10    Middle subscript =      5
Pass #11      Limits are            1-    5    Middle subscript =      3
Pass #12      Limits are            1-    3    Middle subscript =      2
Pass #13      Limits are            1-    2    Middle subscript =      1
Desired number        0 not in file

Enter desired number
30000
Pass # 1      Limits are            1- 5001    Middle subscript =   2501
Pass # 2      Limits are         2501- 5001    Middle subscript =   3751
Pass # 3      Limits are         3751- 5001    Middle subscript =   4376
Pass # 4      Limits are         4376- 5001    Middle subscript =   4688
Pass # 5      Limits are         4688- 5001    Middle subscript =   4844
Pass # 6      Limits are         4844- 5001    Middle subscript =   4922
Pass # 7      Limits are         4922- 5001    Middle subscript =   4961
Pass # 8      Limits are         4961- 5001    Middle subscript =   4981
Pass # 9      Limits are         4981- 5001    Middle subscript =   4991
Pass #10      Limits are         4991- 5001    Middle subscript =   4996
Pass #11      Limits are         4996- 5001    Middle subscript =   4998
Pass #12      Limits are         4998- 5001    Middle subscript =   4999
Pass #13      Limits are         4999- 5001    Middle subscript =   5000
Desired number 30000 not in file

Enter desired number
--> EOD code <--
STOP
```

The original top limit is higher by one than the number of elements so that the truncation resulting from the division by 2 does not prevent the middle pointer from reaching the last element of the array. The test run checks to make sure that the first and last elements are checked and also shows a successful run.

5A.3.2 Generalized binary search subprogram

Now let's set up a generalized subprogram for this search. Since the only value that will be returned is the location of the element in the array (or file), a function subprogram can be used. A positive returned value indicates that the desired value has been found; a zero value indicates that the value is not in the array.

```
C             Function LBSRCH:  binary search for array element
C
      FUNCTION  LBSRCH  (LRAY, NNUM, NUMDES)
C
C                     Glossary
C                     --------
C             LRAY:   an array of sorted values
C             NNUM:   number of elements in the array
C             NUMDES: desired value
```

```
C
      LBOT    = 1
      LTOP    = NNUM + 1
      NPASS   = ALOG (FLOAT (NNUM)) * 1.4427  +  1.0
C               loop through passes
      DO 100  IPASS = 1,NPASS
          LBSRCH = (LBOT + LTOP) / 2
          IF  (NUMDES .EQ. LRAY(LBSRCH))  RETURN
          IF  (NUMDES .LT. LRAY(LBSRCH))  LTOP = LBRSCH
          IF  (NUMDES .GT. LRAY(LBSRCH))  LBOT = LBRSCH
  100 CONTINUE
C               number not found
      LBRSCH = 0
      RETURN
      END
```

Before we leave this topic, it is important to emphasize one point. These techniques work as given with sorted files of unique values. If the desired value appears more than once, these routines will find it only once. In a sequential sort, the first element will be found and the programmer can include code to search the succeeding elements for an identical value. In the binary search, the first occurrence will not necessarily be the one found, so the code must include both a forward and backward search.

5A.4 Bracketing

Bracketing is a type of table lookup in which there are not unique values to be found, but rather limiting values for a range. For example, a typical grading scheme that converts numeric grades to letter grades might be based on the following ranges:

numeric range	letter grade
90 and greater	A
80 to 89	B
70 to 79	C
65 to 69	D
less than 65	F

A more elaborate scheme is encapsulated in most taxing situations that use a graduated income tax. For example, the Federal withholding tax for single wage earners is based on weekly (1986) wages as follows:

gross wage	withholding tax
$0.00	
	$ 0.00
$ 28.00	
	$ 0.00 + 12% of (Wage − 28.00)
$ 87.00	
	$ 7.08 + 15% of (Wage − 87.00)
$192.00	
	$ 22.83 + 19% of (Wage − 192.00)
$302.00	
	$ 43.73 + 25% of (Wage − 302.00)
$457.00	
	$ 82.48 + 30% of (Wage − 457.00)
$577.00	
	$118.48 + 34% of (Wage − 577.00)
$687.00	
	$155.88 + 37% of (Wage − 687.00)
no limit	

At the border of each range, the tax is the same whether computed from the preceding formula or the one following the limit. The code must locate which range the income falls in and extract the correct constants to make the computation from a table of values. Since these tax tables can change as often as every six months, professional programmers usually set the program up so that it is easy to change and also leave room for the possibility of more brackets.

```
C               Function TXFED:  Federal Withholding Tax Computation
C                                Single taxpayer, paid weekly (1986)
C

      FUNCTION  TXFED  (GROSS, NDEP)
C
C                   Glossary
C                   --------
C          GROSS:   weekly gross pay
C          NDEP:    number of dependents claimed
C
C
      DIMENSION  TXWAGE(10),  TXRATE(10),  TXBASE(10)
C
      DATA  TXWAGE/  28.,  87., 192., 302., 457.,  577.,  687., 3*0./
      DATA  TXBASE/ 0.00, 7.08,22.83,43.73,82.48,118.48,115.88, 3*0./
      DATA  TXRATE/ 0.12, 0.15, 0.19, 0.25, 0.30,  0.34,  0.37, 3*0./
      DATA  NUMBRK/ 7/,   DPRATE/ 20.77/
C
```

```
C              calculate taxable wage after subtracting deduction
      TXABLE = GROSS - FLOAT(NDEP) * DPRATE
      IF  (TXABLE .GT. TXWAGE(1))  GO TO 100
C              no tax
      TXFED = 0.00
      RETURN
C              tax computation
  100 DO 140  I = 2,NUMBRK
          IF  (TXABLE .LE. TXWAGE(I))  GO TO 180
  140 CONTINUE
      I = NUMBRK + 1
  180 I = I - 1
      TXFED = TXBASE(I)  +  TXRATE(I) * (TXABLE - TXWAGE(I))
C
      RETURN
      END
```

The code works by finding the first limit that is greater than the wage and then stepping back one bracket to get the correct constants from the table (DATA statements); the bracket decrement is done at statement 180. However, if the wage is greater than the maximum in the table ($687.00), no greater limit is available and the DO loop is exhausted, at which time the value of the index (I) may become undefined. The statement I = NUMBRK + 1 sets the index at one greater than the number of brackets so that when the next statement decreases it by one, it ends up having the correct value.

An alternative approach might have been to have used seven different IF statements to determine the correct bracket and perform the calculation. However, this would lead to longer, albeit easier to read, code. More critical, however, is the difficulty in changing that code in case the number of brackets is changed. Another approach would have been to use an IF statement with both upper and lower limits given so as to improve readability. These choices become a matter of programmer taste. The code given here was written in an early version of FORTRAN, with the two logical IFs substituted some years later; it has been working for over 20 years and, quoting the byword of most programmers, "If it ain't broke, don't fix it!"

5A.4.1 Exercise

Exercise 5A–2
Write a program to analyze the random data generated and filed in exercise 5–1. The allowable range of X-coordinates was from 8000 to 20000; find the distribution (number of points) in the ranges 8000 to 10000, 10000 to 12000, 12000 to 14000, 14000 to 16000, 16000 to 18000, and 18000 to 20000. This distribution gives us an approximate measure of the effectiveness of the random

number generator. Repeat the same process for the Y-coordinates, again using brackets of 2000 units, although there will only be five brackets for Y since its range is 10000 to 20000. Set up the logic carefully to prevent the possibility of a coordinate being in two brackets.

5A.5 Merging

Merging refers to the collation of two or more sorted arrays into a single sorted array. Of course, the obvious method is to stack one array behind the other in a new array and then sort the new array. Although this is a perfectly logical solution, sorting requires so much execution time that the method is most inefficient from the standpoint of the computer. In the view of the programmer, however, this solution is so simple that many use it anyway.

The more efficient merging techniques use pointers for each of the input arrays and for the output array. Thus we need two input pointers and one output pointer. Looking at the sample data below

	input 1		*input 2*		*output*
→	(12)	→	(14)	→	( )
	(16)		(15)		( )
	(21)		(21)		( )
	(32)		(35)		( )
			(49)		( )
					( )
					( )
					( )
					( )

we find four values in the first input array and five in the second. The pointers initially point to the first element of each array, and these two input values are compared to find the smaller. That smaller one is moved into the output array, and then the pointers of both the array the value came from and the output array are moved up for the next comparison:

	input 1		*input 2*		*output*
	(12)	→	(14)		(12)
→	(16)		(15)	→	( )
	(21)		(21)		( )
	(32)		(35)		( )
			(49)		( )
					( )
					( )
					( )
					( )

The process continues until one of the arrays is exhausted

input 1		input 2		output
(12)		(14)		(12)
(16)		(15)		(14)
(21)		(21)		(15)
(32)	→	(35)		(16)
		(49)		(21)
→				(21)
				(32)
			→	( )
				( )

and the logic then changes to transferring the remainder of the unexhausted array to the output array:

input 1		input 2		output
(12)		(14)		(12)
(16)		(15)		(14)
(21)		(21)		(15)
(32)		(35)		(16)
		(49)		(21)
→				(21)
	→			(32)
				(35)
				(49)
			→	

There are two ways to effect the coding for this process, a more direct method requiring a lot of logic and a slightly "gimmicky" method yielding simpler coding. We will look at the direct method first.

```
C                MERGE of two sorted files
C
      DIMENSION  IN1(1000), IN2(1000), IOUT(2000)
      DATA       IP1, IP2, IP3/ 3 * 1/
C
C                input routine to read up to 1000 elements into IN1
C                      with number of elements set at N1
                              :
                              :
C                input routine to read up to 1000 elements into IN2
C                      with number of elements set at N2
                              :
                              :
```

```
C
C                comparison
   20 IF  (IN1(IP1) .GT. IN2(IP2))  GO TO 40
C                     array one element to be transferred
          IOUT(IP3) = IN1(IP1)
          IP1 = IP1 + 1
             GO TO 60
C                     array two element to be transferred
   40     IOUT(IP3) = IN2(IP2)
          IP2 = IP2 + 1
C                     check for exhausted array
   60     IP3 = IP3 + 1
      IF  (IP1 .LE. N1  .AND.  IP2 .LE. N2)  GO TO 20
      IF  (IP2 .LE. N2)  GO TO 100
C
C                transfer balance of array one
      DO 80  I = IP1,N1
          IOUT(IP3) = IN1(I)
   80 IP3 = IP3 + 1
      GO TO 140
C                transfer balance of array two
  100 DO 120  I = IP2,N2
          IOUT(IP3) = IN2(I)
  120 IP3 = IP3 + 1
C
  140 N3 = IP3 - 1
C                output routine to write IOUT to a disk file
                        :
                        :
C                termination
      STOP
      END
```

Now we will look at the gimmicky approach, which consists of putting an extra value that is larger than any of the other input values at the end of each input array; this sentinel value serves as an end-of-data (EOD) marker and only needs to be big enough to be greater than all the valid elements. To provide space for the extra element, the dimension of each of the input arrays is expanded by one. Termination of the logic takes place when the number of transferred elements corresponds to the total number of valid input elements.

This routine is notably shorter, and it is less efficient only when one array is exhausted significantly before the other, since comparisons are necessary even beyond that exhaustion.

```
C                 MERGE of two sorted files, VERSION 2
C
      DIMENSION   IN1(1001), IN2(1001), IOUT(2000)
      DATA        IP1, IP2, IP3/ 3 * 1/
C
C                 input routine to read up to 1000 elements into IN1
C                        with number of elements set at N1
                              :
                              :
C                 input routine to read up to 1000 elements into IN2
C                        with number of elements set at N2
                              :
                              :
C
C                 set EOD marks
      IN1(N1+1) = 9999
      IN2(N2+1) = 9999
C                 comparison
   20 IF  (IN1(IP1) .GT. IN2(IP2))  GO TO 40
C                        array one element to be transferred
         IOUT(IP3) = IN1(IP1)
         IP1 = IP1 + 1
            GO TO 60
C                        array two element to be transferred
   40    IOUT(IP3) = IN2(IP2)
         IP2 = IP2 + 1
C                        check for exhausted array
   60    IP3 = IP3 + 1
      IF  (IP3 .LE. (N1 + N2))  GO TO 20
C
      NP3 = IP3 - 1
C                 output routine to write IOUT to a disk file
                              :
                              :
C                 termination
      STOP
      END
```

5A.6 Summary and additional exercises

The applications presented in this chapter represent some of the most usual ones found in most scientific and commercial computer installations. But they only scratch the surface of the myriad of applications to be found in the real world.

In this chapter, we have covered the following new programming concepts:

topic	_section_
binary search	5A.3
bracketing	5A.4
merging	5A.5
searching	5A.2
sort keys	5A.1
sorting	5A.1

5A.6.1 Exercises

Exercise 5A–3

Using the data file generated in exercise 5–1, perform a descending sort on the Z-coordinate and then have the program determine bracketing values for the top 20%, the next 20%, and so forth. Run the data through the brackets and print out the X, Y, and Z-coordinates within each of the Z-coordinate brackets. With 20 data points, there should be exactly 4 in each bracket.

Exercise 5A–4

Using the same data base, write a program to accept a Y-coordinate and find any point within 600 feet of that value. The points should be sorted on the Y-coordinate for fast access.

Exercise 5A–5

Using the same random number generator used in exercise 5–1, generate a second set of coordinates within the same ranges. Sort each set in ascending order by X-coordinate. Then merge the two files.

6

The art of programming

6.1 Introduction

We will now step back from the technique of programming and look at the art of programming. There is a significant difference between the two. The technique of programming is the development of the necessary logic and the implementation of that logic into code. Furthermore, we can quantitatively measure programming technique with such questions as:

1. Does the logic do the job?
2. Is the code efficient?
3. Are the hardware resources used effectively?
4. Is the documentation adequate?

All of these questions can be answered quantitatively with a yes or a no or perhaps a rating on a scale from 1 to 10.

The art of programming involves measures that are more qualitative and often a matter of opinion or taste. Among the questions that could be asked are:

1. Does the program yield user satisfaction?
2. Is the input easy to enter?
3. Is the output descriptive and clear?
4. Is the program operation simple?
5. Are the error messages informative?
6. Is the program idiot-proof?
7. Are the recovery procedures easy to implement?
8. Are the backup procedures adequate in case of a bomb-out?

For any one program and a multitude of programmers and users, one would expect the answers to these questions to reflect a diversity of opinion.

The old adage about the impossibility of satisfying all of the people all of the time certainly applies to programming, but it is important to try to satisfy as many as practical. A program that is not liked will not be used; thus it might just as well not have been written!

In this chapter we intend to examine the nonquantifiable (or artistic) aspects of programming activity. In the preface, we stated:

> The overall theme of this text is that the computer is a tool whose usefulness depends on how carefully the programs are fashioned to the needs of the user. A program is a means of communicating information from the user, through the tool, and back to the user; the program (and the computer) serve as the medium through which the information passes and is manipulated. The program is not created and does not exist for itself, but only to serve the user.
>
> Now this is not to deny that programming can be a creative and satisfying activity; it certainly is. After over twenty years, the author still loves this kind of work. But the ultimate satisfaction should be looked for not in the sophistication of the code but in the ease with which the program can be used.
>
> Thus we look at programming not as a machine-oriented function but as one deeply involved with human communication. Our first priority is people, not machines. Although the term *user-friendly* has been overused and abused, it describes what we are striving for. Our activities are guided by human psychology and perception.

6.2 Systems analysis

The term *systems analysis* has many meanings, not all of which are involved with computers. Systems analysis is involved with all aspects of some system, whether it be the operations on a loading dock in a trucking firm, the flow of information in an accounting department, or the setting up of a hardware system to meet job requirements. Systems analysis is interested not only with individual actions, but with the interrelationship of those actions with all others involved in the task.

The type of systems analysis that we are concerned with involves the flow of information through a computer system. To direct this flow of information, there are three questions that must be answered:

1. What do we know?

2. What do we want to know?

3. How do we manipulate what we know to get what we want to know?

The computer and the program are the tools that we use to implement the answer to question 3. Of course, if we cannot answer question 3 precisely, then the computer serves no purpose whatsoever! Also note that a computer is not absolutely necessary for solving any problem; it is only a tool that makes the solution easier and faster. The critical point to remember is that if the problem cannot be solved manually, it cannot be solved on the computer!

Once these three questions are answered and a decision has been made to solve the problem on the computer, then there are some other questions to be asked and to be answered by the systems analyst:

1. How should what we know be input into the machine?
2. How should the machine present what we want to know?
3. What information should be permanently stored (in disk files)?
4. What language should be used?
5. What work force should be used to program and document the system?
6. Into what modules should the programming system be broken?
7. What systems utilities should be used?
8. What algorithm should be used?
9. How should the operation work?
10. What error procedures should be included?
11. What recovery procedures are necessary?
12. What backup procedures are necessary?

And usually there are many others.

The fourth question is probably the only one we can answer immediately; obviously we will use FORTRAN, not because it is necessarily the best language for every application, but because it is the language we are learning.

It is immediately clear that a systems analyst (or team thereof) must possess many talents. There must be a knowledge of the user's field, whether it be mathematics, engineering, science, or accounting. There must also be a talent for forms design. Operational procedures must be known, and there must be an intimate knowledge of hardware capabilities. The software systems, including the operating system, the system utilities, and the FORTRAN compiler must also be very well known. But most of all, the systems analyst must be a bit of a psychologist in order to anticipate the human reactions to what is being developed, and he or she must make those judgments that fit the tool to the mind of the user.

To illustrate the programming considerations discussed in this chapter, we will use two real-life examples (programming systems that were actually written and used, although they have been somewhat modified for pedagogical reasons), one commercial application and one engineering application. Neither example contains any difficult mathematical procedures, so the user can concentrate on the system, not the algorithms.

6.2.1 Example 1: job costing and payroll

Although many technically oriented professionals would like not to think so, money matters have a very great influence over their activities. Scientists and engineers without a background in accounting, economics, and management often find themselves at a disadvantage in understanding many of the activities of industry. The New York State Professional Engineers examination has a required section on economic analysis, an indication of the importance of such topics. And whereas most professionals can appreciate the importance of a payroll application, the job costing applications may not be as obvious.

Job costing has two very important roles in the technical environment. Since so many activities are directed toward the public sector and research grants, it is usually necessary to justify the costs of a job. It is not unusual for a government or grant-giving agency to call for an audit of those costs, and since most activities in this area are labor-intensive, the payroll is the first area examined. Business and research organizations are required to keep separate records for different jobs so that an employee's activities on any particular job can be isolated from other jobs the employee worked on. Contracts for jobs are usually based on estimates of hours of work and labor costs, and an examining agency is entitled to see where the actual expenses have differed from the estimate. Evidence of fraud and improperly charged expenses are also looked for. And, of course, there may be cost overruns, for which all expenses must be documented and justified. Careful job cost records must be kept for extended periods of time, often as much as ten years.

The secondary purpose of job costing is to provide good information for future job estimates. A comparison of estimated and actual hours indicates the accuracy of the original estimate, and many jobs, if not companies, rise or fall due to the accuracy (or inaccuracy) of their cost proposals. Its importance cannot be exaggerated in those areas in which competitive bidding takes place.

Thus the tracking of labor costs is probably the most important accounting procedure in most business, especially those in the technical field.

Our job costing and payroll example will assume the following:

1. A personnel file (F0101) contains all information pertaining to each employee. This information would include such items as name, address, activity status (active, part-time, temporary, discharged, and so forth), pay rate, tax status, payroll deductions, accumulated quantities (gross pay, taxes, deductions, and so forth). The file is accessed by the employee number, a number in the range 1–999. For the sake of continuity, an employee number is maintained for ten years after an employee leaves the firm.

2. All source records are appended to a labor summary file (F0131, with index F131A), which serves as the historical source for all future access to such records. There is a separate set of files for each year. The information in this file includes the date, the employee number, the job number worked on, a task identification (designing, drafting, training, and so forth), an overtime indicator, the hours worked, and the rate paid. Although the employee's pay rate is in the personnel file, that rate may

change during the years in which the job is active; thus the rate is kept for each charge.

3. An active job file (F0102) is kept so that input records can be checked for validity such that no charges can be made to a job that does not exist. Job numbers are four-digit numbers.

4. A temporary file (T0180) is generated for payroll purposes; it contains only the employee number and gross salary for the pay period, assumed to be a week. This is all the information needed, other than what is on the personnel file, for the generation of a payroll. This file is destroyed by the running of the payroll so that the payroll cannot be run more than once (a protection against embezzlement).

5. The input will be edited for:
   a. Active employee number
   b. Active job number
   c. Valid task number
   d. Valid number of hours
   e. Valid overtime status.

6. The output will consist of:
   a. The temporary payroll file
   b. The records that will update the permanent historical file and its index
   c. A printed payroll report with grand total
   d. A cost distribution report consisting of three sections, each with subtotals, totals, and grand totals:
      1. sorted by employee
      2. sorted by job
      3. sorted by task

6.2.2 Example 2: cross-section analysis

In many areas of engineering, cross sections are used to describe structures and earth shapes. A cross section consists of three dimensions: a station marking the location of the perpendicular cross section along a baseline, an offset representing the distance along the cross section to the left or right of the baseline, and the elevation (the vertical distance) from a horizontal datum. For our example, we will deal with earthwork calculations similar to those used in highway design, construction, and geological exploration.

In a standard earthwork situation, a baseline is laid through the area being investigated. Usually it is a straight line, but it can follow a highway or railroad alignment and go around curves as well. This baseline is "stationed" by assigning increasing numbers every 100 feet; for example, if we assume that the stationing starts with a value of 1000 (usually 0 is not used to avoid negative stations in case the surveyors have to move to a point prior to the beginning station) that station is defined as 10+00. The station 100 feet farther down the line is 11+00, then 12+00, and so forth. Intermediate stations are described as 11+53.872, for example. Insertion of the plus sign has become conventional for surveyors, but otherwise the numbers are no different from what we would expect.

At some desired interval, say every 50 feet, a cross section is taken on the existing ground perpendicular to the baseline. Someone must determine how far to go and how many points are needed to accurately describe the ground as a series of straight lines approximating the uneven surface; the points are usually taken at the tops of ridges and the bottoms of valleys. Points to the left of the baseline are given a negative offset; points to the right, a positive one. Elevations are transcribed at each of the offsets to give a three-dimensional coordinate system describing each point (see fig. 6.1).

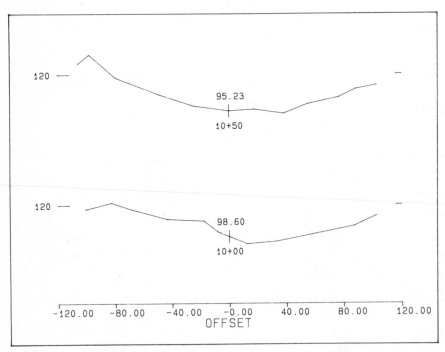

Figure 6.1   Original ground cross-sections

We should mention at this point that cross sections can be obtained by a number of methods other than sending a surveying crew out in the field. Stereo aerial photographs are a source of fairly accurate data at much lower cost; this method is called *photogrammetry*. Geologists may use seismic surveys or aerial geophysical methods using magnetometers and Geiger counters to determine the locations of underground layers. Underwater surveys use sonic soundings, and surveys of distant surfaces use radar. After the data is obtained, it is coordinated and put together in a digital terrain model (DTM). The cross-sectioning method we will describe is a very simple form of DTM. Eventually the methods of DTM lead to the ability to draw contour maps of such things as the surface of the earth, the surface of the moon, radioactivity, or infrared (heat) emissions.

In our example, we will consider a highway design example in which cross sections are taken of the original ground and correlated with a series of highway cross sections designed by an engineer. We will be interested in the differences between the design section and the ground surface as a means of determining earthwork, that is, how much earth must be removed when the highway is below the earth surface (cut) and how much earth must be added when it is above the ground surface (fill).

Our example will assume the following:

1. The input program for entering the existing ground surface will edit for order of data, sufficiency of data, and valid values. The raw data will be stored in an original ground file (OGIN.DAT) and written to a new, indexed direct access file OG.DAT with index INDXOG.DAT.

2. A highway profile program will generate the elevations of the highway at each of the critical cross-sections. The parameters for the highway template (the design surface) will be stored in an input file (DSIN.DAT) and written to a new, indexed direct access file DS.DAT with index INDXDS.DAT.

3. A program will correlate the two sets of data and edit for sufficiency and validity of that data. If the data is correct, it will compute the areas of cut and fill at each cross-section and the total volume of cut and fill.

6.3 Data preparation

To develop a good input procedure, the systems analyst must understand the details of the information going into the system and must consider the user's ability to handle the computer. If the user is expected to be very familiar with the machine, less sophisticated input methods can be used. On the other hand, the occasional user may need to be prompted when entering data. One must also consider the complexity of the data and the probability of bad data coming into the system. The examples described in the previous section represent the two extremes of strictly versus loosely defined data.

For our purposes, we will assume that all input data will be placed on a disk file prior to being processed and combined with any other files. The raw data will be entered at the keyboard by the user of the program, not the analyst or the programmer, so the input procedure must be user-friendly and idiot-proof.

There are two basic approaches to data preparation. The first uses a general purpose editor that is usually supplied with the operating system. This approach requires no programming effort and is usually used for noncritical data. For instance, in our second example (cross section analysis), our input data consists of station, offset, and elevation for each of the existing ground points. Entering three values per record is relatively simple, and since a program will edit the data later for validity, the necessity for immediate (on-line) editing (that is, editing each data value as it comes in) is not as critical as it is in the first example (job costing and payroll).

Assuming that the editor will be used, there is yet another critical decision to make: should the data be entered in free-format or formatted form? Free-formatted input (input that is not column dependent but requires a blank or comma between each of the three values) is easier to input but more prone to value error; in addition, a missing comma or blank will cause values from two different records to be combined. We will discuss this topic at much greater length when we consider the coding.

Formatted input, on the other hand, is often more difficult for the person doing the data entry because the data must be placed in the correct columns and, if integer, must be right-justified. Some editors have tab settings that make the data entry easier. However, the programming is easier with formatted input. Unfortunately, there is always a trade-off, and the systems analyst must make this often difficult decision.

There is even an argument for using an on-line input program as an aid to the input process, not so much to edit as to reduce the keystrokes necessary to enter the data. If there are 50 points on a cross section, the station must be entered 50 times, once for each point, a task that is very repetitious and subject to error. Using a program rather than the editor would allow the user to enter the station once and then enter the elevation and offset for all the points on that cross section. Thus 50 points would require only 101 values, compared to 150 values if using the editor.

Decisions, decisions! That's the name of the game. For the cross section example, we will decide (that is, the author did decide) to use the editor with free-format input. However, as we get into the coding and into more advanced topics, we will develop input techniques that will eliminate not only unnecessary keystrokes, but errors as well.

On the other hand, the job costing example should use an on-line input program because of the criticalness of the data. For each employee there will probably be a number of detailed job/hour entries; each employee number must be checked against the personnel file to see if the employee is active. But what if the data enterer puts in the wrong number? Then we want to double-check against the employee name. Each job entry and task entry must be checked for validity. The hours worked must be checked for size, and the total hours worked by each employee must also be checked; after all, there are only 168 hours in the week. Maybe the validity of the overtime indicator should be checked?

For this example, we will use an on-line input program. But what should happen if a time sheet is improperly filled out? Should the data preparer stop everything and try to get the manual sheet corrected? No! First of all, the person who made the mistake is probably out of the building or on coffee break, and secondly, the data preparation process is a pressurized task in which no time should be wasted. Our on-line program must allow bad data to be forced into the system and must contain a secondary edit that lists the errors in the input and prevents the generation of a file to be used by later programs; that file should be generated only if all the data edit correctly.

Another consideration is the amount of on-line prompting that should be given the user. Again, prompting is very useful for the occasional user, but for the experienced user, prompting for every piece of input is quite tedious. It would be excellent if the programmer could produce a user interface that allowed the user to enter data at will, avoiding prompts when multiple values are added.

And one more consideration must be brought up. There are a number of ways in which input data can be destroyed before it is filed. There is always the chance of the system going down due to hardware or power failure; a software bug may cause the program to abort before filing the good data; a time-out procedure may close down a terminal that has not been used for some specified period of time (usually 20 to 40 minutes), aborting the program. The input procedures developed by the systems analyst must contain provisions for catastrophes like these. In some cases the data preparer could file from the editor every few minutes; if an on-line input program is used, it could update the file for every tenth entry, for example.

All of these considerations affect the programming of a system. Although the reader may be enmeshed in the problems of coding, believe me, the coding becomes the easiest part of the programming process.

6.4 Output design

Now the systems analyst becomes an artist. Information that is output must be complete, properly annotated, and easy to read. Columns and headings should be properly lined up, and subtotals, totals, and grand totals properly delineated.

The problem with output design is that it is a matter of taste. It would be so nice if the person describing the program would do the output design for us, but unfortunately that is not usually the case. All too often, the systems analyst draws up the output form only to find that after all the code has been written, the user decides that some columns should be moved around, some additional information should be added, or another set of subtotals should be included. Well, that's the name of the game, and that's why a program is called "software"— because it has to be changed so often!

Of course, if the systems analyst has done a good forms design, the reaction usually is, "Hey, that's nice. But can you also add in a column for. . ." It has always been the attitude of the author that even if no money is made on a programming project when originally written, you "get 'em on the revisions." We are still at a stage in the use of computer information where a good systems analyst can tell the user what can be done instead of the user asking the analyst for it. A good systems analyst sets the system up so that any information that might be useful in the future is available in the program.

Nonetheless, there are some hard decisions to be made. One question to be asked is, How much hardcopy? Should all the available information be printed, or should only a summary be printed with the ability to extract other details when necessary? Computers have the power to produce so much hard copy, especially on the new laser printers, that the alternative of outputting directly onto micro-film and thus saving thousands of reams of paper becomes economically attractive.

If we assume, as we will do here, that all of the information we are inputting and generating is important, then we need only look at the artwork required to produce that information on paper or screen. We must concern ourselves with the layout of the information and its clarity and readability. We do not want to generate too much paper, so we should use the full size of the printer sheet to make the information easier to physically access. Sometimes one must compromise between number of sheets and amount of information on each sheet; again, it is a matter of judgement. Similarly, double-spacing may make the output look less "busy," but it causes more pages to be printed. Again, more decisions, but in this case they are cluttered with esthetic judgments; and the more people involved, the more judgments.

Fortunately for the reader, the author will make the esthetic judgments here (except for the exercises and projects). I will assume that all of our output will be in 80-column form so that it may also be displayed on the screen. (Actually 79 columns is safer, since writing to the 80th column on many screens may cause an extra blank line to appear after each line.)

Consider the following possible output for the main report for example 1 (job costing and payroll). All three of the main reports will have the same form; only the sort key will be different. Our sample report is sorted by employee, with subtotals by job. An abridged form is shown, but it is sufficient for our purposes.

```
                Job Costing by Employee

                Continental Congress

                Week of 06/14/76


Employee              Job      Task          Hours      Rate        Cost
   1  J. Hancock      1034      107          12.50     $22.50    $  281.25
   1  J. Hancock      1034      109          17.50     $22.50    $  393.75
                      1034   Subtotal:       30.00*              $  675.00*

   1  J. Hancock      1375      107          10.00     $22.50    $  225.00
   1  J. Hancock      1375      218 Overtime  5.00     $33.75    $  168.75
                      1375   Subtotal:       15.00*              $  393.75
```

1	J. Hancock	Total:		45.00**		$1,068.75**
2	J. Adams	1034	213	40.00	$19.75	$ 790.00
		1034	Subtotal:	40.00*		$ 790.00*
2	J. Adams	Total:		40.00**		$ 790.00**
14	T. Jefferson	1034	213	16.50	$20.75	$ 342.38
14	T. Jefferson	1034	218	12.00	$20.75	$ 249.00
		1034	Subtotal:	28.50*		$ 591.38*
14	T. Jefferson	Total:		28.50**		$ 591.38**

Grand Totals: 113.50*** $2,450.13***

A printout of the cross section data may have the following form:

Lincoln Highway Cross Sections

Station   10+00.00

Offset	Elevation	Offset	Elevation	Offset	Elevation
-100.8	117.25	-82.7	121.62	-67.9	116.86
-43.2	110.33	-18.0	109.16	-7.8	101.77
0.0	98.60	12.4	93.55	32.7	95.22
57.8	100.01	87.3	105.74	92.6	108.17
102.5	112.54				

Station   10+50.00

Offset	Elevation	Offset	Elevation	Offset	Elevation
-105.6	127.54	-97.8	133.45	-79.3	117.83
-49.2	106.52	-24.7	98.56	0.0	95.23
17.5	96.32	38.4	93.48	55.4	99.97
76.7	104.32	88.4	109.87	103.0	112.55

Station   11+00.00

    :   :   :   :   :   :

Data of this type is generally output to a disk file for later printing or, if possible, directly to the printer. However, it is sometimes practical, especially during the development and debugging processes, to send the output simultaneously to the screen so that the programmer can see errors immediately.

It is also recommended that the program be written so that the user can note progress on the screen. Some programs may run for a few minutes, and to a user used to seeing immediate results, it can be frightening to see the computer ap-

parently doing nothing. Thus, in our first example, we will display the following
descriptions and milestones on the screen:

```
Job Costing & Payroll for week of 06/14/76
Enter 1 to edit, 2 for final run
2

  181 records to be processed
Sorting by employee
Generating payroll file
Sorting by job
Adding to summary file
Sorting by task

Job complete
```

6.5 File structure

FORTRAN allows us to use a variety of file structures and data storage methods.
First of all, we can store numeric information either in formatted form as characters or in pure binary as shown in chapter 3. For example, consider the storage
of the labor summary records. In formatted (or character) form, we set up columns for each of the fields, just as we would if printing the record out, except
that spaces between the fields are not necessary:

columns	stored information
1–2	month
3–4	day (usually first or last of week)
5–7	employee number
8–11	job number
12–14	task number
15	overtime indicator
16–20	hours worked
21–25	rate

The first record (J. Hancock) would appear as:

`06140011034107012.5022.50`

and require 25 bytes for storage. If we use the methods of chapter 3 with short
integers and standard precision reals, the same information could be stored in
the following way:

field	bytes	stored information
1	1–2	data (month and day combined into a single value)
2	3–4	employee number

3	5–6	job number
4	7–8	task number
5	9–10	overtime indicator
6	11–14	hours worked (standard precision real)
7	15–18	rate (standard precision real)

The same record would appear in hexadecimal (with each byte shown vertically) as:

```
060000060086008500
2614A0B0044005A00
```

Eighteen bytes are required, a 28% reduction in storage space, and more importantly, the information is somewhat secure from prying eyes because it appears to be in code.

A further advantage of storing in pure binary is that the time to read from the disk and write to the disk is significantly reduced since it is not necessary to do any translation to and from characters; the information is stored on disk just as it is stored in memory.

The systems analyst, when making a decision about how the data is to be stored, must decide between these two methods of storage. Both forms may be patched in the editor, although a knowledge of hex is needed for the latter. Character storage provides readability and ease of checkout; binary storage provides reduced storage requirements and faster access.

6.5.1 File access methods

Another choice that must be made involves the access method used to transfer information to and from disk files. Up until now, we have only used the sequential access method, that is, we have read files from beginning to end, moving sequentially through the records; this method is very similar to the way in which a tape cartridge is used to record and playback video or music. But there is a second method called *direct access,* which, like a phonograph record, lets us move directly to some location in the middle of the file and access only that selected information; all we need to know is the record number.

Let's consider the personnel file in our job costing application. We could store the information sequentially, with each record having the employee number as its first data field. Thus, even though we have 999 available employee numbers, we need only 200 records if there are only 200 employees. However, to update the file with new accumulated quantities at the end of our payroll run, we will have to read the entire file in at the beginning of the program (for which we would need a lot of memory), somehow get back to the beginning of the file, and then rewrite all of the records sequentially with the new values.

The alternative is to have a direct access file with 999 records, one for each employee number. Then when information is needed about an employee, only his or her record need be accessed and read. When writing updated figures to the file, only that record is written to. However, when there are only 200 employees, only about 20% of the file is actually used. The required storage space is much greater, but the ease of programming and speed of access are so much improved that the trade-off is usually in favor of the direct access file for this kind of application.

For input and output, sequential access files are usually used for a different reason. Whereas direct access files must have fixed-length records, sequential access uses an end-of-line character (or other means) to determine the length of each line. Thus, only as many characters as are in the record are stored. For example, an 80-column output report stored in a direct access file would require an 80-character record for each line; in a sequential file, a blank line would only require the end-of-line marker. Thus, sequential access results in a significant saving of file space with files of variable record length.

Files are accessed for different purposes, and most operating systems protect the files by having the programmer declare the type of access being made to the file when opening it. Furthermore, if a file is opened for writing or updating, that is, modifying the contents, no other user is allowed to open it simultaneously, thus preventing the use of the information that is being changed. The various types of file access include:

type of file access	action taken
INQUIRE	check for existence of file
OPEN	open file for access
READ	read from file
WRITE	write to file
UPDATE	read from and write to same file
TRUNCATE	cut off file after last record accessed
CLOSE	close file, allowing access to others
APPEND	add to existing file
COPY	copy file to one with new name
RENAME	give existing file a new name
DELETE	delete file

Some of these options are in the operating system, and some are included in FORTRAN.

For our job costing and payroll example, we will use the following files:

file name	description	access		storage mode
F0101	personnel	direct	read	binary
F0102	active job file	direct	read	binary
F0104	labor input	sequential	read	character

F0131	labor summary file	direct	update	character
F131A	labor summary index	direct	update	character
R0134	output file to be printed	sequential	write	character
T0180	temporary file for payroll	sequential	write	character

For our earthwork example, we will use the following files:

file name	*description*	*access*		*storage mode*
OGIN.DAT	raw original ground data	sequential	read	character
OG.DAT	original ground X-sections	direct	update	character
INDXOG.DAT	index of OG.DAT	sequential	update	character
DSIN.DAT	design surface parameters	sequential	read	character
DS.DAT	design surface X-sections	direct	update	character
INDXDS.DAT	index of DS.DAT	sequential	update	character

6.5.2 File backup

Another concern of the systems analyst is the backup and recovery procedures to be used in case of a catastrophe during the run or in the event that a file is destroyed accidentally. It is also possible that bad information may be entered into the system, making the updated file incorrect; it would be handy to go back to the file as it existed before the update and run again, this time with correct information. A well-written procedure will make recovery possible by generating a copy of the file prior to its updating. Depending on the system, file operations such as copying, renaming, and so forth, can be done by the operating system, if not by the program.

Generally most shops keep magnetic tape backups of all of the files on at least a daily basis. However, it is much safer and faster to create a copy of the file to be updated and leave it on disk for a set period, after which it can be deleted. The magnetic tapes are then used for historical storage only and not for temporarily generated files.

6.6 Documentation

Documentation is probably the most controversial area of programming. How much, what type, and where it is put are the questions most often posed. The success of a program often rests on how well it is documented.

Many different persons in the data processing cycle need documentation, but they do not all need the same documentation. Although there may be common features required by all, it is best to tailor the documentation to the task being performed.

6.6.1 System manager's documentation

The system manager is the person responsible for the overall operation of not only the hardware, but the system software as well. This person sets up the recovery procedures in case of hardware failure and oversees all operational procedures, even though he or she may not actually do the running. The system manager needs to know the name of the program, the frequency of its use, the files accessed by the program, and how they are accessed. The system manager should have the following type of documentation:

```
L0134: Weekly Job Costing & Payroll - System Documentation
                                September 18, 1987

Running Frequency & Schedule: Weekly, usually on Wednesday afternoon
                 File      Access     Comments
                 F0101     Read
                 F0102     Read
                 F0104     Read
                 F0131     Update
                 R0134     Write       Printer Output
                 T0180     Write

Associated Program: L134A: Input generation for file F0104
```

```
L0404: Earthwork Analysis - System Documentation
                     September 18, 1987

Running Frequency & Schedule: As needed

            File          Access     Comments
            OG.DAT        Read
            INDXOG.DAT    Read
            DS.DAT        Read
            INDXDS.DAT    Read
            R0404         Write       Printer Output

Associated Program: PREPOG: Edit and convert raw cross section data

            File          Access     Comments
            OGIN.DAT      Read
            OG.DAT        Write
            INDXOG.DAT    Write

Associated Program: PREPDS: Generate design surface from parameters

            File          Access     Comments
            DSIN.DAT      Read
            DS.DAT        Write
            INDXDS.DAT    Write
```

6.6.2 Operator's documentation

The operator's documentation is for the person who is going to run the program. It may well be the same person who is identified as the user, but the operational documentation is significantly different from the user documentation. The operator's documentation is concerned strictly with the run, its success and failure, and the printing of the reports. The user is concerned with the validity of the data and the effect of the data on the file contents. The operator's documentation might be something like this:

```
L0134: Weekly Job Costing & Payroll - Operator's Documentation
                                   September 18, 1987

Running Frequency & Schedule: Weekly, usually on Wednesday afternoon

Sample Screen (underlined entries are operator input):

+++++++++++++++++++++++++++++++++++++++++++++++++++++++++++
+                                                         +
+    RUN L0134                                            +
+                                                         +
+    Job Cost & Payroll Input for  10/03/87               +
+                                                         +
+    Enter 1 to edit, 2 for final run                     +
+    2                                                    +
+                                                         +
+      181 records to be processed                        +
+    Sorting by employee                                  +
+    Generating payroll information                       +
+    Sorting by job                                       +
+    Adding to summary file                               +
+    Sorting by task                                      +
+                                                         +
+    Job complete                                         +
+                                                         +
+++++++++++++++++++++++++++++++++++++++++++++++++++++++++++

Print Report File R0134, 3 copies.

In case of any errors, record error message and report to
user. Close all files and print output file.
```

6.6.3 User's documentation

The user's documentation is far more detailed. It must describe all of the input file structure and the record layout. The size of the input fields and the allowable ranges must also be stated, as well as the order of the records, if that is critical.

```
L0134: Weekly Job Costing & Payroll - User's Documentation
                                  September 18, 1987

Running Frequency & Schedule: Weekly, usually on Wednesday afternoon

Input File: F0104 - Sequential, character
     Record(s) Columns     Description, Range and/or Format
        1          1 -  8:  nn/nn/nn
                  11 - 44:  'WEEKLY JOB COSTING & PAYROLL INPUT'
      2 - n        1 -  3:  employee number (1 to 999)
                   6 -  9:  job number (1 to 9999)
                  11 - 13:  task number (101 to 399)
                      15:   overtime indicator: 0 = regular
                                                 1 = time + 1/2
                                                 2 = double time
                  16 - 20:  hours worked (real), nn.nn

Date will be verified by operator when running program.
Employee number and job will be checked against valid data in files
     F0101 and F0102.
All other fields will be checked against allowable ranges.

Output Files:  F0131 (Labor Summaries) updated with new input.
               F131A (Labor Summary Index) updated accordingly.
               R0134 (Report File) to be sent to printer, 3 copies.
               T0134 (Payroll File) to be used later during Payroll
                     generation.

Report: consists of three outputs, by employee, by job and by task
        with appropriate subtotals and totals.
```

6.6.4 Programmer's documentation

The programmer's documentation is the most detailed of all. There are two theories as to where this documentation should appear. Some experts claim that the documentation should be placed external to the program in a separately maintained document. However, experience has shown that documentation external to the program is not as well maintained as documentation within the program. Comments within a program are kept up-to-date more often than external documentation because when the programmer is modifying the program, it is much easier to remember to adjust a comment than to change another document at some later time. Programmers are notoriously sloppy about documentation, so it is important to devise methods that are easy to follow.

The comments in the body of the FORTRAN program should be considered the programmer's documentation. A well-documented program will include the following:

1. Title: the program name and title
2. Abstract: a short description of the program
3. Files accessed and their mode of access (read, write, and so forth)
4. Subprograms called
5. Glossary of variables and arrays
6. Module headers placed before each module or subprogram call
7. Dates of modifications made and statements affected

One very handy mechanism for documentation is to enter all the comments that are part of the documentation with a unique character in column 2 (for example, an apostrophe), and then have a simple program that reads the FORTRAN source program and prints out only the lines beginning with C'. In this way external documentation can be obtained directly from the program without the need for the programmer to access a second document.

Examples of semiadequate programmer documentation have appeared in previous examples in this text, but more adequate documentation will appear in later chapters.

6.6.5 File documentation

Finally, it is necessary to document the files that are used. In the case of input files generated by the user, the user documentation should contain such information as shown above. However, there must also be file documentation for files that are either read or written by the program. Since these files may be used by many different programs, file documentation is usually kept separately to provide a common source of information to the programmers who are concerned with the file structure. File documentation is usually quite simple, and some was shown in section 6.5. Character files are usually described in terms of columnar layout, binary files in field and byte layout.

6.7 Modularity

Modularity is critical in program writing today because it is the most effective tool against programming errors and bugs. Modularity means that coding is reduced to a collection of small modules, each semi-independent of those around it; thus testing and understanding of the code are markedly simpler.

Modularity has two components: subprograms and structure. We have already looked at subprograms in some detail. Structure is concerned with the writing of code within a program module and will be discussed in section 6.8.

First of all, programming effort is greatly reduced by using subprograms already in the library. This eliminates the writing and testing of new code and also reduces the number of program modules used in a shop. Furthermore, the programmer then develops the attitude that he or she is writing not only for himself or herself, but also for the programmers who may later be responsible for maintaining (debugging and enhancing) the code. Since all other programmers will be familiar with the system program library, their effort in understanding the program is likewise reduced.

In many instances, the mainline program will simply be a collection of calls to subprograms to handle various tasks. In our job costing and payroll example, we will use the following subroutines:

subroutine	purpose
LA134	input data from F0104 and edit
LSORT	sort data by employee number
LB134	generate output by employee
LC134	pack data and generate payroll file T0180
LSORT	sort data by job number
LD134	generate output by job
LE134	add to Labor Summary File F0131
LSORT	sort data by task
LF134	generate output by task

The mainline L0134 consists of a sequence of CALLs to the subroutines plus checking for the existence of files and rearranging the data for the second and third sorts (as we will see in the next three chapters). Note that the same sort routine is used for all three sorts, so even though there are nine CALLs to subprograms, only seven subprograms are used.

When a programming system (a mainline and its called subprograms) like this one is set up, it is critical that we keep careful track of the information that is common to all of the routines. However, in this application the only information common to all routines is the information read from the input file F0104, the rates read from the personnel file F0101, and the computed costs; of course, we must also know the number of records. In addition, the date and possibly the page number must be carried into the output routines so that the pagination can be properly sequenced. In sections 4.3 and 5.8 we saw how information can be transmitted to a subprogram through the argument list; in section 8.4 we will look at another method, which assigns shared information to an area of memory common to all routines.

A close inspection of the above subprogram list and the preceding sections on documentation might cause the reader to wonder about the letter L that appears before each of the modules. One of the jobs of the software manager is to avoid having different programmers write subprograms with similar names. (When the author first began writing programs, the department he headed had seven programmers, all sharing the same disk space. Thus a subprogram written by one programmer would destroy a subprogram with the same name written by a different programmer. To clear up the chaos, a system was devised in 1965 in which all programs began with the letter L, which was the first letter in the name of the company; mainlines were L0*nnn* and the associated subprograms were LA*nnn,* LB*nnn,* and so forth. Other associated mainlines were L*nnn*A, L*nnn*B, and so forth. Files were F0*nnn*, FA*nnn*, FB*nnn*, F*nnn*A, F*nnn*B, and so forth. Temporary files began with T and report files with R. The software manager gave all subprograms in the company's subprogram library a nonconflicting reserved name that could not be used for any other purpose. LSORT was the first sort written for this library, and we will be looking at it in section 9.4. This system has lasted through the years and is still in operation.)

In addition to avoiding the problem of conflicting subprogram names, it is also critical that there be a similarity of operation in all modules written for a given environment. It would be quite confusing if a requested yes/no response required all letters to be in uppercase in one application, while another would accept a Y or N in either uppercase or lowercase. It often doesn't matter what standard is selected; what does matter is that a standard be selected and adhered to.

Error handling, error messages, and documentation should also be standardized to avoid conflicts and confusion. A strong-willed but non-standard-following programmer will write programs that are difficult to use and thus of little value.

6.8 Structured programming

The idea of structured programming is to break the code into small semi-independent modules in which a single process is performed; there should be no branching into a module except at the beginning and no branching out of it except at the end. Furthermore, backward branches, that is, branches to a previous statement, are to be eliminated as much as possible. As a general rule, no section of code should be longer than one page (about 56 lines), and they should preferably be only 20 lines.

The adoption of a new version of FORTRAN in 1977 was not so much an attempt to improve the language as it was to try to eliminate some of the inherent chaos that programmers had engendered while using this most flexible language. The usual complaint was "spaghetti code," code in which the branching went forwards and backwards, conflicting, crossing, jumbled up, convoluted, and so forth. Since it was necessary to have the new version "upward compatible" with the older version, it was impossible to do away with the main culprit, the GO TO statement. The approach of the new version of the language is to try to make the GO TO unnecessary by providing additional facilities that would lead to better structure.

The main facility added to the language was the IF..THEN..ELSE..ENDIF, as discussed in section 2.11. The programmer no longer has to use a negative approach (IF *NOT* the case, GO TO nn) but can now encapsulate the positive decision (and its negation) with clarity. From the standpoint of many professionals, this construct was the most critical addition to the language; it does not eliminate the crazy branching in all cases, but it certainly has lead to more easily written and understood code.

However, a number of enhancements were forthcoming. Even while FORTRAN 66 was still the standard, a number of enhanced versions (MAD: Michigan Algorithmic Decoder, WATFOR: University of Waterloo FORTRAN, its successor, WATFIV, and many others) influenced the members of the committee who developed the specifications for FORTRAN 77. Some of the enhancements had great significance; others did not. Among them (all of which we will discuss in later sections) were:

1. The CHARACTER data type (still not nearly as convenient as BASIC's string variable)

2. Arrays of up to seven dimensions

3. Unrestricted subscript expressions, including reals; subscripts can also be subscripted

4. Permissible mixed-mode expressions

5. Firmly specified DO loop implementation (method 2 of section 2.12), and negative incrementation

6. Free-format (list-directed) input/output

7. Some new format field specifications

8. Standardized file access methods

However, the full FORTRAN 77 implementation was so large that again two levels of implementation were set up, the full set and the subset. In the real world, the programmer will seldom see a pure implementation of any of the standard FORTRANs but is more likely to find some between FORTRAN 66 and 77 (usually on the micros), some FORTRAN 77s that are subsets of the subsets, some between full 77 and its subset, and even some that are enhanced beyond the full FORTRAN 77.

We can only repeat the advice heard many years ago, "When all else fails, read the manual!" Most properly written manuals will list the FORTRAN features that have been omitted from that particular implementation and give a list of additional features provided. However, as all of us in the business know, language manuals are notoriously inadequate. There is no substitute for personal experience and experimentation ("E and E").

All in all, the new facilities of FORTRAN 77 are very helpful in reducing the task of programming, testing, and debugging. From here on, we will be working in at least the subset of the 1977 specifications (with the exception of chapter 10, where the subset character facilities cannot perform as well as FORTRAN 66), and the user with only the 66 implementation will have to make the necessary adjustments in his or her programs.

6.9 Debugging techniques

The most frustrating task for a programmer is debugging. Writing code is easy, since we seem to possess perfect logic at that point. It's only during the testing, when we find that our logic is not perfect, that egos suffer and tempers wear thin. There are two things a programmer learns quickly—humility and how to curse! And the cursing is not at the computer or at the world, but at his or her own stupidity for making mistakes.

We will present a number of very powerful debugging techniques in this section, but none is more powerful than carefully thought-out, modularized, structured code. Good, direct, unsophisticated, well-documented code is still the easiest to write, test, and debug.

The attitude of the professional is that code written at any time is subject to logical flaws; thus a program must be written with the intention of having to debug it. A good programmer places debugging statements directly in the program.

6.9.1 Echo check

The first debugging technique is an echo check of the incoming data. We may know what the input data looks like, but we must find out how the computer sees it; improperly formatted input data is most often the cause of problems (GIGO—garbage in, garbage out). In cases where the original data is part of the output, it may not be necessary to handle the echo check separately; however, where it isn't, it is best to either display, file, or print it during the initial test runs. It is critical to be able to separate I/O errors from computational ones.

As an example, our program to handle job costing and payroll may have the following routine to input and echo check the detail data:

```
                  :
C                       input detail records
      READ  (11,1002, END = 20)
    1       (IEMP(I), JOB(I), ITASK(I), IOVRTM(I), HOURS(I), I = 1,2001)
 1002 FORMAT  (I3, 2X, I4, 1X, I3, 1X, I1, F5.2)
         WRITE  (1,1004)
 1004       FORMAT  (//1H0',EXCESS DATA  -   RUN ABORTED!')
         STOP
   20 NREC = I - 1
      WRITE  (1,1020)
    1       (I, IEMP(I), JOB(I), ITASK(I), IOVRTM(I), HOURS(I), I = 1,NREC)
 1020 FORMAT  (1H ,5I6, F7.2)
                  :
```

The echo check provided by the WRITE to the screen does not have a fancy or annotated FORMAT; it is used just for programmer checkout. Once the programmer is convinced that the input routine is working, the WRITE and its associated FORMAT can be commented out with a C in column 1, but they should not be removed. These statements should be left in the code just in case additional testing indicates that the input routine is not perfect. It is much easier to remove the C's than to reenter the statements.

There are even more sophisticated ways to switch in and out of the debugging mode. In the following code, a header must be read prior to reading the detail records. A debugging indicator in column 9 is read in as part of the header:

```
                  :
C                       input header and approve
      READ   (11,1000) (IDATE(J), J = 1,3), INDBG
 1000 FORMAT  (I2,1X,I2,1X,I2, I1)
      WRITE  (1,1001)  IDATE
 1001 FORMAT  (1H0,'Job Cost & Payroll for week of', I3,2('/',I2)/
                 1H0,'Enter 1 to edit, 2 for final run')
      READ  (1,*)  IOPT
          IF  (IOPT .LT. 1  .OR.  IOPT .GT. 2)  STOP
C                       input detail records
      READ  (11,1002, END = 20)
    1       (IEMP(I), JOB(I), ITASK(I), IOVRTM(I), HOURS(I), I = 1,2001)
 1002 FORMAT  (I3, 2X, I4, 1X, I3, 1X, I1, F5.2)
          WRITE  (1,1004)
 1004       FORMAT  (//1H0',EXCESS DATA  -   RUN ABORTED!')
          STOP
   20 NREC  =  I - 1
```

```
C                       optional echo check
      IF  (INDBG .NE. 0)
   1  WRITE  (1,1020)
   1     (I, IEMP(I), JOB(I), ITASK(I), IOVRTM(I), HOURS(I), I = 1,NREC)
 1020  FORMAT (1H ,5I6, F7.2)
                     :
```

If the value in column 9 of the input header is blank or zero, the debugging output will not be triggered; if column 9 contains a digit greater than zero, it will be. Thus the programmer need only modify the data file to switch back and forth from debugging mode to regular mode.

An even better way might be to use the approval value:

```
                     :
C                     input header and approve
      READ  (11,1000) (IDATE(J), J = 1,3)
 1000 FORMAT  (I2,1X,I2,1X,I2)
      WRITE  (1,1001)  IDATE
 1001 FORMAT  (1H0,'Job Cost & Payroll for week of', I3,2('/',I2)/
   1             1H0,'Enter 1 to edit, 2 for final run')
      READ  (1,*)  IOPT
      IF  (IOPT .GE. 0)  THEN
                INDBG  =  0
          ELSE
                INDBG  =  1
                IOPT   =  -IOPT
      ENDIF
          IF  (IOPT .LT. 1 .OR. IOPT .GT. 2)  STOP
                     :
```

Here a negative value will trigger the debugging output, a positive value won't. Only the programmer will know the effect of the negative value; there is no need to put it into the prompt.

As a minimum, the number of records read should be displayed as part of the output, whether in debug mode or not; this will tell the person running the program that the input routine has been completed successfully.

```
                   :
      WRITE  (1,1022) NREC
 1022 FORMAT  (1H0,I4,' records to be processed')
                   :
```

The option of outputting intermediate results should be used throughout the program; then results can be checked along the way and we will not be required to locate errors from only the final results.

6.9.2 Milestones

In section 6.4 we mentioned the practice of displaying milestones while a program is being executed. This is especially useful in long, manipulative routines in which infinite loops are a possibility. If an infinite loop does occur, we will know from the milestone display how far the program got and we can interrupt the execution with at least some knowledge of where to look for the problem.

Fortunately, the ease of placing output statements in FORTRAN programs makes FORTRAN one of the easier languages to debug (only BASIC is easier).

6.9.3 Symbolic debugger

However, in many of the more sophisticated systems there is another tool available that is a tremendous aid when debugging; this exemplary tool is called a *symbolic debugger*. The symbolic debugger allows the programmer to examine memory locations by symbol (variable name). The symbol table developed to keep track of variable addresses is usually destroyed after a program is compiled, but in debug mode, the table is saved so that it can be used during execution. The program is run under the control of this debugger and gives the programmer a number of options:

1. Halting the program at any statement
2. Displaying the contents of any memory location
3. Stepping through the program one statement at a time
4. Displaying any variable whenever it is modified
5. Indicating when a subprogram is accessed.

And there are many other options, depending on the system.

It would be impossible for us to describe all of the symbolic debuggers available on the many computer systems used to run FORTRAN. But we would comment that this tool, which can be used with any of the languages on a computer, including assembly, is usually worth whatever its cost might be. We recommend that the reader check his or her system to see if a symbolic debugger is available and, if it is, learn it, if not for FORTRAN then for some of the more difficult languages.

6.10 Summary and projects

We have attempted to describe some of the noncoding aspects of programming; all too often they are ignored in texts and manuals, and the new programmer in industry finds himself ill prepared for professional work. In the hierarchy of professionals, the coder is at the bottom of the scheme, the programmer (who is responsible primarily for the logic of the software) in the middle, and the systems analyst on top. The most fun is making decisions, not implementing someone else's!

In the projects below, we are looking for simple solutions. Certainly at this stage in the reader's training, we cannot expect sophistication. Some of these projects will reappear later in the text when the reader will have gained more knowledge and insight. Thus, when attacking the projects, avoid complexities and keep the solutions simple.

6.10.1 Projects

Project 6-1

A file keeps track of sales of eggs by a combination retail/wholesale outlet. The file header (the first record) contains the date (month and year) and the three costs associated with the sale of the eggs: the cost per gross, the cost per dozen, and the cost per unit. For example, the sale of 305 eggs would be charged as 2 gross, 1 dozen, and 5 individual eggs. The rest of the records in the file consist of three items: the customer number, the day of the sale, and the number of eggs. Two reports are required each month. The first is a listing by customer itemizing each sale, with subtotals by customer of eggs bought (gross, dozen, and units) and cost and similar grand totals for the month. The egg totals must be reduced to proper amounts, that is, 2 gross, 14 dozen, 65 units becomes 3 gross, 7 dozen, and 5 units. The cost totals should be the sum of the detail costs, not a recomputation from the egg totals. The second report is a chronological one, listing the total eggs sold each day and the cost as well as grand totals (which should agree with the ones from the previous report).

Determine which functions or subroutines might be handy for this application; document them and the mainline in terms of what algorithms are to be used and what I/O is to take place within them. Design the output reports.

Project 6-2

A direct access file consists of 40 records, each consisting of 80 bowling scores for one bowler. (If you don't know what bowling is, let me just say that it is a frustrating game in which scores range from 0 to 300.) Design a programming system to output each bowler's scores, determine the number of 300 games, determine the lowest score of all the bowlers, and tabulate a distribution for the ranges 0–50, 51–90, 91–130, 131–170, 171–210, 211–250, 251–290, and 291–300 (that is, determine the total number of games in each range).

Determine which subprograms might be useful for this system and document them. Design the output report.

Project 6-3

A sales journal is to be produced from a file that contains multiple records with three items each, the salesperson's number, the identification number of the item sold, and the number of items sold. A table lookup is to be used to determine the price of the item from the identification number. The cost is the number of items times the price, the tax is 8% of the cost, and the total cost is the sum of the cost and the tax. The salesperson's commission is 10% of the cost (before tax) if the cost is greater than or equal to $1000 and 6% if the cost is less than $1000.

Design the mainline and subprograms to be used in the system. Also design a report to output all of the input and computed quantities with totals for cost, tax, and commission.

Project 6–4

A computer use report is to be generated from the information in a file that contains multiple records with the items:

    user number
    year
    month
    day
    log on time, nn.nn, military time (00.00 to 23.59)
    log off time, nn.nn, military time (00.00 to 23.59)

The output report should list the above information and compute the time used in hours and minutes and a cost based on rates of $0.25 per computer minute for the first 120 minutes and $0.15 per computer minute thereafter. Totals for time use and cost should be output as well.

Design the system and the output report. Assume that no log on/log off time extends across two days.

Project 6–4A

Revise the charging mechanism above so that log on/log off can extend across midnight but cannot last more than 24 hours. Any time charged between 6 p.m. and 8 a.m. is to be charged at a reduced rate of 80%.

Project 6–5

A system is to be devised to send out parking violation notices. The input file consists of records with the license plate number and a code for the violation. Another file contains a table of the violation codes with a description and amount of fine for each. A third file contains the license plate numbers and the names and addresses associated with them.

Design a system to input the first file, sort the information by license plate, and then print out notices to be mailed to violators. Design the file structures needed and the output.

7

File access

7.1 Introduction

A file is a medium for inputting information to or outputting information from the memory of the computer. Files can be external input/output devices such as printers, card readers, terminals, magnetic tape units, and so forth, or they can be disk files used to store information on line, that is, readily accessible for either input or output without requiring any manual manipulation.

A permanent file is a collection of data (sometimes called a data base) that is divided into records. Each record contains one or more fields of data. The records may all possess the same data structure, that is, the corresponding fields of each record contain the same data item, or different records may contain different information. As an example of a file where the records have identical structure, recall the file discussed in section 6.5 (F0131), which was used to store the labor summary information. Regardless of the storage mode of the information (binary or character), each of the records will be identical in structure (but not in values). In section 6.6, we described the input file (F0104), which consists of two types of records, a header with one layout of information and the detail records, which all have a similar structure different from that of the header.

The storage of data and programs in a form accessible to the computer at some later time is critical in data processing. The early microcomputers, which had no means of program and data storage, were little more than toys; it was not until some means of saving information permanently was developed that they began to be taken seriously.

Our concern in this chapter is how data can be stored efficiently and effectively so that it can be easily accessed by the program. There are a number of ways in which data can be stored, and we will be discussing these different methods, demonstrating how each is used.

Unfortunately, FORTRAN was developed so early in computer history that file access was often system dependent, and it was not until the adoption of FORTRAN 77 that any kind of compatibility was specified. Fortunately (or unfortunately, depending upon your point of view), IBM dominated the early FORTRAN market, so competitors often had to emulate IBM's file access methods in order to compete. (Not too different from today's microcomputer market, is it?) Before FORTRAN 66, there were commands like READ MAGNETIC TAPE, PUNCH PAPER TAPE, and so forth, but FORTRAN 66 specified a single I/O command for input and one for output, using the logical unit number to indicate the particular device. However, we still see archaic commands like PRINT and ACCEPT, which are holdovers from the early days.

In FORTRAN, a data file on disk is accessed by a logical unit number, the same way that a physical device is accessed. In FORTRAN 66, the connection between the logical unit number and the I/O device or file name is system dependent and usually done with subprograms supplied by the manufacturer. In this chapter, we will work strictly with the compatible access methods now existing in FORTRAN 77 and leave it to the reader who is still working in FORTRAN 66 to do his or her own research. The concepts are the same, only the implementation of file access is different: all of the previously covered FORTRAN commands relating to I/O (and those to be covered in the future) are almost the same, and only the commands for describing the file structure and "connecting" the file to a logical unit number will differ.

7.2 Device characteristics

With the earliest computers, we first had to use punched paper tape; later, cards were used. Both of these media allowed only sequential I/O of the data. Furthermore, they were expensive (relatively) for data storage and took up a lot of space. Magnetic tape was the next major peripheral device; it provided a far more economical medium for data storage and much faster transfer of data to and from the main memory. But tape was also sequential in nature and required a great deal of manual handling to find a desired file. (The users of microcomputers with tape cassette storage are more than aware of some of the problems of tape storage.) Whereas tape provided a very effective means of storing input and output files, permanently stored data too large to fit into the computer's internal memory was not efficiently accessible.

The arrival of magnetic disks and drums changed the whole concept of data storage. Since it was possible to provide an index of the information stored and the hardware could move the read/write device to any desired location on the disk or drum, access to a file was not only faster, but more importantly, direct. To understand the significance of this improvement, the reader need only think of trying to play a recording of a piece of music that is not at the beginning of the recording medium. With a tape cassette, searching must be done, using the fast forward and reverse, but with a phonograph, the tone arm can be moved to the exact location quickly. Although some tape configurations allowed for a tape index at the beginning of the tape, fast forwarding a magnetic tape is a matter of minutes, even if the computer knows the location of the desired file.

(The concept of using magnetic surfaces as memory is not new. One computer with which the author is familiar is the old Bendix G-15. Like the washing machines Bendix used to make with their rotating drum to hold the clothes, this magnetic rotating drum served as primary memory to hold the program and data. A good programmer would allocate his or her variable storage so that the data transfer rate and location of variables to be read sequentially were coordinated and excessive drum rotations avoided.)

The early disks stored on the order of a megabyte or two on a 15-inch platter. Drums, which could provide much more storage, served temporarily until the technology could provide better data packing. The years have witnessed marked improvements, with disk platters being reduced in size and with data being more compressed until, as users of microcomputers know, 20 megabytes squeezed onto a small disk drive mounted on a circuit board for less than $1000 is not unusual. The development of flexible disks (floppies or diskettes) with low-cost drives made the microcomputer a serious contender in the marketplace. The new removable disk cartridges (called Bernoulli boxes because of their use of the Bernoulli principle to prevent contact between the surface of the disk and the read/write head) have further revolutionized storage methods by providing high speed and the flexibility of a removable medium at a relatively economical price.

(As a comparison in the area of data packing, the reader is reminded that the early tape recorders used a quarter inch wide tape at 7.5 inches per second, whereas the current tape cassettes use an eighth inch tape at 1.75 inches per second and get better sound quality. The packing ratio is 8 to 1.)

As a result of the cost-effectiveness of disk media, magnetic tape has been reduced to two prime purposes. The first is backup of the information stored on disk. Disks are subject to occasional failure due to internal defects, the wearing out of the surface, or to hardware or power failure. Tape storage as backup is very economical and quite fast.

The second purpose of magnetic tape is data transfer between computers. Unfortunately, disk formats are system dependent; although physically similar disks are used for different computers, the information on the disk is layed out (formatted) differently for different operating systems. Disk formatting may even be different on different models by a single manufacturer. Thus the most effective way of transferring data from one computer to another is writing a character file on tape and then reading it in on the second computer. (Unfortunately, there are some manufacturers whose operating systems do not allow a transferable tape image to be made easily; they attempt to bind their customers to their systems when making any future purchase in order to preserve the value of the customer's tape library.)

In our discussion, we will ignore magnetic tape and concentrate strictly on the more practical disk (or diskette) medium. A disk surface is divided into tracks or cylinders, each representing a location where the read/write head can be positioned; the term *cylinder* comes from the concept of reading the top and bottom of the disk surface and from the idea of stacked disk platters on the same central axis (or spindle). Each track is broken down into sectors, and each sector can contain a specified number of bytes. Each sector can be accessed or addressed;

the operating system checks the disk index, locates the read/write head on the proper track, and begins the I/O operation when the beginning of the sector passes under the head.

A number of procedures can be used to check the correctness of the data transfer to and from the disk. First of all, the sector address is usually written at the beginning of the sector so that the computer can double-check the location of the read/write head prior to any data transfer; this assures that no data transfer takes place due to mispositioning of the head or due to destruction of the sector address and probably of the data stored therein. Then a checksum, a count of the number of one bits (that is, bits that are on) in the sector, is used to verify that the number of bits transferred corresponds to the number of bits stored. Another verification process can be used during a disk write operation: the information written to the disk is read back from the disk and checked against the original to ensure that the write operation, which is far more critical than the read operation, has occurred correctly.

7.3 READ and WRITE revisited

Thus far, we have used relatively simple READ and WRITE commands that are compatible with all versions of FORTRAN starting with the 1966 version. Fortunately, file access methods became standardized with FORTRAN 77. We will now redefine these simple I/O commands in terms of the more recent standard. Both the READ and WRITE commands are followed by two lists:

1. The control information list

2. The input/output list (optional)

We are already familiar with the I/O list, in which there are no changes. But the control information list has some new features. Looking at the most extensive FORTRAN 66 input command, we might see:

```
READ (8,1000, END=20, ERR=80) i/o list
```

As we know, the first number is the logical unit number, and the second is the associated FORMAT statement number; the logical unit number is required, as is the FORMAT statement number for formatted I/O. The END= and ERR= clauses are optional and are defined with *keywords,* that is, with character strings stating which option refers to which statement number. As a result, one or the other or both may appear, in any order. The following statement is also acceptable:

```
READ (8,1000, ERR=80, END=20) i/o list
```

FORTRAN 66 also has a provision for providing the record number required for input and output to and from a direct access file (to be described fully in section 7.5); the record number follows the FORMAT statement reference and is preceded by an apostrophe. Thus the command to read record 52 would be

```
READ (8,1000'52, ERR=80) i/o list
```

The END= clause is omitted, since it has no meaning for a direct access file.

In the full FORTRAN 77 specification, all of the items in the control list can be specified by keywords; they can be entered in any order:

control item	*description*
UNIT = *n*	required; *n* could be an integer variable.
FMT = *f*	required for formatted I/O only; *f* can be a statement number or a variable name to which the statement number will be assigned by the program (using the ASSIGN command, which will be described in section 8.8); *f* can also be a character string (except in the subset) or an asterisk (*) to denote list-directed I/O (except in the subset or with direct access files).
REC = *rn*	record number required for direct access file.
IOSTAT = *ios*	input/output status indicator (*ios* is an integer variable) that is set to zero if no error occurs, positive if an error condition is encountered, and negative if end-of-file, but no error, is encountered (not included in subset).
ERR = *s*	causes a branch to statement *s* if an error occurs during the I/O, including invalid data characters (not included in subset).
END = *s*	causes a branch to statement *s* if end-of-file is encountered (does not apply to output files).

If the UNIT= keyword is missing, the first item in the list is taken to be the logical unit number (LUN). If the FMT= keyword is missing, the second item in the list is taken to be the associated FORMAT number and the first item, the LUN. To allow compatibility with FORTRAN 66, some implementations will permit the keyword REC= to be replaced with an apostrophe.

In the FORTRAN 77 subset, the keywords UNIT and FMT are not available and the I/O commands are written as described for FORTRAN 66.

Examples

```
READ (UNIT=10, FMT=1000, ERR=80, END=20, IOSTAT=IND) i/o list
```

is identical to

```
READ (10,1000, IOSTAT=IND, END=20, ERR=80) i/o list
```

Both read from file 10 according to FORMAT 1000, branching to statement 20 if end-of-file is detected or to 80 if an error is encountered, with the I/O status placed in the variable IND.

```
WRITE (UNIT=12,FMT='(1H0,2I5)') I, J
```

skips a line and writes the values of I and J in columns 1–5 and 6–10, respectively.

```
WRITE (FMT='(1H0,5X,''I      J''/1H ,2I6)', UNIT=12) I,J
```

writes the same thing as the preceding WRITE statement but adds headings. Note that the FMT format specifications are enclosed in single apostrophes. The double apostrophes are needed within the FMT parentheses because the compiler would consider a single apostrophe to be the end of the format; the double apostrophes (do *not* use quotation marks) are the equivalent of single apostrophes in a less complicated case.

There are also other variations in the full FORTRAN 77 that can be used in very simple I/O operations, requiring only the format reference and the I/O list. The I/O is directed from and to the system's principal I/O device(s), usually the terminal. These variations are very useful for obtaining quick and dirty I/O, usually during the testing and debugging cycle. The programmer can use the character string option and specify a complete I/O operation with just one statement, for example

```
I = 10
J = -20
PRINT *, 'I =', I, ', J =', J
```

or

```
WRITE (5,*) 'I =', I, ', J =', J
```

will output:

```
I =    10, J =    -20
```

using a system-dependent default spacing. Similarly,

```
READ *, A, B, C
```

will perform a free-format read from the system's principal input device.

7.4 Sequential access files

In section 6.5, we briefly presented some of the features of file storage and described the difference between sequential and direct file access. Here we will go into more detail and present more specific illustrations of sequential access files.

7.4.1 Variable length records

Usually sequential files use a variable length record, thus providing the most efficient means of data storage. The record stores the individual data fields followed by some indication of end-of-record, usually the code for carriage return (hex 0D).

Sequential file storage on DEC systems, however, is quite different; a variable length record begins with a byte counter containing the number of bytes in the record, followed by the bytes themselves with no end-of-record indicator. This method of storage is also used on magnetic tapes generated by the DEC operating system, making them difficult to read on non-DEC systems.

As an example of variable record length, think of our earthwork example, in which each cross section may have a different number of points. The record might be set up according to the following layout:

Columns 1–8: station

Columns 9–10: number of points in section

Columns 11–17, 26–32, 41–47, . . . (as needed): offsets

Columns 18–25, 33–40, 48–55, . . . (as needed): elevations

The reason for the second field (number of points in section) has nothing to do with the file structure, but with the implementation of FORTRAN, as we will discuss momentarily.

With the variable record length shown, three points per cross section would use 55 columns; four points, 70 columns; five points, 85 columns, and so forth. One problem to watch for is the limit each system has for the number of bytes per record. Actually, this kind of structure is not practical in situations where there may be a large number of points per cross section, but it does allow us to illustrate one of the applications of FORTRAN I/O.

Although the FORTRAN READ can detect end-of-file, it cannot detect end-of-record. Thus there is no way for us to test for the number of points in the cross section being read. If the number of points were not given (that is, if it were not available in columns 9–10), we could assume the maximum and set up the format accordingly. For a maximum of 50 points, we would have to read through 660 columns:

```
    READ (8,1000, END=20) STATN, (OFFSET(I), ELEV(I), I=1,50)
1000 FORMAT (F8.2, 2X, 50(F7.1, F8.2))
```

If there were only 42 points in the record, FORTRAN would fill the unreadable fields with zeros; the program could then scan backwards through the arrays to find the first nonzero pair of coordinates.

When the number of points is given, as in the preceding record layout, we can use the point counter and write the code:

```
      READ (8,1000, END=20) STATN, NP, (OFFSET(I), ELEV(I), I=1,NP)
 1000 FORMAT (F8.2, I2, 50(F7.1, F8.2))
```

This coding is much simpler and less prone to problems arising from unusual conditions, such as valid 0.0, 0.0 coordinates. However, the bad news is that the data file is harder to create because either the user will have to put the point counter in using an editor or a program will have to be written to analyze the input and write the point counter to the file. As in most situations, there is not always a perfect answer!

7.4.2 Fixed-length records

Fixed-length records are much simpler. An alternative file structure (the one we will use) would be:

Columns   1–8: station

Columns   9–15: offset

Columns   16–23: elevation

The data can be read into three arrays as follows:

```
      READ  (8,1000, END=20) (STATN(I), OFFSET(I), ELEV(I), I=1,10001)
 1000 FORMAT (F8.2, F7.1, F8.2)
```

where the program is able to handle up to 10,000 total points. As we have discussed before, the input routine will cycle through the FORMAT statement, reading three values per record until the end-of-file is reached. The program will later establish the number of points per station. This file structure is much simpler, not only because the size of the record is known, but also because the file can be generated very easily in an editor just by entering one point at a time. Additional points can be added or excess points deleted very easily, and points can be modified quickly.

There are three FORTRAN commands that are useful with files. BACK-SPACE moves the record pointer back one record, allowing a reread of the record just read. Additional BACKSPACEs will continue to move the file pointer backwards; it will stop, of course, when it gets to the first record. REWIND resets the record pointer to the beginning of the file; the next READ will start at record 1. ENDFILE puts an end-of-file mark at the next record; this is necessary when writing over an existing file, otherwise data beyond the new data written may be read also; this command truncates the file so that it contains only the newly written information.

7.4.3 Sample input program

The partial sample program below accepts earthwork data in free format from the keyboard, writes it to a sequential file, truncates the file, then rewinds the file and echo checks it back to the screen.

```
C                    Input Earthwork Data
C
C              open file and connect to unit 8 (to be shown later)
C
C              prompt user
      WRITE  (1,1000)
 1000 FORMAT  (1H ,'Enter station, offset, elevation in free-format'/
     1               '  0.,0.,0. to terminate')
C              input loop
      DO 20  I  =  1,10001
          READ  (2,*, END = 40)  STATN, OFFSET, ELEV
          IF  (STATN .EQ. 0.0  .AND.  OFFSET .EQ. 0.00  .AND.
     1          ELEV .EQ. 0.0)    GO TO 40
          WRITE  (8,1002)  STATN, OFFSET, ELEV
 1002     FORMAT  (F8.2, F7.1, F8.2)
   20 CONTINUE
          WRITE  (1,1020)
 1020     FORMAT  (1H ,'EXCESSIVE INPUT  -  RUN TERMINATED')
          STOP
C              end of data found
   40 NREC  =  I - 1
      ENDFILE 8
      REWIND 8
C              echo check
      WRITE  (1,1040)  NREC
 1040 FORMAT  (1H0,I5,' points filed:')
      DO 60  I  =  1,NREC
          READ  (8,1002)  STATN, OFFSET, ELEV
   60 WRITE  (1,1060)  STATN, OFFSET, ELEV
 1060 FORMAT  (1H ,F8.2, F7.2, F8.2)
C              close file (to be shown later) and terminate
      STOP
      END
```

7.4.4 Null input value

FORTRAN 77 has a feature that can be quite useful in reducing the effort of data entry in the above program. Free-format (or list-directed) input in FORTRAN will accept values separated by either blanks or commas. A *null value* results when there are no characters between two commas (the commas can be adjacent to each other, or they can be separated by blanks). When a null value occurs, the value left in the variable is its previous value. Furthermore, a slash in the value list causes all fields after the slash to be treated as nulls. For example, the program:

```
    DO 20 N = 1,4
        READ (2,*) I, J, K
20  WRITE (1,*) I, J, K
    STOP
    END
```

with data:

```
1, 2, 3
11,,13
,22,,
31/
```

will yield the following output:

```
 1       2      3
11       2     13
11      22     13
31      22     13
```

Thus, the original ground data shown in section 6.4 might be entered as:

```
1000, -100.8,117.25
, -82.7,121.62
, -67.9,116.86
            :
            :
,102.5,112.54
1050, -105.6,127.54
            :
            :
```

Notice that integer-valued reals may be entered without a decimal point.

Warning

The author has discovered that there are exceptions to these rules regarding the null value on certain systems. For example, in DEC VAX FORTRAN, a null string entered at the terminal follows the rules of FORTRAN 77, but when entered from a disk file, the null value becomes a zero. It is not difficult to make an adjustment in the above program to correct for this:

```
C                  input loop
      DO 20  I  =  1,10001
           READ  (2,*, END = 40)  STATN, OFFSET, ELEV
           IF  (STATN .EQ. 0.0  .AND.  OFFSET .EQ. 0.00  .AND.
     1          ELEV .EQ. 0.0)     GO TO 40
           IF  (STATN .EQ. 0.0  .AND.  I .NE. 1)  STATN  =  SAVSTN
           SAVSTN  =  STATN
           WRITE  (8,1002)  STATN, OFFSET, ELEV
 1002      FORMAT  (F8.2, F7.2, F8.2)
   20 CONTINUE
```

This example should emphasize the importance of checking out the null value implementation on any machine the programmer uses!

7.5 Direct access files

Direct (or random) access files allow access to any record individually, provided the record number is known. The records must be of fixed length; within that fixed length, however, the information layout may differ. Direct access files may be formatted or unformatted, the former providing easier readability, the latter generally using less disk space and having improved access time and security.

One of the major disadvantages of a direct access file is that its generation, modification, and access are quite rigidly controlled. Sequential access records contain an end-of-record mark, but direct access records do not; access to those records depends strictly on the specified record length. The location of a given record is computed as

$$\text{record length} \times (\text{record number} - 1) + 1$$

Once a direct access file is set up, the programmer must consider the record length a constant. Furthermore, any change to the file or to the records in the file can be made only with a program and not with a text editor, although a patch utility can modify record contents. List-directed (free-format) I/O is not possible with direct access files.

(Some systems allow the record length to differ among different programs that access the same file; this does have limited application. Other systems store the record length as part of the file description in the user directory, and any attempt to access it with a different record length specified will cause an I/O error; once the file has been generated on those systems, the programmer need not specify the record length in any other program, since it will be taken from the file description.)

Direct access files must be generated by a program. Editors are designed for sequential file generation using the end-of-record mark. Furthermore, the data may go through a compaction scheme to eliminate a long series of blanks or to make use of tab settings; thus the user may think he or she is putting in a fixed number of characters, only to find that the actual number of characters stored is different. Thus direct access files must not be modified in an editor. Some implementations allow the user to "create" a file before using it by commanding the operating system to set aside space for the file; no data is placed into such a file, and it should be assumed that it contains garbage. Other systems require that the file be written sequentially, beginning with the first record and continuing until the end; such a system does not permit a record to be written unless the previous one has been established first, but this can be done with a dummy program that just writes garbage to the file.

For demonstration purposes, let us assume that we have decided to treat the cross section data file as a direct access file. There are some distinct advantages to this: we can index the file (we'll show how in section 7.7) and can then get to a particular station quickly without having to read the entire file into memory (see section 7.8). The syntax of an unformatted direct access file WRITE is

```
WRITE (8, REC=I) STATN, OFFSET, ELEV
```

or, for FORTRAN 66 compatibility:

```
WRITE (8'I) STATN, OFFSET, ELEV
```

These statements will write to the record numbered with the contents of the variable I. Of course the record number could be an integer constant instead of a variable.

The formatted direct access write to the same record is:

```
     WRITE (8,1000, REC=I) STATN, OFFSET, ELEV
1000 FORMAT (F8.2, F7.2, F8.2)
```

Those programmers using a version of FORTRAN 66 with IBM compatibility will find a statement called DEFINE FILE, which is used to specify the parameters of direct access files. The general form is:

```
DEFINE FILE nu (nr, nl, fc, ivar)
```

where:

  nu is the logical unit number of the file

  nr is the number of records in the file

  nl is the size of the records

  fc is the format code: U is unformatted, E is formatted

ivar is an associated integer variable name that will contain the record number one higher than the previous record accessed; it can be used to simulate sequential I/O.

In this version, the READ and WRITE statements do not use the keywords UNIT, FMT, or REC; they use the comma to separate the logical unit number and format statement number (for formatted I/O) and the apostrophe before the record number, for example

```
WRITE (8,1000'I) STATN, OFFSET, ELEV
```

FORTRAN 66 also contained a statement of the form:

```
FIND (8'102)
```

which was used to speed up file access by moving the read/write head of the disk to the proper sector location while other processing was going on. In this case, it would seek out the location of record 102 in file 8. However, with virtual memory and shared disk access, this command would only cause additional wasted head movement.

7.6 Auxiliary I/O statements

The following commands are used to inquire about, connect, and disconnect disk files to and from a program. Each of the statements needs a list of specifiers, many of which are common to all three. The table below lists the specifiers and the commands where they are active. The default is assumed if the parameter is not specified. Furthermore, the table indicates which of the specifiers are in the full set and the subset with the following codes:

I: used in INQUIRE (not in subset)

O: used in OPEN

C: used in CLOSE (not in subset)

S: available in subset version of OPEN

Parameter	Used in	Description
UNIT = n	I O C S	n is logical unit number. In subset, keyword not used.
FILE = *name*	I O	*name* is the name of the file, given either as a character string or a variable. In the subset, a processor-determined default file is connected.
ERR = s	I O C	s is statement number branched to if an error occurs.

IOSTAT = *ios*	I O C	*ios* is an integer variable into which the I/O status is placed. See section 7.3 for values used.
STATUS = *str*	O C	for OPEN, *str* may be OLD, NEW, SCRATCH, or UNKNOWN. For OLD or NEW, the FILE = parameter must be used. If NEW, the file must not exist; successful opening converts it to OLD; if OLD, it must exist. If SCRATCH, the file is destroyed at end of run. If UNKNOWN, status is system dependent. for CLOSE, *str* may be KEEP (default) or DELETE. KEEP cannot be used if file was opened as SCRATCH.
ACCESS = *str*	I O S	*str* is either SEQUENTIAL (default) or DIRECT in full set, DIRECT only in subset.
FORM = *str*	I O	*str* is either FORMATTED or UNFORMATTED. If SEQUENTIAL, default is FORMATTED; if DIRECT, default is UNFORMATTED.
RECL = *n*	I O S	*n* is the record length. If FORMATTED, given in bytes; if UNFORMATTED, given in processor-dependent units.
BLANK = *str*	I O	*str* is either NULL (default) or ZERO. If NULL, all blanks in numerically formatted input fields are ignored, except that a field of all blanks is treated as zero; if ZERO, all nonleading blanks are treated as zeros.
EXIST = *log*	I	*log* is a logical variable in which will be placed either TRUE if file exists or FALSE if it does not.
OPENED = *log*	I	*log* is a logical variable that is TRUE if the file is open, FALSE if not.
NUMBER = *n*	I	*n* is an integer variable in which the number of the file is placed, if known.
NAMED = *log*	I	*log* is a logical variable that is TRUE if the file is named, FALSE if not.
NAME = *str*	I	*str* is the name of the file, if known.
SEQUENTIAL = *str*	I	*str* is a character variable that is given the value YES if the file can be I/Oed sequentially; otherwise, NO.

DIRECT = *str*	I	*str* is a character variable that is given the value YES if the file can be I/Oed by direct access; otherwise, NO.
FORMATTED = *str*	I	*str* is a character variable that is given the value YES if formatted, NO if unformatted.
UNFORMATTED = *str*	I	*str* is a character variable that is given the value YES if unformatted, NO if formatted.
NEXTREC = *n*	I	*n* is an integer variable that is assigned the value one higher than the last record read if connected for direct access.

We can now complete the code for opening and closing the files in our input program from section 7.4:

```
C                       Input Earthwork Data
C
C               open output file
      OPEN  (UNIT = 8, FILE = 'OGIN.DAT', STATUS = 'NEW',
     1                 FORM = 'FORMATTED', ERR = 920)
C               prompt user
      WRITE  (1,1000)
 1000 FORMAT  (1H ,'Enter station, offset, elevation in free-format'/
     1               ' 0.,0.,0. to terminate')
C               input loop
      DO 20  I  =  1,10001
           READ  (2,*, END = 40) STATN, OFFSET, ELEV
           IF  (STATN .EQ. 0.0  .AND.  OFFSET .EQ. 0.00  .AND.
     1           ELEV .EQ. 0.0)    GO TO 40
           WRITE  (8,1002) STATN, OFFSET, ELEV
 1002      FORMAT  (F8.2, F7.2, F8.2)
   20 CONTINUE
           WRITE  (1,1020)
 1020      FORMAT  (1H ,'EXCESSIVE INPUT  -  RUN TERMINATED')
           STOP
C               end of data found
   40 NREC = I - 1
C                   truncate file and then return pointer to beginning
      ENDFILE 8
      REWIND 8
```

```
C              echo check
      WRITE  (1,1040)  NREC
 1040 FORMAT  (1H0,I5,' points filed:')
      DO 60   I = 1,NREC
           READ  (8,1002)  STATN, OFFSET, ELEV
   60 WRITE  (1,1060)  STATN, OFFSET, ELEV
 1060 FORMAT  (1H ,F8.2, F7.2, F8.2)
C              close file
      CLOSE  (UNIT = 8, ERR = 940)
C              terminations
      STOP
  920     WRITE  (1,1920)
 1920     FORMAT  (1H0,'ERROR IN OPENING FILE  -   PROGRAM ABORTED')
      STOP
  940     WRITE  (1,1940)
 1940     FORMAT  (1H0,'ERROR IN CLOSING FILE')
      STOP
      END
```

If the file is to be an unformatted but direct access file, we must supply a record length. For unformatted files, the record length is given in processor-dependent units; on a system that stores four bytes per system unit (that is, a 32-bit machine), the 23 columns (the file structure is given in section 7.4.2) requires 6 units. The OPEN command then becomes

```
OPEN (UNIT=8, FILE='OGIN.DAT', STATUS='NEW',
1                          ACCESS='DIRECT', RECL=6, ERR=920)
```

We have made use of all of the defaults in the above OPENs; some programmers like to spell out all of the parameters as a documentation aid.

In the following section, we will present a number of examples of the use of the file access commands combined with the associated I/O commands.

7.7 File applications

Of course, once we get into applications, the complications arise.

There are some points that we must discuss before we present a complete program illustrating some of the methods of file access. We cannot open an output file as a NEW file if it already exists. It is quite common in a production environment to write new information to existing data files, either to bring them up to date or because they are used to temporarily hold output reports. Thus some method must be devised for defining the file as either NEW if it does not exist or OLD if it does. Fortunately, the INQUIRE command allows us to check for the existence of a file.

The existence parameter (EXIST=*log*) of the INQUIRE command sets a logical variable as either TRUE or FALSE. Although this text will not thoroughly cover logical variables until section 8.2 (you can peek ahead if you want to), suffice it to say that we can define a variable as a logical with the statement

```
LOGICAL EXST
```

let the INQUIRE command set the value of EXST, and then use it in the program in the following way:

```
IF (EXST) ......
```

If EXST is true, the THEN option of the IF will be executed; if false, the ELSE option (if there is one) is executed. The false condition can be tested for with:

```
IF (.NOT. EXST) ......
```

The final problem is that there is no way of determining from a direct access file exactly how many records are in the file. The END= clause of the READ is inoperative with such files. In the majority of cases where direct access files are used, the number of records is fixed, as in the personnel file we discussed above. But in our earthwork application, this is not the case. Somehow, we will have to store the number of total records in the file so that we do not attempt to I/O beyond that number.

The following program illustrates a number of file commands and is part of our cross section analysis application. The input file (OGIN.DAT) was created by the preceding program. This program (PREPOG) edits the original data and creates three output files: OG.DAT contains the original data in formatted form, INDXOG.DAT is an index file, and PREPOG.TXT is a sequential, formatted file that contains the number of points and offset range for each station, along with error messages regarding any errors found by the editing process.

```
C                       PREPOG:  program to input, edit and file
C                                original ground data
C
C       Abstract:       input free-format data from OGIN.DAT.
C                       edit data and write to direct access file.
C
C       Input file OGIN.DAT:    free-format
C                               field 1:  station
C                                  "   2:  offset
C                                  "   3:  elevation
C
C       Edited for:     1.   stations increasing
C                       2.   offsets increase from left to right
```

```
C                     3.   zero offset exists
C                     4.   elevation vary by no more than 10' between
C                               adjacent points
C
C     Output files
C         OG.DAT:  direct access, formatted
C                     records 1 - n:  cross-section points:
C                         columns  1 - 8:  station   (xxxxx.xx)
C                            "     9 - 15:  offset   (xxxxx.x)
C                            "     16 - 23:  elevation (xxxxx.xx)
C         INDXOG.DAT:  sequential access, formatted
C                     records 1 - n:  index
C                         columns  1 - 8:  station
C                            "     10 - 14:  record number of last point
C                                               in station
C         PREPOG.TXT:  sequential, formatted report file:
C                     1.   stations with number of points and
C                            extremes
C                     2.   record number for station
C                     3.   error messages
C                         summary of run
C
C
      LOGICAL  IEX
C
      DIMENSION  STATN(10001), OFFSET(10001), ELEV(10001)
      DIMENSION  STATI(2000), INDEX(2000)
C
      DATA  NUMSTA, NUMPTS/ 2*1/,  NUMERR/ 0/
C
C                         begin processing
      WRITE  (1,1000)
 1000 FORMAT (///1H0,'Program PREPOG:  convert raw original ground')
C                         check existence of input file, open if there
      INQUIRE  (FILE='OGIN.DAT', EXIST=IEX)
      IF  (.NOT. IEX)  THEN
          WRITE  (1,1002)
 1002     FORMAT  (1H0,'File OGIN.DAT does not exist  -  ABORT RUN!')
          STOP
      ENDIF
      OPEN  (UNIT=11, FILE='OGIN.DAT', FORM='FORMATTED', STATUS='OLD')
C
```

```
C                      input routine
      READ  (11,*, END=20)  (STATN(I), OFFSET(I), ELEV(I), I=1,10001)
           WRITE  (1,1006)
 1006      FORMAT  (1H0,'EXCESSIVE DATA   -   ABORT RUN!')
           CLOSE  (UNIT=11)
           STOP
   20 CLOSE  (UNIT=11)
      NUMPTS = I - 1
      WRITE  (1,1020)  NUMPTS
 1020 FORMAT  (1H0, I5,' records')
      IF  (NUMPTS .EQ. 0)  STOP
C                      open report file
      INQUIRE  (FILE='PREPOG.TXT', EXIST=IEX)
      IF  (IEX)  THEN
              OPEN  (UNIT=12, FILE='PREPOG.TXT', FORM='FORMATTED',
     1                   STATUS='OLD')
         ELSE
              OPEN  (UNIT=12, FILE='PREPOG.TXT', FORM='FORMATTED',
     1                   STATUS='NEW')
      ENDIF
      WRITE  (12,1022)  NUMPTS
 1022 FORMAT  (1H1,'Preparation of Original Ground Data',
     1             I10,' points on file'//
     2          1H0,' Station  Records',8X,'Range', 20X,'Errors'/)
C
C                      develop index
      STATI(1) = STATN(1)
      DO 40  I = 2,NUMPTS
          IF  (STATN(I) .NE. STATI(NUMSTA))  THEN
              INDEX(NUMSTA) = I - 1
              NUMSTA = NUMSTA + 1
              IF  (NUMSTA .GT. 2000)  THEN
                  WRITE  (1,1024)
 1024             FORMAT  (1H0,'EXCESSIVE STATIONS   -   ABORT RUN!')
                  STOP
              ENDIF
              STATI(NUMSTA) = STATN(I)
          ENDIF
   40 CONTINUE
      INDEX(NUMSTA) = NUMPTS
C
```

```
C                        edit points in section, with output
       NP1 = 1
       DO 200  N = 1,NUMSTA
            NP2 = INDEX(N)
            WRITE  (12,1060)  STATI(N), NP1,NP2, OFFSET(NP1),OFFSET(NP2)
 1060       FORMAT  (1H0,F8.2, I7,'-',I5, 4X, F7.1,' to ',F7.1)
C                          edit for increasing station
            IF  (N .NE. 1  .AND.  STATI(I) .LE. STATI(I-1))  THEN
                WRITE  (12,1062)
 1062           FORMAT  (1H+, 50X,'STATION')
                NUMERR = NUMERR + 1
            ENDIF
C                          edit for increasing offsets
            NPP = NP1 + 1
            DO 100  I = NPP,NP2
                IF  (OFFSET(I) .LE. OFFSET(I-1))  THEN
                    WRITE  (12,1064)
 1064               FORMAT  (1H+, 60X,'OFFSET')
                    NUMERR = NUMERR + 1
                ENDIF
  100       CONTINUE
C                          edit for zero offset
            DO 120  I = NP1,NP2
                IF  (OFFSET(I) .EQ. 0.00)  GO TO 200
  120       CONTINUE
                WRITE  (12,1120)
 1120           FORMAT  (1H+, 70X,'ZERO')
                NUMERR = NUMERR + 1
  200 NP1 = NP2 + 1
C
C                    discontinue processing if there are errors
       IF  (NUMERR .GT. 0)  THEN
            WRITE  (12,1200)  NUMERR
            WRITE  (1,1200)  NUMERR
 1200       FORMAT  (1H0,'Edit completed with at least', I4,' errors'/
      1              1H0,'Report file:  PREPOG.TXT'/
      2              1H0,'Output files not generated!')
            STOP
       ENDIF
```

```
C                     check existence of output files and open
      INQUIRE  (FILE='OG.DAT', EXIST=IEX)
      IF  (IEX)  THEN
              OPEN  (UNIT=21, FILE='OG.DAT',FORM='FORMATTED',
     1                 STATUS='OLD', ACCESS='DIRECT', RECL=23)
          ELSE
              OPEN  (UNIT=21, FILE='OG.DAT',FORM='FORMATTED',
     1                 STATUS='NEW', ACCESS='DIRECT', RECL=23)
      ENDIF
      INQUIRE  (FILE='INDXOG.DAT', EXIST=IEX)
      IF  (IEX)  THEN
              OPEN  (UNIT=22, FILE='INDXOG.DAT',FORM='FORMATTED',
     1                 STATUS='OLD')
          ELSE
              OPEN  (UNIT=22, FILE='INDXOG.DAT',FORM='FORMATTED',
     1                 STATUS='NEW')
      ENDIF
C            write to output files
      DO 220  I = 1,NUMPTS
  220 WRITE  (21,1220, REC=I)  STATN(I), OFFSET(I), ELEV(I)
 1220 FORMAT  (F8.2, F7.1, F8.2)
      WRITE  (22,1222)  (STATI(I), INDEX(I), I=1,NUMSTA)
 1222 FORMAT  (F8.2, I6)
C            close files
      ENDFILE 22
      CLOSE  (UNIT=22)
      CLOSE  (UNIT=21)
      WRITE  (5,1224)
 1224 FORMAT  (1H0,'Output files OG.DAT and INDXOG.DAT written'/
     1            1H0,'Report file:  PREPOG.TXT'/
     2            1H0,'Processing complete')
      ENDFILE 12
      CLOSE  (UNIT=12)
C            termination
      STOP
      END
```

The output written to the PREPOG.TXT file has the following form:

```
Station  Records       Range                        Errors
1000.00      1-   13   -100.8 to   102.5
1050.00     14-   25   -105.6 to   112.55
1100.00      :    :       :    :       :
```

The beginning record number for each station (NP1) is calculated as one more than the ending record number of the previous station (NP2). The three possible error messages (STATION, OFFSET, and ZERO) begin (when they occur) in columns 51, 61, and 71, respectively, on the same line as the station.

To determine the number of records in the file OG.DAT, it is only necessary to read in the sequential file INDXOG.DAT using the END= clause of the READ statement to determine the number of stations. Then the index value associated with the last station is the number of points.

7.7.1 Exercise

Exercise 7–1

Set up a free-format data input file for the two stations given in section 6.4. (See section 7.4 for the easiest way to enter it.) Write a program to read the file and write it in the formatted fashion shown in section 6.4 to a disk file for later display and/or printing. Use file names of your own choosing, not default file names that may exist on your system.

7.8 File searching

In the last section we developed an index for our cross section file. This index allows us to access the file much more quickly. In an application involving this file, we could (provided we have enough memory) bring the entire file into the memory. But even with large memories, whether real or virtual, there is a limit. Especially in a multiuser environment, the need for large segments of memory by one program degrades the speed of all programs using the computer. Thus it is in the best interests of all concerned to utilize memory efficiently. In the case of large files, the use of an index that allows us to access the file quickly without overloading the memory is recommended.

As an example, let's look at a program that is intended to search out a particular point in the file. Recall the similar discussion (section 5A.3) on searching techniques for one-dimensional arrays. We could take the same approach here: scan the file starting at the beginning, reading one record at a time, and compare that record against a search key. Since our cross section file is sorted, the search is speeded up because once we search beyond the station in the search key (or beyond the offset in the same station as the search key), we know that the record is not there. We could go a step further and conduct a binary search of the file, thus significantly reducing the number of file accesses.

However, it is far more efficient to use an index for a sorted file. The method we will demonstrate involves reading the index into memory and accessing only the file records for the station we want. We then have a program that does not use too much memory but at the same time is quick and efficient.

```
C                    DISPLOG:  display selected points
C
C
C     Abstract:        input a desired point (station, offset)
C                      display record and record number
C
C     Input files:  OG.DAT:   direct access, formatted
C                      records 1 - n:  cross-section points
C                         columns  1 - 8:  station   (xxxxx.xx)
C                            "    9 - 15:  offset    (xxxxx.x)
C                            "   16 - 23:  elevation (xxxxx.xx)
C                      limit of 500 points per station assumed
C                   INDXOG.DAT:  sequential access, formatted
C                      records 1 - n:  index
C                         columns  1 - 8:  station   (xxxxx.xx)
C                            "   10 - 14:  record number of last
C                                          point in station
C
C     Input from keyboard in free format
C
C     Output:  display record and record number on screen
C
C
      DIMENSION  STATI(2001), INDEX(2001), RKEY(2)
      DIMENSION  OFFSET(500), ELEV(500)
C
      DATA  STATLS/ -1.00/
C
C
C               input index, determine number of stations and points
      OPEN  (UNIT=22, FILE='INDXOG.DAT', FORM='FORMATTED',
     1                STATUS='OLD')
      READ  (22,1000, END=20)  (STATI(I), INDEX(I), I=1,2001)
 1000 FORMAT  (F8.2, 1X, I5)
         WRITE  (1,1002)
 1002    FORMAT  (1H0,'EXCESSIVE STATIONS  -  RUN ABORTED')
         CLOSE  (UNIT=22)
         STOP
   20 CLOSE  (UNIT=22)
      NUMSTA = I - 1
      NUMPTS = INDEX(NUMSTA)
      WRITE  (1,1020)  NUMSTA, NUMPTS
 1020 FORMAT  (1H0,I5,' stations and', I6,' points on file')
```

```
C                    open point file
      OPEN  (UNIT=21, FILE='OG.DAT', FORM='FORMATTED', STATUS='OLD',
     1                 ACCESS='DIRECT', RECL=23)
C
C                    input loop
  100 WRITE  (1,1100)
 1100 FORMAT  (1H0,'Enter station, offset in free-format'/
     1                ' use end-of-data code to terminate')
      READ  (2,*, END=900, ERR=100)  RKEY
C                    if same as station in memory, don't re-read
      IF  (ABS (RKEY(1) - STATLS) .LT. 0.01)  GO TO 170
C                    search index
      DO 120  I = 1,NUMSTA
          IF  (ABS (RKEY(1) - STATI(I)) .LT. 0.01)  GO TO 140
  120 CONTINUE
          WRITE  (1,1120) RKEY(1)
 1120     FORMAT  (1H0,'Station', F9.2,' not on file')
          GO TO 100
C                    read in station
  140 IN2 = INDEX(I)
      IF  (I .EQ. 1)  IN1 = 1
      IF  (I .NE. 1)  IN1 = INDEX(I-1) + 1
      NP = IN2 - IN1 + 1
      IF  (NP .GT. 500)  THEN
          WRITE  (1,1140)
 1140     FORMAT  (1H0,'More than 500 points in section.',
     1                ' Only first 500 will be input.')
          NP = 500
      ENDIF
      DO 160  I = 1,NP
          READ  (21,1142, REC=IN1)  OFFSET(I), ELEV(I)
 1142     FORMAT  (8X, F7.1, F8.2)
  160 IN1 = IN1 + 1
C                    search for offset
  170 DO 180  I = 1,NP
          IF  (ABS (KEY(2) - OFFSET(I)) .LT. 0.01)  GO TO 200
  180 CONTINUE
          WRITE  (1,1180) RKEY
 1180     FORMAT  (1H0,'Station',F9.2,', offset',F8.1,' not on file')
          GO TO 100
```

```
C                      display record
  200 NREC = IN2 - NP + I
      WRITE  (1,1200)  RKEY, ELEV(I), NREC
 1200 FORMAT  (1H0,'Station',F9.2,' at offset',F8.1,
    1                       ' has an elevation of',F9.2,' at record',I6)
C                      save value of station in memory
      STATLS = RKEY(1)
      GO TO 100
C
C                      close file and terminate
  900 CLOSE  (UNIT=21)
      STOP
      END
```

In this program, there is no need to read in the station from the point file, since the only points read will automatically be at that station. As another time-saving device, the station in memory is saved so that a request for another point at the same station does not require a reread of the same records. To speed up the process even more, a binary search of the offsets could be used.

7.9 Summary and additional exercises

We have given all of the FORTRAN 77 file access commands and will illustrate additional applications in upcoming chapters. In addition, almost all systems provide a number of file subprograms and routines that simplify programming; however, they are not part of the FORTRAN specifications and can destroy the portability of a program. And again, we must warn of system-dependent exceptions to the rules.

topic	*section*
ACCESS=	7.6
BLANK=	7.6
DEFINE FILE	7.5
DIRECT=	7.6
END=	7.3
ERR=	7.3, 7.6
EXIST=	7.6
FILE=	7.6
FIND	7.5
FMT=	7.3
FORM=	7.6
FORMATTED=	7.6
IOSTAT=	7.3, 7.6
LOGICAL	7.7

NAME=	7.6
NAMED=	7.6
NEXTREC=	7.6
NUMBER=	7.6
OPENED=	7.6
PRINT	7.3
READ	7.3
REC=	7.3, 7.5
RECL=	7.6
SEQUENTIAL=	7.6
STATUS=	7.6
WRITE	7.3
UNFORMATTED=	7.6
UNIT=	7.3, 7.6

7.9.1 Exercises

Exercise 7–2

Write a program to generate two identical files, one a NEW file, the other a SCRATCH file. In each file, write the numbers from 1 to 100 in four columns, 25 lines in the format:

```
 1     26     51     76
 2     27     52     77
 :      :      :      :
 :      :      :      :
25     50     75    100
```

After the execution is finished, check the directory to see if the NEW file is still there, but the SCRATCH file is not.

Exercise 7–3

Write a program to read the above file into a one-dimensional array such that the first element is 1, the second is 2, and so forth. Write onto a new file in the format:

```
 1     2     3     4     5     6     7     8     9    10
11    12    13    ..    ..    ..    ..    ..    ..    ..
..    ..    ..    ..    ..    ..    ..    ..    ..    ..
..    ..    ..    ..    ..    ..    97    98    99   100
```

8

Tools and techniques

8.1 Introduction

This chapter is a grab bag of assorted topics intended to pull together many of the details that we have passed over either for the sake of simplicity or because of limited application. By this time, however, the reader has gained enough sophistication to appreciate many of them and see their application. Furthermore, the work of the last two chapters allows us to demonstrate their usefulness instead of just presenting a collection of unapplicable commands. Again we will concentrate almost entirely on FORTRAN 77, but we will indicate the availability of these tools and techniques in the earlier versions.

This chapter contains some very detailed explanations, and the reader is cautioned not to skip over them too lightly. We will review a number of statements in order to examine alternatives and additional properties. As in any "foreign" language, there are little quirks and idioms that are familiar to the experienced, but not to the neophyte. The author has been working in this language for over 24 years and still finds that there is much to learn.

8.2 Variable typing

Unless the program specifies otherwise, FORTRAN automatically defaults to the type INTEGER if the variable name starts with the letters I, J, K, L, M, or N and to type REAL if the variable name starts with any letter in the range A–H or O–Z.

The number of bits associated with a particular variable is a function of the architecture of the machine. The specifications for FORTRAN 77 simply state that one numeric storage unit is to be used for any standard numeric variable (INTEGER, REAL, or LOGICAL) and two storage units for DOUBLE PRECISION or COMPLEX reals. Since some micro- and older minicomputers are 16-bit machines (16 bits is too small for a real variable), they use the 32-bit definition. Thus we assume a minimum of 32 bits for the storage unit. Although the larger mainframes may go as high as 60 bits, we will use the 32-bit standard for our explanations since it will be adequate for the majority of applications.

We thus assume that the default integer is one of 32 bits with a range of $-2,147,483,648$ to $+2,147,483,647$. However, most of the values that we work with will easily fit within the 16-bit range of -32,768 to $+32,767$. Smaller storage requirements not only save memory and disk space but also compute faster. It behooves us as responsible programmers to control our space and time requirements, and so most programmers prefer to work with the shorter integer except where the longer one is necessary. Some systems can be forced to default to the 16-bit integer with a system-dependent directive placed directly in the program; on the IBM PC, for example, $STORAGE:2 will do just that. FORTRAN 77 provides us with only a single type command for INTEGER, but most implementations provide more control—the INTEGER*2 type command for the 2-byte or 16-bit integer and INTEGER*4 for the 4-byte or 32-bit integer. Although it is not a feature of FORTRAN 77, some implementations permit a BYTE type that uses 8 bits with a range from -128 to $+127$.

With reals there are no inconsistencies, since there are standard precision reals (REAL) and double precision reals (DOUBLE PRECISION). Complex numbers (COMPLEX) are made up of two standard precision reals and are stored in two storage units; however, some implementations have double precision complex (DOUBLE COMPLEX), which combines two double precision reals.

The type statements also allow the user to add the dimension value, although the user has the option of using a type statement and a dimension statement for the same purpose. For example,

```
DOUBLE PRECISION X(50), Y(50)
```

is the same as

```
DOUBLE PRECISION X, Y
DIMENSION X(50), Y(50)
```

8.2.1 LOGICAL type

The LOGICAL variable is used to store only one bit that represents either true or false. Certainly using a 32-bit storage unit would be quite wasteful. Thus there are implementations with such types as LOGICAL*1, LOGICAL*2, and LOGICAL*4, the last being the default. There are a number of ways in which the bipolar state is stored: values of 0 and 1 may represent false and true, respectively; another implementation may use 0 and -1 (all bits on) for false and true; yet another uses even and odd, the last bit being the critical one. To the programmer it should not matter how the information is stored since he or she uses it only for logical purposes.

The application of the LOGICAL type is different from that of the numeric types, although it is grouped with the numeric data types since it contains a numeric value. The programmer can store the results of logical expressions in logical variables and can test them with very simple IF statements, as we did in section 7.7. Two logical constants, .TRUE. and .FALSE., are available to be used in either data or assignment statements. For example, the following program segment uses logical variables to keep track of errors:

```
LOGICAL ERRORS, PROBLM
          :
DATA   ERRORS, PROBLM/ 2 * .FALSE./
          :
          :
IF  (A .LT. 0.00) ERRORS = .TRUE.
          :
PROBLM = NUMPTS .NE. NUMREC .OR. TOTAL .LT. 0.00
          :
IF  (ERRORS .OR. PROBLM) STOP
          :
```

Summary of numeric data types

Data Type	Storage Requirements (Bytes)
BYTE	1
LOGICAL	4
LOGICAL*1	1
LOGICAL*2	2
LOGICAL*4	4
INTEGER	4
INTEGER*2	2
INTEGER*4	4
REAL	4
DOUBLE PRECISION	8
COMPLEX	8

8.2.2 The IMPLICIT statement

Not only can the programmer control the size of storage, but he or she can also dictate the data type, overriding the default. There are two ways to do this. An IMPLICIT statement allows the user to define either an individual letter or a range of letters as the beginning letter for a data type. General type statements like those shown above can also be used to set the type (or mode) of any individual variable name. The following code gives examples of both methods:

```
        IMPLICIT INTEGER*2       (I, J, M, N)
        IMPLICIT INTEGER*4       (K)
        IMPLICIT LOGICAL         (L)
        IMPLICIT REAL            (A-H)
        IMPLICIT DOUBLE PRECISION (O-Z)
C
        REAL     LENGTH
        INTEGER  UNITS
```

In this program segment, all variables starting with I, J, M, and N are short integers and those starting with K are long integers. All variables starting with L are logicals, with the exception of LENGTH, which is individually declared as a real. All variables beginning with a letter in the range A–H are single precision reals, and those beginning with a letter in the range O–Z are double precision reals, with the exception of UNITS, which is individually typed as integer. These *type statements* must be the first statements in the program (except for PARAMETER statements, which will be covered in section 8.3). Of course, no letter may appear in two IMPLICIT statements. Actually, in the above example, the IMPLICITs for INTEGER*4 and REAL are unnecessary.

8.2.3 Intrinsic functions

Each intrinsic function comes in a number of versions. Usually there will be a version for real, one for double precision, and one for complex. For example, FORTRAN 77 calls for the absolute value functions ABS, DABS, and CABS for standard precision real, double precision real, and complex, respectively, as well as IABS for integer. On systems that can define both INTEGER*2 and INTEGER*4, there must be two versions of the integer absolute value function; the generic name IABS will usually refer to the INTEGER*4 version, and the system will have its own names for the two versions. For example, the DEC VAX has IIABS for INTEGER*2 and JIABS for INTEGER*4, the latter identical to IABS.

(See the appendix B for a list of the intrinsic functions defined in FORTRAN 77.)

IMPLICIT statements do not apply to intrinsic functions. Thus using an IMPLICIT statement to define the letter A as an integer does not change the type of the intrinsic function ABS. Arithmetic statement functions and internal functions can have their names typed to change the mode from the usual default mode. Within a function itself, the type may be controlled by either a type statement or a header like:

```
      DOUBLE PRECISION FUNCTION RND2 (AMOUNT)
C
      IMPLICIT DOUBLE PRECISION (A-H, U-Z)
                    :
```

All real variables are typed as double precision except those in the range O–T; the function name RND2 has been explicitly typed as double precision since R is not in that range.

8.2.4 Review questions

8–1. For the following type declarations:

```
      IMPLICIT INTEGER*2 (I-K)
      IMPLICIT DOUBLE PRECISION (A-D, W-Z)
      INTEGER*2 HEIGHT, WIDTH, LENGTH
      REAL XIN, YIN, ZIN
```

what are the types of the following variables?

a. DIST	d. WIDTH	g. NOTO
b. WIN	e. JOINT	h. LBIG
c. HITE	f. MONEY	i. ZIN

8–2. Determine the results (.TRUE. or .FALSE.) that are stored in the logical variable LGG.

```
      LOGICAL LGG
   a. LGG = 10 .GT. 5 .AND. -10 .GT. -5
   b. LGG = 10 .EQ. 10 .AND. 10 .NE. 10
   c. LGG = 10 .EQ. 10 .OR. 10 .NE. 10
   d. LGG = .TRUE.
   e. LGG = .NOT. 10 .GT. 5
```

8.3 The PARAMETER statement

In the earlier versions of FORTRAN, the DATA statement was often used to set a constant. It was much easier to set a variable to a constant value than to repeat that value a number of times throughout the program. Using a variable name instead of the value also serves as a documentation aid. However, a variable set in a DATA statement, like one defined in an assignment statement, can be modified during execution.

In FORTRAN 77, the PARAMETER statement looks like an assignment statement, but it actually represents a string substitution. For example, in the following program

```
      PARAMETER (PI = 3.14159265, TWOPI = 2.00 * PI)
C
   20 READ   (2,*, END=90) RADIUS
      AREA    = PI * RADIUS * RADIUS
      CIRCUM  = TWOPI * RADIUS
      WRITE (1,*) AREA, CIRCUM
      GO TO 20
C
   90 STOP
      END
```

the string 'PI' is replaced by '3.14159265' whenever it appears as an apparent variable name; any place the string 'TWOPI' appears, it is replaced with '2.00 * PI', which in turn becomes '2.00 * 3.14159265'. Thus to the compiler, the two statements following the READ appear to be:

```
AREA = 3.14159265 * RADIUS * RADIUS
CIRCUM = 2.00 * 3.14159265 * RADIUS
```

Thus, since the PARAMETER statement defines a variable that remains constant throughout a program, it is more appropriate than the DATA statement for representing constants.

A PARAMETER equivalence consists of a symbolic name, an equal sign, and either a constant, the symbolic name of a constant, or a constant expression. The constant may be a logical .TRUE. or .FALSE. if the symbolic name is defined as a logical.

A constant set by a PARAMETER statement may not be used in a FORMAT statement, but it can be used anywhere else, including the DATA statement. The PARAMETER statement must appear after any type statement that affects it and before it is used elsewhere in the program.

The PARAMETER statement does not exist in the subset of FORTRAN 77.

8.4 COMMON

An alternative method for transmitting data from one module of a programming system to another is to store it in a section of the memory accessible by all modules. The information to be stored in this common area is listed in and allocated to memory by a COMMON statement.

In the older, single-user computers, the COMMON variables were stored in high memory, starting at the top of memory and working downward; in contrast, the rest of the program and data were laid out starting at the lower end of memory just above the operating system and moving upward. If the two areas overlapped, the program would not fit in memory. In our newer, virtual memory, multiprogramming computers, the location of COMMON is not as rigidly defined, but the results are the same to the programmer.

Basically, COMMON works by allocating the memory downward in the order of the listed variables. For example,

```
COMMON A, B, C
```

would allocate the highest four bytes of memory (assuming a 32-bit real) to the variable A, the next highest four bytes to B, and the next highest four to C. Then if we have a subprogram such as

```
SUBROUTINE SUBR

COMMON R, S, T
```

the variable addressed as A in the mainline program is addressable as R in the subprograms, likewise for B and S, C and T. Thus, as in argument lists, the location of the variable in the list is the important point, not the actual symbolic name.

There are two types of COMMON. The type we have just shown is called blank (or unnamed) COMMON. The rules imply that the mainline must contain all of the elements in COMMON; the subprograms can contain abbreviated lists but must still maintain corresponding locations.

8.4.1 Named COMMON

The other type of COMMON is called named COMMON; it has an identifying name that appears in all subprograms using it. Furthermore, the list of variables must be of the same length in all modules using a particular named COMMON (although the variable names themselves need not be the same). Named COMMON does *not* start necessarily at the top of memory but at some alternatively defined location; thus not all COMMONs need be listed in a routine. It is very possible to have:

```
        COMMON A, B, C
        COMMON /ERRORS/ NUMERR, NMPTER, NMSTER
        COMMON /FLAGS/ IFLAG, JFLAG, KFLAG, LFLAG


        SUBROUTINE SUBR2
C
        COMMON /FLAGS/ IFLAG, JFLAG, KFLAG, LFLAG
```

This method relieves the necessity of listing all COMMONs in a subprogram that may only use one or two blocks. The COMMONs can be listed in any order, which may differ from module to module. An alternative syntax for blank common is:

```
COMMON // A, B, C
```

The dimension of an array may be included in the COMMON statement, or it may be left in the DIMENSION statement with only the array name in the COMMON statement.

An EQUIVALENCE statement may be used in conjunction with the COMMON statement, but it cannot extend COMMON in either direction beyond what has been defined as COMMON.

8.4.2 Application of COMMON

To illustrate the use of COMMON, let us break down the large program in section 7.7 into four subroutines and a mainline. The CALLs to the subroutines have been underlined:

```
C                     PREPOG:  program to input, edit and file
C                              original ground data
C
C    Abstract:        input free-format data from OGIN.DAT.
C                     edit data and write to direct access file.
C
C                          :
C                          :
C
C                     ****    MAINLINE    ****
C
     LOGICAL  IEX
C
     COMMON   STATN(10001), OFFSET(10001), ELEV(10001),
    1            NUMPTS, NUMSTA
C
     COMMON   /STNDX/  STATI(2000), INDEX(2000)
C
C                     initialize counters
     NUMSTA = 1
     NUMPTS = 1
     NUMERR = 0
C
C                     begin processing
                          :
                          :
```

```
C
C                         input routine
      CALL INPTOG
C                         open report file
                              :
                              :
C
C                         develop index
      CALL DEVNDX
C
C                         edit points in section, with output
      CALL EDITPT (NUMERR)
C
C                         discontinue processing if there are errors
                              :
                              :
C                         check existence of output files and open
                              :
                              :
C               write to output files
      DO 220  I = 1,NUMPTS
  220 WRITE  (21,1220, REC=I)  STATN(I), OFFSET(I), ELEV(I)
 1220 FORMAT  (F8.2, F7.1, F8.2)
      CALL WRNDX (NUMSTA)
C               close files
                              :
                              :
C               termination
      STOP
      END




                     SUBROUTINES



C                         INPTOG:  input original ground
C
      SUBROUTINE  INPTOG
C
      COMMON  STATN(10001), OFFSET(10001), ELEV(10001), NUMPTS
```

```
C
      READ  (11,*, END=20)  (STATN(I), OFFSET(I), ELEV(I), I=1,10001)
          WRITE  (1,1006)
 1006     FORMAT  (1H0,'EXCESSIVE DATA  -  ABORT RUN!')
          CLOSE  (UNIT=11)
          STOP
   20 CLOSE  (UNIT=11)
      NUMPTS = I - 1
      WRITE  (1,1020) NUMPTS
 1020 FORMAT  (1H0, I5,' records')
      IF  (NUMPTS .EQ. 0)  STOP
C                   return
      RETURN
      END
C                 DEVNDX:  develop index
C
      SUBROUTINE  DEVNDX
C
      COMMON  STATN(10001), OFFSET(10001), ELEV(10001),
     1          NUMPTS, NUMSTA
      COMMON  /STNDX/  STATI(2000), INDEX(2000)

      STATI(1) = STATN(1)
      DO 40  I = 2,NUMPTS
          IF  (STATN(I) .NE. STATI(NUMSTA))  THEN
              INDEX(NUMSTA) = I - 1
              NUMSTA = NUMSTA + 1
              IF  (NUMSTA .GT. 2000)  THEN
                  WRITE  (1,1024)
 1024             FORMAT  (1H0,'EXCESSIVE STATIONS  -  ABORT RUN!')
                  STOP
              ENDIF
              STATI(NUMSTA) = STATN(I)
          ENDIF
   40 CONTINUE
      INDEX(NUMSTA) = NUMPTS
C                 return
      RETURN
      END


C                 EDITPT:  edit points
C
      SUBROUTINE  EDITPT (NUMERR)
```

```
C
      COMMON  STATN(10001), OFFSET(10001), ELEV(10001),
     1          NUMPTS, NUMSTA
      COMMON  /STNDX/  STATI(2000), INDEX(2000)

C                   edit points in section, with output
      NP1 = 1
      DO 200  N = 1,NUMSTA
          NP2 = INDEX(N)
          WRITE  (12,1060)  STATI(N), NP1,NP2, OFFSET(NP1),OFFSET(NP2)
 1060     FORMAT  (1H0,F8.2, I7','',I5, 4X, F7.1,' to ',F7.1)
C                       edit for increasing station
          IF  (N .NE. 1 .AND. STATI(I) .LE. STATI(I-1))  THEN
              WRITE  (12,1062)
 1062         FORMAT  (1H+, 50X,'STATION')
              NUMERR = NUMERR + 1
          ENDIF
C                       edit for increasing offsets
          NPP = NP1 + 1
          DO 100  I = NPP,NP2
              IF  (OFFSET(I) .LE. OFFSET(I-1))  THEN
                  WRITE  (12,1064)
 1064             FORMAT  (1H+, 60X,'OFFSET')
                  NUMERR = NUMERR + 1
              ENDIF
  100     CONTINUE
C                       edit for zero offset
          DO 120  I = NP1,NP2
              IF  (OFFSET(I) .EQ. 0.00)  GO TO 200
  120     CONTINUE
              WRITE  (12,1120)
 1120         FORMAT  (1H+, 70X,'ZERO')
              NUMERR = NUMERR + 1
  200 NP1 = NP2 + 1
C
C                   return
      RETURN
      END


C                   WRINDX:  write index
C
      SUBROUTINE  WRINDX (NUMSTA)
```

```
C
      COMMON  /STNDX/  STATI(2000), INDEX(2000)
C
      WRITE  (22,1222)  (STATI(I), INDEX(I), I=1,NUMSTA)
 1222 FORMAT  (F8.2, I6)
C              return
      RETURN
      END
```

In this program the arrays were all dimensioned directly in the COMMON statement. Because a DATA statement cannot be used at all for variables in blank common, the three variables NUMSTA, NUMPTS, and NUMERR, which were previously defined in a DATA statement, had to be defined in assignment statements. However, there is a way (to be discussed in the next section) to DATA variables in named COMMON.

The routine INPTOG does not access the variable NUMSTA, which is therefore left out of the COMMON in the subprogram. In the routine EDITPT, the variable NUMERR was transmitted to the subprogram by placing it in an argument list. The routine WRINDX needed only the named common and the variable NUMSTA from the blank common; the latter was transmitted in an argument list.

In many computer systems, especially mini- and micro-computer systems, where the data is paged or stored in separate banks of the memory, any array larger than a given size must be placed in COMMON. This requirement is system dependent; neglecting to follow it may not always yield an error message, but the program will not run correctly.

8.4.3 Exercise

Exercise 8–1

Redo exercise 4–14 at the end of chapter 4 (section 4.8) by placing the variables NGROSS, NDOZEN, and NUNITS in COMMON. The other variables in the argument lists should be left there.

8.5 BLOCK DATA and SAVE

We mentioned in the previous section that it is possible to use a DATA statement to initialize a variable in named COMMON. This requires a separate module called BLOCK DATA. For example, to initialize the arrays STATI and INDEX to zero, we could use the following module:

```
      BLOCK DATA INITLZ
C
      COMMON /STNDX/ STATI(2000), INDEX(2000)
```

```
C
      DATA STATI, INDEX/ 2000*0.00, 2000*0/
C
      END
```

A BLOCK DATA can contain only specification statements such as the type statements IMPLICIT, PARAMETER, DIMENSION, COMMON, EQUIV-ALENCE, and DATA. There can be no executable statements in this module, but it must terminate with an END statement. This module must be compiled and then linked in with the mainline and subprograms.

Variables that appear in only one module of a programming system are called *local* variables. Those appearing in COMMON or in argument lists are called *global* variables. (It is the location that is global, not the variable. It is possible to use the same variable name in two routines; as long as the variables are not related through either COMMON or the subprogram variable lists, they are local in each routine.) The rules of FORTRAN state that a local variable contained in a subprogram need not be saved by the system when the RETURN is executed. Although most systems do so and most programmers do expect that to happen, it is safer to resort to the proper mechanism—using a SAVE statement. The variables listed in the SAVE statement are preserved after the execution of the routine and can be reaccessed upon returning to the subprogram. If SAVE appears without a variable list, all local variables in the subprogram are saved.

We will illustrate the SAVE statement with a subprogram that checks a key against the records in a file. Since this subprogram is intended to be used in many applications, it is efficient to have the subprogram also read in the file. However, it would be wasteful to read in the file each time the subprogram is accessed. A good solution would be to read in the file only the first time the subprogram is accessed and not thereafter. We can do this by placing a counter in the routine and initializing it to zero in a DATA statement; since a DATA statement is *not* executable, reentering the subprogram does not reset the counter to zero. However, a SAVE is needed to ensure that the counter is not destroyed.

```
C              FINDPT:  Fuction to return elevation of desired point
C
C    Abstract: searches for a point in the original ground arrays
C                    returns elevation if point there
C                    returns -9999.00 if point not on file
C                    reads in file on first entrance
C
      FUNCTION  FINDPT  (RKEY)
C
      LOGICAL  IEX
C
      COMMON  STATN(10001), OFFSET(10001), ELEV(10001), NUMPTS
      DIMENSION  RKEY(2)
```

```
C
      SAVE  NTIMES
      DATA  NTIMES/ 0/
C
C                    on first entrance, check existence of input file,
C                        open if there and input
      IF  (NTIMES .EQ. 0)  THEN
          INQUIRE  (FILE='OGIN.DAT', EXIST=IEX)
          IF  (.NOT. IEX)  THEN
              WRITE  (1,1002)
 1002         FORMAT  (1H0,'File OGIN.DAT does not exist!')
              STOP
          ENDIF
          OPEN  (UNIT=11, FILE='OGIN.DAT', FORM='FORMATTED',
     1                      STATUS='OLD')
C
C                    input routine
          READ  (11,*, END=20)
     1    (STATN(I), OFFSET(I), ELEV(I), I=1,10001)
              WRITE  (1,1006)
 1006         FORMAT  (1H0,'EXCESSIVE DATA  -  ABORT RUN!')
              CLOSE  (UNIT=11)
              STOP
   20     CLOSE  (UNIT=11)
          NUMPTS = I - 1
          IF  (NUMPTS .EQ. 0)  STOP
      ENDIF
C
C                    enter here after first time
      NTIMES = NTIMES + 1
```

```
C                       binary search to find point
      LBOT = 1
      LTOP = NUMSTA + 1
      FINDPT = -9999.00
      DO 100   I = 1,14
          LMID = (LBOT + LTOP) / 2
          IF  (ABS (RKEY(1) - STATN (LMID)) .LT. 0.01  .AND.
     1          ABS (RKEY(2) - OFFSET(LMID)) .LT. 0.01)  THEN
                  FINDPT = ELEV(LMID)
                  RETURN
          ENDIF
          IF  (RKEY(1) - STATN(LMID)  60, 20, 40
   20     IF  (RKEY(2) .LT. OFFSET(LMID))  GO TO 60
   40     LBOT = LMID
          GO TO 100
   60     LTOP = LMID
  100 CONTINUE
C                       termination
      RETURN
      END
```

8.6 INTRINSIC and EXTERNAL

The INTRINSIC statement allows the programmer to use an intrinsic function supplied by the system library (with the exception of the type conversion, lexical relationship, and minimum and maximum functions) as an argument to a subprogram. The EXTERNAL statement allows the programmer to indicate that an argument to a subprogram is actually a user-written subprogram. As examples, we will use the intrinsic functions SIN and COS and the user-written function PERI in the application below to determine the two sides and perimeter of a triangle from the hypotenuse and one angle.

```
C               sides and perimeter of a triangle
C
      PARAMETER  (D2R=3.14159 / 180.00)
      EXTERNAL  PERI
      INTRINSIC  SIN, COS
C
```

```
C
   20 WRITE   (1,1020)
 1020 FORMAT  (1HO, 'Enter hypotenuse, angle (degrees)')
      READ   (2,*, END=90)  HYPOT, ANGLE
         ANGLE=D2R * ANGLE
         CALL TRIANG  (HYPOT, ANGLE, SIN, OPPOS)
         CALL TRIANG  (HYPOT, ANGLE, COS, ADJCNT)
         CALL TRIANG  (HYPOT, ANGLE, PERI, PERIM)
         WRITE  (1,1022)  OPPOS, ADJCNT, PERIM
 1022    FORMAT (1H ,'Sides =', 2F8.2, '    Perimeter =', F8.2)
      GO TO 20
C
   90 STOP
      END


             SUBROUTINE  TRIANG  (H, A, F, S)
C
      S = H * F (A)
      RETURN
      END


             FUNCTION  PERI  (A)
C
      PERI = SIN(A) + COS(A) + 1.00
      RETURN
      END
```

The INTRINSIC and EXTERNAL statements must appear before any executable statements.

8.7 PAUSE and STOP

The PAUSE statement allows the programmer to cause a temporary halt in the operation of a program; entering a system-dependent command (usually CONTINUE) then causes the program to continue. The PAUSE may include a number of up to five digits or a character constant to present a display on the screen:

```
      :
PAUSE  8
      :
```

An alternative method that requires less input effort to restart the program is to request input that can consist of just a RETURN:

```
              :
    WRITE  (1,1000)
1000 FORMAT  (1H ,'Press RETURN to continue display')
    READ  (2,1002)  IDUMMY
1002 FORMAT  (I1)
              :
```

This type of coding is useful to stop a screen from scrolling after displaying 20 lines, for example, giving the user time to read the data before proceeding to the next "page."

The PAUSE is very useful in an operation in which printer output is sent directly from the computer. Here the temporary halt is useful for changing forms or testing forms lineup.

Similarly, the STOP statement may also include a number of up to five digits or a character constant:

```
              :
STOP   'end of run'
END
```

8.8 Computed and assigned GO TO

The computed GO TO is a conditional branch instruction based on the integer value of an index. The syntax of the instruction is:

```
GO TO (n1, n2, n3, n4, ..., nm), index
```

If *index* = 1, the branch is made to the first statement, the one numbered *n1;* if *index* = 2, the branch is made to the second statement, numbered *n2,* and so forth up to a value of *index* = *m*. If the value of index is less than 1 or greater than *m* (the number of branches in the list), execution continues with the next sequential statement. The index may be an integer variable or expression.

(In earlier versions of FORTRAN, the results of an out-of-range index were not defined and became system dependent. One possibility was that the rule above adopted in FORTRAN 77 was implemented; another possibility was to use the first branch for values less than 1 and the last branch for values greater than the limit; another possibility was a bomb-out in the form of an infinite loop or a halt.)

The computed GO TO is very useful in situations where selections are to be made from a menu, as in the following program segment:

```
         :
100 WRITE  (1,1100)
1100 FORMAT   (1H0,'Enter 1 for listing'/
   1          1H ,' 2 for edit'/
   2          1H ,' 3 to summarize'/
   3          1H ,' 4 to write file onto disk'/
   4          1H ,' 8 to terminate run')
    READ (2,*, ERR=100) IOP
         GO TO (200, 300, 380, 700, 100, 100, 100, 900), IOP
         GO TO 100
         :
```

8.8.1 ASSIGN statement

The ASSIGN statement lets us use a variable statement number. The assigned GO TO statement has a variable rather than a statement number and comes in two forms, unconditional and computed, both shown below. That variable, however, can be given a value only by an ASSIGN statement, for example

```
       :
ASSIGN 450 TO IBRANCH
       :
       :
GO TO IBRANCH
       :
       :
GO TO IBRANCH, (100, 200, 450, 900)
       :
```

In the case of the computed version of the assigned GO TO, the specifications state that the value assigned to the variable must appear in the list; there is nothing said about what happens if it does not.

The ASSIGN is also used to link a statement number with the FMT= clause of an I/O command:

```
         :
    ASSIGN 1200 TO NSFMT
1200 FORMAT  (1H0, 3I8)
         :
         :
    WRITE  (6, FMT=NSFMT) I, J, K
         :
```

8.9 The FORMAT statement revisited

We have touched upon various features of the FORMAT statement in many of the previous sections. At this point we will give a thorough treatment of one of the most important statements in the language. Despite its complexities, the FORMAT statement provides the programmer with more flexibility with less coding than is found in any other language. The emphasis in this section will be on output, since input is sufficiently covered in sections 2.7 and 3.8.

8.9.1 Integer edit descriptors: Iw and Iw.m

The I edit descriptors are used to input or output integer variables. w represents the field width, for example, the number of columns allocated to the value. m represents the minimum number of digits output and has no effect on input. Unless a minimum field is specified, the output value is preceded by blanks; the value 0 yields a single zero. A negative value has a minus sign preceding the first printed digit.

Examples

value	format	output
		Columns: 123456
64	I4	64
64	I4.3	064
0	I4	0
0	I4.0	all blank
−64	I4	−64
−6420	I4	****

8.9.2 Real and double precision edit descriptors: Fw.d, Ew.d, Dw.d, and Gw.d

These edit descriptors are used to input and output real, double precision, and complex values. In each case, w represents the field width and d the number of significant digits. A complex variable is I/Oed as two reals, requiring two edit descriptors.

In F format, the number appears in standard decimal form, rounded to d decimal places. The value is right-justified and preceded by blanks. Values less than 1.0 have a zero preceding the decimal point. Space must be left for a minimum of d digits, the decimal point, the leading digit, and a possible minus sign; thus the general rule is that w must be greater than or equal to $d+3$.

Ew.d and Dw.d (exponential and double) editing are identical; each is used to input or output real numbers in exponential format. The value is rounded to d significant digits and is right-justified in normalized form, with the decimal point to the left of the first significant digit; this is followed by the exponent, which consists of either a D or an E, the appropriate sign, and the power of 10. Space must be allowed for the four-character exponent, the d digits, the decimal point, the leading zero, and a possible sign; thus the general rule is that w must be greater than or equal to $d+7$.

Another allowable form of the E format is E$w.d$E$e,$ where e represents the number of digits in the exponent. This form is useful for those computers that handle a very large range of reals where the exponent can be more than the usual two digits.

The G$w.d$ and G$w.d$Ee formats (g for *general* editing) combine the E and F formatting specifications and adjust the output form to the value of the number. Magnitudes less than 0.1 are output in exponential format, as are values that would not fit in the specified field if F format were used; otherwise, the output is the same as if F format had been specified.

Examples

value	format	output 1........12
		Columns: 12345678901234567890
123.456	F8.2	123.46
123.456	E12.5 or D12.5	0.12346E+03
−123.456	G12.5	-123.45600
−123.456	E16.5E4	-0.12346E+0003
0.0	F6.0	0.
−0.01	G9.2	-0.10E-01
−0.49	F6.0	-0.

8.9.3 Scaling: kP

As an aid to the input and output of very large and very small real numbers, FORTRAN provides a scale factor, represented here by k. k is a positive or negative number that indicates how many places the decimal point should be moved during the scaling operation; using the scale factor is equivalent to multiplying the number by the kth power of 10 or 10**k. P formatting applies only to real values. The scale factor, once expressed, applies to all of the following real format specifications until a new scale factor is specified. To return to the default scale factor of 10**0, a scaling factor of 0P must be specified.

In input formats, the scale factor only applies where the input value does not have an exponent; the input value is divided by the *k*th power of 10.

Examples

	input	1........12	*format*	*stored as*
Columns:	12345678901234567890			
	123.456		2PF10.2	1.23456
	123.456		−2PE10.2	12345.6
	123.456E2		5PE10.2	12345.6

On output, the value is multiplied by 10**k*. The statements:

```
     A = -123.456
     WRITE (1,1000) A, A, A, A
1000 FORMAT (1H ,F10.2, 2PF10.2, F12.2, -2PF10.2)
```

will produce the following output:

```
                    1........12........23........34..
Columns:  1234567890123456789012345678901234567890 12
            -123.46 -12345.60    -12345.60      -1.23
```

8.9.4 Logical edit descriptor: Lw

The logical edit descriptor is used to input or output the two possible values of a logical variable. For input, the value may begin with optional blanks but must contain a period followed by either a T or an F. Additional characters may follow the T or F; thus it is not unusual for a user to spell out .TRUE. or .FALSE. even though the first two characters are sufficient.

As output, a T or an F will be printed or displayed, preceded by *w*-1 blanks.

8.9.5 Positional editing: nX, Tc, TLc, and TRc

In addition to the skip edit (*n*X), which skips over spaces, leaving them blank, there are tab (T) edits that give the programmer more positive control of the location of the input/output field. Consider a pointer that points to the next column to be accessed. All of the previously mentioned numeric and logical edits leave the pointer at the column following the last one in the numeric or logical field. The tab edit allows the user to reset the pointer at any desired column, including one already processed. For example:

```
     READ (2,1000) AMOUNT, IDOLAR, ICENTS
1000 FORMAT (F6.2, T1,I3,1X,I2)
```

reads the real variable AMOUNT from columns 1 through 6; then the pointer is moved back to column 1 and the integer variables IDOLAR and ICENTS are read from columns 1 through 3 and columns 5 through 6, respectively, skipping column 4 where the decimal point is assumed to be placed.

There are two alternative tab edits: TLc, which moves the pointer c columns to the left (limited to moving only as far back as column 1), and TRc, which moves the pointer c columns to the right. Using these edits, the above program segment would be written as:

```
     READ (2,1000) AMOUNT, IDOLAR, ICENTS
1000 FORMAT (F6.2, TL6,I3, TR1,I2)
```

T format is very useful for output because it saves a great deal of counting when locating values and literal fields. However, as is always the case when dealing with any output involving carriage control, the programmer must remember that the carriage control column is considered column 1. Therefore, to begin a field in printing column 21, the programmer must specify T22. For example,

```
     WRITE (3,1000)
1000 FORMAT (T12,'X Coordinate', T32,'Y Coordinate', T1,'1')
```

will place the headings in columns 11 through 22 and 31 through 42, respectively, and the carriage control '1' will cause movement to a new page before printing. If a carriage control character had not been specified, that column would have been left blank, resulting in a movement to the next line before printing.

```
     WRITE (3,1002) AREAL
1002 FORMAT (1H ,F7.0, T8,' ')
```

overwrites a blank in the column in which the decimal point had been placed and makes the output of a real look like an integer value, that is, it is printed without the decimal point.

Obviously, the tab edit forces us to restudy just how the I/O is handled. During input, the line image is placed into a buffer, a series of locations in memory used to store the input characters temporarily. The FORMAT statement, in conjunction with the variable list in the READ statement, then scans through the buffer in the order specified by the format descriptors, converting to the internal storage methods of the particular computer. Thus there is no problem moving backward in the buffer to reread information. During output, the WRITE and FORMAT statements set up the characters in a previously blanked output buffer in the order specified by the FORMAT; thus, there is no difficulty replacing one character with another if the specified fields overlap.

8.9.6 Sign edits: S, SP, and SS

In the numeric edits, the placement of a plus sign in an output value is system dependent. In the majority of cases, a leading plus sign is not normally output for the magnitude of the number but may appear in the exponent portion of exponential or general output. The use of SP in the format forces the placement of a plus sign wherever it is possible, and the use of SS forces the suppression of an output plus sign in all possible positions. The use of S returns the compiler to its system-dependent status.

8.9.7 Zero/blank edits: BN and BZ

During numeric input, the BN specifier causes all leading, embedded, and trailing blanks to be ignored, with the remaining digits treated as though they were right-justified. The BZ specifier causes all blanks to be treated as zeros. For example:

```
      READ (2,1000) I, J, K
1000 FORMAT (BN,2I6, BZ,I6)
```

with the following input line:

```
         1.......1
123456789012345678

 1 2   1 2   3 1 23
```

will result in the values I = 12, J = 123, and K = 10230.

8.9.8 Colon editing: :

In a situation where the variable list is shorter than the number of variable fields specified in the FORMAT statement, I/O ceases when the first unsatisfiable variable field is reached. Thus, the program segment

```
      X = 123.45
      WRITE  (1,1000) X
1000 FORMAT (1H , 'X =', F8.2, 5X, 'Y =', F8.2)
```

yields the output:

```
X =  123.45     Y =
```

To correct the error of the unnecessary literal field (without having to write an additional WRITE and FORMAT pair), the colon can be used to cause output to cease when the variable list is exhausted:

```
1000 FORMAT (1H , 'X =', F8.2,:,5X, 'Y =', F8.2)
```

8.9.9 Reversion

If the variable list is longer than the number of variable fields specified in the FORMAT statement, the closing parenthesis serves as both an end-of-record and a command for the computer to revert back into the FORMAT for additional specifications. FORMAT control reverts to the rightmost opening parenthesis. For example:

```
      WRITE  (1,1000) I, J, K, L, M
1000 FORMAT (1H0,2I6/ 1H ,2I6)
```

reverts back to the 1H0 and produces the output:

line	columns 1–6	columns 7–12
2	value of I	value of J
3	value of K	value of L
5	value of M	

skipping line 4. Modifying the FORMAT to:

```
1000 FORMAT (1H0,2I6/ (1H ,2I6))
```

reverts back to the 1H (blank) and produces the output:

line	columns 1–6	columns 7–12
2	value of I	value of J
3	value of K	value of L
4	value of M	

For output FORMATs, the point of reversion must contain a carriage control character. In fact, it is possible to overprint in the following way:

```
      WRITE (3,1000)
1000 FORMAT (1H ,'O'/ 1H+,'X')
```

With printed output, an O will first be printed in column 1 and then an X directly on top of it. Writing this to a screen will result in the last defined character in the field being displayed.

Warning: it is possible to generate infinite output if a variable is specified without a corresponding format field:

```
      WRITE (3,1000) X
1000 FORMAT (1H1,'HEADING')
```

With this code, the literal HEADING is printed at the top of a new page. Because the end of the FORMAT is reached without outputting the variable, reversion takes place, beginning an infinite process.

8.9.10 Review questions

8–3. For the following program segment, show the output that will be produced by the WRITE statement interacting with the various FORMAT statements:

```
        COMPLEX  CMPLX
        LOGICAL  LGCL
C
        DATA    CMPLX,              LGCL,   IN,  RL/
       1        (56.798, -823.45),  .TRUE., -12, 86.427/
C
        WRITE   (1,5)  RL, LGCL, IN, CMPLX
```

  a. 5 FORMAT (1H , F8.2, L7, I10.5, -2PE12.4, E12.4)

  b. 5 FORMAT (1H0, E7.0, T52,L1, T12,I5, TR5, 2F5.0)

  c. 5 FORMAT (1H , 3PF10.1, L10/ 1H+, T12,I5, 20X,2E12.4)

  d. 5 FORMAT (1H , ' Value =',F12.4, T2,L1, TR30,I2/ 1H0, 2F8.2)

  e. 5 FORMAT (1H , F6.1, L6, TL4,I3/ (1H ,G12.5))

  f. 5 FORMAT (1H0, F12.5, L1, I7/ 1H0, F12.5)

8–4. Using the type, DATA and WRITE statements from question 8–3, determine the FORMATs needed to produce the following output:

```
                  1........12........23........34
        Columns: 12345678901234567890123456789012345678 90
```

a.	T -12 -823.45 56.798 86.427
b.	-0012T 86427. 56798. -823450.
c.	Real = 0.864270E+02 ** T
	Complex = 0.567980E+02 -0.823450E+03

8.10 Format specifiers

There are a number of alternative ways of specifying a format with a READ or WRITE statement. Up to this point we have always specified the format associated with such a statement by placing the FORMAT statement number in the I/O command. One alternative method is to specify a variable for the number, which can be given a value by an ASSIGN statement. For example:

```
            :
        IF  (I .LT. J) ASSIGN 1002 TO IFRMT
        IF  (I .GE. J) ASSIGN 1004 TO IFRMT
        WRITE  (1,IFRMT) I, J
            :
   1002 FORMAT   (1H0,'Condition 1', 2I6)
   1004 FORMAT   (1H0,'Condition 2', I6, I12)
```

It is also possible to include the format directly in the I/O command by treating it as a literal field:

```
IF (I .LT. J) WRITE (1,'(1H0,''Condition 1'', 2I6)') I, J
IF (I .GE. J) WRITE (1,'(1H0,''Condition 2'', I6, I12)') I, J
```

The double apostrophes within the format are necessary because the compiler would treat a single one as the end of the format string. The disadvantage of placing the format directly in the I/O command is that the format cannot be used by another I/O command. Nonetheless, some programmers use this construction quite often, especially for debugging statements.

In both of the above cases, it would be possible to precede the implied format (which must be placed in the second field of the I/O command) with FMT =, thus allowing it to be placed in any position in the I/O command.

There is yet another format method involving character variables that will be covered in section 10.10.

8.11 ENTRY and alternative RETURN

(Neither of these statements are supported in the subset.)

The ENTRY statement allows a subprogram to be entered at different points depending on the accessing statement. This feature is useful for grouping a number of routines in a single subprogram unit; the grouped routines may or may not share some of the logic of the subroutine.

Suppose we have a system in which three area routines are needed, one for right triangles, one for rectangles, and one for circles. The input is in feet, and the area is to be computed in both square feet and acres. Since each of the routines is quite small, they will be combined into a single subprogram unit headed by the entry for triangles but containing separate entry points for the other two computations.

```
C               Subroutine ATRNGL: computes area of right triangle
C               Entry      ARCNGL: computes area of rectangle
C               Entry      ACRCLE: computes area of circle
C                          areas returned in square feet and acres
C
      SUBROUTINE ATRNGL (SIDE1, SIDE2, SQFT, ACRES)
      SQFT = 0.5 * SIDE1 * SIDE2
      GO TO 100
C
      ENTRY ARCNGL (SIDE1, SIDE2, SQFT, ACRES)
      SQFT = SIDE1 * SIDE 2
      GO TO 100
C
      ENTRY ACRCLE (RADIUS, SQFT, ACRES)
      SQFT = 3.14159265 * RADIUS * RADIUS
C
```

```
C                         convert square feet to acres and return
  100 ACRES = SQFT / 43560.0
      RETURN
      END
```

The subprogram can be accessed by statements like:

```
      :
CALL ACRCLE (R, FEET, ACRES)
      :
CALL ATRNGL (X, Y, FEET, ACRES)
      :
CALL ARCNGL (X, Y, FEET, ACRES)
      :
```

If we had wanted the area only in square feet, a function could have been used:

```
C               Function ATRNGL: computes area of right triangle
C               Entry     ARCNGL: computes area of rectangle
C               Entry     ACRCLE: computes area of circle
C                         area returned in square feet
C
      FUNCTION ATRNGL (SIDE1, SIDE2)
      ATRNGL = 0.5 * SIDE1 * SIDE2
      RETURN
C
      ENTRY ARCNGL (SIDE1, SIDE2)
      ARCNGL = SIDE1 * SIDE 2
      RETURN
C
      ENTRY ACRCLE (RADIUS)
      ARCRCL = 3.14159265 * RADIUS * RADIUS
      RETURN
      END
```

The function would be accessed by statements like:

```
ACRETR = ATRNGL (X, Y) / 43560.0
```

The full FORTRAN 77 allows for alternative RETURNs from a subprogram to statements other than the one following the subprogram accessing statement. For example, the following mainline includes error messages that are triggered by the conditions noted in the subprogram:

```
      :
      CALL COMPUT (X, Y, Z, &800, &820)
C               continue computations
      :
      :
```

```
C              error messages
  800 WRITE  (1,1800)
 1800 FORMAT  (1H0,'INVALID INPUT DATA - COMPUTATION NOT PERFORMED')
      GO TO nn
  820 WRITE  (1,1820)
 1820 FORMAT  (1H0,'DIVISION BY ZERO ATTEMPTED')
      GO TO nn
                :
              SUBROUTINE  COMPUT  (A, B, C, *, *)
      IF  (B .LT. 0.00)  RETURN 1
      IF  (B .EQ. 0.00)  RETURN 2
      C = A / B
      RETURN
      END
```

The two asterisks in the subroutine header indicate that statement numbers are referenced in the calling statement. The first statement number corresponds to RETURN 1, the second to RETURN 2. In the calling statement, the statement numbers are preceded by ampersands (&) to distinguish them from constants; asterisks (*) may also be used. A RETURN 1 condition will cause a branch to the statement numbered 800; a RETURN 2 condition will cause a branch to the statement numbered 820. Should the subroutine progress to the normal RETURN, execution continues with the statement following the CALL to the subprogram.

Alternative RETURNs cannot be implemented with functions.

8.12 Compound decision making

In section 2.11, we discussed the IF ... THEN ... ELSE ... ENDIF construction. It is possible to compound these decision makers with the combination of ELSE and IF to produce alternative logical paths. Consider the sample symbolic condition:

```
IF  (condition 1)  THEN
          block 1
      ELSE IF  (condition 2)  THEN
          block 2
      ELSE IF  (condition 3)  THEN
          block 3
      ELSE
          block 4
ENDIF
```

conditions

1	2	3	*executed*
T			Block 1
F	T		Block 2
F	F	T	Block 3
F	F	F	Block 4

If the last ELSE had been an ELSE IF testing condition 4, block 4 would have been executed only if that condition were true; if all conditions had been false, no block would have been executed.

The blocks can contain any statement except an END. Branches can be made to the ENDIF but only from within one of the blocks; branches can also be made within a block but not from block to block. A block IF can be nested completely within another Block IF, but the constructs must not overlap.

The following program segment

```
WRITE (3,'(1H ,I3)') IGRADE
IF (IGRADE .GE. 90) THEN
        WRITE (3,'(1H+, T7,''A'')')
    ELSE IF (IGRADE .GE. 80) THEN
        WRITE (3,'(1H+, T7,''B'')')
    ELSE IF (IGRADE .GE. 70) THEN
        WRITE (3,'(1H+, T7,''C'')')
    ELSE IF (IGRADE .GE. 65) THEN
        WRITE (3,'(1H+, T7,''D'')')
    ELSE
        WRITE (3,'(1H+, T7,''F'')')
ENDIF
```

will output the numeric grade in columns 1–3 and the letter grade in column 6 of the same print line.

8.12.1 Exercise

Exercise 8–2

Repeat exercise 3–6 (section 3.13) using a compound IF.

8.13 Summary

The purpose of this chapter was to cover a number of assorted and sometimes unrelated topics so that the reader can use these advanced tools and techniques as we move toward more sophisticated programming. In this chapter we have either covered or amplified the following topics:

topic	section
BLOCK DATA	8.5
COMMON	8.4
COMPLEX	8.2
DOUBLE PRECISION	8.2
ELSE	8.12
ELSE IF	8.12
ENDIF	8.12
ENTRY	8.11
EXTERNAL	8.6
FORMAT	8.9,10
GO TO (computed and assigned)	8.8
IF	8.12
IMPLICIT	8.2
INTEGER, INTEGER*2, INTEGER*4	8.2
INTRINSIC	8.6
LOGICAL, LOGICAL*1, LOGICAL*2, LOGICAL*4	8.2
PAUSE	8.7
PARAMETER	8.3
REAL	8.2
Alternative RETURN	8.11
SAVE	8.5
STOP	8.7

We are now prepared to concentrate on new applications with almost all of FORTRAN's tools available to us.

9

Multidimensional arrays

9.1 Introduction

In chapter 5, we introduced the concept of arrays and developed multiple applications using one-dimensional arrays. In this chapter we will expand both the array concept and our ability to write cost-effective and efficient software.

While a one-dimensional array can be thought of as a column (or a row) of values, a two-dimensional array is more like a matrix of values arranged in rows and columns. A three-dimensional array can be visualized as layers of two-dimensional arrays or, as often described, a matrix of values arranged in rows, columns, and pages. Nor need we limit ourselves to the three visual dimensions; a four-dimensional array is a collection of three-dimensional arrays arranged in volumes or files. There is theoretically nothing that prevents a compiler, as we will shortly see, from implementing as many dimensions as desired.

FORTRAN 77 allows up to seven dimensions in its full implementation and up to three dimensions in its subset. Although there were some very early versions of FORTRAN that supported only two dimensions, the overwhelming majority supported three, so that became the minimum.

We have purposely delayed the presentation of this material (it could have been placed immediately after or combined with the material on one-dimensional arrays) so that our applications would be on the highest possible level of sophistication. For the sake of compatibility, we will work with no more than three dimensions, although the reader is encouraged to try more if the facilities are available.

The rules pertaining to multidimensional arrays are very similar to those for one-dimensional arrays. A DIMENSION statement must declare the number and size of the array; the total number of elements that can be stored in the array is the product of the dimensions. For example, the arrays declared by the statement

```
DIMENSION J(3,4), K(4,5,2)
```

have 12 and 40 elements respectively. Any DATA statement initializing multi-dimensional arrays must reflect the array size, for example

```
DATA K/ 40 * 0/
```

Similarly, an I/O statement that uses only the array name will have to handle the 12 and 40 elements, respectively.

With a two-dimensional array, one is tempted to ask which dimension stands for the row and which for the column, and with a three-dimensional array, one might also ask which dimension represents the page. The author will resist answering these questions for two reasons: (1) any such definition is artificial, since the programmer has absolute control over how the information is input or output, and (2) there is a better way to think of the dimensions in light of our applications. It is much more important for the sophisticated programmer to understand how the information is stored in memory and the techniques for controlling that information's I/O.

9.2 The mapping function

In reality, there is no such thing as a multidimensional array! Such arrays are figments of the programmer's imagination. The computer's memory is one big one-dimensional array, and all data, both single values and arrays, must be stored accordingly. Thus a multidimensional array must be rearranged into a single list of values by some consistent method. The *mapping function* is the formula that maps multidimensional arrays into one dimension.

For example, let's look at a simple two-dimensional array:

```
DIMENSION IJ(3,4)
```

The mapping function states that the order of storage of this array is:

IJ(1,1), IJ(2,1), IJ(3,1), IJ(1,2), IJ(2,2), IJ(3,2), IJ(1,3), IJ(2,3), IJ(3,3), IJ(1,4), IJ(2,4), IJ(3,4)

To remember the order of storage, note that the first subscript changes most often and the second subscript changes only when the range of the first subscript is exhausted (the first subscript is then reset to 1).

The order of storage of a three-dimensional array is defined in the same way. For example:

```
DIMENSION NN(2,3,2)
```

is stored in the order

NN(1,1,1), NN(2,1,1), NN(1,2,1), NN(2,2,1), NN(1,3,1), NN(2,3,1),
NN(1,1,2), NN(2,1,2), NN(1,2,2), NN(2,2,2), NN(1,3,2), NN(2,3,2)

again with the earlier subscripts changing most often.

The mapping function for element $IJ(m,n)$ in the two-dimensional array $IJ(M,N)$ defines the displacement from the beginning of the array as:

$$M * (n-1) + m - 1$$

Taking our array $IJ(3,4)$, let's see how this works:

IJ(m,n):	1,1	2,1	3,1	1,2	2,2	3,2	1,3	2,3	3,3	1,4	2,4	3,4
address:	1	2	3	4	5	6	7	8	9	10	11	12

Element $IJ(2,3)$ has a displacement of $3 * (3-1) + 2 - 1 = 7$. Adding this displacement to the address of the beginning of the array (1), we get address 8, and lo and behold, that is where $IJ(2,3)$ is stored! Try a few more examples to convince yourself of the consistency of this scheme.

Furthermore, notice that the value of N does not even appear in our formula, indicating that the value of the last dimension is not critical. This observation brings us to a new way of defining what our dimensions stand for in terms of the data structure.

Let's consider a situation in which we are analyzing temperature data. We want a data base to hold the high, low, and mean temperatures for each day in some period. That period can be a week (7 days), a month (28, 29, 30, or 31 days), a year (365 or 366 days), or some part of a year. Each day will have three data elements; these three data elements constitute a record. However, the number of records can vary depending on the period selected. Since the value of N, the second dimension in a two-dimensional array, does not come into the mapping formula, we can make maximum use of the mapping function by setting the first dimension to be the constant one. Thus we will assume that the first dimension stands for the number of items in a record and the second for the number of records. Then the formula of the mapping function does not vary, even though the number of records may.

We can diagram the situation in two ways:

Record: 1   2   3   4   5

Item 1

Item 2

Item 3

or

Item: 1   2   3

Record 1:

Record 2:

Record 3:

Record 4:

Record 5:

Obviously, we can look at the item/record orientation as either row/column or column/row.

Look back for a moment at the diagram that shows the layout of the two-dimensional array IJ(3,4). If we consider the mapping formula without the −1 at the end, we find that the formula gives the address below the diagram, which represents an equivalent one-dimensional array. With this in mind, we now present a function that can return either the maximum value of a one-dimensional array or the maximum value of any item in a two-dimensional array.

```
        FUNCTION  RMAX  (A, N, NITEMS, ITEM)
C
C       Abstract:  returns maximum value from a one-dimensional array
C                              or
C                  returns maximum value of one item in a two-
C                                            dimensional array
C
C       Glossary:  A:      a real array, one or two dimensions
C                  N:      number of records
C                  NITEMS: number of items
C                  ITEM:   item whose maximum is desired
C
C       For one-dimensional array, NITEMS = 1, ITEM = 1
C
C

        DIMENSION  A(1)
```

```
C
      RMAX = -1.00E+38
      DO 20  I = 1,N
          LOC = NITEMS * (I - 1) + ITEM
          IF  (A(LOC) .GT. RMAX)  RMAX = A(LOC)
   20 CONTINUE
C
      RETURN
      END
```

Note how the equation for LOC reduces to LOC = 1 when NITEMS and ITEM both equal 1. The function is accessed as follows:

```
              :
      DIMENSION TEMP1(366), TEMP3(3,366)
              :
C                 find maximum of TEMP1
      TMAX = RMAX (TEMP1, 366, 1, 1)
              :
C                 find maximum of item 2 in TEMP3
      TEMPMX = RMAX (TEMP3, 366, 3, 2)
              :
```

In a later section, we will apply this concept again in a number of very useful general purpose subprograms.

The mapping function for the element IJ(k,m,n) in the three-dimensional array IJ(K,M,N) has a displacement from the first element of:

$$K * M * (n-1) + K * (m-1) + k - 1$$

Note again that the last dimension (N) does not appear in the mapping function. Ignoring the -1 at the end, we get the location in the equivalent one-dimensional array.

Not much effort is required to extend the function into the higher dimensions. For example, Microsoft Disk Basic on the micro-computers allows as many dimensions as the programmer desires; the mapping function in BASIC is the same as in FORTRAN.

9.2.1 Review question

9–1. For the given arrays:

```
DIMENSION M(3,4,6), N(5,3)
```

determine the displacements of the following elements from the first element of that array.
a. N(4,2)
b. N(5,3)
c. M(1,3,2)
d. M(2,3,5)

9.2.2 Exercise

Exercise 9–1

Write a subroutine ASUM (A, N, NITEMS, SUMS) that determines the sum of a one-dimensional array or the sum of the individual items in a two-dimensional array. The variable SUMS is an array for the sums of the individual items; it can be dimensioned as 1 in the subroutine but should have the appropriate dimension in the calling program. Write a driver program to test the subroutine.

9.3 I/O of multidimensional arrays

As we mentioned earlier in the chapter, the programmer has full control over which dimension represents the row or the column (or the page). To input or output multidimensional arrays, we can use any of the tools we mentioned in chapter 5: the DO loop, the implied DO loop, or the entire array method, or any combination of methods. The implied DO loop can have as many indices as there are dimensions; the programmer must include the appropriate number of paired parentheses to keep the syntax correct. When the entire array method is used, the I/O order agrees with the order of storage, namely, the earlier subscripts change most often. Thus, for:

```
DIMENSION  IA (3,2)
           :
WRITE  (1,*)  IA
```

the order of output is: IA(1,1), IA(2,1), IA(3,1), IA(1,2), IA(2,2), IA(3,2).

Using our temperature data as an example, let us assume that the highs and lows for each day represent an input record and that a record is filed on one line with the high temperature in columns 1–5 and the low temperature in columns 6–10, right-justified; the temperatures are entered without a decimal point, although they will be read in as real numbers. There are as many lines in the file as there are input records and since each record represents a day, each line is a day.

```
C                 Input and echo check temperature data
C
      DIMENSION  TEMP3 (3,367)
C
C                 open input file and read data
      OPEN  (UNIT=7, FILE='TEMPIN', FORM='FORMATTED', STATUS='OLD')
      READ  (7,1000, END=20)  ((TEMP3(J,I), J=1,2), I=1,367)
 1000 FORMAT  (2F5.0)
           STOP 'excessive data'
   20 NUMDAY = I - 1
      CLOSE (UNIT=7)
C                 compute mean temperatures
      DO 40  I = 1,NUMDAY
   40 TEMP3(3,I) = (TEMP3(1,I) + TEMP3(2,I)) / 2.00
C                 open output file and echo check
      OPEN  (UNIT=8, FILE='TEMPOUT', FORM='FORMATTED', STATUS='NEW')
      WRITE  (8,1040)  ((TEMP3(J,I), J=1,3), I=1,NUMDAY)
 1040 FORMAT  (1H1,'Temperature Data'//
     1          1H0,'  High    Low    Mean'//
     2          (1H , 3F7.1))
      CLOSE (UNIT=8)
C                      termination
      STOP
      END
```

Notice how concise the I/O routine is. The output pair includes title, headings, and data, all neatly lined up.

The next application shows how a very short program can utilize the tools of FORTRAN to develop a rather large report from an unlimited amount of input. It works with the three-dimensional array AMT(12,31,2), which stores two values for each day of the year. The reader can think in terms of 12 pages (months), each with up to 31 lines (days) and two columns. Each of the storage locations is first cleared (set to zero), then each data item is added into the proper location as it is read. The array allows for up to 31 days per month, but the output routine restricts the number of days printed out to the actual number in each month, as stored in the array MDAY; for simplicity, February is assumed to have 29 days.

```
C                    Program to Demonstrate Multi-Dimensionsed Arrays
C
C          Abstract: a program to display sales and returns for a chain
C                    of retail stores by printing a chronological
C                    listing of activities on a daily basis with monthly
C                    and annual totals.
C
C          Input:    columns 1 - 2:  month (integer, range 1 - 12)
C                       "    4 - 5:  day   (integer, range 1 - 31)
C                       "   11 - 20:  amount of sales   (real)
C                       "   21 - 30:  amount of returns (real)
C              Input has been previously edited for proper ranges.
C              Data is unsorted.
C              There are multiple records for each day.
C
C          Output:  12 pages, one for each month.
C                   Up to 31 lines, one for each day.
C                   Monthly totals on each page.
C                   Annual totals on final page.
C
C
      IMPLICIT DOUBLE PRECISION  (A-H, O-Z)
      DIMENSION  AMT(12, 31, 2), TOTM(12, 2), TOTA(12,2), XIN(2), MDAY(12)
C
      DATA  AMT, TOTM, TOTA/ 770 * 0.00/
      DATA  MDAY/ 31,29,31, 30,31,30, 31,31,30, 31,30,31/
C
C                    input loop
      OPEN  (UNIT=4, FILE='SRIN', FORM='FORMATTED', STATUS='OLD')
   20 READ  (4,1020, END=100) MO,    IDAY,   XIN
 1020          FORMAT        (I2, 1X, I2, 5X, 2F10.2)
          DO 40  I=1,2
   40      AMT(MO,IDAY,I)=AMT(TO,IDAY,I) + XIN(I)
      GO TO 20
  100 CLOSE (UNIT=4)
C
C                    compute totals
      DO 140  I=1,2
          DO 140  J=1,12
              DO 120  K=1,31
  120          TOTM(J,I)=TOTM(J,I) + AMT(J,K,I)
  140 TOTA(I)=TOTA(I) + TOTM(J,I)
C
C                    output
      OPEN  (UNIT=3, FILE='SROUT', FORM='FORMATTED', STATUS='NEW')
```

```
C                                loop through months, new page for each
       DO 200  I=1,12
             WRITE  (3,1140)  I
 1140        FORMAT  (1H1, 'SALES & RETURNS for Month', 13//
      1               1HO, 'Day', 7X, 'Sales', 5X, 'Returns'/)
             NDAYS=MDAY(I)
C                                loop through days
             DO 160  J=1,NDAYS
  160        WRITE  (3,1160)  J, (AMT(I,J,K), K=1,2)
 1160        FORMAT  (1H, 13, 2F12.2)
C                          monthly totals
  200 WRITE  (3,1200)  (TOTM(I,J), J=1,2)
 1200 FORMAT  (1HO, 3X, 2F12.2, 4X, 'Totals')
C                       annual totals
      WRITE  (3,1202) TOTA
 1202 FORMAT  (//1HO, 3X, 2F12.2, 4X, 'Grand Totals')
C
C                       termination
      CLOSE (UNIT=3)
      STOP  'end-of-run'
      END
```

Note the various methods of I/O used, including implied DO loops and whole arrays. The module for computing the monthly and annual totals is very efficient and is similar to the way a sophisticated calculator user with one available memory location would work. The outer loop sets up the calculation first for sales, then later for returns. The sales for the first month are added up, and that sum added to the annual sales; then sales for the second month are added up, and the sum is again added to the annual sales; the process continues through all twelve months. Then the outer loop is set to returns and the process is repeated. Having two of the three loops terminate on the same statement (140) may be confusing to the reader, but not to the machine; the same results would be obtained with the following code, which might be more understandable:

```
C
C                  compute totals
      DO 140 I = 1,2
           DO 130 J = 1,12
               DO 120 K = 1,31
  120          TOTM(J,I) = TOTM(J,I) + AMT(J,K,I)
  130      TOTA(I) = TOTA(I) + TOTM(J,I)
  140 CONTINUE
C
```

Another interesting application involving multidimensional arrays is the generation of a table of squares:

Value	Square	Value	Square
1	1	51	2601
2	4	52	2704
:	:	:	:
:	:	:	:
50	2500	100	10000

The program is remarkably short. Note the clever use of the triply implied DO loop!

```
C                 TABLE OF SQUARES
C
      DIMENSION  ISQ(2,100)
C
C                 generate values
      DO 20  I = 1,100
           ISQ(1,I) = I
   20 ISQ(2,I) = I * I
C                 output routine
      WRITE  (3,1020)  (((ISQ(J,I), J=1,2), I=N,100,50), N=1,50)
 1020 FORMAT  (1H1,2('Value', 5X,'Square', 9X)/(1H ,I5,I11, I14,I11))
C                 termination
      STOP
      END
```

9.3.1 Review questions

9–2. Indicate the order of output for the following WRITE statements:

   a. WRITE (1,1000) ((A(J,I), J=1,10,2), I=1,3)
   b. WRITE (1,1000) ((A(J,I), I=1,3,2), J=1,10,4)

9–3. An array J(3,5) stores a matrix of three rows and five columns. Give the WRITE and FORMAT statements necessary to display the array in that geometric form.

9–4. Assume that same array J(3,5) has five rows and three columns. Give the WRITE and FORMAT statements necessary to display the array in that geometric form.

9.3.2 Exercise

Exercise 9–2

Write a program to input a tax rate in percent and produce a table in the following format:

```
                    TAX  TABLE  for  7.50%

Amount    Tax     Amount    Tax     Amount    Tax     Amount    Tax
  0.01   0.00       0.26   0.02       0.51   0.04       0.76   0.06
  0.02   0.00       0.27   0.02       0.52   0.04       0.77   0.06
    :      :          :      :          :      :          :      :
  0.05   0.00       0.30   0.02       0.55   0.04       0.80   0.06

  0.06   0.00       0.31   0.02       0.56   0.04       0.81   0.06
    :      :          :      :          :      :          :      :
    :      :          :      :          :      :          :      :
    :      :          :      :          :      :          :      :
  0.25   0.02       0.50   0.04       0.75   0.06       1.00   0.08
```

Skip a line after every multiple of five cents.

9.4 Access to subprograms

When we discussed transmitting one-dimensional arrays to subprograms through the argument list (section 5.9), we pointed out that a dimension of 1 was sufficient to indicate to the compiler that a variable was an array. Since the mapping function for one-dimensional arrays is so simple, no complications arise.

In contrast, the mapping function for multidimensional arrays requires that every dimension but the last be exactly defined. Thus, if we transmit an array A(20,100) from a calling program, the subprogram must have as a minimum

```
DIMENSION A(20,1)
```

since the first subscript is used in the mapping function. This requirement significantly reduces the ability to write general purpose subprograms for multidimensional arrays.

However, there is a way around this problem. If the subprogram treats the array as one-dimensional and includes the mapping function in the code, then we can construct very general purpose routines much like function RMAX in section 9.2.

In section 5A.2, we presented a generalized ascending integer sort for one-dimensional arrays. Now we present the same sorting algorithm in a form that accesses either one- or two-dimensional arrays.

```
C              LSORT:  1-d or 2-d Ascending integer sort with carry-alongs
C
       SUBROUTINE  LSORT  (KEY,NREC,NITEM, ICARY,INDI, RCARY,INDR)
C
       DIMENSION  KEY(1), ICARY(1), RCARY(1)
C
C                        Glossary
C                        --------
C              KEY:     the integer array upon which the sort acts
C              NREC:    the number of records (last dimension) in the
C                         arrays
C              NITEM:   the number of items (first dimension) in the
C                         key array
C              ICARY:   the integer carry-along array
C              INDI:    the number of items in the integer carry-along
C                         0 if no carry-along, >0 if a carry-along
C              RCARY:   the real carry-along array
C              INDR:    the number of items in the real carry-along
C                         0 if no carry-along, >0 if a carry-along
C              All arrays may be one or two-dimensional
C              Where an array is one-dimensional, number of items = 1
C
C
       M = NREC
   20 M = M / 2
       IF (M .EQ. 0)  RETURN
C
       K = NREC - M
       J = 1
C
   60 I = J
C
   80 L = I + M
C                        comparison
       DO 100  JK = 1,NITEM
           II = NITEM * (I-1) + JK
           LL = NITEM * (L-1) + JK
           IF (KEY(II) .GT. KEY(LL))  GO TO 120
           IF (KEY(II) .LT. KEY(LL))  GO TO 200
  100 CONTINUE
       GO TO 200
```

```
C                        interchange key
   120     DO 140  JK = 1,NITEM
               II = NITEM * (I-1) + JK
               LL = NITEM * (L-1) + JK
               ITEMP  = KEY(II)
               KEY(II) = KEY(LL)
   140     KEY(LL) = ITEMP
C                          interchange integer carry-along, if necessary
          IF (INDI .GT. 0)  THEN
          DO 160  JK = 1,INDI
               II = INDI * (I-1) + JK
               LL = INDI * (L-1) + JK
               ITEMP    = ICARY(II)
               ICARY(II) = ICARY(LL)
   160     ICARY(LL) = ITEMP
          ENDIF
C                          interchange real carry-along, if necessary
          IF (INDR .GT. 0)  THEN
          DO 180  JK = 1,INDR
          II = INDR * (I-1) + JK
          LL = INDR * (L-1) + JK
          TEMP     = RCARY(II)
          RCARY(II) = RCARY(LL)
   180     RCARY(LL) = TEMP
          ENDIF
C                          reset for next comparison
       I = I - M
          IF (I .GE. 1)  GO TO 80
   200 J = J + 1
          IF (J - K)  60,60,20
C
      END
```

We will illustrate the use of this sort in the job costing and payroll programming system described in chapter 6. The input, which is read in subroutine LA134, has five input fields; the sixth field, cost, is calculated in subroutine LB134.

field	*variable*
1. employee number	JOBIN(1,n)
2. job number	JOBIN(2,n)
3. task number	JOBIN(3,n)
4. overtime indicator	JOBIN(4,n)
5. hours worked	HRSCST(1,n)
6. cost	HRSCST(2,n), calculated in LB134

Subroutine LSORT sorts the key array JOBIN in the order of the items in the array. The order of the input fields corresponds to the order of the desired first sort (that is, the first sort is by employee number, with job number as a secondary key and task number as a tertiary key), so the sort routine can be called without any preliminary manipulation. However, the program requires two other sorts, one by job number with the task number as the secondary key and employee number as the tertiary key, and the other by task with the job and employee numbers as the secondary and tertiary keys. Thus the items in each record must be rearranged accordingly before the second and third sorts.

The mainline, L0134, accesses the required subprograms and also sets up and calls the sort:

```
C                  L0134:  Job Costing & Payroll Mainline
C
      IMPLICIT INTEGER*2  (I-N)
      COMMON  HRSCST(2,2001)
C              HRSCST(1,n): Hours
C              HRSCST(2,n): Cost
      COMMON  JOBIN(4,2001), IDATE(3), NREC, IOPT, NUMERR, INDBG
C
C                      input file F0104
      CALL LA134
C                      sort by employee number
      CALL LSORT (JOBIN,NREC,4, ICARY,0, HRSCST,2)
C                      optional debugging output
      IF (INDBG .NE. 0) WRITE (1,1000)
     1           (I, (JOBIN(J,I), J=1,4), HRSCST(1,I), I=1,NREC)
 1000     FORMAT (1H0,'After Sorting:'/ (1H , 5I6, F7.2))
C                      open personnel file for later access
      OPEN (UNIT=12, FILE='F0101', ACCESS='DIRECT',
     1                STATUS='OLD', RECL=5)
C                      open printer output file
      OPEN (UNIT=21, FILE='R0134', FORM='FORMATTED', STATUS='NEW')
C                      output by employee
      CALL LB134
C                      pack data and generate payroll file
      CALL LC134
C                      sort data by job, task, employee numbers
      DO 20  I = 1,NREC
          ITEMP     = JOBIN(1,I)
          JOBIN(1,I) = JOBIN(2,I)
          JOBIN(2,I) = JOBIN(3,I)
   20 JOBIN(3,I)     = ITEMP
      CALL LSORT (JOBIN,NREC,4, ICARY,0, HRSCST,2)
```

```
C                       output by job
      CALL LD134
C                       add to labor summary file
      CALL LE134
C                       sort data by task, job, employee numbers
      DO 40  I = 1,NREC
          ITEMP      = JOBIN(1,I)
          JOBIN(1,I) = JOBIN(2,I)
   40 JOBIN(2,I)      = ITEMP
      CALL LSORT (JOBIN,NREC,4, ICARY,0, HRSCST,2)
C                       output by task
      CALL LF134
C                       close files and terminate
      CLOSE  (UNIT=12)
      CLOSE  (UNIT=21)
      STOP   'end-of-run'
      END
```

9.4.1 Exercises

Exercise 9–3

Enter LSORT into your library and test it with a simple one-dimensional array as the key and no carry-alongs. The data can be put directly into your mainline with a DATA statement.

Exercise 9–4

Generate a short data file consisting of five integer items and two real items per record. Treat the first two integer items as a two-dimensional key and the last three as a two-dimensional carry-along array; the two real items form another two-dimensional carry-along array. Use LSORT to sort the data and then output it.

9.5 Advanced programming systems

Except for variable alphameric data, which we will cover in chapter 10, we have now covered all of the necessary material to demonstrate how an advanced programming system is put together. We will continue to use the job costing and payroll application and will illustrate various techniques by presenting, with explanation, the first three subprograms, LA134, LB134, and LC134.

LA134 serves primarily as the input routine; it checks for the existence of the input file, allows selection of options (actual run, edit only, or abort run if date is incorrect) by the user, including optional debug output, and edits the data. If there are any errors or if only an edit is desired, execution ends in the subroutine. If there are no errors and an actual run has been requested, return is made to the mainline L0134.

```
C                    LA134:  input and edit data from file F0104
C
      SUBROUTINE  LA134
C
      IMPLICIT INTEGER*2  (I - N)
      LOGICAL   LEX
C
      COMMON  HRSCST(2,2001)
      COMMON  JOBIN(4,2001), IDATE(3), NREC, IOPT, NUMERR, INDBG
C
      DATA  NERR/ 0/
C
C                    check existence of input file
      INQUIRE  (FILE='F0104', EXIST=LEX)
      IF  (.NOT. LEX)  THEN
          WRITE  (1,9999)
 9999     FORMAT  (1H0,'File F0104 does not exist!')
          STOP   'Run Aborted'
      ENDIF
C                    open input file
      OPEN  (UNIT=11, FILE='F0104', FORM='FORMATTED', STATUS='OLD')
C                    input header, request approval and options
      READ  (11,1000)  IDATE
 1000 FORMAT  (I2, 1X, I2, 1X, I2)
      WRITE  (1,1001)  IDATE
 1001 FORMAT  (1H0,'Job Cost & Payroll for week of', I3,2('/,'I2) /
     1         1H0,'Enter 1 to edit, 2 for final run, 0 to abort')
      READ  (2,*)  IOPT
      IF  (IOPT .EQ. 0  .OR.  IABS(IOPT) .GT. 2)  THEN
              CLOSE  (UNIT=11)
              STOP   'Run Aborted'
          ELSE IF  (IOPT .LT. 0)  THEN
              INDBG = 1
              IOPT = -IOPT
          ELSE
              INDBG = 0
      ENDIF
C                    input detail records
      READ  (11,1002, END=20)
     1                ((JOBIN(J,I), J=1,4), HRSCST(1,I),  I = 1,2001)
 1002 FORMAT  (I3, 2X, I4, 1X, I3, 1X, I1, F5.2)
          WRITE  (1,1004)
 1004     FORMAT  (//1H0,'EXCESS DATA')
          CLOSE  (UNIT=11)
          STOP   'Run Aborted'
```

```
C                         close file, display number of records
   20 CLOSE  (UNIT=11)
      NREC = I - 1
      WRITE  (1,1020) NREC
 1020 FORMAT  (1H0,I4,' records to be processed')
C                         optional echo check
      IF  (INDBG .NE. 0)  WRITE  (1,1022)
     1            (I, (JOBIN(J,I), J=1,4), HRSCST(1,I), I = 1,NREC)
 1022     FORMAT  (1H , 5I6, F7.2)
C
C                  edit
      DO 40  I = 1,NREC
C                         task range:  101 to 299
          IF  (JOBIN(3,I) .LT. 101 .OR.  JOBIN(3,I) .GT. 299)  THEN
              WRITE  (1,1030)  I, (JOBIN(J,I), J=1,4), HRSCST(1,I)
 1030         FORMAT  (1H ,'Record',I4, 4I6,F8.2,':  INVALID TASK')
              NERR = NERR + 1
          ENDIF
C                         overtime indicator:  0, 1 or 2
          IF  (JOBIN(4,I) .GT. 2)  THEN
              WRITE  (1,1032)  I, (JOBIN(J,I), J=1,4), HRSCST(1,I)
 1032         FORMAT  (1H ,'Record',I4, 4I6,F8.2,
     1                      ':  INVALID OVERTIME INDICATOR')
              NERR = NERR + 1
          ENDIF
C                         hours worked on one entry must be <= 40
          IF  (HRSCST(1,I) .GT. 40.00)  THEN
              WRITE  (1,1034)  I, (JOBIN(J,I), J=1,4), HRSCST(1,I)
 1034         FORMAT  (1H ,'Record',I4, 4I6,F8.2,':  EXCESSIVE HOURS')
              NERR = NERR + 1
          ENDIF
   40 CONTINUE
C
C                     if final run and no errors, return
      IF  (IOPT .EQ. 2 .AND.  NERR .EQ. 0)  RETURN
C                     display message, giving error count
      IF  (NERR .GT. 0)  WRITE  (1,1040) NERR
 1040     FORMAT  (1H0,'At least',I3,' errors in input data')
      IF  (NERR .EQ. 0)  WRITE  (1,1042)
 1042     FORMAT  (1H0,'Edit complete with no apparent errors')
      STOP
      END
```

Note the cautiousness with which the error count messages are given; they are
so phrased to warn the user that some errors may have escaped detection.

LB134 is the first output routine. However, it must first compute the cost (that is, hours times rate, with possible overtime adjustment) for each employee. The rates and the employee names are stored in the personnel file, F0101, which will have to be accessed. To reduce running time, file F0101 is accessed only when a new employee is encountered, while the variable LASTEM keeps track of the previous employee. As we will see in the next chapter, each employee record consists of the pay rate (4 bytes), a 14-character name and the activity indicator, for a total of 20 bytes. In the mainline, L0134, where we opened the file (section 9.4), the record length of 5 corresponds to 20 bytes (5 × 4 bytes) since direct access unformatted files must be specified in terms of the system's basic storage unit (which we have assumed to be 32 bits).

Another concept introduced here is the *level break*, that is, totals and sub-totals are output at certain changes of the key. In this case, we will produce a total for each employee and a subtotal within each employee for each job worked on. There are a number of ways of performing the necessary coding, but this author prefers the *look-ahead* approach: after each detail record is printed, we look at the next record to see if a level break is justified. There is no problem with this approach until we reach the last record, when we are looking ahead to a nonexistent record; the solution is to dummy up the record following the last valid one with a key different (usually higher) from the last valid one, thus using it as an end-of-data indicator.

We will also use a line count to limit our pages to 50 lines plus the title and heading. Efficiency of coding is accomplished by initializing the line count at 50 or higher and using the same code as used to check the incremented line count.

Because we have not yet covered alphameric variable data, our output will be exactly like that shown in section 6.4 without the employee names and over-time descriptions; those will be added in the next chapter.

```
C                    LB134:  output by employee
C
      SUBROUTINE  LB134
C
      IMPLICIT INTEGER*2  (I - N)
C
      COMMON  HRSCST(2,2001), JOBIN(4,2001), IDATE(3), NREC
C
      DIMENSION  STOT(2), TOT(2), GTOT(2)
C
      DATA  STOT, TOT, GTOT/ 6 * 0.00/,  LASTEM,LINE/ 0,50/
C
C              set end-of-data indicator
      JOBIN(1,NREC+1) = 1000
C
C              loop through records
      DO 100  I = 1,NREC
```

```
C                       new page if 50 or more lines used
              IF  (LINE .GE. 50)  THEN
                    WRITE  (21,1000)  IDATE
  1000             FORMAT  (1H1,30X,'Job Costing by Employee'/
      1                    1H0,32X,  'Continental Congress'/
      2                    1H0,34X,    'Week of',I3, '/', I2, '/', I2 //
      3                    1H0,'Employee', 13X,'Job', 6X,'Task',
      4                        11X,'Hours', 8X,'Rate', 8X,'Cost'/)
                    LINE = 0
              ENDIF
C                       get new employee rate
              IF  (JOBIN(1,I) .NE. LASTEM)  THEN
                    READ  (12, REC=JOBIN(1,I))  RATE
                    LASTEM = JOBIN(1,I)
              ENDIF
C                       compute cost, with overtime factor
C                           if JOBIN(4,I) = 0, multiplier = 1.0
C                           if      ''      = 1,        ''     = 1.5
C                           if      ''      = 2,        ''     = 2.0
              FACTOR = FLOAT (JOBIN(4,I) + 2) / 2.00  *  RATE
              HRSCST(2,I) = HRSCST(1,I) * FACTOR
C                       output detail line
              WRITE  (21,1002)  (JOBIN(J,I), J=1,4), HRSCST(1,I),
      1                         FACTOR, HRSCST(2,I)
  1002        FORMAT  (1H ,I3, 16X, I5, I10, I2, 7X, F7.2,
      1                         6X, '$',F5.2, 3X, '$',F8.2)
C                       add to sub-totals
              STOT(1) = STOT(1) + HRSCST(1,I)
              STOT(2) = STOT(2) + HRSCST(2,I)
              LINE = LINE + 1
C                       sub-total routine, if new employee or new job
              IF  (JOBIN(1,I) .NE. JOBIN(1,I+1)  .OR.
      1          JOBIN(2,I) .NE. JOBIN(2,I+1))                 THEN
                    WRITE  (21,1004)  JOBIN(2,I), STOT
  1004             FORMAT  (1H ,20X,I4,' Sub-total:', F15.2,' *',
      1                                 13X, '$',F8.2,' *'/)
                    LINE = LINE + 2
C                       add to totals, clear sub-totals
                    DO 20  J = 1,2
                        TOT(J) = TOT(J) + STOT(J)
    20              STOT(J) = 0.00
              ENDIF
```

```
C                     total routine, if new employee
          IF  (JOBIN(1,I) .NE. JOBIN(1,I+1))   THEN
                WRITE  (21,1020)  JOBIN(1,I), TOT
    1020        FORMAT  (1H ,I3, 16X,' Total:', F24.2,' **',
        1                           12X,'$',F8.2,' **'//)
                LINE = LINE + 4
C                   add to grand totals, clear totals
                DO 40   J = 1,2
                    GTOT(J) = GTOT(J) + TOT(J)
      40        TOT(J) = 0.00
          ENDIF
  100 CONTINUE
C             grand totals
      WRITE  (21,1100)  GTOT
 1100 FORMAT  (1H0,'Grand Totals:,' F37.2,' ***',
    1                     11X,'$', F8.2,' ***')
C             return
      RETURN
      END
```

LC134 packs the job costing data into a file to be used for payroll. Payroll needs only the employee number and the total salary and is not concerned with the distribution of those costs. The approach is to set the first employee number and cost into the variables to be used, the second of which will be used to accumulate the gross salary as the sum of all of the costs for that employee. When a new employee number is found, the stored number and gross salary are written to the file and the new employee's first record replaces the sum for the previous employee. We must remember to file the last employee's information after the loop is exhausted.

```
C             LC134:  pack data and store in T0180
C
      SUBROUTINE  LC134
C
      IMPLICIT INTEGER*2  (I - N)
C
      COMMON  HRSCST(2,2001), JOBIN(4,2001), IDATE(3), NREC
C
C             open file T0180 for payroll information
      OPEN  (UNIT=13, FILE='T0180', FORM='FORMATTED', STATUS='NEW')
C             set up first employee
      IEMPNO = JOBIN(1,1)
      GROSS  = HRSCST(2,1)
```

```
C               loop through rest of records
      DO 100  I = 2,NREC
          IF  (JOBIN(1,I) .EQ. IEMPNO)  THEN
                  GROSS = GROSS + HRSCST(2,I)
              ELSE
                  WRITE  (13,1000)  IEMPNO, GROSS
 1000             FORMAT  (I3, F9.2)
                  IEMPNO = JOBIN(1,I)
                  GROSS  = HRSCST(2,I)
          ENDIF
  100 CONTINUE
C               file last employee
      WRITE  (13,1000)  IEMPNO, GROSS
C               close file and return
      ENDFILE 13
      CLOSE  (UNIT=13)
      RETURN
      END
```

The other output subroutines in the system, LD134 and LF134, are very similar to LB134; in fact, most programmers would copy LB134 into those two files and make any necessary adjustments to them rather than writing them from scratch. Subroutine LE134, which writes the records to the labor summary file, is very similar to the debugging output, since the already sorted records are written as is to that file.

9.6 Additional exercises

Exercise 9–5
Write a program to read up to 100 records of three real items each. Multiply all of the items by the number of records and write a new file with these values.

Exercise 9–6
Write a program to work with a matrix of 12 values arranged in 4 rows and 3 columns. Compute the 4 row sums and the 3 column sums, and compute the grand total of all values. Output the array in the geometrical form described with the sums in the appropriate locations and explicitly annotated.

Exercise 9–7
An input file can store up to 100 records of integer values defined as follows:
   Item 1: student number
   Item 2: first examination grade
   Item 3: second examination grade
   Item 4: third examination grade

This information will be part of a two-dimensional array of size (7,100). Item 5 is the integer average of the three exams, rounded. Item 6 is the average of the second and third exams. Item 7 is the largest of items 4, 5, and 6 and will be used to generate the final letter grade. Write a program to read in the input data, generate the last three items, and print out the entire array.

Exercise 9–8

An input file consists of the following information:

    Record   1: Item 1: number of rows of a matrix
                 Item 2: number of columns of a matrix
    Records 2–n: each record consists of one row of values.

Write a program to read in the matrix and print it out in the geometrical form described. Then print it in inverted form, that is, row 1 becomes column 1, row 2 becomes column 2, and so forth, such that the number of rows and columns becomes interchanged.

Exercise 9–9

The formula for compound interest is:

total amount = principal * (1 + interest in decimal) ** number of years

Using a two-dimensional array (8,5), develop a table of interest based on a principal of $100 for interest rates of 6% to 20% incrementing by 2% and years from 5 to 25 in increments of 5 years. Then print out the table as show below:

```
                    Table of Interest
            6%    8%    10%    12%    14%    16%    18%    20%
 5 years   nnn.  nnn.  nnn.   nnn.   nnn.   nnn.   nnn.   nnn.
10 years   nnn.  nnn.  nnn.   nnn.   nnn.   nnn.   nnn.   nnn.
15 years
20 years
25 years   nnn.  nnn.  nnnn.  nnnn.  nnnn.  nnnn.  nnnn.  nnnn.
```

10

Alphameric data

10.1 Introduction

All the data used in the previous chapters was numeric; the only nonnumeric information was in the literal or Hollerith fields in FORMAT statements. Yet we have talked of using names, as in the cost distribution and payroll application, where they would be read from a file and printed out. Thus we must develop techniques for treating nonnumeric or alphameric information as a variable. (The term *nonnumeric* refers to information that need not be numeric, and the term *alphameric* refers to information that may be alphabetic or numeric; thus, these two terms may be used interchangeably.)

Unfortunately, we are caught on the horns of a dilemma. As originally designed, FORTRAN was intended to be used as a number cruncher, not for list processing or other applications involving nonnumeric manipulation. Alphameric characters are stored as numbers in FORTRAN, so FORTRAN programmers learned how to massage alphameric information in a manner not unlike that used by assembly language programmers, that is, by working with one character at a time. The FORTRAN programmer became expert in the different internal codes used and developed techniques that depended on those values. FORTRAN IV provided the programmer with an alphameric constant embedded in apostrophes (like literal format), eliminating the necessity of using the internal codes in many cases, but the manipulations still required a character-by-character approach.

FORTRAN 77 tried to simplify the situation by including the CHARACTER variable, which could be set to a defined length, and adding a few techniques for the manipulation of such data, including concatenation of strings and accessing substrings. However, the facilities added provided nothing like the flexibility of string handling in BASIC, and although they were useful in many situations, they could not replace the character-by-character techniques in many applications. Furthermore, the ability to concatenate and to access substrings was not included in the subset of FORTRAN 77!

Our dilemma is caused by the incompatibility of CHARACTER storage with other modes of storage, as well as the varied methods presented by FORTRAN

66, the FORTRAN 77 subset, and full FORTRAN 77. In order that this chapter not become a volume within itself, we will compromise and implement most of our applications using CHARACTER*1 such that they will work on all machines; when either BYTE or INTEGER*2 mode is substituted, FORTRAN 66 will work also.

(INTEGER*2 is wasteful for storing one character per variable, but storing two characters in each location involves some complications when manipulating that information. Some implementations of FORTRAN reverse the characters when they are stored two per variable, others leave them in the correct order; thus an alpha sort may work in one environment and not in another. Thus it is my recommendation that where INTEGER*2 is required, waste the space and keep the code simple and portable.)

Some terminology must be introduced here. A *string* is a collection (or array) of characters that are put together as a unit; a *substring* is part of a string. Blanks are perfectly valid characters within a string and are not to be ignored. (FORTRAN ignores blanks in its instructions, except in literal and Hollerith fields, which are constant strings.) In FORTRAN, as in most other languages, fixed-length variable locations are set aside for storing strings, which may not exceed that length.

This author has always found that alphameric coding is the most interesting and the most challenging of all FORTRAN programming; it certainly beats what is often the very dull manipulation of numeric data. In this chapter we will see some of the many applications programs written over the past two decades to ease data input and produce better looking output.

10.2 Alphameric codes

All information, including alphameric data, is stored as numbers. Thus we must begin by looking at some of the codes used for that storage.

The simplest and one of the earliest codes used was Binary Coded Decimal (BCD). This code consists of four-bit groupings that are capable of storing the 10 decimal digits from 0 to 9, plus codes for the + and − signs. This is strictly a numeric code, but it could be used for storing characters by combining two digits, providing codes for up to 100 characters.

IBM also developed an internal six-bit code to store its keypunch information. This code was capable of storing 64 different combinations of bits, allowing for 64 characters including the 26 uppercase letters, the 10 digits, a blank, and a number of special characters. In time this code proved insufficient for the needs of the data processing community. Eventually (in the early 1960s), IBM moved to an expanded code, Extended Binary Coded Decimal Interchange Code (EBCDIC), an eight-bit code that provided up to 256 characters, more than enough for both upper- and lowercase letters, the digits, all of the special characters, and many other characters used for device control and communications. But because EBCDIC was an extension of an existing code designed not specifically for computers but merely for information storage, it has some inherent problems such as the inability to sort properly.

There is also a seven-bit code called American Standard Code for Information Interchange (ASCII); it was designed specifically for data processing and is far more logical in its layout. This code allows for 128 characters, of which the first 32 are for device control and communications, the next 95 are for printable characters (including upper- and lowercase letters, numbers, and punctuation characters), and the last is the delete code (backspace and erase). When it became apparent that the industry was moving toward an eight-bit (byte) standard, an eight-bit version of ASCII appeared in which the first bit was ignored; unfortunately, some manufacturers made that bit a one bit rather than a zero bit, leaving eight-bit ASCII nonstandard.

In our programming work, we will make every attempt to write our programs so that they work regardless of the method of data storage (EBCDIC or ASCII), but in some cases that will not be possible and we will have to produce programs tailored to one code or the other. Appendix A includes tables of both major codes and will have to be consulted from time to time in order to understand the programs. Fortunately most devices, even some IBM computers, now use ASCII.

On microcomputers, which were invented after the eight-bit byte had become standard, the full 256 codes are used, with the last 128 used for graphic characters (symbols produced on the screen) or letters in foreign languages. However, these additional codes are not standardized.

There did exist another code called Baudot, a five-bit code used on the old teletypes. Although it had only 32 possible characters, additional characters were obtained by using two of the codes to shift back and forth between numeric and alphabetic information. The term *Baud* (used in data transmission) stems from this code. The Baud rate divided by ten gives an approximation of the number of characters transmitted per second.

10.3 Storage of alphameric data

The *byte,* an eight-bit configuration capable of storing non-negative values from 0 to 127, has become the standard building block for almost all computers; the byte is synonymous with the *character*. Multiple characters can be stored in any variable, integer or real, depending on how many bits that variable uses. (On some nonstandardized computers, other configurations were possible; for example, on the 36-bit DEC 20, five ASCII coded characters using seven bits each could be stored in one storage unit.) No special variables are used for alphamerics. FORTRAN 77 introduced a new mode of storage, CHARACTER, which is used strictly for storing nonnumeric information. Thus FORTRAN allows characters to be stored in the following data types:

data type	characters storable	notes
BYTE	1	nonstandard*

INTEGER*2	2	
INTEGER*4	4	
REAL	4	
DOUBLE PRECISION	8	
CHARACTER	1	FORTRAN 77 only
CHARACTER*n	n*	FORTRAN 77 only

*The value of n can range from 1 to a system-dependent maximum, which may be 127, 255, or even as high as 4095. BYTE mode is the same as CHARACTER*1.

   Real and double precision variables are useful only for storing alphameric information; they cannot be used for alphameric manipulation, in which the characters in the variable can be examined and/or modified.
   The type statement for CHARACTER has a number of variations. There can be a separate statement for each string length, or the different string lengths can be combined according to the following syntax:

```
CHARACTER*4 ISTRING(18)
CHARACTER*9 JSTRING
```

is equivalent to

```
CHARACTER ISTRING(18)*4, JSTRING*9
```

And, of course, the IMPLICIT statement can be used for grouped variables.

10.3.1 Alphameric specification: Aw

The format specification for alphameric information is Aw, where w is the field width. If any attempt is made to place more characters in a variable than it can store, only the leftmost characters are stored. Placing fewer characters into a variable than its capacity allows will cause padding with blanks in the remaining rightmost positions. If an output field is longer than required, the field is padded with leading blanks.
   As examples of how alphameric information can be input and output, let us look at a number of ways in which a 40-column title can be read in from a file numbered 4 and written to a file numbered 5 in printout format, centered at the top of a new page of 80-column width:

```
     INTEGER*2 ITITLE(20)  or  INTEGER*4 ITITLE(10)
            :
     READ (4,1000) ITITLE
1000 FORMAT (20A2)         or  FORMAT (10A4)
     WRITE (5,1002) ITITLE
1002 FORMAT (1H1,20X, 20A2) or  FORMAT (1H1,20X, 10A4)
```

A real variable would use the same 10A4 format specification as the IN-TEGER*4; a double precision variable would use 5A8. Using character mode, the FORTRAN code would be

```
      CHARACTER ITITLE(40)      or    CHARACTER*40 ITITLE
                          :
      READ  (4,1000)  ITITLE
 1000 FORMAT  (40A1)            or    FORMAT (A40)
      WRITE  (5,1002)  ITITLE
 1002 FORMAT  (1H1,20X, 40A1) or      FORMAT (1H1,20X, A40)
```

Using some of the blank padding features with A format can lead to useful I/O techniques. For example, reading into an array in A1 format and outputting into a larger A field will yield spaces between the characters. Note that the output characters are right-justified:

```
      CHARACTER  HEADNG(6)
                      :
      READ  (4,1000)  HEADNG
 1000 FORMAT  (6A1)
      WRITE  (5,1002)  HEADNG
 1002 FORMAT  (1H0, 6A2)
```

```
                                                        111
 Input columns:   123456      Output columns:   123456789012
                  LENGTH                        L E N G T H
```

10.3.2 Internal storage codes

If you are not sure what code is used in your computer, or if you want to determine the values of any of the characters used (including some of the special keys on your keyboard, like the function keys), the following program is useful. The variable is declared as INTEGER*2 so that we can show the direct relationship between character and numeric storage.

```
C               Program to display alphameric code value
C
      INTEGER*2  IC
C
C
   20 WRITE  (1,1020)
 1020 FORMAT  (1H0,'Enter desired character:')
      READ  (2,1022, END=90)  IC
 1022 FORMAT  (A1)
      WRITE  (1,1024)  IC, IC
 1024 FORMAT  (1H ,'Internal code for character ',A1,' =',I6)
      GO TO 20
```

```
C
   90 STOP
      END
```

If your computer implements hexadecimal output format (*Zn*), this code would be useful for examining the method of storage, checking for the padding blank; otherwise it will be necessary to convert the decimal answer to two separate eight-bit values.

To illustrate the possible variations of storage methods, entering the character 0 (zero) with the above program can lead to four different decimal values: 8240 (hex 2030), 12320 (hex 3020), −24400 (hex A0B0), and −20320 (hex B0A0). The first two are blank,zero and zero,blank; the last two are exactly the same, except that the leading bit of each group of eight is on, yielding a negative number. Although the seven-bit code for the character 0 is standard, the eighth bit and the location of the byte in the integer are not! (This program is very useful in determining how FORTRAN sees some of the special keys on the keyboard, such as the function keys, thus allowing the programmer to include their use in an application; however, be forewarned that these special key codes are not standardized and thus not portable from terminal to terminal.) The apparent reversal of characters is due to the practice in some implementations of storing arrays in reverse order, with the first element in the highest memory location and the array ascending in descending memory locations; thus two characters, whether stored as A2 or as 2A1, end up in the same locations.

10.3.3 Intrinsic conversion functions

Thus we can see the advisability of using the CHARACTER mode supplied by FORTRAN 77 wherever possible, since its implementation is transparent to the programmer. In fact there is no way of displaying the internal code used except by accessing the intrinsic function ICHAR, which converts the character to its numeric ASCII equivalent. Converting the above program to CHARACTER mode, we get:

```
C                   Program to display alphameric code value
C
      CHARACTER  IC
C
C
   20 WRITE   (1,1020)
 1020 FORMAT   (1H0,'Enter desired character:')
      READ   (2,1022, END=90)  IC
 1022 FORMAT   (A1)
      WRITE   (1,1024)  IC, ICHAR(IC)
 1024 FORMAT   (1H ,'Internal code for character ',A1,' =',I6)
      GO TO 20
```

```
C
  90 STOP
     END
```

There is also an intrinsic function CHAR, which converts a numeric code from 0 to 127 to CHARACTER mode; its application will appear in subsequent sections.

10.3.4 Review question

10–1. For the given program segment and the input field shown, determine the contents of each variable and the output lines:

```
      CHARACTER IN(8)*1, JN*4
      READ (4,1000) IN, JN
 1000 FORMAT (8A1, 2X, A3)
      WRITE (5,1002) (IN(K), K=1,8,2), JN
 1002 FORMAT (1H ,4A1, 2X, A5)
      WRITE (5,1004) (IN(K), K=5,7), JN
 1004 FORMAT (1H ,7A1)

                  1.......1
Input columns:    12345678901 2345678
                  ABCDEFGHIJKLMNOPQR
```

10.4 Assignment of alphameric data

A character can be assigned to a location just as a numeric value is; the character is placed between two apostrophes, as illustrated in the following program, which determines a letter grade for a given numeric one. The first version is more direct, but less sophisticated; the second uses arrays and the DATA statement.

```
C     Program to determine letter grade
C
C     For numeric grade between 90 and 100, letter grade = A
C        ''     ''    ''      ''   80 and 89,    ''     '' = B
C        ''     ''    ''      ''   70 and 79,    ''     '' = C
C        ''     ''    ''      ''   65 and 69,    ''     '' = D
C        ''     ''    ''     less than 65,       ''     '' = F
C

                   Version 1

      CHARACTER   GRADE
C
```

```
C                input loop
   20 WRITE   (1,1020)
 1020 FORMAT   (1H0,'Enter numeric grade')
      READ    (2,*, END=90) IGRADE
C                check ranges
      IF  (IGRADE .GE. 90)                      GRADE = 'A'
      IF  (IGRADE .GE. 80  .AND.   IGRADE .LE. 89)  GRADE = 'B'
      IF  (IGRADE .GE. 70  .AND.   IGRADE .LE. 79)  GRADE = 'C'
      IF  (IGRADE .GE. 65  .AND.   IGRADE .LE. 69)  GRADE = 'D'
      IF  (IGRADE .LT. 65)                      GRADE = 'F'
C                output
      WRITE   (1,1022)  GRADE
 1022 FORMAT   (1H ,'Letter grade is ',A1)
      GO TO 20
C                termination
   90 STOP
      END
```

Version 2

```
      CHARACTER   GRADE(5)
      INTEGER*2   RANGE(4)
C
      DATA   GRADE/ 'A', 'B', 'C', 'D', 'F'/,
     1       RANGE/ 90,  80,  70,  65/
C
C                input loop
   20 WRITE   (1,1020)
 1020 FORMAT   (1H0,'Enter numeric grade')
      READ    (2,*, END=90)  IGRADE
C                check ranges
      DO 40  I = 1,4
           IF  (IGRADE .GE. RANGE(I))   GO TO 60
   40 CONTINUE
      I = 5
C                output
   60 WRITE   (1,1060)  GRADE(I)
 1060 FORMAT   (1H ,'Letter grade is ',A1)
      GO TO 20
C                termination
   90 STOP
      END
```

Another useful application involves the output of monetary values in a form appreciated by most accountants, that is, with a trailing CR for credit instead of a leading minus sign for negative values. The following subprogram does just that:

```
      SUBROUTINE CREDIT (XIN, TRAILR)
C
C                returns a positive value unchanged with trailing blanks
C                   ''   absolute value of negative with trailing 'CR'
C
      CHARACTER*2 TRAILR

      IF  (XIN .GE. 0.00) THEN
              TRAILR = '  '
          ELSE
              XIN     = -XIN
              TRAILR = 'CR'
      ENDIF
      RETURN
      END
```

The calling program might look something like this:

```
      CHARACTER*2  ICR(6)
      DIMENSION    AMOUNT(6)
                      :
                      :
      DO 180  I = 1,6
  180 CALL CREDIT (AMOUNT(I), ICR(I))
      WRITE (3,1180) ((AMOUNT(I), ICR(I), I=1,6)
 1180 FORMAT (1H0, 6(F10.2,A2))
                      :
```

Once characters are defined, they can be treated just like other variables. Their use in IF statements looks no different from that of numeric variables, except that a character constant is placed between apostrophes to distinguish it from a variable name or a numeric constant. Thus the number zero (in the first IF below) and the character zero (in the second IF below) are two distinct entities.

```
CHARACTER  CNUM
INTEGER*2  INUM
                :
IF  (INUM .EQ. 0) ...
IF  (CNUM .EQ. '0') ...
                :
```

Interestingly, on a system whose internal character code is ASCII, an alpha sort can be performed by the same subprogram used to do an ascending integer sort; this sort can also be applied to characters stored in INTEGER*2 mode as long as only one character is stored in each location, regardless of whether stored in order or reversed, or with leading bit off or on.

Another very useful function determines the length of the contents of an array of characters, defining that length as the location of the last nonblank character in the string. The algorithm is optimized by scanning the array in reverse. Note the alphameric comparison with a blank character.

```
      FUNCTION LENSTR (STRING, LS)
C
C     Abstract: determines the last nonblank character in a string
C                    STRING of length LS.
C
      CHARACTER STRING(1)
C
      DO 40 L = 1,LS
          LENSTR = LS - L + 1
          IF (STRING(LENSTR) .NE. ' ') RETURN
   40 CONTINUE
      LENSTR = 0
      RETURN
      END
```

Using the decrementing DO loop, the DO 40 loop can be modified to:

```
      DO 40 LENSTR = LS,1,-1
          IF (STRING(LENSTR) .NE. ' ') RETURN
   40 CONTINUE
```

Another interesting subprogram is the one below, which converts all lowercase letters to uppercase. Note how the arithmetic statement function is written so that the program works in any internal code (ASCII or EBCDIC) by defining the difference between the code for lowercase and uppercase as the difference between those cases for any letter; we used A in this program, but any other letter could have been used.

```
C                 Subroutine L2U:  lower to upper case conversion
C
C         Abstract: converts the lower case letters in array ICIN of
C                    length NCIN to upper case.
C
      SUBROUTINE  L2U  (ICIN, NCIN)
C
      CHARACTER  ICIN(1), IC, LOW2UP
      INTEGER*2  NCIN
```

```
C
C                 arithmetic statement function to perform conversion
      LOW2UP (IC) = CHAR (ICHAR(IC) - (ICHAR('a') - ICHAR('A')))
C
      DO 40  I = 1,NCIN
          IF  (ICIN(I) .GE. 'a'  .AND.  ICIN(I) .LE. 'z')
     1                          ICIN(I) = LOW2UP (ICIN(I))
   40 CONTINUE
C
      RETURN
      END
```

The next program shows how a message can be built up from an assortment of strings. The function LENSTR (developed above) is used here. In the next section we will show the same program using some of the facilities offered by the full FORTRAN 77 language.

```
C                 Program Salutation
C
C     Abstract:  displays a salutation based on time of day and
C                        user's name.
C
C
      CHARACTER  NAME(18), MESSGE(42), HOWDY(12), SALUT(9,3)
      INTEGER*2  LENSAL(3), LNAME
C
      DATA  LENSAL/ 7,9,7/
      DATA  SALUT/'m','o','r','n','i','n','g',' ',' ',
     1            'a','f','t','e','r','n','o','o','n,'
     2            'e','v','e','n','i','n','g',' ',' '/
      DATA  HOWDY/'h','o','w',' ','a','r','e',' ','y','o','u','?'/
C
C                      enter name, get length
      WRITE  (1,1000)
 1000 FORMAT  (1H0,'Please enter your name (up to 18 characters')/
     1                        1H , 18('-'))
      READ  (2,1002)  NAME
 1002 FORMAT  (18A1)
      LNAME = LENSTR (NAME, 18)
```

```
C                    enter time as real number, determine part of day
      WRITE  (1,1004)
 1004 FORMAT  (1H0,'Enter military time (00.00 to 23.99)')
      READ  (2,*)  TIME
      ITIME = TIME
      ITIME = ITIME / 6
      IF  (ITIME .EQ. 0)  ITIME = 1
C                    move salutation into output string
      LSAL = LENSAL (ITIME)
      DO 20  I = 1,LSAL
   20 MESSGE(I) = SALUT(I,ITIME)
C                    blank rest of output line
      L = LSAL + 1
      DO 40  I = L,42
   40 MESSGE(I) = ' '
C                    transfer name into output line
      DO 60  I = 1,LNAME
         L = L + 1
   60 MESSGE(L) = NAME(I)
      L = L + 1
      MESSGE(L) = ','
      L = L + 1
C                    transfer greeting into output line
      DO 80  I = 1,12
         L = L + 1
   80 MESSGE(L) = HOWDY(I)
C                    output message
      WRITE  (1,1080)  MESSGE
 1080 FORMAT  (1H0,'Good ',42A1)
C     termination
      STOP
      END
```

A sample run is shown below:

```
Please enter your name (up to 18 characters)
------------------
G. Washington

Enter military time (00.00 to 23.99)
18.53

Good evening G. Washington, how are you?
```

10.4.1 Exercises

Exercise 10–1

Write a program with terminal I/O that reads in a four-digit integer number and converts it to words, for example

input	*output*
1704	One Seven Zero Four
16	One Six

Exercise 10–2

Write a program that reads in an eight-character date sequence and outputs it in words, as shown below. It might be found advantageous to input some of the numbers numerically and the rest alphamerically or, using T format, both ways.

input	*output*
10/12/86	October 12, 1986
07/01/87	July 1, 1987

Exercise 10–3

Write a program that generates a FORTRAN program source file from inputted abbreviated instructions, substituting the full string into the output file; use the following abbreviations:

abbreviation	*full character string*
<D	DIMENSION
<W	WRITE
<R	READ
<G	GO TO
<S	STOP and (on new line) END

For example,

input	*output*
<D IN(80)	`DIMENSION IN(80)`
<S	`STOP`
	`END`

10.5 Strings and substrings

FORTRAN 77 allows us to define CHARACTER variables capable of storing very large strings. This ability is extremely useful when handling information that remains constant, but it can cause problems when that string is to be examined and/or manipulated. To make manipulation of long strings easier, the full FORTRAN 77 allows the programmer to define substrings, that is, strings that are part of other strings, and perform many of the manipulations on them. However, the subset of FORTRAN 77 does not include the ability to work with substrings and must use other methods to perform the same process.

Let us reiterate and review some of the concepts of assignment involving strings of different length. The action of the statement

```
STRNGA = STRNGB
```

depends on the lengths of the variables storing the strings. If STRNGA and STRNGB are defined as character variables of the same length, the contents of the two locations represented by these variables become the same upon execution of the instruction. But if STRNGA is defined as shorter than STRNGB, STRNGA will contain only the leftmost characters of STRNGB, truncating the string when no more characters will fit into STRNGA. If STRNGA is defined as longer than STRNGB, the contents of STRNGB will be left-justified in STRNGA with blank padding on the end. Note that this placement is just the opposite of what happens when a string is output into a field bigger than it needs— then the string will be right-justified and padded with leading blanks. Thus the programmer must be cognizant of the difference in handling strings in assignment and in output, as illustrated in the following example.

```
C                    Example of String Assignment & Output
C
      CHARACTER   STR10*10, STR8*8, STR4*4
      DATA STR8/ 'ABCDEFGH'/
C
      STR10 = STR8
      STR4  = STR8
      WRITE  (1,1000) STR10, STR8, STR4, STR4,
     1                STR8, STR4, STR10, STR10
 1000 FORMAT  (1H ,A10, 2X, A8, 2X, A4, 2X, A7)
      STOP
      END

                         1........12........23........3
       Output:   12345678901234567890123456789012345678 9
                 ABCDEFGH     ABCDEFGH   ABCD      ABCD
                   ABCDEFGH        ABCD   ABCD   ABCDEFG
```

The full FORTRAN 77 (but not the subset) allows the user to access substrings by using range specifiers separated by a colon and embedded in a set of parentheses. For example, using STR8 as defined above,

STR8(3:6) refers to 'CDEF'

STR8(:6) refers to 'ABCDEF' (same as STR8(1:6))

STR8(3:) refers to 'CDEFGH' (same as STR8(3:8))

STR4 = STR8(2:4) yields 'BCD '

STR4 = STR8(2:8) yields 'BCDE'

STR4 = STR8(7:9) is illegal since range specifier is too big

STR8(2:5) = STR4 yields 'AABCDFGH'

STR8(2:5) = ' ' yields 'A   FGH'

STR8 = ' ' yields '   '

Note in the last case how a substring substitution can take place.

If the character variable is an array, the syntax is CVAR(*subscript*)(*range*), as in:

```
CHARACTER ASTR*10(4)
          :
ASTR(2)(5:7)=' '
```

which puts blanks into characters 5, 6, and 7 of the second element of array ASTR.

10.5.1 Additional intrinsic functions

There are a number of functions that pertain directly to string handling. Two of them, ICHAR and CHAR, have already been mentioned in section 10.3. If ICHAR has a string greater than one character as an argument, only the first character is converted to numeric code.

Because of the inability to sort correctly when EBCDIC code is used, there are four lexical comparison functions that refer to the ASCII collating (sorting) order even when EBCDIC code is used for internal storage. The four functions are:

LLT for lexically less than

LLE for lexically less than or equal to

LGT for lexically greater than

LGE for lexically greater than or equal to

The syntax of these functions is:

L*aa* (STRNG1, STRNG2)

where STRNG1 and STRNG2 are character variables and appear in such statements as:

```
IF (LLT (STRNG1, STRNG2)) IFLAG = 2
```

This is equivalent to

```
IF (STRNG1 .LT. STRNG2) IFLAG = 2
```

The logical operators .EQ. and .NE. are not affected by which internal storage code is used and may be programmed without hesitation. If the compared character variables are of different length, the shorter one is padded with trailing blanks so that the strings compared are of equal length.

Another available function is LEN (*character expression*), which returns the length of a character expression. LEN can determine either the number of characters in a character variable or the number of characters storable in a string constant, as illustrated in the program segment below, where both L1 and L2 will be assigned the value 10:

```
CHARACTER*10  STRNG
          :
L1 = LEN (STRNG)
L2 = LEN ('characters')
```

This function has limited usefulness and does not appear in the subset. However, it can be used in a subprogram to determine the length of a transmitted character variable.

INDEX is a more valuable function that also does not exist in the subset; it locates a substring (the second argument) within a string (the first argument) by locating the position of the first substring character in the full string. If the substring is not there, a value of 0 is returned. In the program segment below, L1 will contain the value 4 and L2 will contain a 0:

```
L1 = INDEX ('character', 'ract')
L2 = INDEX ('character', 'race')
```

A final character-handling facility that exists only in the full FORTRAN 77 is concatenation, which allows us to add character strings. The concatenation operator is a double slash (//), and the concatenation operation allows the programmer to include sets of parentheses for purposes of clarity or documentation, but they are ignored. For example:

```
CHARACTER*10  STRNG
STRNG = 'Good'//'-'//'Afternoon'
```

will place the string "Good-After" into STRNG, which has been defined as having 10 characters. Again, if the storage location is larger than the generated string, the location is padded with trailing blanks.

Since the LEN function does not give us the length of the nonblank character string contained in a character variable, it might be useful to have a function similar in operation to function LENSTR, which was described in section 10.4.

We will also introduce here a feature of FORTRAN 77 for which we have had very little use previously—the use of an assumed size dimension wherein the value of the dimension *and* the length of a character variable are unspecified in the subprogram and taken from the calling program.

```
CHARACTER*(*)  STRING    refers to a single string in a subprogram
        of unknown length.
CHARACTER*(*)  STRING(1) refers to an array string in a subprogram
        of unknown length.
```

It is in this type of situation that the function LEN becomes valuable.

```
      FUNCTION  LNSTR (STRING)
C
C     Abstract:  determines the last non-blank character in a character
C                variable of any length.
C
      CHARACTER*(*)  STRING
C
C             get size of character variable
      LENGTH = LEN (STRING)
C             pass through string backwards looking for last non-blank
      DO 40  LENSTR = LENGTH,1,-1
          IF  (STRING(LENSTR:LENSTR) .NE. ' ')  RETURN
   40 CONTINUE
      LNSTR = 0
      RETURN
      END
```

Now we can rewrite our salutation program using these new tools:

```
C             Program Salutation
C
C     Abstract:  displays a salutation based on time of day and
C                user's name.
C
C
      CHARACTER  NAME*18, MESSGE*47, HOWDY*12, SALUT*9(3)
      INTEGER*2  LENSAL(3), LNAME
C
      DATA  LENSAL/ 7,9,7/
      DATA  SALUT/'morning  ',
     1            'afternoon,'
     2            'evening  '/
      DATA  HOWDY/'how are you?'/
```

```
C
C                    enter name, get length
      WRITE  (1,1000)
 1000 FORMAT  (1H0,'Please enter your name (up to 18 characters')/
     1                        1H , 18('-'))
      READ  (2,1002)  NAME
 1002 FORMAT  (A18)
      LNAME = LNSTR (NAME)
C                    enter time as real number, determine part of day
      WRITE  (1,1004)
 1004 FORMAT  (1H0,'Enter military time (00.00 to 23.99)')
      READ  (2,*)  TIME
      ITIME = TIME
      ITIME = ITIME / 6
      IF  (ITIME .EQ. 0)  ITIME = 1
C                    concatenate output string
      LSAL = LENSAL (ITIME)
      MESSGE = 'Good '//SALUT(ITIME)(1:LSAL)//' '//NAME(1:LNAME)//
     1          ', '//HOWDY
C                    output message
      WRITE  (1,1080)  MESSGE
 1080 FORMAT  (1H0, A47)
C                    termination
      STOP
      END
```

10.5.2 Exercises

Exercise 10–4

If you have the full FORTRAN 77 available, repeat exercise 10–1 using the techniques described above.

Exercise 10–5

If you have the full FORTRAN 77 available, repeat exercise 10–2 using the techniques described above.

10.6 Internal files

Since it does not have the ability to work with substrings, the subset of FORTRAN 77 would be very handicapped if it were not for another feature that allows the use of the I/O facilities to modify strings. This facility is derived from two commands that were implemented in some earlier versions of FORTRAN, ENCODE and DECODE.

For example, let's consider how we might implement the INDEX function in the FORTRAN 77 subset, where it does not exist as an intrinsic function. We would need some way of converting the information in a long character variable into an array of CHARACTER*1. One way of doing this is to write the information into a disk file record using one format and read it back with another into the array. In the function below, we open a temporary (or scratch) direct access file just for that purpose; in the subset, a file is automatically closed at the end of the execution of the program and a scratch file is automatically deleted. A scratch file is set up by not specifying a file name.

```
C                       Function INDEX for FORTRAN '77 Subset
C
      FUNCTION  INDEX  (STRING, SUBSTR, LSUBST)
C
C     Abstract:  determines location of Substring SUBSTR (CHAR*1 array)
C                     of length LSUBST in String STRING (CHAR*n).
C                     Limit of 80 characters.
C
      CHARACTER  STRING*(*), SUBSTR(80)*1, TMPSTR(80)*1
C
C                     open scratch file 99
      OPEN  (99, ACCESS='DIRECT', FORM='FORMATTED', RECL=80)
C                         write to file
      WRITE  (99,1000, REC=1)  STRING
 1000 FORMAT  (A80)
C                         read from file
      READ   (99,1002, REC=1)  TMPSTR
 1002 FORMAT  (80A1)
C                         search for substring
      LSTR   = LENSTR (TMPSTR,80)
      NSERCH = LSTR - LSUBST + 1
      IF  (NSERCH .LT. 1)  GO TO 120
      DO 100  INDEX = 1,NSERCH
         II = INDEX
         DO 60  J = 1,LSUBST
            IF  (SUBSTR(J) .NE. TMPSTR(II))  GO TO 100
   60    II = II + 1
         RETURN
  100 CONTINUE
  120 INDEX = 0
      RETURN
      END
```

The value of NSERCH is determined in such a way that any attempt to go beyond the main string is prevented.

10.6.1 ENCODE/DECODE

Writing a record to a disk file and then reading it is rather time-consuming, involving extra physical effort by the computer. The ENCODE statement allowed the translation of any data in any format to character data; the DECODE statement allowed the translation of character data to data in any format. The general forms of these statements are:

```
ENCODE (c, f, b) variable-list
DECODE (c, f, b) variable-list
```

where c is the number of characters, f is the format statement number, and b is the character array.

Most implementations of these statements still use the old FORTRAN 66 method of character storage of two characters in an INTEGER*2 variable. Thus the above program for the function INDEX becomes:

```
C                        Function INDEX for FORTRAN '77 Subset
C
      FUNCTION  INDEX  (STRING, SUBSTR, LSUBST)
C
C     Abstract:  determines location of Substring SUBSTR (CHAR*1 array)
C                of length LSUBST in String STRING (CHAR*n).
C                Limit of 80 characters.
C
      CHARACTER  STRING*(*), SUBSTR(80)*1, TMPSTR(80)*1
      INTEGER*2  ITEMP(40)
C
C                        ENCODE to character array
      ENCODE (80,1000, ITEMP)  STRING
 1000 FORMAT  (A80)
C                        DECODE to character*1 array
      DECODE (80,1002, ITEMP)  TMPSTR
 1002 FORMAT  (80A1)
C                        search for substring
                            :
                          etc.
```

10.6.2 "Memory" files

The program given above is much faster in that no disk access is required. However, FORTRAN 77 did not implement the ENCODE and DECODE commands (although some manufacturers did for the sake of upward compatibility). Instead, FORTRAN 77 uses the concept of an internal file in which the logical unit number of a file is replaced with a character variable corresponding to the size of the desired record. This method accesses a series of locations in memory instead of a disk file, and thus it works very much like the ENCODE/DECODE pair. Again, revising the above program:

```
C                       Function INDEX for FORTRAN '77 Subset
C
      FUNCTION  INDEX  (STRING, SUBSTR, LSUBST)
C
C     Abstract:  determines location of substring SUBSTR (CHAR*1 array)
C                of length LSUBST in string STRING (CHAR*n).
C                Limit of 80 characters.
C
      CHARACTER     STRING*(*), SUBSTR(80)*1, TMPSTR(80)*1
      CHARACTER*80  INTFLE
C
C                     write to internal file
      WRITE  (INTFLE, 1000)  STRING
 1000 FORMAT  (A80)
C                     read from internal file
      READ   (INTFLE, 1002)  TMPSTR
 1002 FORMAT  (80A1)
C                     search for substring
                        :
                      etc.
```

Before we leave this subject, let us look at one very practical implementation of the internal file. Suppose we are inputting data and wish to edit it before formatting it numerically; this is sometimes necessary because the implementation of the ERR= clause may not trap invalid characters the way we might expect. Thus one solution is to input a line alphamerically, check to make sure that all characters are valid, and then, using an internal file, reformat the input. The subprogram below is a simple example of this type of application:

```
C               Subroutine INPTI4:  edits input & converts to I4 format
C
      SUBROUTINE  INPTI4  (IOUT, NERR)
C
C     Abstract:  inputs a 40 column field.  checks that all characters
C                are either numbers, minus, plus or blank.
C                Returns an array of 10 integer values if ok,
C                otherwise all zeros and a positive error counter.
C                If end-of-file, NERR = -1
C
      CHARACTER  IN(40)*1, INTFLE*40
      DIMENSION  IOUT(10)
```

```
C
C                    clear array and error counter
      DO 20  I = 1,10
   20 IOUT(I) = 0
      NERR    = 0
C                    input into character array
      READ (3,1020, END=90)  IN
 1020 FORMAT (40A1)
C                    edit for valid characters
      DO 40  I = 1,40
         IF (IN(I) .GE. '0'  .AND.  IN(I) .LE. '9')  GO TO 40
         IF (IN(I) .EQ. '-'  .OR.  IN(I) .EQ. '+'  .OR.
    1         IN(I) .EQ. ' ')                        GO TO 40
         NERR = NERR + 1
   40 CONTINUE
      IF (NERR .GT. 0) RETURN
C                    convert to I4 format
      WRITE (INTFLE,1020)  IN
      READ  (INTFLE,1040)  IOUT
 1040 FORMAT (10I4)
      RETURN
C                    end-of-file
   90 NERR = -1
      RETURN
      END
```

10.6.3 Exercise

Exercise 10–6

Write a program to input a monetary value and compute a tax at 5% and a total cost. Then print out the answer with a space between each character. For example, for an input of 52.40 the output would be:

5 2 . 4 0   w i t h   t a x   o f   2 . 6 2   =   5 5 . 0 2

10.7 Decoding

In the previous sections we covered all of the commands and features of FORTRAN that facilitate alphameric manipulation. Now we will look at a series of applications. However, there are so many possible applications that it is difficult to choose which would be of greatest interest and usefulness. The author has chosen to present a number of subprograms that illustrate techniques that have proven useful over the last two decades of practical programming. These subprograms should present enough insight into the myriad of possible applications to fire the imagination of the reader!

Decoding is the process whereby information is extracted from a record. For example, we are all familiar with operating system commands that are entered in free format and may be abbreviated. The program that interprets the command must parse it into its component parts and extract what is needed to continue with its processing. Let's start with a function that receives a string of alpha characters in A1 format and returns the number derived from it.

```
      FUNCTION  GETVAL (ISTR, NSTR)
C
C     Abstract:  receives a string of A1 characters and returns value
C                extracted from it.  All non-numeric values are
C                ignored
C
C     Glossary: ISTR:   a string of characters in A1 format
C               NSTR:   number of characters to be scanned
C
      IMPLICIT INTEGER*2  (I-N)
      CHARACTER  ISTR(1)
C
C                    initialize value and indicators
      GETVAL = 0.0
      SGN    = 1.0
      NDEC   = 0
C                loop through characters
      DO 20  I = 1,NSTR
C                    check for plus, minus signs and decimal point
          IF  (ISTR(I) .EQ. '+')  GO TO 20
          IF  (ISTR(I) .EQ. '-')  THEN
              SGN = -1.0
              GO TO 20
          ENDIF
          IF  (ISTR(I) .EQ. '.')  THEN
              NDEC = NDEC - 1
              GO TO 20
          ENDIF
C                        eliminate non-digits
          IF  (ISTR(I) .LT. '0'  .OR.  ISTR(I) .GT. '9')  GO TO 20
C                        convert from internal code to number
          VALUE = ICHAR (ISTR(I)) - ICHAR ('0')
C                        if before decimal point, add new digit
          IF  (NDEC .EQ. 0)  GETVAL = 10.0 * GETVAL  +  VALUE
```

```
C                        if after decimal point, add in power
         IF (NDEC .LT. 0) THEN
              GETVAL = GETVAL  +  VALUE * 10.0 ** NDEC
              NDEC = NDEC - 1
         ENDIF
   20 CONTINUE
C                     adjust for sign and return
      GETVAL = SGN * GETVAL
      RETURN
      END
```

This function does have a possible bug, depending on the way in which it is called: all of the digits are considered valid, even if a nonnumeric character is embedded in them. Thus 12/a34BB5 would be interpreted as 12345, and because each entered decimal point decrements the power of 10 applied to the next digit, 12...34 would be interpreted as 12.0034. A more sophisticated function could stop evaluation upon reaching the first invalid character (which would include multiple decimal points) once the numeric value has been started; writing such a function would be an excellent student exercise.

Now let's use this technique to demonstrate how the necessary data can be extracted from a command line. Let's assume that we have an application that accepts four possible commands, two of which require a pair of numeric values for their execution. Because of the paucity of commands, we can select their names in such a way that we can key on the first letter of the command, although the user can enter the full command or any other word that starts with the same letter. Once we have isolated each of the necessary numeric values, a call to GETVAL will evaluate them:

```
C             Program FILEDESC:  display certain file parameters
C
C    Abstract: Reads a command line from keyboard.  Interprets line and
C              branches to appropriate routine.  Possible commands:
C                 NUMBER to display number of active records in
C                                      direct access file
C                 LIST nnn1 nnn2  to display records nnn1 to nnn2
C                 SUM nnn1 nnn2  to display sum of real field in
C                                      records nnn1 to nnn2
C                 EXIT to terminate execution of program
C
C    Glossary of indices:    I is column pointer
C                            J is key number
C                            K is counter for numeric values
C
```

```
C
      IMPLICIT INTEGER*2  (I-N)
      CHARACTER   IN(80), KEY(4)
      DATA            KEY/ 'E', 'L', 'N', 'S'/
C
C                      open file, find number of active records
      OPEN  (................
                     :
C                     :        routine to determine number of active records
C                     :                NREC
C
C                 enter command
   20 WRITE  (1,1020)
 1020 FORMAT   (1H0,'Enter:   NUMBER'/
     1         1H ,8X,      'LIST  nnn1  nnn2'/
     2         1H ,8X,      'SUM   nnn1  nnn2'/
     3         1H ,8X,      'EXIT')
      READ  (2,1022,END=990)  IN
 1022 FORMAT  (80A1)
C                       search for first letter (upper or lower case)
         DO 40  I = 1,80
             IF  (IN(I) .GE. 'A'  .AND.  IN(I) .LE. 'Z')  GO TO 60
             IF  (IN(I) .GE. 'a'  .AND.  IN(I) .LE. 'z')  THEN
                 IN(I) = CHAR(ICHAR(IN(I))
     1                    (ICHAR('A') - ICHAR('a')))
                 GO TO 60
             ENDIF
   40    CONTINUE
C                       no letters entered
         GO TO 20
C                       letter found, check for valid one
   60    DO 80  J = 1,4
             IF  (IN(I) .EQ. KEY(J))  GO TO 100
   80    CONTINUE
C                       invalid key
         WRITE  (1,1080)
 1080    FORMAT (1H ,'INVALID COMMAND  -  RETRY!')
         GO TO 20
```

```
C                       valid key.
   100      IF  (J .EQ. 1)  THEN
              CLOSE  (....
              STOP
           ENDIF
           IF  (J .EQ. 3)  THEN
              WRITE  (1,1100)  NREC
  1100           FORMAT  (1H0,I5,' records in file!)
              GO TO 20
           ENDIF
C                     for commands L and S, determine record numbers
           DO 200  K = 1,2
C                            find first digit
              II = I
              DO 120  I = II,80
                 IF  (IN(I) .GE. '0'  .AND.  IN(I) .LE. '9')
     1                                          GO TO 140
   120        CONTINUE
C                             no numeric field
                 GO TO 800
C                        find end of numeric field
   140        ISTART = I
              II    = I
              DO 160  I = II,80
                 IF  (IN(I) .LT. '0'  .OR.  IN(I) .GT. '9')
     1                                          GO TO 180
   160        CONTINUE
              I = 81
C                        evaluate number
   180        LENGTH = I - ISTART
              NN(K) = GETVAL (IN(ISTART), LENGTH)
C                        see if room in line for second value
              IF  (I .GE. 79  .AND.  K .EQ. 1)  GO TO 800
              I = I + 1
   200     CONTINUE
C                     distribute to appropriate routine
           IF  (J .EQ. 2)  GO TO routine to list records
           IF  (J .EQ. 4)  GO TO routine to summarize records
                    :
                    :
C                          no numeric field
   800        WRITE  (1,1800)
  1800        FORMAT  (1H0,'MISSING NUMERIC FIELD  -  RETRY!')
              GO TO 20
```

```
C
  990 STOP
      END
```

A few comments are in order here. Care must be taken to assure that we do not try to read beyond column 80 of the input line. Thus the careful reader will find places where the same input column is checked twice when scanning for the numeric fields; it was a choice of checking twice or adding more elaborate code that would not save any execution time, and the author, being lazy, chose to have the computer do more work than the programmer. Also note the call to GETVAL; by subscripting the array, the specified element becomes the first element in the subprogram's array, thus providing an alternative method of accessing substrings.

Finally, we will present a general decoding routine written over twenty years ago and still in use. It extracts multiple numeric data from an input line, assuming that all nonnumeric characters serve as delimiters, that is, separators of numeric fields; the coding actually treats those nonnumerics as blanks. Multiple signs or decimal points embedded in a number are treated both as what they represent and as delimiters. Thus, 12.3.4 becomes 12.3 and 0.4; 12--34 becomes 12, 0, and -34.

```
C                 Subroutine DCODE:  converts from A1 to real numeric
C
      SUBROUTINE DCODE (IN, JBEGN, JEND, NDATA, DATA, IND)
C
      CHARACTER   IN(1)
      REAL        DATA (1)
C
C         IN:      input array of A1 characters
C         JBEGIN:  first element in array to be decoded
C         JC:      indicator for last symbol (+ - .) found
C         JEND:    last    "   "   "   "   "      "
C         NDATA:   maximum number of values to be extracted
C         DATA:    output array for values
C         IND:     overflow indicator  -  if 0, no overflow
C                              if >0, number of excessive values
C
C   Glossary: IC       column pointer
C             IFLAG    if 1, value not begun
C                      if 2, in process of developing value
C                      if 3, + - or . as only delimiter
C                      if 4, end of input reached
C             ISGN     sign indicator: 1 = +, -1 =
C             JPNT     if 1, developing integer portion
```

```
C                              if 2, developing decimal portion
C                    N         counter of value being generated
C                    NDPLAC    decimal place locator
C                    VAR       temporary location to develop value
C
C
C                         initialization of counters, indicators and values
      IND = 0
      N   = 0
      IC  = JBEGIN
C
C                         initialization for new value
   10 IFLAG  = 1
      ISGN   = 1
      VAR    = 0.0
      NDPLAC = 0
      JPNT   = 1
C                    isolate + - .
   20 JC = 0
      IF  (IN(IC) .EQ. '+')   JC = 1
      IF  (IN(IC) .EQ. '-')   JC = 2
      IF  (IN(IC) .EQ. '.')   JC = 3
      IF  (JC      .EQ. 0)    GO TO 200
C                         + - or . at beginning of value
      IF  (IFLAG .NE. 2)  THEN
          IFLAG = 2
          IF  (JC .EQ. 2)  ISGN = -1
          IF  (JC. EQ. 3)  JPNT = 2
          GO TO 300
      ENDIF
C                    + - or . within input field
      IF (JC .EQ. 1)  GO TO 320
      IF (JC .EQ. 2 .OR.  (JC .EQ. 3  .AND.  JPNT .EQ. 2))  THEN
              IFLAG = 3
              GO TO 320
          ELSE
              JPNT = 2
              GO TO 300
      ENDIF
C
C                    check for delimiter
  200 IF (IN(IC) .LT. '0'  .OR.  IN(IC) .GT. '9')
     1                                        GO TO (300, 320), IFLAG
```

```
C                     digit found
      XNUM = ICHAR(IN(IC)) - ICHAR('0')
      IF  (IFLAG .EQ. 1)  IFLAG = 2
      IF  (JPNT .EQ. 1)  THEN
              VAR = 10.0 * VAR  +  XNUM
          ELSE
              NDPLAC = NDPLAC - 1
              VAR = VAR  +  XNUM * 10.0 ** NDPLAC
      ENDIF
C
C                     increment location in input array
  300 IC = IC + 1
      IF  (IC .LE. JEND)  GO TO 20
      IFLAG = 4
      IF  (VAR .EQ. 0.00)  GO TO 400
C                     place in output array, if room
  320 N = N + 1
      IF  (N .LE. NDATA)  THEN
              DATA(N) = VAR + FLOAT(ISGN)
          ELSE
              IND = IND + 1
      ENDIF
C                     set up for next value
  350 IF  (IFLAG .LE. 3)  GO TO 10
C
C                     fill unused fields with 0.00
  400 N = N + 1
      IF  (N .LE. NDATA)  THEN
          DO 420  I = N,NDATA
  420         DATA(I) = 0.00
      ENDIF
C                     return
      RETURN
      END
```

10.7.1 Exercise

Exercise 10–7

A computer system allows a date to be entered in a variety of ways, all of which use free format but have certain distinctive characteristics. Develop a series of subprograms that accept an input date and return three values: a number from 1 to 12 to represent the month, another from 1 to 31 to represent the day, and a third from 1921 to 2020 to represent the year. Tie all of the subprograms into a driver mainline that inputs the line, branches to the appropriate routine, and outputs the results. The date can be entered in any of the following forms:

a. Numeric input with slashes, spaces, or hyphens between the numbers. Allowable forms include:
   11/2/86   11/02/86   11 2 86   11-02-86   3-22-88
   There may be additional blanks within the string but not embedded in the numbers. Leading zeros may be included with one-digit numbers.

b. Numeric sorted order with year, month, day as one constant length string of six characters, for example, 880322.

c. Alphameric form, such as February 2, 1988 or MAR.22,1988. The first three characters of the month can be used as the key, but both uppercase and lowercase letters are valid. There may also be a period if the month is abbreviated, and the blanks shown may be omitted. The comma is required.

d. A form such as 22MAR88, in which the constant length string always begins with a two-digit day, a three-character month, and a two-digit year trailer.

10.8 Encoding

Encoding is a process in which numeric data is converted to alphameric form so that it can be manipulated character by character. When dealing with output, the term *editing* is often used to describe this process. The only difficulty we may run into is that the FORTRAN 77 subset does not have the CHAR routine, which converts the equivalent character code into a digit, and even where we do have it, it will not work with EBCDIC code. Thus we must develop our own equivalent routine.

On an ASCII machine, the conversion to alphameric is very easy since the character code for a digit is 48 higher than the value of the digit itself. On non-ASCII computers or in FORTRAN 66, the equation varies depending on how the value is stored. The function below is guaranteed to work in all cases, even in FORTRAN 66, where INTEGER*2 must be substituted for CHARACTER*1:

```
      CHARACTER*1 FUNCTION MYCHAR(N)
C
C     Abstract: returns the character code for the digit received
C               Works with all internal storage codes
C
      CHARACTER  CH(10)
      INTEGER*2  N
      DATA       CH/ '0','1','2','3','4', '5','6','7','8','9'/
C
      MYCHAR = CH(N+1)
      RETURN
      END
```

This function is designed to be used only in the controlled situation where the value of N transmitted to it is within the range 0 to 9. We will use this function in the applications below. The reader is advised to experiment with CHAR and to write individual arithmetic statement functions for his or her own internal code.

The routine presented below allows FORTRAN to output real numbers in commercial format, that is, with commas in the appropriate places and a floating dollar sign (just to the left of the first significant digit). Leading zeros are suppressed except for the one immediately before the decimal point if the value is less than $1.00. Zero values are left blank, and values that overflow the field (as well as invalid options) result in the field being filled with asterisks. Negative values have the option of sign suppression, a trailing minus, a trailing CR, or enclosing parentheses. The input is limited to 12 significant digits, thus allowing values up to almost $10 billion. The output field in the calling program is larger than necessary for a single value, thus allowing a number of values to be placed in the same output array for output of a single line of multiple values.

```
C                 Subroutine MONEY:  reformats real values to money output
C
        SUBROUTINE  MONEY  (VALUE, IOUT, LEND, NCOL, IOP)
C
C        VALUE:     real value to be edited
C        IOUT:      output array in Character mode
C        LEND:      end position in output array
C        NCOL:      number of available columns in output array
C        IOP:       positive for floating '$', negative for none
C                         +/-1, sign suppression
C                         +/-2, trailing '-'
C                         +/-3, trailing 'CR'
C                         +/-4, enclosing parenthesis
C
        IMPLICIT INTEGER*2  (I-N)
        IMPLICIT DOUBLE PRECISION  (A-H, O-Z)
        CHARACTER  IOUT(1), IDIG(12)
C
        DIMENSION  NDIG(12), KOP(4)
        DATA                KOP/ 0, 1, 2, 1/
C
C   Glossary: NDIG      twelve individual digits, obtained from VALUE
C             IDIG      the characters obtained from NDIG
C             IS        sign indicator (+1 or -1)
C             JD        number of digits following leading zeros
C             KOP       amount of shift from end of field due to
C                             negative value indicator used
```

```
C                 L          column pointer
C                 LBEG       beginning of output field
C                 ND         number of columns needed
C
C                    check option value
      JOP = IABS (IOP)
      IF (JOP .EQ. 0 .OR. JOP .GT. 4) GO TO 90
C                    find beginning of field and clear field
      LBEG = LEND - NCOL + 1
      DO 10  I = LBEG,LEND
   10 IOUT(I) = ' '
C                    breakdown number (rounded) into 12 digits,
C                       convert to 12 characters
      IS = DSIGN (1.D+00, VALUE)
      X  = DABS  (VALUE * 100.00) + 0.50
      IF (X .GT. 1.D+12)  GO TO 90
      DO 20  I = 1,12
          DIV    = 10.0 ** (12-I)
          NDIG(I) = X / DIV
          X       = X  -  DIV * FLOAT (NDIG(I))
   20 IDIG(I) = MYCHAR(NDIG(I))
C                    find number of digits (JD), needed columns (ND)
C                       convert leading zeros to blanks
      DO 30  I = 1,9
          IF (IDIG(I) .NE. '0')  GO TO 50
   30 IDIG(I) = ' '
      JD = 3
      ND = 4
C                    if zero, leave blank and return
      DO 40  I = 10,12
          IF (IDIG(I) .NE. '0')  GO TO 60
   40 CONTINUE
             RETURN
C
C                    not zero
   50 ND = 14 - I
      JD = 13 - I
C                    adjust for commas and for trailer
   60 ND = ND  +  (ND-4) / 3
      ND = ND  +  KOP (JOP)
C                    adjust for leading parenthesis and/or '$'
      IF (JOP .EQ. 4  .AND.  IS .LT. 0)  ND = ND + 1
      IF (IOP .GT. 0)                    ND = ND + 1
```

```
C                       check for overflow
      IF  (ND .LE. NCOL)  GO TO 110
C                         insert asterisks and return
   90 DO 100  I = LBEG,LEND
  100 IOUT(I) = '*'
                RETURN
C
C                     locate position of end of number
  110 L = LEND
      IF  (IS .GT. 0)  THEN
                L = L - KOP(JOP)
          ELSE
C                         insert trailer
            IF  (JOP .EQ. 2)  THEN
                    IOUT(L) = '-'
                    L = L - 1
            ENDIF
            IF  (JOP .EQ. 3)  THEN
                    IOUT(L)   = 'R'
                    IOUT(L-1) = 'C'
                    L = L - 2
            ENDIF
            IF  (JOP .EQ. 4)  THEN
                    IOUT(L) = ')'
                    L = L - 1
            ENDIF
      ENDIF
C                     relocate digits, inserting commas and decimal point
      II = 12
      DO 190  I = 1,JD
          IOUT(L) = IDIG(II)
          L  = L  - 1
          II = II - 1
                GO TO (190,170,190, 190,180,190,
     1                  190,180,190, 190,180,190), I
  170     IOUT(L) = '.'
          L = L - 1
                GO TO 190
  180     IF  (I .LT. JD)  THEN
                IOUT(L) = ','
                L = L - 1
          ENDIF
  190 CONTINUE
```

```
C                       add floating '$'
      IF  (IOP .GT. 0)  THEN
          IOUT(L) = '$'
          L = L - 1
      ENDIF
C                     add leading parenthesis, if necessary
      IF  (JOP .EQ. 4  .AND.  IS .LT. 0)  IOUT(L) = '('
C                         return
      RETURN
      END
```

10.8.1 Exercises

Exercise 10–8

Write a program that accepts as input an integer value in the range of 0 to 32767 and outputs the equivalent four-character hexadecimal value.

Exercise 10–9

Write a program that inputs a positive integer value and breaks it down into gross (144 units), dozen (12 units), and units. The output should be in the form shown below.

input	*output*
512	3 gross, 6 dozen, 8 units
120	10 dozen
118	9 dozen, 10 units
290	2 gross, 2 units

Exercise 10–10

Write a program that inputs a positive real number in centimeters and converts it to feet and inches, rounding to the nearest eighth of an inch and reducing the fraction where possible to halves or quarters. Use the equivalency 2.54 centimeters = 1 inch. The output should have the form:

input	*output*
100	3 feet, 3 3/8 inches
499	16 feet, 4 1/2 inches
8	3 1/8 inches
61	2 feet
127	4 feet, 2 inches

10.9 **Text editing**

Text editing is another active area for programmers. Text editing actually refers to all alphameric work, but we are concentrating here on the manipulation of text without the mixture of alpha and numeric work that we have looked at in the previous two sections. Text editing, in its simplest form, is done by the editors that most programmers use when entering and modifying a program through a terminal. In its most advanced form, it includes word processing and typesetting.

As an example, we will look at an application that reads a file and substitutes text where desired. Even an application like this has many options. For example, we might do a string substitution (like most editors), or we might do a word substitution where we substitute only for a full word. For example, in a string substitution, the string "the" will substitute for "the," "there," "their," "then," "other," and so forth. In a word substitution, the string "the" will substitute for the string "the" only when it is surrounded by blanks and/or punctuation. We must also consider upper- and lowercase: should the string "the " also substitute for "The" or "THE"?

We will do a word substitution ignoring case, that is, we will substitute for any word of the same length as the desired string with the same letters, regardless of whether the letters are upper- or lowercase. This adds complications to the program but also makes it more interesting. We will also avoid the problems of input and output by writing a subroutine that acts under the following assumptions:

1. The input array of CHARACTER*1 will be defined in the calling program and transmitted to the subroutine with its number of valid characters (that is, ignoring the trailing blanks).

2. There will be an output array of CHARACTER*1 defined in the calling program and transmitted to the subroutine with its storage capacity in characters so that the subroutine will not try to store more characters in it than it can handle. It is expected that the output array will be larger than the input array so that substitutions of longer strings can be accommodated, within reason.

3. Two CHARACTER*1 arrays with their respective lengths will be sent to the subroutine; they represent the word to be searched for and its replacement.

4. There will be a returned indicator of the number of characters stored in the output array. Should the output array become filled to capacity, that indicator will be given a negative value.

5. It is assumed that any nonletter except an apostrophe or hyphen is a word delimiter.

```
C                  Subroutine  SUBSTR:  makes string substitutions
C
       SUBROUTINE  SUBSTR (STRIN, LENIN,    STROUT, LENOUT,
      1                    STROLD, LENOLD,  STRNEW, LENNEW,  NCHAR)
C
       IMPLICIT    INTEGER*2  (I-N)
       CHARACTER  STRIN(1), STROUT(1), STROLD(1), STRNEW(1),
      1           UPBUFF(80,2), LOW2UP, IC
C
C      Glossary: String     Length    Description
C                STRIN      LENIN      input string
C                STROUT     LENOUT     output string
C                STROLD     LENOLD     word to be replaced
C                STRNEW     LENNEW     replacement word
C
C          NCHAR:   number of new characters in output array.  If
C                     storage overflow, NCHAR becomes negative.
C          NIN:     input array pointer
C          INDOV:   overflow indicator
C          LENWRD:  length of word found
C          UPBUFF:  temporary area to store upper case equivalents of
C                     old word and found word
C
C                  statement function to convert lower to upper case
       LOW2UP (IC) = CHAR(ICHAR(IC) - (ICHAR('a') - ICHAR('A')))
C                  initialize parameters
       NIN   = 0
       NCHAR = 0
       INDOV = 1
C                  move old word into upper case buffer
       DO 20  I = 1,LENOLD
           IF  (STROLD(I) .GE. 'a'  .AND.  STROLD(I) .LE. 'z')  THEN
                   UPBUFF(I,1) = LOW2UP (STROLD(I))
               ELSE
                   UPBUFF(I,1) = STROLD(I)
           ENDIF
    20 CONTINUE
C
```

```
C                       begin processing:  look for first letter of word
  100 NIN = NIN + 1
      IF  ((STRIN(NIN) .GE. 'A'  .AND.  STRIN(NIN) .LE. 'Z')  .OR.
     1     (STRIN(NIN) .GE. 'a'  .AND.  STRIN(NIN) .LE. 'z'))
     2                                                   GO TO 140
      NCHAR = NCHAR + ISIGN (INDOV,1)
          IF  (NCHAR .GT. LENOUT)  THEN
              INDOV = -1
              NCHAR = -NCHAR
          ENDIF
      IF  (INDOV .GT. 0)  STROUT(NCHAR) = STRIN(NIN)
      IF  (NIN    .LT. LENIN)  GO TO 100
          RETURN
C                 letter found.  look for end of word
  140 II = NIN + 1
      DO 160  I = II,LENIN
      IF  (.NOT. (STRIN(I) .EQ. '-'  .OR.  STRIN(I) .EQ. ''''
     1     .OR.  (STRIN(I) .GE. 'A'  .AND.  STRIN(I) .LE. 'Z')
     2     .OR.  (STRIN(I) .GE. 'a'  .AND.  STRIN(I) .LE. 'z')))
     3                                                   GO TO 200
  160 CONTINUE
C                 end of input array
      I = LENIN + 1
C                 check length of found word
  200 LENWRD = I - NIN
      IF  (LENWRD .NE. LENOLD)  GO TO 300
C                 length matches.  put into upper case buffer
      DO 220  I = 1,LENWRD
          II = NIN - 1 + I
          IF  (STRIN(II) .GE. 'a'  .AND.  STRIN(II) .LE. 'z')  THEN
                UPBUFF(I,2) = LOW2UP (STRIN(II))
            ELSE
                UPBUFF(I,2) = STRIN(II)
          ENDIF
  220 CONTINUE
C                 compare buffer contents
      DO 240  I = 1,LENWRD
          IF  (UPBUFF(I,1) .NE. UPBUFF(I,2))  GO TO 300
  240 CONTINUE
```

```
C                       word match found.  do replacement
      DO 260  I = 1,LENNEW
           NCHAR = NCHAR + ISIGN (1,INDOV)
           IF  (NCHAR .GT. LENOUT)  THEN
                INDOV = -1
                NCHAR = -NCHAR
           ENDIF
           IF  (NCHAR .GT. 0)  STROUT(NCHAR) = STRNEW(I)
  260 CONTINUE
      NIN = NIN + LENWRD - 1
           GO TO 400
C                       no match found.  transfer old characters
  300 DO 320  I = 1,LENWRD
           II = NIN - 1 + I
           NCHAR = NCHAR + ISIGN (1,INDOV)
           IF  (NCHAR .GT. LENOUT)  THEN
                INDOV = -1
                NCHAR = -NCHAR
           ENDIF
           IF  (NCHAR .GT. 0)  STROUT(NCHAR) = STRIN(II)
  320 CONTINUE
C                       check for end of input array
  400 NIN = II
      IF  (NIN .LT. LENIN)  GO TO 100
           RETURN
C
      END
```

10.9.1 Exercises

Exercise 10–11

Write a sort subroutine for an alphameric key. The sort shown in section 9.4 (LSORT) can be adjusted to handle character data with the appropriate type statements and the insertion of ICHAR in the comparison. All else stays the same. If you are using FORTRAN 77 with INTEGER*2 mode for the alpha data stored in ASCII internal code, LSORT can be used as is.

Exercise 10–12

A sometimes useful research technique is to produce a concordance, that is, a list of all of the different words used in a text and a count of how many times each appears. Write a program to read in from a sequential text file and produce a concordance of the words used. Do not distinguish between upper- and lower-case. It will be useful to keep a letter count of each word in order to simplify the logic, as we did in the preceding program. List each word that appears and the number of times it appears. As an additional exercise, sort the concordance so that the words are in alphabetical order.

Exercise 10–13
Generally textbook material is passed through a program that tabulates the length of the words used and produces a frequency distribution of word size; this is used as an indication of the level of reading skills required of the reader. Write a program to read in from a sequential text file and produce such a frequency distribution, displaying the number of words 1 letter long, 2 letters long, 3 letters long, and so forth, up to 12 letters, placing all longer words into a group of words longer than 12 letters.

Exercise 10–14
Still another analysis technique used in analyzing text is to count the number of words per sentence. Write a program to read in from a rather long sequential text file and produce a word per sentence count.

10.10 Format identifiers

A format identifier is a character variable or array containing the characters that make up a valid format statement. Since we have seen how character variables can be input as data or modified, we now have the ability to modify formats during execution. In previous versions of FORTRAN where this was possible, such formats were called *run-time* formats.

In simplest form, we might see a code sequence like:

```
CHARACTER*11 FRMT1
        :
DATA   FRMT1/ '(1H0, 2I10)'/
        :
WRITE  (1, FRMT1) I, J
```

However, FORTRAN 77 gives us the facility to modify the format within the program:

```
FRMT1(10:10) = '2'
```

Now we are specifying 2 fields of 12.

The ability to input a format into a character variable allows us to read in a data file that contains as its first record the input format to be used. Characters in the format beyond the closing parenthesis are ignored, so we have no difficulty in reading into a long character variable. For example, the program segment:

```
      CHARACTER*66  INFRMT
      INTEGER*2     IDATA(2000)
           :
      READ  (3,1000)  INFRMT
1000 FORMAT  (A66)
      READ  (3,INFRMT, END = 120) (IDATA(I), I=1,2000)
           STOP 'excessive data'
  120 NREC = I - 1
           :
```

with data looking like this:

```
(4I6)
   123     52  1546  8852
 32767 26852-19058  -881
    -1  -850  1175
```

will read in four fields of six columns per record.

10.11 Summary

If this chapter doesn't whet the appetite of the reader, I don't know what will! If nothing else, it indicates why FORTRAN has had the staying power to survive many predictions of its death. Professional FORTRAN programmers see it as one of the most flexible general purpose languages; it offers challenges to the programmer, but there are very few situations in which a solution cannot be found. Fortunately, most manufacturers have taken the attitude that FORTRAN will be around for a long time yet and have developed FORTRAN interfaces with their operating systems so that it can use many of the file- and device-handling procedures available, as well as many of the system routines.

Nor have we seen the end of these techniques. They will be necessary in the next chapter, and the projects at the end of the text are replete with more exercises involving alphamerics.

topic	*section*
ASCII	10.2
Baudot	10.2
BCD	10.2
case conversion	10.4
CHAR	10.3
CHARACTER	10.3
concatenation	10.5
EBCDIC	10.2
ICHAR	10.3
INDEX	10.5
LEN	10.5
lexical functions LGE, LGT, LLE, LLT	10.5
substrings	10.5

11

Advanced input/output

11.1 Introduction

When FORTRAN first appeared, programmers were happy to be able to read punched cards, punch out answers onto cards, and write to a typewriter. The addition of on-line printers and magnetic tape required that new I/O commands be added to the language. Disk access was a slightly different matter, however, since disk formatting and hardware facilities differed so greatly; eventually most manufacturers supplied subprograms for disk access that either simulated the usual READs and WRITEs or required the transfer of information through buffers. With FORTRAN 77, a standard method of disk I/O finally became a reality. (For upward compatibility, some versions of FORTRAN 77 include some of the old FORTRAN 66 methods so that program revision is not necessary.)

However, additional output devices, particularly graphics hardware, were difficult to blend into any language. BASIC programmers using the microcomputers, who are accustomed to being able to place graphic symbols anywhere on the screen, find that other languages (and even BASIC on mainframes) are seriously lacking in that facility. In order to perform such procedures as erasing a given portion of a line or placing a prompt at any desired position, the FORTRAN programmer must resort to manufacturer-supplied software, and that software may pertain only to limited specific hardware (usually the manufacturer's own). In many cases, such software is not even available for non-BASIC languages, even on the micros.

For a hardware device to be supported by a computer system, the device must have a piece of software called a *driver,* which converts the ASCII or EBCDIC code transmitted to it to the actual hardware codes needed to drive the device electrically. (Sometimes this software is called a *filter* because it allows some signals to go through unchanged and others to be appropriately converted.) Computer manufacturers supply the drivers needed for the devices supplied with their systems. Devices not supported by the manufacturer also require a driver; that software may be obtainable from the manufacturer of the device or it may have to be written by the user. The latter prospect is usually not too enjoyable, since most drivers and/or filters must be written in assembly language.

In this chapter we will discuss some of the output devices available and attempt to guide the reader as to how to find solutions in specialized I/O situations. The only real "graphics" we will consider concerns the placing of standard alphameric characters on the screen or printer to simulate a drawing or graph; we will do this in the next section. All other graphics is hardware-dependent, and we can only offer some general hints. Our discussion will be limited to standard output devices such as the alphameric screen, the character printer, and the digital plotter and will not concern itself with the more sophisticated graphics screens that are usually supported with FORTRAN-callable routines supplied by the manufacturer.

11.2 Character graphics

Character manipulation can easily be used to produce graphical output on either the screen or the printer. The fundamental idea is to divide the output space into a number of pixels (picture elements) corresponding to the number of character positions on the particular device. On most continuous forms printers, it is usually possible to use 132 columns and an unlimited number of rows. On a screen, the user should limit the output to 79 columns (using 80 columns usually will cause a skipped line, since most screens "wrap-around" to the next line before issuing the end-of-line) and 23 rows (most screens will automatically move to the 24th line; an attempt to display more than 24 lines will cause the top lines to scroll off the screen unless the user manually controls the scrolling).

Now the quality of the graphics produced in this manner is no great shakes! However, it is easy to program, the output is rapid, and it often produces enough of a picture to convey information very efficiently. On the printer, the ability to overprint using the + carriage control allows the programmer to produce a better product; however, the programming effort becomes much more extensive.

Our approach will be to work within a matrix of characters, placing the desired character in the right location before outputting the matrix. The major difficulty will be realizing that row 1 of the matrix is at the top of the output and the row numbers increase going downward. Below is a simple example in which the parabola represented by $3y = x^{**}2 - 8x + 19$ is plotted in the range from $x = 1$ to $x = 7$. The output is:

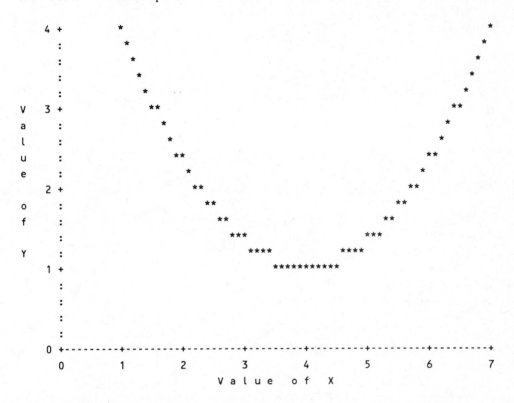

As we said, no great shakes, but the program that produced it is quite simple.

```
C               Screen Display of Graph:  3y = x**2 - 8x + 19
C
      CHARACTER  MOUT(79,23), IANNO(10), IN
C
      DATA  MOUT/ 1817 * ' '/
      DATA  IANNO/'V','a','l','u','e',' ','o','f',' ','X'/
C
C                  horizontal axis
      DO 20  I = 10,79
   20 MOUT(I,21) = '-'
      DO 40  I = 9,79,10
         MOUT(I,21) = '+'
   40 MOUT(I,22) = CHAR (I/10 + ICHAR('0'))
```

```
C                     vertical axis
      DO 60  I = 1,20
   60 MOUT(9,I) = ':'
      DO 80  I = 1,21,5
           MOUT(9,I) = '+'
   80 MOUT(7,I) = CHAR (5 - (I+4)/5 + ICHAR('0'))
C                     annotation
      DO 100  I = 1,10
           MOUT(2*I+33,23) = IANNO(I)
  100 MOUT(3,I+5) = IANNO(I)
      MOUT(3,15)  = 'Y'
C                     curve
      DO 120  I = 10,70
           X = FLOAT(I) / 10.0
           Y = (X*X - 8.0*X + 19.0)
           J = 5.0 * Y  +  0.5
           L = 21 - J
  120 MOUT(I+9,L) = '*'
C                     display
      WRITE (1,2000)  MOUT
 2000 FORMAT (1X, 79A1)
C                     dummy read to stop scrolling
      READ  (2,2002)  IN
 2002 FORMAT (A1)
      STOP
      END
```

The reader will note that some pixels have been defined twice (the plus signs on the axes and the character Y in the annotation); the latter definition is the one that will be displayed. Defining some pixels twice makes the program shorter and less complex, and therefore easier to write; the few microseconds wasted while running will hardly be noticeable. In this example, a point is plotted for each value of *x,* and the value of *y* is rounded to the nearest multiple of the row, that is 0.2, by the calculation of J; that value is converted to the matrix row, the value L. The dummy READ stops the scrolling; pressing the end-of-record key (usually labeled RETURN or ENTER) will continue the execution of the program. This latter step is necessary because some implementations skip a line or two and display a message indicating that the STOP has occurred, thus reducing the number of lines that can be displayed on one screen.

One issue is avoided in the above program: what should be done with points out of range of the "window" or plotting area. This problem can be resolved by inserting two instructions to check that the computed column and row values are within the proper range, proceeding to a CONTINUE statement at line 120 if they are not; the statement now at 120 defining the pixel would be moved up into the body of the DO loop.

This small demonstration is just designed as an eye-opener to the possible applications. Bar graphs, which are even more effective, will be demonstrated in the exercise below.

11.2.1 Exercises

Exercise 11–1
Write a program to display a bar graph whose vertical axis has values from 1 to 20 and horizontal axis shows cases A, B, C, D, and E. Plot the following data on the graph, using a triple column of X's above each case.

case	value
A	14
B	9
C	10
D	19
E	4

Exercise 11–2
Write a program to display a circle on the screen. Measure the pixel sizes of your particular piece of hardware and adjust your row and column values to produce as circular a picture as possible.

11.3 Screen control

Although most of the computer field has striven for some kind of compatibility, the area in which the absence of hardware compatibility stands out most flagrantly is that of terminals. Most glaring is the absence of compatibility of keyboards. Although most keyboards have the so-called QWERTY layout (named for the first six keys of the upper, left-hand row), the placement of the special characters and keys, such as the RETURN or ENTER, the break, the control, and the arrow keys, often differs. Computer users must quite often get used to a number of keyboard layouts. We will not take the time to deplore the extremely poor layouts found on some terminals, but we would urge a movement of the industry toward some kind of standard color coding.

Terminal screens often have facilities that sophisticated programmers find most useful. For example, the author likes to start the operation of a program on a clean screen and prefers a screen that does not scroll and has particular lines for particular pieces of information. Most users find that sophisticated applications programs have this control, which usually requires specialized assembly language programming, but that high-level languages, like FORTRAN, cannot duplicate this facility. However, this is not necessarily true. For example, two of the ASCII codes distinctly refer to screen control: 12 (hex 0C), called the *form feed,* will generally clear the screen, and 7 (hex 07), called the *audible signal,* will generally cause a beep. In order to effect this operation, the codes must be sent to the terminal as characters. The following program segment should cause a clean screen and an audible signal:

```
      CHARACTER  BEL, CLR
      DATA       BEL, CLR/ 7, 12/
                      :
      WRITE (1,1000)  CLR, BEL
1000 FORMAT (1H+,2A1)
```

The 1H+ carriage control prevents the cursor from moving down a line before effecting the operation, although it will move down at the end of the operation since a carriage return is always included with terminal output.

    Furthermore, it is possible to write routines to effect other screen controls. Most terminals (and printers) generate special controls by using an *escape sequence,* in which the escape code, decimal 27 = hex 1B, is followed by a series of control characters. These control characters can usually be found in the terminal manual. We will present a subroutine below implemented on the VAX computer for the VT 52 terminal.

    On this terminal there are three escape sequences used for controlling the screen:

Escape 78 to erase from the cursor position to the end of the screen.
Escape 75 to erase from the cursor position to the end of the line.
Escape 89 to indicate that positioning coordinates are forthcoming.

The positioning coordinates are:

Line number + 32 for vertical position
Column number + 32 for horizontal position

The lines are numbered from 0 to 23, the columns from 0 to 79.

    To implement the above facilities accurately required the use of a $, a special VAX FORTRAN format specifier, at the end of the format; this leaves the cursor at the position set.

```
      SUBROUTINE  SCREEN  (IOP, LINE, ICOL)
C
C     Abstract: allows program to position cursor and execute a number
C               of optional actions onto a fixed screen.
C
C          IOP = -2: set cursor and erase rest of screen
C          IOP = -1: erase whole screen and set cursor at home position
C          IOP =  0: set cursor at home position (line 0, column 0)
C          IOP =  1: set cursor
```

```
C            IOP =  2: set cursor and erase rest of line
C            IOP =  3: sound audible
C            IOP > 31: set cursor and display ASCII character
C
C
      CHARACTER  ESCAPE(2), ERASSC(2), ERASLN(2)
C
      DATA       ESCAPE,    ERASSC,    ERASLN/
     1           27,89,     27,78,     27,75/
      DATA       AUD,  LUN/
     1            7,    1/
C
C                     check for valid options
      IF (IOP .LT. -2  .OR.  IOP .GT. 127)  RETURN
      IF (IOP .GT. 3 .AND. IOP .LE. 31)   RETURN
C                audible
      IF (IOP .EQ. 3)  THEN
          WRITE (LUN,1001) AUD
 1001     FORMAT (1H+, A1, $)
          RETURN
      ENDIF
C                define setting position
      IF (IOP .EQ -1  .OR.  IOP .EQ. 0)  THEN
              IL = 0 + 32
              IC = 0 + 32
          ELSE
              IF (LINE .LT. 0  .OR.  LINE .GT. 23  .OR.
     1             ICOL .LT. 0  .OR.  ICOL .GT. 79) RETURN
              IL = LINE + 32
              IC = ICOL + 32
      ENDIF
C                set cursor
      IF (IOP .EQ. 0  .OR.  IOP .EQ. 1)
     1    WRITE (LUN,1004) ESCAPE, IL, IC
 1004     FORMAT (1H+, 4A1, $)
C                    erasing rest of screen or line
      IF (IOP .LT. 0)  WRITE (LUN,1006) ESCAPE, IL, IC, ERASSC
      IF (IOP .EQ. 2)  WRITE (LUN,1006) ESCAPE, IL, IC, ERASLN
 1006     FORMAT (1H+, 6A1, $)
C                place character
      IF (IOP .GT. 31) WRITE (LUN,1005) ESCAPE, IL, IC, IOP
 1005     FORMAT (1H+, 5A1, $)
C                    return
      RETURN
      END
```

The above routine is not only for a particular terminal, but requires a particular nonstandard FORTRAN option. Another approach to screen placement is shown below, where a subroutine generates the location parameters for an ADDS 40 terminal on a Prime. Here the control characters are generated for use in a later WRITE statement. On the Prime, the control characters are INTEGER*2 variables and are output in A2 format; note that the Prime does not require carriage control for terminal output.

```
C          Subroutine SCRNLC:  returns controls for positioning cursor
C
      SUBROUTINE  SCRNLC  (LINE, ICOL, LNCNTL, ICCNTL)
C
C          Input:  Line (0 - 23), column (0 - 79)
C          Output: Controls for positioning
C          Sample usage:  places AMT on line 8 in columns 20-29
C                    CALL SCRNLC (8, 20, LL, LC)
C                    WRITE (1,10) LL, LC, AMT
C   10               FORMAT (2A2, F10.2)
C
      IMPLICIT INTEGER*2 (I - N)
C
C                    transfer into working variables
      LNCNTL = LINE
      ICCNTL = ICOL
C                    if out of range, use position 0
      IF  (LNCNTL .LT. 0  .OR.  LNCNTL .GT. 23)  LNCNTL = 0
      IF  (ICCNTL .LT. 0  .OR.  ICCNTL .GT. 79)  ICCNTL = 0
C                    line location, add 2816
      LNCNTL = LNCNTL + 2816
C                    column location, add 16 * digit 1 + digit 2
      LCCNTL = LCCNTL + 16*(ICOL/10) + MOD(ICOL, 10)
C                    return
      RETURN
      END
```

11.4 Incremental plotters

Since the 1950s, computers have been used to drive incremental plotting devices that are capable of drawing lines and alphamerics in different color inks, with different pen types, and at speeds and accuracies far in excess of those of a draftsperson. By an incremental device, we mean one that can instruct the writing implement to move a defined distance in a number of possible directions. Whereas lower-precision devices may move 0.01 inch in any one of 8 possible directions (multiples of 45 degrees), more precise devices move in increments of 0.001 inch (or even less) in as many as 24 different directions (multiples of 15 degrees).

Straight-line drawing speeds can exceed 24 inches per second, and it is not unusual to use a factor of 8 to 1 in estimating plotter output over human output.

Curved lines, like alphamerics, are actually a collection of straight lines, but if the increment is small, the human eye will have difficulty detecting that. The programmer is responsible, however, for defining the length of the straight lines that make up the curves (but not the alphamerics).

Since plotting devices are not standardized, the programming interface is not either. However, history plays a role here. In the very early days, there was only one company making incremental plotters, the California Computer Company (CalComp). Since FORTRAN had become available soon after the hardware was released, CalComp supplied (or sold) the necessary driver subprograms written so that they could be called from FORTRAN. As later manufacturers entered the market, they found that they could not compete unless they were able to supply compatible interfaces so that existing applications software could be utilized without change. Thus some manufacturers produce what they call "industry standard" subprograms, which is just a way of acknowledging that CalComp got there first!

Basically, plotting software consists of three main routines that the programmer sees:

SYMBOL: moves the pen to a specified point with either pen up (no line drawn) or pen down (thus drawing a line from the previous point to the specified point).

SYMBOL: plots a single symbol or a character string starting at any point, of any size, and at any angle.

NUMBER: converts a number to a character string and then performs all of the functions included in SYMBOL.

On plotters with multiple pens, there is another command:

NEWPEN: changes the pen type or color; the pens are stored in a reservoir with several (usually 2, 4, or 8) numbered slots.

There may be additional commands used to initialize the plot. Some more advanced systems also have software for drawing sets of axes and curved lines through defined points.

In programming a plot, the programmer must make sure that no attempt is made to go beyond the physical size of the sheet on which the plot is made. (While some hardware is "intelligent" enough to ignore those commands and only time is wasted, others will lose their origin and the plot will be incorrect.) The subprogram provided below is very useful for determining the parts of a line that appear within a given plot. It is called a "clipping" algorithm because it returns the clipped points, that is, the points beyond which the line is clipped. The area within the boundaries of the plot is called the "window."

This particular algorithm uses a binary pattern of four bits to locate a point:

bit on *location of point*	

bit on	location of point
1	above window
2	below window
3	right of window
4	left of window

1001 = 9	1000 = 8	1010 = 10
0001 = 1	0000 = 0	0010 = 2
0101 = 5	0100 = 4	0110 = 6

Thus a bit pattern of 0000 indicates that a point is within the window.

The program furthermore uses a very interesting technique of logically combining two variables using the connective .AND., producing a new value that is the *logical* result of the operation. A logical relationship between values is based on a bit-by-bit comparison, not an arithmetic combination, and is implemented by the following truth tables:

	.AND.	.OR.	.NOT.
	0 1	0 1	
0	0 0	0 1	1
1	0 1	1 1	0

Thus 1010 .AND. 1100 yields 1000, 1010 .OR. 1100 yields 1110, and .NOT. 1100 yields 0011.

A line completely above, below, to the left of, or to the right of the window yields nonzero values (1000, 0100, 0001, and 0010, respectively) when the patterns for its endpoints are ANDed. The pattern of a single endpoint, when ANDed with either an 8, a 4, a 1, or a 2, will locate it either above, below, to the left of, or to the right of the window. Note the extraordinary efficiency of this approach in the IF statement three lines after statement 20, as well as in the first IF in each group.

```
      SUBROUTINE  CLIPPR  (XMIN,XMAX, YMIN,YMAX,
     1                     X1,Y1, X2,Y2, XY, IND)
C
C     Input:    borders of window - XMIN, XMAX, YMIN, YMAX
C               endpoints of line - X1, Y1  and  X2, Y2
C
C     Output:   endpoints of clipped line - XY(2,2)
C                  XY(1,1): x-coordinate of first point
C                  XY(2,1): y-coordinate of first point
C                  XY(1,2): x-coordinate of second point
C                  XY(2,2): y-coordinate of second point
C               indicator - IND
```

```
C                           = 0 if line does not pass through window
C                           = 1 if first point within window
C                           = 2 if second point within window
C                           = 3 if both points within window
C                           = 5 if first point in, second out of window
C                           = 6 if second point in, first out of window
C                           = 8 if both outside of window, but line passes
C                                   though window
C
C      Glossary: IPAT(2) - integer equivalent of binary pattern
C                TX, TY  - temporary values of clipped coordinate
C
C
       DIMENSION  IPAT(2), XY(2,2)
C
C                   statement function to get intersection point
       T (W1,W2,W3,W4, WM) =
      1           W1 + (W2 - W1) * (WM - W3) / (W4 - W3)
C
C                   move points to working locations
       XY(1,1) = X1
       XY(2,1) = Y1
       XY(1,2) = X2
       XY(2,2) = Y2
C                   generate pattern
       DO 20  I = 1,2
           IPAT(I) = 0
           IF  (XY(2,I) .GT. YMAX)  IPAT(I) = IPAT(I) + 8
           IF  (XY(2,I) .LT. YMIN)  IPAT(I) = IPAT(I) + 4
           IF  (XY(1,I) .GT. XMAX)  IPAT(I) = IPAT(I) + 2
           IF  (XY(1,I) .LT. XMIN)  IPAT(I) = IPAT(I) + 1
    20 CONTINUE
C                   if line outside of window, return
       IND = 0
       IF  ((IPAT(1) .AND. IPAT(2))  .NE.  0)  RETURN
C                   adjust indicator if either point within window
       IF  (IPAT(1) .EQ. 0)  IND = IND + 1
       IF  (IPAT(2) .EQ. 0)  IND = IND + 2
C                   return if both points in window
       IF  (IPAT(1) .EQ. 0  .AND.  IPAT(2) .EQ. 0)  RETURN
C                   loop through points to get border intersections
       DO 200  I = 1,2
C                       ignore points in window
           IF  (IPAT(I) .EQ. 0)  GO TO 200
```

```
C                          left border
         IF  ((IPAT(I) .AND. 1)  .EQ.  0)  GO TO 120
             TY = T (XY(2,1), XY(2,2), XY(1,1), XY(1,2), XMIN)
             TX = XMIN
             IF  (TY .GE. YMIN  .AND.  TY .LE. YMAX)  GO TO 180
C                          right border
   120   IF  ((IPAT(I) .AND. 2)  .EQ.  0)  GO TO 140
             TY = T (XY(2,1), XY(2,2), XY(1,1), XY(1,2), XMAX)
             TX = XMAX
             IF  (TY .GE. YMIN  .AND.  TY .LE. YMAX)  GO TO 180
C                          lower border
   140   IF  ((IPAT(I) .AND. 4)  .EQ.  0)  GO TO 160
             TX = T (XY(1,1), XY(1,2), XY(2,1), XY(2,2), YMIN)
             TY = YMIN
             IF  (TX .GE. XMIN  .AND.  TX .LE. XMAX)  GO TO 180
C                          upper border
   160   IF  ((IPAT(I) .AND. 8)  .EQ.  0)  GO TO 200
             TX = T (XY(1,1), XY(1,2), XY(2,1), XY(2,2), YMAX)
             TY = YMAX
             IF  (TX .GE. XMIN  .AND.  TX .LE. XMAX)  GO TO 180
         GO TO 200
C                     point on window edge found
   180   IPAT(I) = 0
         XY(1,I) = TX
         XY(2,I) = TY
         IND = IND + 4
   200 CONTINUE
C                          return
     RETURN
     END
```

11.5 Graphics screens, printers, and plotters

Graphics screens, plotters, and printers use an extremely small pixel to produce a digital picture of much finer precision than the standard character plots discussed in section 2 of this chapter. Graphics screens are very similar to television tubes, which have sufficient resolution to produce a very lifelike picture. Graphics printers use dot matrix techniques to produce output with a resolution of approximately 60 points per inch. Graphics plotters, which are usually referred to as electrostatic plotters because they "burn" the image into the medium by causing a spark to jump onto specially treated paper, can have resolutions of about 200 points per inch. In comparison, there are 10 character pixels per inch horizontally and 6 to 8 per inch vertically; thus, the images produced on these devices are significantly more detailed. Even some of the economically priced printers sold for microcomputer systems are capable of medium quality graphics.

In most applications, plotting uses the industry standard routines described in the previous section; the subprograms generate information in a form such that the output can be converted to the necessary dots and then sent to the device. Thus the plotting subroutines are called from the FORTRAN program, and the rest of the operation is transparent to the programmer.

With the development of more graphically oriented I/O such as CAD (computer-aided design), CAM (computer-aided manufacturing), computer-aided mapping, and computer-aided drafting, most producers of this hardware and software supply (or sell) a set of FORTRAN-interfacing routines so that the user may produce his or her own programs to drive the graphics devices.

12

Projects

The projects in this chapter are designed to provide large scale exercises performable either by individuals or by programming teams. Each project section has a reference (in parentheses) indicating the chapter containing the highest-order material required. The reader is encouraged to modify the conditions of the projects to provide greater challenges or more practical applications.

12.1 Project 1: bowling scores

This project generates a file of bowling scores, in which each record contains 80 scores for a single bowler. (If you don't know what bowling is, let me just say that it is a very frustrating game in which the scores range from 0 to 300.) These scores are to be analyzed and a graph of their distribution produced.

To generate a representative collection of scores, the random number function defined in chapter 2 (section 16) is incorporated into another function that uses 12 random values to calculate a normally distributed value. A normally distributed set of values has a higher number of values in the middle of the range, with the number of values trailing off as we move from the middle toward each of the ends; the graph of the distribution is a bell-shaped curve. Normally distributed data is typical for the distributions of such quantities as weight, height, and exam scores and is perfect for a collection of bowling scores.

The distribution is described by two parameters, the mean and the standard deviation; the former cuts the data in half, and the latter measures the spread of the values. As a general rule, three standard deviations on each side of the mean encompass 99.9% of the values. Thus a mean of 170.5 and a standard deviation of 40.5 produce an excellent distribution for our purposes.

The following function uses the random number routine to generate a normal distribution:

```
C            Function DSTRNML:  generates normally distributed values
C

      FUNCTION  DSTRNML (XMEAN, STDEV)
C
C     Input:    XMEAN     mean or average of the distribution
C               STDEV     standard deviation
C
C                    initialize seed (negative value)
      SAVE  SEED
      DATA  SEED/ 0.00/
      SEED = SEED - 1.0
C                    set first random number
      DSTRNML = RAN(SEED)
C                    add in eleven more random numbers
      DO 10  I = 2,12
   10 DSTRNML = DSTRNML + RAN(1.0)
C                    get average and adjust with deviation and mean
      DSTRNML = STDEV * (DSTRNML - 6.0)  +  XMEAN
      RETURN
      END
```

To get a new normally distributed number it is only necessary to code:

```
VALUE = DSTRNML (170.5, 40.5)
```

12.1.1 Generation of normally distributed test data (chapter 7)

Write a program to generate a direct access file of 40 records, each containing 80 bowling scores, using the normal distribution function defined above (or any other supplied with your system or of your own invention). Make sure that all of the scores are in the range of 0 to 300 either by excluding those out of range or by modifying them to 0 or 300.

12.1.2 File patching (chapter 7)

Write an interactive patch program that will allow the user to display any desired score for any bowler. The input, entered at the keyboard, should include the bowler number (record number in the file) and the game number. The program should contain an option to change that score after displaying it. Use this routine to plant at least two 300 games in the file.

12.1.3 Dump file routine (chapter 7)

Write a program to print out a partial or entire file. Each page should include a page number, title, and up to eight bowler records. The user should enter the first and last records to be printed. Each record should be identified with the bowler number, and the output should be designed for clarity and compactness.

12.1.4 Analyze with two-dimensional array (chapter 9)

Write a program to read the entire bowler file into a two-dimensional array of (80,40). Determine the averages of each of the bowlers, and output the highest average and the number of the bowler who achieved it. Also output the lowest score with the number of the bowler who scored it and the game number in which it was scored. In addition, output a list of the bowlers who bowled a 300 game.

12.1.5 Distribution of values (chapter 9)

Modify the above program so that it also produces a distribution of the scores; use the following ranges:

```
  0 to  50
 51 to  90
 91 to 130
131 to 170
171 to 210
211 to 250
```

251 to 290

291 to 300

Output each of the ranges and the number of scores in each range.

12.1.6 Graphical output (chapter 11)

Draw a bar graph of the above results on a printer. The horizontal axis should show the eight ranges; the vertical axis, the number of games. Use a scale of 1 line = 25 games, with any remainder in numeric form on top of the graphing element. For example, a bar for 62 games in the range of 51 to 90 might be output as:

```
    12
    **
    **
- - - - - - - - - - - - -
    51
    90
```

12.2 Project 2: computer time accounting

The following programming system requires a mainline and two subprograms that are used to produce a report of computer time used and the charges incurred. The program uses an input file with the following file structure:

Record 1:   columns 1– 9:   month (alphameric)
                 columns 11–14:   year

Records 2–*n*:   columns   1–2:   user number (range: 1 to 20)
                 columns   4–5:   day of month (range: 1 to 28, 30, or 31)
                 columns 7–10:   log-on time, minutes since midnight
                                  (range: 0 to 1439)
                 columns 12–15:   log-off time, minutes since midnight
                                  (range: 0 to 1439)

If log-off time is less than log-on time, log-off is assumed to be on next day.

12.2.1 Generation of random test data (chapter 7)

Using the random number generator, generate a sequential access file of data sorted by day of month and log-on time to be used in this application. Generate about 50 records. Then, using an editor, insert the header record with the date.

12.2.2 Subroutine for integer conversion (chapter 4)

Write the subroutine described by the following specifications:

```
      SUBROUTINE M2HM (MIN, NEWHRS, NEWMIN)
C
C     Abstract: reduces minutes to hours and minutes
C
C     Input:    MIN        minutes since midnight
C
C     Output:   NEWHRS     hours since midnight
C               NEWMIN     remainder of minutes
C
C     Example:  if MIN = 535, NEWHRS = 8 and NEWMIN = 55
```

12.2.3 Function to compute cost (chapter 4)

Write the function to compute the computer time cost:

```
      FUNCTION CMPCST (MIN, RATE)
C
C     Abstract: computes the cost of computer time
C               from the minutes used
C
C     Input:    MIN        minutes since midnight
C               RATE       basic rate per minute
C
C     Output:   CMPCST     based on RATE * MIN for first 120 minutes and
C                               80% of RATE for balance of minutes
C
C     Example:  if MIN = 90 and RATE = 2.50, CMPCST = 90 * 2.50
C               if MIN = 150 and Rate = 2.50,
C                    CMPCST = 120 * 2.50 + 0.80 * 30 * 2.50
```

12.2.4 Mainline to generate report with totals (chapter 9)

Write a mainline program to read the file and generate a chronological report. Use an array MT(9,2000) to hold the input data and the calculated values as follows:

$MT(1,n)$ = user number
$MT(2,n)$ = day of month
$MT(3,n)$ = log-on time, in minutes since midnight
$MT(4,n)$ = log-off time, in minutes since midnight
$MT(5,n)$ = time used in minutes = log-off − log-in. If log-off less than log-on, add 1 day (1440 minutes) to log-off time.
$MT(6,n)$ = log-on time, in hours

$MT(7,n)$ =   and minutes since midnight

$MT(8,n) =$ time used, in hours

$MT(9,n) =$ and minutes

An additional array will be required to hold the generated costs.

    The mainline is to be written in modular form. Module 1 will input up to 2000 records, using the END= clause to terminate the READ. If there is excessive data, the program should terminate with an error message. Module 2 will calculate items 5 to 9 in array MT and the cost. The total time use and the rate will also be necessary. Module 3 should produce the output report in the following format, with times in hours and minutes:

```
COMPUTER TIME USE REPORT FOR aaaaaaaaa, 198n

User        Day      Time       Usage          Cost

 nn          n      nn.nn       nn.nn         nn.nn
 nn          n      nn.nn        n.nn          n.nn
  n          n      nn.nn       nn.nn        nnn.nn
 nn         nn      nn.nn        n.nn         nn.nn
  .          .        .           .             .
  .          .        .           .             .
  .          .        .           .             .
 nn         nn      nn.nn       nn.nn        nnn.nn

Totals                         nnnn.nn     nnnnnn.nn
```

12.2.5 Re-sort data, generate report with subtotals (chapter 9)

Re-sort the above data by user, day, and log-on time. Reprint the report with subtotals by user for time use and cost and grand totals for all records. The subtotals should be printed to the right of the cost columns and a line should be skipped before a new user.

12.2.6 Modify function in 12.2.3 (chapter 4)

Adjust Function CMPCST to apply a prime-time surcharge of 25% for any time charged between 8 A.M. and 6 P.M.

12.3 Project 3: automatic teller machine

An automatic teller machine is used by a system of banks to dispense cash in multiples of $10. The user of the machine inputs the account number and the amount desired. The program calculates the number of each denomination of bill needed to meet that amount and keeps a record of the money distributed by account and by denomination. A fee is charged against the account but is not deducted from the money given out.

12.3.1 Subroutine for integer conversion (chapter 4)

Write the following subroutine:

```
        SUBROUTINE BRKDWN (IAMT, N50, N20, N10)
C
C       Abstract: reduces a dollar amount (multiple of $10) to the
C                 appropriate number of $50, $20, and $10 bills.
C
C       Input:    IAMT        amount, a multiple of $10
C
C       Output:   N50         number of $50 bills dispensed
C                 N20         number of $20 bills dispensed
C                 N10         number of $10 bills dispensed
C
C       Example:  if IAMT = $180, use 3 $50, 1 $20, and 1 $10
```

12.3.2 Function to compute cost (chapter 4)

Write the following function:

```
        FUNCTION CALCFE (IAMT)
C
C       Abstract: calculates a fee to be applied to the account
C
C       Input:    IAMT        amount of money dispensed
C
C       Output:   CALCFE   fee charged according to:
C                             if IAMT < $100, fee = $2.00
C                             if IAMT >= $100, fee = 2% of IAMT
C
```

12.3.3 Mainline to accept input, edit, write record (chapter 5)

Write a mainline that:

1. prompts for a numeric account number and amount, using the ERR=
   clause to ensure that data is numeric and the END= clause to terminate
   input.

2. verifies that the amount is a multiple of 10, displaying an error message
   and returning for another READ if not. Also sets a limit of $400.

3. accesses subroutine BRKDWN to get the breakdown of bills to be
   dispensed and the function CALCFEE to determine the fee to be charged,
   displaying the results.

4. writes a record to a sequential access file containing the following items:

> account number
>
> amount
>
> number of $50 bills dispensed
>
> number of $20 bills dispensed
>
> number of $10 bills dispensed
>
> fee applied

all but the last item should be integer.

12.3.4 Mainline to generate report (chapter 5)

Write a mainline to read the above sequential file and output a printed report in the following format:

Transaction Register

Account	Amount	$50	$20	$10	Fee
nnnnn	nnn	n	n	n	n.nn
nnnnn	nn	n	n	n	n.nn
.	.	.	.	.	.
.	.	.	.	.	.
.	.	.	.	.	.
nnnnn	nnn	n	n	n	n.nn
Totals:	nnnnn	nnn	nnn	nnn	nnnn.nn

12.3.5 Check input data for validity (chapter 7)

Generate a direct access file in which each record contains:
   Item 1: account number (use 0 in last record to indicate end-of-file)
   Item 2: balance in account (real)
Modify the mainline program to check for a valid account number, preventing any further action if a number is invalid. If the account number is valid, check the balance in the account before dispensing any money. Both the desired amount and the fee must be considered. If there are insufficient funds, display the balance in the account and prompt for a new amount; an entry of 0 cancels the request. If money is dispensed, display the balance after that money and the fee are deducted, and update the file with the new balance.

12.3.6 Modify mainline (12.3.3) (chapter 8)

Modify the mainline program to accept as its first input the number of bills of the three denominations stored in the machine at the beginning of the day. Use

COMMON to store those values. Modify subroutine BRKDWN to contain the COMMON variables and to adjust the denomination amounts when it runs out of certain denominations of bills, reducing the amount distributed if it cannot meet the desired amount and displaying a message to that effect.

12.4 Project 4: parking violations

A parking ticket system consists of two permanent files; one contains the information necessary for describing and charging for parking violations, and the other keeps a record of car registrations in a state. A third temporary file keeps track of all outstanding (unpaid) tickets.

The parking violation description file is a sequential file structured as follows:

columns   1–2: violation code (alpha)
columns   5–34: violation description (alpha)
columns 39–40: amount of fine (integer)

It contains the following entries:

code	description	fine
OV	Overtime unmetered parking	5
OM	Overtime parking at meter	5
PD	Parked in driveway	15
PF	Parked at fire hydrant	25
PB	Parked in bus stop	15
PX	Parked in crosswalk	10
PR	Parked in restricted area	15
PT	Parked on railroad tracks	30
PH	Parked in handicapped spot	20
P2	Parked in two spots	10

The license plate file has the following structure:
columns   1–8: license plate number (alpha)
columns 11–28: name of car owner (alpha)
columns 31–48: address of car owner (alpha)
columns 51–62: town
columns 64–65: state code
columns 66–70: zip code
The reader may have the pleasure of setting up his or her own license plate file as a direct access file. The last valid record should be followed by one that has an end-of-data indicator in one of its fields.

The file for outstanding traffic violations is also a direct access file and has the following structure:

columns   1–8: license plate number (alpha)

column   10: deletion code: nonblank if fine is paid and record is to be deleted

columns 11–18: date (alpha) *nn/nn/nn*

columns 19–20: violation code

columns 21–22: fine

12.4.1 *Function to access file (chapter 10)*

Write the following function:

```
      FUNCTION NUMVIO (VCODE)
C
C     Abstract: on blank entry, reads in violation description file into
C               COMMON arrays for code, description, and fine. On
C               nonblank entries, returns subscript of violation.
C
C     Input:    VCODE    Violation code (CHARACTER*2)
C
C     Output:   NUMVIO   Subscript of violation in table. Return 0 if
C                        violation not in table. (Integer)
C
```

12.4.2 *Subroutine to search array (chapter 10)*

Write the following subroutine:

```
      SUBROUTINE NUMLIC (LIPLAT, NAME, ADDRSS, TOWN, STATE, ZIP)
C
C     Abstract: returns license plate information.
C
C     Input:    LIPLAT   license plate (CHARACTER*8)
C
C     Output:   name, address, town, state and zip code of
C               vehicle owner.
C               returns blank NAME if plate not on file
C
```

12.4.3 *File maintenance (chapter 10)*

Write a mainline program to accept keyboard input and add to the outstanding violation file. The input for each record should include the license plate number, the violation code, and the date; the program should leave the deletion code blank and should insert the appropriate fine into the record. Valid violation codes and license plate numbers should be verified using the other files.

12.4.4 Interactive mainline (chapter 10)

Write a mainline program that accepts as input a license plate number from the keyboard and displays all tickets, paid and unpaid, as well as the name and address of the violator. The total outstanding fines should also be displayed. The program should then give the user the option of indicating the payment of an outstanding fine; the file should be updated when a fine is paid by setting the deletion code to nonblank.

12.4.5 Mainline to generate report (chapter 10)

Write a mainline program to produce a listing of all unpaid violations sorted by license plate, with subtotals by license plate. To save memory, a key sort should be used in which the license plate is the key and the record number in the file is the integer carry-along; after sorting, the order of the record numbers is the order in which the file should be read.

12.4.6 Mainline to pack file (chapter 10)

Write a mainline program to generate an updated outstanding violation file in which the paid violations (the records marked for deletion) are eliminated. This can be done with a single file by simply writing over the records to be deleted in a simple packing procedure.

Appendix A:
Character Code Tables

As discussed in section 10.2, there are two major coding methods for characters, ASCII (American Standard Code for Information Interchange) and EBCDIC (Extended Binary Coded Decimal Interchange Code). Complete tables for each code follow. The tables include:

character or abbreviation (mnemonic)

keyboard entry to enter the character (ASCII only)

binary code (7-bit for ASCII, 8-bit for EBCDIC)

octal code (ASCII only)

decimal code

hexadecimal code

definition

ASCII

The user will find ASCII to be the more commonly used code since its internal structure is more logical; it is found in almost all terminals and printers, even in those systems that use EBCDIC internally in memory. ASCII was defined as a 7-bit code, but with the transition to a byte (8-bit) standard, those systems that have made the conversion to 8-bit ASCII (most of the microcomputers, for example) have an additional 128 codes available; however, these codes are defined individually by the manufacturer and do not fit into any general pattern. The additional codes are used primarily for graphics characters (symbols) or foreign language letters and symbols not used in English.

ASCII Terminal character	key	binary	oct	dec	hex	Definition of Use
NUL	CTRL/@	0 000 000	000	0	0	filler; null
SOH	CTRL/A	0 000 001	001	1	1	start of heading; home position
STX	CTRL/B	0 000 010	002	2	2	start of text
ETX	CTRL/C	0 000 011	003	3	3	end of text
EOT	CTRL/D	0 000 100	004	4	4	end of transmission
ENQ	CTRL/E	0 000 101	005	5	5	enquiry
ACK	CTRL/F	0 000 110	006	6	6	acknowledge
BEL	CTRL/G	0 000 111	007	7	7	bell
BS	CTRL/H	0 001 000	010	8	8	backspace; ← arrow
HT	CTRL/I	0 001 001	011	9	9	horizontal tabulation
LF	CTRL/J	0 001 010	012	10	A	line feed; ↓ arrow
VT	CTRL/K	0 001 011	013	11	B	vertical tabulation; ↑ arrow
FF	CTRL/L	0 001 100	014	12	C	form feed; clear screen
CR	CTRL/M	0 001 101	015	13	D	carriage return
SO	CTRL/N	0 001 110	016	14	E	shift out
SI	CTRL/O	0 001 111	017	15	F	shift in
DLE	CTRL/P	0 010 000	020	16	10	data link escape
DC1	CTRL/Q	0 010 001	021	17	11	device control 1
DC2	CTRL/R	0 010 010	022	18	12	device control 2
DC3	CTRL/S	0 010 011	023	19	13	device control 3
DC4	CTRL/T	0 010 100	024	20	14	device control 4
NAK	CTRL/U	0 010 101	025	21	15	negative acknowledge
SYN	CTRL/V	0 010 110	026	22	16	synchronous idle
ETB	CTRL/W	0 010 111	027	23	17	end of transmission block
CAN	CTRL/X	0 011 000	030	24	18	cancel
EM	CTRL/Y	0 011 001	031	25	19	end of medium
SUB	CTRL/Z	0 011 010	032	26	1A	substitute
ESC	CTRL/[	0 011 011	033	27	1B	escape
FS	CTRL/\	0 011 100	034	28	1C	file separator
GS	CTRL/]	0 011 101	035	29	1D	group separator
RS	CTRL/^	0 011 110	036	30	1E	record separator
US	CTRL/__	0 011 111	037	31	1F	unit separator
SP	SPACE	0 100 000	040	32	20	space; blank
!	!	0 100 001	041	33	21	exclamation mark
"	"	0 100 010	042	34	22	double quote
#	#	0 100 011	043	35	23	number symbol
$	$	0 100 100	044	36	24	dollar symbol
%	%	0 100 101	045	37	25	percent symbol
&	&	0 100 110	046	38	26	ampersand
'	'	0 100 111	047	39	27	single quote; apostrophe
(	(	0 101 000	050	40	28	left parenthesis
)	)	0 101 001	051	41	29	right parenthesis
*	*	0 101 010	052	42	2A	asterisk
+	+	0 101 011	053	43	2B	plus symbol
,	,	0 101 100	054	44	2C	comma
-	-	0 101 101	055	45	2D	minus symbol; hyphen
.	.	0 101 110	056	46	2E	period; decimal point
/	/	0 101 111	057	47	2F	divide symbol; slash; virgule
0	0	0 110 000	060	48	30	digit zero
1	1	0 110 001	061	49	31	digit one
2	2	0 110 010	062	50	32	digit two
3	3	0 110 011	063	51	33	digit three
4	4	0 110 100	064	52	34	digit four
5	5	0 110 101	065	53	35	digit five
6	6	0 110 110	066	54	36	digit six
7	7	0 110 111	067	55	37	digit seven

8	8	0 111 000	070	56	38	digit eight
9	9	0 111 001	071	57	39	digit nine
:	:	0 111 010	072	58	3A	colon
;	;	0 111 011	073	59	3B	semicolon
<	<	0 111 100	074	60	3C	less than symbol; left caret
=	=	0 111 101	075	61	3D	equal symbol
>	>	0 111 110	076	62	3E	greater than symbol; right caret
?	?	0 111 111	077	63	3F	question mark
@	@	1 000 000	100	64	40	at sign
A	A	1 000 001	101	65	41	uppercase letter A
B	B	1 000 010	102	66	42	uppercase letter B
C	C	1 000 011	103	67	43	uppercase letter C
D	D	1 000 100	104	68	44	uppercase letter D
E	E	1 000 101	105	69	45	uppercase letter E
F	F	1 000 110	106	70	46	uppercase letter F
G	G	1 000 111	107	71	47	uppercase letter G
H	H	1 001 000	110	72	48	uppercase letter H
I	I	1 001 001	111	73	49	uppercase letter I
J	J	1 001 010	112	74	4A	uppercase letter J
K	K	1 001 011	113	75	4B	uppercase letter K
L	L	1 001 100	114	76	4C	uppercase letter L
M	M	1 001 101	115	77	4D	uppercase letter M
N	N	1 001 110	116	78	4E	uppercase letter N
O	O	1 001 111	117	79	4F	uppercase letter O
P	P	1 010 000	120	80	50	uppercase letter P
Q	Q	1 010 001	121	81	51	uppercase letter Q
R	R	1 010 010	122	82	52	uppercase letter R
S	S	1 010 011	123	83	53	uppercase letter S
T	T	1 010 100	124	84	54	uppercase letter T
U	U	1 010 101	125	85	55	uppercase letter U
V	V	1 010 110	126	86	56	uppercase letter V
W	W	1 010 111	127	87	57	uppercase letter W
X	X	1 011 000	130	88	58	uppercase letter X
Y	Y	1 011 001	131	89	59	uppercase letter Y
Z	Z	1 011 010	132	90	5A	uppercase letter Z
[	[	1 011 011	133	91	5B	left bracket
\	\	1 011 100	134	92	5C	back slash; back slant
]	]	1 011 101	135	93	5D	right bracket
^	^	1 011 110	136	94	5E	circumflex; ↑ up arrow
_	_	1 011 111	137	95	5F	underscore; underline
`	`	1 100 000	140	96	60	back quote; grave accent
a	a	1 100 001	141	97	61	lowercase letter a
b	b	1 100 010	142	98	62	lowercase letter b
c	c	1 100 011	143	99	63	lowercase letter c
d	d	1 100 100	144	100	64	lowercase letter d
e	e	1 100 101	145	101	65	lowercase letter e
f	f	1 100 110	146	102	66	lowercase letter f
g	g	1 100 111	147	103	67	lowercase letter g
h	h	1 101 000	150	104	68	lowercase letter h
i	i	1 101 001	151	105	69	lowercase letter i
j	j	1 101 010	152	106	6A	lowercase letter j
k	k	1 101 011	153	107	6B	lowercase letter k
l	l	1 101 100	154	108	6C	lowercase letter l
m	m	1 101 101	155	109	6D	lowercase letter m
n	n	1 101 110	156	110	6E	lowercase letter n
o	o	1 101 111	157	111	6F	lowercase letter o
p	p	1 110 000	160	112	70	lowercase letter p
q	q	1 110 001	161	113	71	lowercase letter q
r	r	1 110 010	162	114	72	lowercase letter r

		binary				
s	s	1 110 011	163	115	73	lowercase letter s
t	t	1 110 100	164	116	74	lowercase letter t
u	u	1 110 101	165	117	75	lowercase letter u
v	v	1 110 110	166	118	76	lowercase letter v
w	w	1 110 111	167	119	77	lowercase letter w
x	x	1 111 000	170	120	78	lowercase letter x
y	y	1 111 001	171	121	79	lowercase letter y
z	z	1 111 010	172	122	7A	lowercase letter z
{	{	1 111 011	173	123	7B	left brace
l	l	1 111 100	174	124	7C	vertical bar; logical OR
}	}	1 111 101	175	125	7D	right brace
~	~	1 111 110	176	126	7E	tilde
DEL	DEL	1 111 111	177	127	7F	delete; rub out

EBCDIC

In the EBCDIC table below, only the standardized characters are given; thus not all 256 available codes are present. This code derives partially from the old 6-bit code used in IBM keypunches and thus lacks the more logical arrangement found in ASCII. For example, one finds a difference of one between all letters of the alphabet with the exception of I to J and R to S, where the differences are 8 and 9, respectively. Also, the sorting order based on the numeric values will place lowercase letters before uppercase ones and letters before digits. Furthermore, when stored in byte mode or in any configuration that places the desired character first followed by blanks, the letters and numerals will store as negative numbers (look at the binary or hex representations, which show that the first, or sign, bit is on), thus sorting the letters and numerals before the special characters, most notably the blank. Special sorts may thus be required when using EBCDIC code.

EBCDIC char	hex	Equivalent Forms binary	decimal	Definition of Use
NUL	00	0000 0000	0	filler; null
SOH	01	0000 0001	1	start of heading; home position
STX	02	0000 0010	2	start of text
ETX	03	0000 0011	3	end of text
SEL	04	0000 0100	4	select
HT	05	0000 0101	5	horizontal tab
RNL	06	0000 0110	6	required new line
DEL	07	0000 0111	7	delete
GE	08	0000 1000	8	graphic escape
SPS	09	0000 1001	9	superscript
RPT	0A	0000 1010	10	repeat
VT	0B	0000 1011	11	vertical tab; ↑ arrow
FF	0C	0000 1100	12	form feed; clear screen
CR	0D	0000 1101	13	carriage return
SO	0E	0000 1110	14	shift out
SI	0F	0000 1111	15	shift in
DLE	10	0001 0000	16	data link escape
DC1	11	0001 0001	17	device control 1
DC2	12	0001 0010	18	device control 2
DC3	13	0001 0011	19	device control 3
RES/ENP	14	0001 0100	20	restore; enable presentation

NL	15	0001 0101	21	new line acknowledgment
BS	16	0001 0110	22	backspace
POC	17	0001 0111	23	program-operator communication
CAN	18	0001 1000	24	cancel
EM	19	0001 1001	25	end of medium
UBS	1A	0001 1010	26	unit backspace
CU1	1B	0001 1011	27	customer use 1
IFS	1C	0001 1100	28	interchange file separator
IGS	1D	0001 1101	29	interchange group separator
IRS	1E	0001 1110	30	interchange record separator
IUS	1F	0001 1111	31	interchange unit separator
DS	20	0010 0000	32	digit select
SOS	21	0010 0001	33	start of significance
FS	22	0010 0010	34	field separator
WUS	23	0010 0011	35	word underscore
BYP/INP	24	0010 0100	36	bypass; inhibit presentation
LF	25	0010 0101	37	line feed
ETB	26	0010 0110	38	end of transmission block
ESC	27	0010 0111	39	escape
	28	0010 1000	40	reserved
	29	0010 1001	41	reserved
SM/SW	2A	0010 1010	42	set mode, switch
FMT	2B	0010 1011	43	format
	2C	0010 1100	44	reserved
ENQ	2D	0010 1101	45	enquiry
ACK	2E	0010 1110	46	acknowledge
BEL	2F	0010 1111	47	bell
	30	0011 0000	48	reserved
	31	0011 0001	49	reserved
SYN	32	0011 0010	50	synchronous
IR	33	0011 0011	51	index
PP	34	0011 0100	52	presentation position
TRN	35	0011 0101	53	transparent
NBS	36	0011 0110	54	numeric backspace
EOT	37	0011 0111	55	end of transmission
SBS	38	0011 1000	56	subscript
IT	39	0011 1001	57	indent
RFF	3A	0011 1010	58	required
CU3	3B	0011 1011	59	customer use 3
DC4	3C	0011 1100	60	device control 4
NAK	3D	0011 1101	61	negative acknowledge
	3E	0011 1110	62	reserved
SUB	3F	0011 1111	63	substitute
SP	40	0100 0000	64	space; blank
RSP	41	0100 0001	65	required space
¢ or [	4A	0100 1010	74	cents symbol on IBM; left bracket on Burroughs
.	4B	0100 1011	75	period; decimal point
<	4C	0100 1100	76	less than sign; left caret
(	4D	0100 1101	77	left parenthesis
+	4E	0100 1110	78	plus symbol
|	4F	0100 1111	79	logical OR
&	50	0101 0000	80	ampersand
! or]	5A	0101 1010	90	exclamation mark on IBM; right bracket on Burroughs
$	5B	0101 1011	91	currency symbol
*	5C	0101 1100	92	asterisk
)	5D	0101 1101	93	right parenthesis
;	5E	0101 1110	94	semicolon
¬	5F	0101 1111	95	logical NOT symbol
-	60	0110 0000	96	minus sign; hyphen

/	61	0110 0001	97	slash
I	6A	0110 1010	106	vertical line
,	6B	0110 1011	107	comma
%	6C	0110 1100	108	percent symbol
__	6D	0110 1101	109	underscore
>	6E	0110 1110	110	greater than sign; right caret
?	6F	0110 1111	111	question mark
`	79	0111 1001	121	grave accent; back quote
:	7A	0111 1010	122	colon
#	7B	0111 1011	123	number sign
@	7C	0111 1100	124	at sign
'	7D	0111 1101	125	prime; apostrophe
=	7E	0111 1110	126	equal sign
''	7F	0111 1111	127	quotation marks; double quote
a	81	1000 0001	129	lowercase letter a
b	82	1000 0010	130	lowercase letter b
c	83	1000 0011	131	lowercase letter c
d	84	1000 0100	132	lowercase letter d
e	85	1000 0101	133	lowercase letter e
f	86	1000 0110	134	lowercase letter f
g	87	1000 0111	135	lowercase letter g
h	88	1000 1000	136	lowercase letter h
i	89	1000 1001	137	lowercase letter i
j	91	1001 0001	145	lowercase letter j
k	92	1001 0010	146	lowercase letter k
l	93	1001 0011	147	lowercase letter l
m	94	1001 0100	148	lowercase letter m
n	95	1001 0101	149	lowercase letter n
o	96	1001 0110	150	lowercase letter o
p	97	1001 0111	151	lowercase letter p
q	98	1001 1000	152	lowercase letter q
r	99	1001 1001	153	lowercase letter r
~	A1	1010 0001	161	tilde
s	A2	1010 0010	162	lowercase letter s
t	A3	1010 0011	163	lowercase letter t
u	A4	1010 0100	164	lowercase letter u
v	A5	1010 0101	165	lowercase letter v
w	A6	1010 0110	166	lowercase letter w
x	A7	1010 0111	167	lowercase letter x
y	A8	1010 1000	168	lowercase letter y
z	A9	1010 1001	169	lowercase letter z
{	C0	1100 0000	192	opening brace
A	C1	1100 0001	193	uppercase letter A
B	C2	1100 0010	194	uppercase letter B
C	C3	1100 0011	195	uppercase letter C
D	C4	1100 0100	196	uppercase letter D
E	C5	1100 0101	197	uppercase letter E
F	C6	1100 0110	198	uppercase letter F
G	C7	1100 0111	199	uppercase letter G
H	C8	1100 1000	200	uppercase letter H
I	C9	1100 1001	201	uppercase letter I
}	D0	1101 0000	208	closing brace
J	D1	1101 0001	209	uppercase letter J
K	D2	1101 0010	210	uppercase letter K
L	D3	1101 0011	211	uppercase letter L
M	D4	1101 0100	212	uppercase letter M
N	D5	1101 0101	213	uppercase letter N
O	D6	1101 0110	214	uppercase letter O
P	D7	1101 0111	215	uppercase letter P

Q	D8	1101 1000	216	uppercase letter Q
R	D9	1101 1001	217	uppercase letter R
\	E0	1110 0000	224	reverse slash; back slash
S	E2	1110 0010	226	uppercase letter S
T	E3	1110 0011	227	uppercase letter T
U	E4	1110 0100	228	uppercase letter U
V	E5	1110 0101	229	uppercase letter V
W	E6	1110 0110	230	uppercase letter W
X	E7	1110 0111	231	uppercase letter X
Y	E8	1110 1000	232	uppercase letter Y
Z	E9	1110 1001	233	uppercase letter Z
0	F0	1111 0000	240	digit zero
1	F1	1111 0001	241	digit one
2	F2	1111 0010	242	digit two
3	F3	1111 0011	243	digit three
4	F4	1111 0100	244	digit four
5	F5	1111 0101	245	digit five
6	F6	1111 0100	246	digit six
7	F7	1111 0111	247	digit seven
8	F8	1111 1000	248	digit eight
9	F9	1111 1001	249	digit nine

Appendix B:
Intrinsic Functions

The intrinsic functions are functions provided within the FORTRAN library as part of the language. They may thus be accessed as a regular function and are brought into the program during the linking operation.

In FORTRAN 66 and the FORTRAN 77 subset, the functions have specific argument types. In the full FORTRAN 77 language, there are generic names that act on all types of arguments, adjusting the returned value to the appropriate type. For example, the generic name ABS will convert to the specific functions IABS, ABS, DABS, or CABS depending on the mode of the argument (integer, real, double precision, or complex) and return an answer in the corresponding type.

In the table below, the functions are listed in four categories, FORTRAN 66 (66), FORTRAN 77 subset (77s), FORTRAN 77 (77), and FORTRAN 77 generic (77g). The last category contains the generic name where it exists; where it does not, the specific name may be used. Some FORTRAN 66 implementations may contain functions now appearing in FORTRAN 77. The type codes used are as follows:

C   Complex
D   Double Precision
A   Character
I   Integer
L   Logical
R   Real

Table B.1   Type conversion

Description	66	77s	77	77g	Type	Arguments	
Conversion to integer				INT	I	I	1
truncating if numeric		INT	INT	INT	I	R	1
	IFIX	IFIX	IFIX	INT	I	R	1
			IDINT	INT	I	D	1
				INT	I	C	1
		ICHAR	ICHAR		I	A	1
Conversion to real	REAL	REAL	REAL	REAL	R	I	1
	FLOAT	FLOAT	FLOAT	REAL	R	I	1
				REAL	R	R	1
			SNGL	REAL	R	D	1
				REAL	R	C	1
Conversion to double precision				DBLE	D	I	1
				DBLE	D	R	1
				DBLE	D	D	1
				DBLE	D	C	1
Conversion to complex				CMPLX	C	I	1 or 2
if two arguments, must be of same type				CMPLX	C	R	1 or 2
				CMPLX	C	D	1 or 2
				CMPLX	C	C	1 or 2
Conversion to character			CHAR		A	I	1
Nearest integer, rounding		NINT	NINT	NINT	I	R	1
			IDINT	NINT	I	D	1
Imaginary part of a complex number			AIMAG		R	C	1
Double precision product			DPROD		D	R	2

Table B.2   Arithmetic manipulation

Description	66	77s	77	77g	Type	Arguments	
Truncation	AINT	AINT	AINT	AINT	R	R	1
			DINT	AINT	D	D	1
Nearest whole number		ANINT	ANINT	ANINT	R	R	1
			DNINT	ANINT	D	D	1
Remainder (modulo function)	MOD	MOD	MOD	MOD	I	I	2
	AMOD	AMOD	AMOD	MOD	R	R	2
			DMOD	MOD	D	D	2
Positive difference	IDIM	IDIM	IDIM	DIM	I	I	2
$a1-a2$ if $a1 \geq a2$	DIM	DIM	DIM	DIM	R	R	2
0 if $a1 < a2$			DDIM	DIM	D	D	2
Absolute value	IABS	IABS	IABS	ABS	I	I	1
	ABS	ABS	ABS	ABS	R	R	1
			DABS	ABS	D	D	1
			CABS	ABS	C	C	1
Square root	SQRT	SQRT	SQRT	SQRT	R	R	1
			DSQRT	SQRT	D	D	1
			CSQRT	SQRT	C	C	1
Conjugate of a complex argument			CONJG		C	C	1
Transfer of sign	ISIGN	ISIGN	ISIGN	SIGN	I	I	2
ABS($a1$) if $a2 \geq 0$	SIGN	SIGN	SIGN	SIGN	R	R	2
$-$ABS($a1$) if $a2 < 0$			DSIGN	SIGN	D	D	2
Choosing largest value	MAX0	MAX0	MAX0	MAX	I	I	>1
	AMAX1	AMAX1	AMAX1	MAX	R	R	>1
			DMAX1	MAX	D	D	>1
	AMAX0	AMAX0	AMAX0		R	I	>1
	MAX1	MAX1	MAX1		I	R	>1
Choosing smallest value	MIN0	MIN0	MIN0	MIN	I	I	>1
	AMIN1	AMIN1	AMIN1	MIN	R	R	>1
			DMIN1	MIN	D	D	>1
	AMIN0	AMIN0	AMIN0		R	I	>1
	MIN1	MIN1	MIN1		I	R	>1

Table B.3   Mathematical functions

Description	66	77s	77	77g	Type	Arguments	
Exponentiation (e ** a)	EXP	EXP	EXP	EXP	R	R	1
			DEXP	EXP	D	D	1
			CEXP	EXP	C	C	1
Natural logarithm (base e)	ALOG	ALOG	ALOG	LOG	R	R	1
			DLOG	LOG	D	D	1
			CLOG	LOG	C	C	1
Common logarithm (base 10)	ALOG10	ALOG10	ALOG10	LOG10	R	R	1
			DLOG10	LOG10	D	D	1
Sine	SIN	SIN	SIN	SIN	R	R	1
			DSIN	SIN	D	D	1
			CSIN	SIN	C	C	1
Cosine	COS	COS	COS	COS	R	R	1
			DCOS	COS	D	D	1
			CCOS	COS	C	C	1
Tangent		TAN	TAN	TAN	R	R	1
			DTAN	TAN	D	D	1
Arcsine		ASIN	ASIN	ASIN	R	R	1
			DASIN	ASIN	D	D	1
Arccosine		ACOS	ACOS	ACOS	R	R	1
			DACOS	ACOS	D	D	1
Arctangent	ATAN	ATAN	ATAN	ATAN	R	R	1
			DATAN	ATAN	D	D	1
		ATAN2	ATAN2	ATAN2	R	R	2
			DATAN2	ATAN2	D	D	2
Hyperbolic sine		SINH	SINH	SINH	R	R	1
			DSINH	SINH	D	D	1
Hyperbolic cosine		COSH	COSH	COSH	R	R	1
			DCOSH	COSH	D	D	1
Hyperbolic tangent	TANH	TANH	TANH	TANH	R	R	1
			DTANH	TANH	D	D	1

Table B.4   Character manipulation

Description	66	77s	77	77g	Type	Arguments	
Length of a character variable			LEN		I	A	1
Index of a substring			INDEX		I	A	2
Lexically greater than or equal		LGE	LGE		L	A	2
Lexically greater than		LGT	LGT		L	A	2
Lexically less than or equal		LLE	LLE		L	A	2
Lexically less than		LLT	LLT		L	A	2

Appendix C:
An Implementation Test of FORTRAN

Unfortunately, despite the length of the 1977 A.N.S.I. FORTRAN specifications, there are many differing implementations of FORTRAN. The reasons for this are manifold. First of all, there are some hardware differences that may affect precision of reals. Then there is the need for upward compatibility. If a manufacturer had offered a certain feature in an earlier version of FORTRAN, that manufacturer would want a later version to not only implement the new features, but also maintain the old ones. Should those old features differ with the new specifications, a conflict might arise. Thirdly, there are times when the specifications do not cover particular situations; there the software designer must make some independent choices. Thus the user is stuck with certain vagaries.

This section of the text is a guide to the methods that might be used to test for some of the features that might vary from implementation to implementation. We can only discuss those we know about; each user will have to be on the alert for other differences.

topic	section or exercise	feature examined
operating systems	2.15.3	journal or log files
syntax	exercise 2–5	lowercase letters in FORTRAN instructions
input	2.7, exercise 2–8	input of integer values from keyboard
	2.7	list-directed input
	7.7.4	null-value input
output	2.3.1	Hollerith FORMAT descriptor
	2.3.1, 2.14, exercise 2–6	carriage control on peripheral devices
	2.14.1	slash at end of FORMAT
	3.8	rounding
file access	2.15.1	opening and closing of files

arithmetic	3.4, 3.4.1	integer overflow
	3.4, 3.4.2	division by zero
	exercises 3–2, 3–3	precision of Reals
	3.4.1	system error handling
alphameric storage	10.3.2	internal storage codes
logic flow	2.12.2	DO loop: parameter implementation
	2.13	DO loop: branching into range
subprograms	3.9	error handling in intrinsic functions
peripheral devices	11.3	terminal screen controls

Index